P9-DTD-942

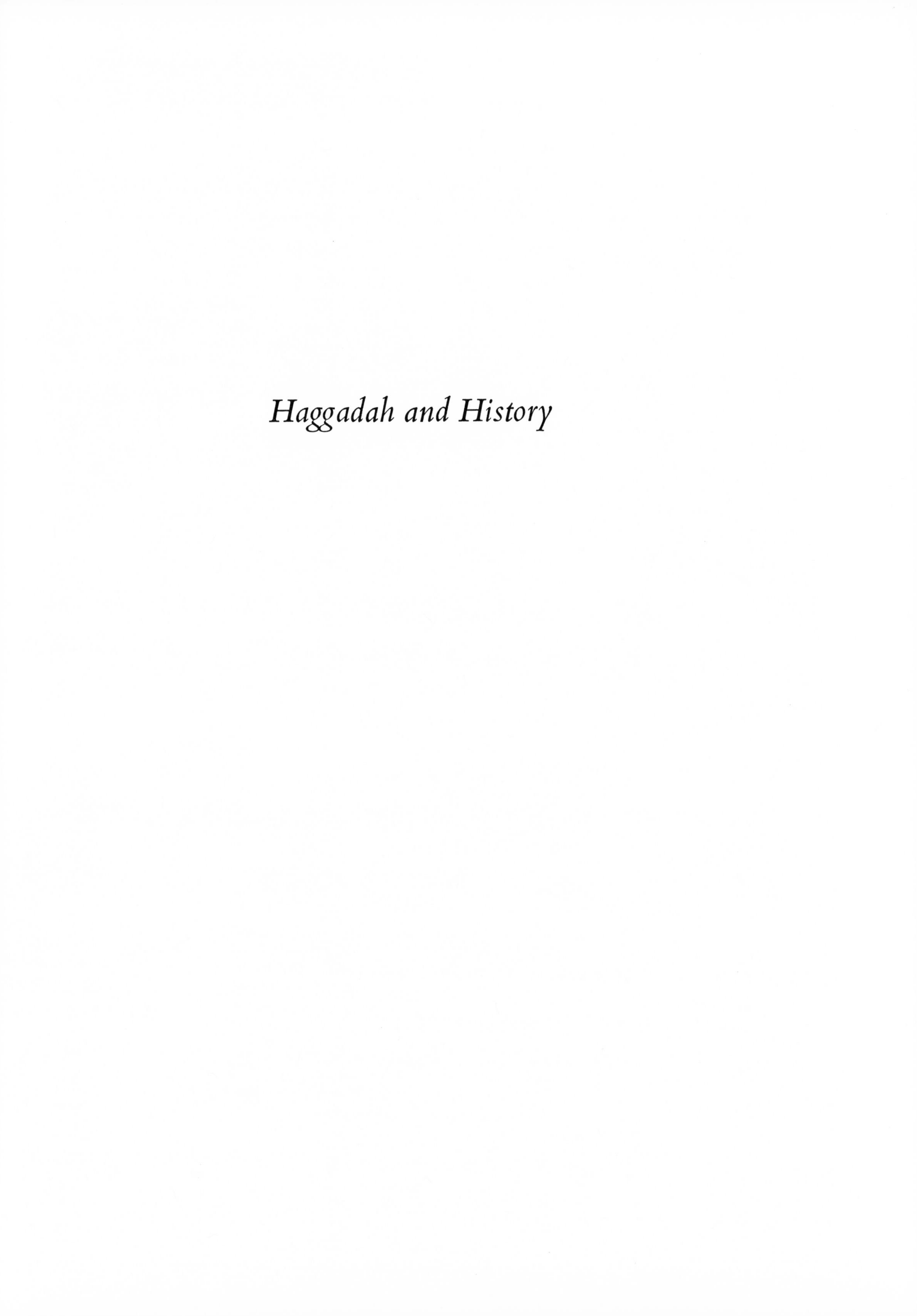

Haggadah and History

Haggadah and History

A Panorama in Facsimile of Five Centuries of the Printed Haggadah from the Collections of Harvard University and the Jewish Theological Seminary of America

BY

YOSEF HAYIM YERUSHALMI

The Jewish Publication Society of America
PHILADELPHIA

Copyright © 1975 by
The Jewish Publication Society of America
First edition · All rights reserved
ISBN 0-8276-0046-1
Library of Congress catalog card no. 73-21169
Manufactured in the United States of America
Second printing, 1975

TO THE MEMORY OF MY MOTHER

לאמי מורתי ז"ל

חוה בת מרדכי ושרה לבית קפלן
מק"ק פינסק

את אהבת הפסח
נטעה בלבי

נפטרה בניו יורק
ערב פסח
שנת תשכ"ח
לפ"ק

Contents

PREFACE

THIS BOOK MARKS the first systematic attempt to offer, by means of facsimile pages from many editions, a representative survey of the development of the Passover Haggadah during the last five centuries. As such it is both a history of the printed Haggadah and an examination of the Haggadah as a reflection of Jewish history, from the end of the fifteenth century to the present. Hence its title: *Haggadah and History*.

The plates have been photographed directly from the originals in two of the world's great Haggadah collections, those of Harvard University and the Jewish Theological Seminary of America. They are arranged in chronological order.

Though I have been concerned here exclusively with the printed Haggadah, I have approached it in its broadest contexts. Thus, in the evolution of Haggadah printing the inclusion of the text in larger liturgical works can sometimes be as significant as its appearance in a separate format. Similarly, for the historical impact of the Haggadah, nontraditional forms, parodies, Israeli kibbutz experiments, and even an occasional Christian version can prove as relevant and revealing as the classical text. All these genres are represented here.

With several thousand Haggadah editions available, the selection of two hundred plates must ultimately remain subjective, though not capricious. Some Haggadahs are of such obvious intrinsic importance as to virtually demand admission. Many others are merely repetitive or otherwise undistinguished. For the rest—my task has sometimes had its pleasant frustrations. More than once I have had rather ruthlessly to exclude a Haggadah that was worthy of reproduction in itself, but that did not fit the overall purpose and structure of this book. Even when a particular Haggadah had already been chosen, the temptation to reproduce yet another interesting or beautiful page had to be stoutly resisted.

Although Haggadah illustrations are a major component of this survey, as the reader will easily ascertain, these alone could not provide the criterion for selection. For reasons that will be set forth in the Introduction, the history of the Haggadah is far more than a history of its woodcuts and engravings. In addition to visual elements, the selections have been based on rarity, historical significance, places of printing, languages, rituals, etc.

The Introduction and the individual plate descriptions are meant to complement one another closely, with the latter focusing on the specific details of the page reproduced. At the bottom of each description are noted the location of the Haggadah from which the facsimile was made, a reference to one of the standard Haggadah bibliographies in which the edition is listed, and the dimensions of the original page. Biblical verses are generally given in the English translation produced in 1917 by the Jewish Publication Society of America, except where the context required some modification for the sake of greater clarity. Translations of all other texts are my own.

This book could not have appeared without the close cooperation of several individuals and institutions.

My friend and colleague Dr. Charles Berlin, Lee M. Friedman Bibliographer in Judaica and head of the Hebrew Division of the Harvard College Library, has been helpful to me at every turn. Himself a connoisseur of the Haggadah, his interest and expertise are reflected in the devotion with which he has developed the Harvard Haggadah collection to its present level of eminence. He was my surest guide through this labyrinth, pausing along the way to point out items I may have missed, ever ready to assist in the technical details and logistics involved in this rather complicated project. His collaboration has been particularly gratifying to me as yet another fruit of an association over the years in which we have deepened our common interest in the Jewish book.

Dr. Menahem Schmelzer, librarian of the Jewish Theological Seminary of America, opened its treasures to me with the customary graciousness that has endeared him to scholars everywhere. I had but to send him my lists of desiderata, and when I arrived in New York all would be ready and waiting for my perusal. From the very outset he dismissed any qualms I may have felt at interrupting his own busy schedule. That my use of the Seminary collection proved feasible and productive is due entirely to his readiness to indulge my most extravagant whims.

To both these distinguished librarians, then, and to the authorities of their respective institutions who released the books for reproduction, my heartfelt thanks. I should only add that all decisions, as well as any attendant defects, are mine alone.

I take special pleasure in recalling that the physical appearance of this volume stems from what has proved, in retrospect, a felicitous encounter. Just at the time when questions of production came onto the agenda, I chanced to meet David Godine, the Boston publisher. One conversation with him brought an immediate meeting of minds, and a glance at the superb books produced by his firm sufficed to convince me that here was the ideal person to be entrusted with the aesthetic and technical aspects of the book. To him and to his staff, as well as to The Meriden Gravure Company and The Stinehour Press, belongs the credit for the handsome result. Their fastidious taste, superlative craftsmanship, and experience in the production of fine books are evident throughout. If among them all, I feel particularly beholden to Carol Goldenberg, it is because only I can appreciate how very much I owe, not only to her talents and hard work, but to her willingness to regard every concern of mine as her own.

I wish also to express my gratitude to the officers of the Jewish Publication Society of America, to its president, Jerome Shestack, its executive vice-president, David Gross, and its editor, Chaim Potok, for their faith in sponsoring so difficult and costly a venture, and for sparing no subsequent effort to assure its successful conclusion.

Kay Powell is the fulfillment of this author's dream of what a copy editor should be. My secretary, Jeanne Onorato, and my student, Bernard Cooperman, shared the burden of typing and proofreading. I am indebted to all of them.

In a final and quite separate category are my wife, Ophra, and my "almost-five-year-old" son, Ariel, who bring joy and encouragement to my life and give meaning to all my endeavors. May this book partly atone for an unprecedented two-month and 6,000-mile separation which they sustained with good grace in Haifa while I completed my work.

YOSEF HAYIM YERUSHALMI
Cambridge, Massachusetts
22 Tammuz, 5733—July 22, 1973

INTRODUCTION

On the Passover Haggadah

THE NIGHT IS "different from all other nights." The book has a special place among all Jewish books.

It is the fourteenth of the Hebrew month Nisan. As evening descends in succession over five continents, Jews have gathered in their homes for the Passover Seder, the one great liturgical celebration entrusted, not to the public worship of the synagogue, but to the intimacy of a family meal. Even before the well-rehearsed questions are asked by the youngest present, all are intuitively aware of the distinctiveness of this night. Less obvious, perhaps, is the singular character of the book held open around the table.

The Haggadah is in many ways the most popular and beloved of Jewish books. Scholars have meditated upon it, children delight in it. A book for philosophers and for the folk, it has been reprinted more often and in more places than any other Jewish classic, and has been the most frequently illustrated. Over 3,500 extant editions have been catalogued thus far through the assiduous labors of bibliographers, and yet hitherto unknown editions continue to come to light. There is hardly a city or town in the world where a Hebrew press once functioned which has not produced at least one Haggadah. It has been translated into almost every language spoken by Jews throughout their global dispersion. As these words are being written, one is confident that Jewish printers in far-flung places are already preparing other Haggadahs for local or foreign markets in anticipation of the Passover to come.

The Book of Remembrance and Redemption

IN THE REALM of books, such a long and ubiquitous career for a single work constitutes a remarkable phenomenon. Mundane factors alone will not explain it. To be sure, the Haggadah is a relatively small book (some twenty to forty pages, depending on the format), and it is thus an easier undertaking for a printer than a Bible or even the Prayer Book. Moreover, it is a notoriously perishable item, readily vulnerable to the stains of spilled wine, the hands of inquisitive children, and other normal hazards of the festive meal, and this factor alone creates a constant need for new copies.

Clearly, however, such considerations are only subsidiary to the central fact—the extraordinary hold that the Passover holiday itself continues to have over the Jewish people even in our own day. Of all the great Jewish rites, the Passover Seder seems to have suffered the least erosion in modern times; of the entire Jewish liturgy, the words of the Haggadah remain for many the most familiar. In one form or another the Seder continues to be celebrated not only by Jews committed to religious tradition, but across the spectrum of religious modernism and revisionism, among secularists of every stripe, even by seemingly alienated Jews whose knowledge of Judaism has otherwise atrophied to that of the Fourth Son in the Haggadah "who knows not what to ask." Separated ordinarily by the widest range of ideology and depth of Jewish commitment, heirs to the atomization of Jewish life since the end of the eighteenth century, they are yet to be found together on the eve of Passover, often at the same table, somehow united in the living reality of the Jewish people. Nostalgia, the congenial opportunity for family reunion, the modern attractiveness of the theme of freedom—all these may play a part. Yet more profound impulses seem to be operative here, set in motion ages ago and sustained through the entire grand and awesome course of Jewish history. However dimly perceived, in the end it is nothing less than the Jewish experience and conception of history that are celebrated here, in that orchestration of symbol, ritual, and recital for which the Haggadah provides the score.

For Passover is preeminently the great historical festival of the Jewish people, and the Haggadah is its book of remembrance and redemption. Here the memory of the nation is annually revived and replenished, and the collective hope sustained. The ancient redemption of Israel from Egypt is recounted and relived, not merely as an evocation from the past, but above all as prototype and surety for the ultimate redemption yet to come. That, indeed, is the basic structure of the Haggadah itself. And so the participant is adjured to regard himself literally "as though he himself had emerged from Egypt," and in that phrase lies the latent power of the Haggadah to move the hearts of Jews. Every oppressor is Pharaoh, and Egypt every exile. On this night time is in radical flux, the generations are linked together around the table and across millennia, past has become present, and the Messianic era is suddenly imminent. "*Next year*—in Jerusalem . . . !"

The Written and the Printed Word

JUST WHEN the arrangement of the Haggadah text as we know it finally came into being is still a matter of conjecture. Curiously, it is not really a book at all, in the sense of a work written at one time by an author or group of authors for the purposes of Passover. It is, rather, a mosaic comprised of passages from Bible, Mishnah, and Midrash, as well as blessings and prayers that already existed, all somehow blending ultimately into a felicitous and harmonious whole. The various layers were progressively edited over the course of many centuries until the whole reached its definitive form, probably in Babylonia. Some hymns appended toward the end (e.g., *Adir hu*) derive from the Middle Ages. The beloved *Ḥad gadya* ("One Kid") and *Eḥad mi yode'a* ("Who Knows One?") are folk songs and were not included until the fifteenth century; perhaps they were originally intended to catch the interest of the children and keep them awake until the conclusion of the Seder.

The earliest manuscripts of the Haggadah, even in its final redaction, have long been lost. The oldest complete version of the main body of the text that we possess is the one found in the prayer book compiled by Saadia Gaon, head of the great academy at Sura in Babylonia in the tenth century. Another complete text appears in the so-called *Maḥzor Vitry,* produced in the twelfth century by disciples of Rashi, the famous French exegete. For basically the Haggadah can appear in two different formats: as a separate entity, or simply as part of a prayer book that contains the various services for Passover and other festivals. Our oldest independent manuscript Haggadahs go back only to the thirteenth and fourteenth centuries. Older fragments have been found, but because of their incomplete character we cannot know whether or not they were once part of some larger liturgical work. The most important of such early leaves are those retrieved from the Genizah, that inexhaustible treasure-trove of manuscripts and documents stored for a millennium in the attic of a Cairo synagogue and discovered early in our own century. Of special importance are those fragments containing remnants of the old Palestinian version of the Haggadah, which fell by the wayside after the ascent of Babylonian Judaism to worldwide hegemony.

Before the latter half of the fifteenth century the pen of the scribe was the only means by which the Haggadah or any other work could be reproduced, be it on parchment or paper. Haggadah manuscripts, some of the utmost beauty in their calligraphy and illumination, are to be found in the world's great libraries and occasionally even in private collections. Regrettably, only a relatively few masterpieces have been adequately studied, and much remains to be done by scholars of both the history of art and of liturgy before we obtain a satisfactory understanding of what exists.

But manuscripts are a field unto themselves. Our present volume is concerned exclusively with the ramifications of one of the truly seminal events in the history of human technology: the invention of printing from movable type in the fifteenth century.

It was Johann Gutenberg of Mainz who, regardless of what abortive attempts may have preceded him, achieved a deserved immortality as father of the craft. Having cast his first types around 1440, he began to print in earnest five years later. In 1455–56 he produced his first Bible. Meanwhile, the technique was taken up by others and spread with great rapidity. It was not long before Jews began to adapt it to their own needs. The first known printed Hebrew book to bear a date is Rashi's commentary to the Pentateuch, which appeared in the Italian town of Reggio di Calabria in 1475. Actually, some extant Hebrew books may have been printed even earlier, but we cannot be certain of this because it was not yet a fixed practice to specify the date in the book itself. (Gutenberg himself did not date a book until his Latin Bible of 1462.)

In the eighth decade of the fifteenth century Hebrew printing came to other parts of Italy, as well as to Spain and Portugal. For sheer aesthetic achievement, many of these Hebrew incunabula ("cradle-prints") have never been surpassed. More important, the art of printing was to have as revolutionary an impact upon Jewish culture as upon European civilization generally. Suddenly it became possible to avoid the costly and tedious work of copying manuscripts by hand, thus enabling even those who were not wealthy to form a collection of books if they were so disposed. For Jewry, among whom the ideal of universal study by ordinary laymen had long been translated into reality, the development was laden with particular significance and potential. By the year 1500 Jewish printers had already issued a veritable library of major Jewish classics—Bibles, tractates of the Talmud, Midrash, exegesis, legal codes, philosophy, liturgy, and even poetry and belles-lettres. The pioneer productions in most of these genres can be dated with a fair degree of precision. It is otherwise with the Haggadah.

The origins of the printed Haggadah remain obscure. What is assumed to be the first extant copy has been ascribed to the Hebrew press in Guadalajara, Spain, around 1482. Consisting of six folio leaves printed on both sides in double columns, it contains no illustrations. The Hebrew text displays no vowel marks. Compared to some of the lavish productions known to us from the Hebrew presses of the Iberian peninsula, this is an extremely modest affair. It is, nevertheless, of obvious historic interest, especially since it survives in a unique copy. Discovered only a generation or two ago, it is now in the Schocken Library in Jerusalem. A complete facsimile was published in 1960 as a separate brochure inserted into A. Yaari's monumental bibliography of the Passover Haggadah. Unfortunately, the attribution to Guadalajara cannot be considered firm. There is no colophon at the end, and consequently no mention of place or date of printing. Even if the surmise is correct, in light of the precarious fate of early Hebrew books we can never be quite sure that the first surviving edition of a work is the true "first." The possibility cannot be excluded that an even older Haggadah may someday dazzle the eyes of its fortunate discoverer.

We are on somewhat firmer ground when we turn back to Italy.

Among the most illustrious of the early Hebrew printers were the various members of the Soncino family. Deriving their name from their place of residence, the town of Soncino in the Duchy of Milan, they set a new standard of excellence in everything they undertook. From the 1480s, when the first Soncino imprints began to appear, to the mid-sixteenth century, several generations worked consecutively at the same craft, moving their press from place to place, first in Italy and later in Turkey.

In 1486, some two or three years after the first Soncino book had come off the press, a small prayer book known as the *Sidorello* (a combination of the Hebrew word *Siddur* with an Italian diminutive ending) was issued. It is now among the very rarest of Hebrew books. As usual, the book concludes with a printer's colophon giving the date and circumstances of publication. However, in the copy owned by the Jewish Theological Seminary of America, this is followed by a Haggadah that is bound in with it. In typography and format it is similar to the *Sidorello* itself and was undoubtedly printed in Soncino in the same year. Whether it was the general practice to bind the two together is hard to say, since only one other copy exists. At any rate, since the Haggadah comes after the colophon of the *Sidorello* proper, it must necessarily be considered a separate and independent work. It contains a lovely woodcut initial word in the passage beginning *Ha laḥma anya*

("This is the bread of affliction"), as well as two others for the matzah and the bitter herbs (see Plates 2–3).

Even earlier, in September 1485, the printers in Soncino had begun the important task of publishing the first edition of the *Maḥzor Roma*, the festival prayers according to the venerable Roman Jewish rite. The work apparently continued while the *Sidorello* was itself in press and was to appear in two imposing volumes. But in 1486, before the first volume was quite finished, and for reasons not known, the printing in Soncino was suspended and transferred to the town of Casalmaggiore. There the whole was brought to completion on August 21, 1486. In the *Maḥzor Roma* the full text of the Haggadah is printed as part of the liturgy for Passover, and here too an occasional word is presented with woodcut embellishment (Plate 4). The practice of printing the Haggadah in festival prayer books continued afterward with the publication of a second edition of the Roman Maḥzor, as well as the Ashkenazic Maḥzor of the Jews following the German rite. It may also be noted that before the end of the fifteenth century the Haggadah was printed in yet another context. It is contained in the two editions (Rome, 1480; Soncino, 1490) of the *Mishneh Torah*, the great code of Jewish law composed by Moses Maimonides, which includes a Haggadah text intended for study and reference. Finally, a remarkable illustrated Haggadah, of which only fragments survive, may have been printed in the fifteenth century; it will be discussed in the next section.

These, then, were the debuts of the Haggadah in the first quarter-century of Hebrew printing, at least as far as our present state of knowledge will allow. The next Haggadah to make its appearance is noteworthy for having been produced in a new setting, with a novel feature in the text, and as a result of a major shift in Jewish destinies.

The final decade of the fifteenth century witnessed the end of open Jewish life in Western Europe and some parts of Central Europe as well. It was the culmination of a process that had begun with the expulsion of the Jews from England in 1290, from the Kingdom of France in the fourteenth century, and subsequently from most of the major German cities. Now, in 1492, the expulsion from Spain overwhelmed the largest and most affluent of all medieval Jewries, a historical catastrophe of the first magnitude. This was followed in 1497 by the brutal forced conversion of all the Jews of Portugal. In 1498 the Jews were expelled from Provence and in the ensuing years from various parts of southern Italy. Only in central and northern Italy were Jewish communities tolerated and Jewish life allowed to continue. Beyond that, the rash of expulsions in Europe necessarily moved the geographical locus of Jewry from the Christian to the Muslim orbit. Fortunately, the prior rise of the Ottoman Turks to the status of a world power now provided Jewish refugees with a safe haven in an ever-expanding empire. A constant stream of migration brought thousands of Jews to the Turkish Balkan provinces and to Turkey itself. Alongside the immigrants from other European countries, refugees from the Iberian peninsula rapidly rebuilt their communal and cultural life in such cities as Adrianople, Salonika, and Constantinople, and in a host of other places. Dominant over all the other groups, Sephardic Jewry was to enjoy in the sixteenth-century Ottoman Empire its second golden age.

With the rise of the new Jewish centers, Hebrew printing did not lag far behind, and it was Constantinople, with its large and thriving Jewish communities, which took pride of place. The first Hebrew book was published in the Turkish capital in 1504. The third, printed only two years later, contained the Passover Haggadah with a commentary to the text entitled *Zebaḥ Pesaḥ* ("The Passover Sacrifice") by Don Isaac Abravanel (Plate 5). Actually, the volume consists of three of his works, the others being his commentary to the Ethics of the Fathers, entitled *Naḥalat abot* ("Inheritance of the Fathers"), and his *Rosh amanah* ("Pinnacle of Faith") on the principles of Jewish belief.

The entire book is of both intrinsic and symbolic importance. It is the very first edition of the Haggadah to appear with a commentary. Its author, Isaac Abravanel, was more than a scholar and philosopher. He was the last of the long and distinguished line of Jewish statesmen in the royal courts of Spain and played a major role in the drama of the Expulsion itself. Having tried desperately to move Ferdinand and Isabella to rescind their decree, he rejected the option of remaining in Spain at the price of conversion and, though advanced in years, became a wanderer. The most famous Jewish figure of his time, his works and his personal example were a source of consolation and strength to an entire generation of exiles. The works printed together in the Constantinople volume appeared while he was still alive and are themselves a partial reflection of his peregrinations. The *Rosh amanah*, he informs us, was composed in Naples in 1495; *Zebaḥ Pesaḥ* and *Naḥalat abot* in the town of Monopoli in 1496. At the end of the latter he writes, succinctly but graphically: "This commentary was completed in the city of Monopoli in the Apulian province of the Kingdom of Naples, to which we came to live because of the tempests of the Expulsion decreed against the Jerusalem Diaspora which was in Spain. And this kingdom at first received us with a fair countenance, but then it turned into an enemy." Forced by the French invasion of Naples to flee once more, he was to go on to other places, finally ending his days in Venice in 1508.

Our interest in this volume as a reflection of the Spanish Expulsion is further enhanced by the fact that its printers, the brothers David and Samuel Ibn Naḥmias, were themselves Spanish exiles, and it is they who founded the Hebrew press in Constantinople. In their own colophon they write with pride and thanksgiving: "It was completed by them on Thursday, the 9th of Kislev, in the year 5266 [1506], in the metropolis of Constantinople, a mother city in Israel, which is under the rule of Sultan Bayazid, may his glory be uplifted and may God be blessed forever, Amen."

Having now followed the Haggadah through the early decades of Hebrew printing, one must be struck by the extreme paucity of editions in this period. In all its various formats we find about six Haggadahs, of which only two or three are separate productions. Even if we grant the possibility that someday a few others may turn up, the meager total seems quite puzzling. Early Hebrew books were usually published in no more than a few hundred copies. Surely the editions we have surveyed did not meet the needs of the contemporary Jewish world, or even of the countries in which they were printed.

The reason for this is, however, quite simple, and a moment's reflection renders it obvious. The advent of printed Haggadahs by no means immediately displaced the writing of manuscripts. In many areas the handwritten text, with its thoroughly personal quality, was still considered superior to the printed one. Among the fastidious there was a certain disdain for that which was "mass produced," and in the ensuing competition it took some time before this elitism succumbed to the manifold advantages of the new process. We know this from the general history of printing, and it was no different among Jews. As a result, manuscripts of the Haggadah continued to be written even when the rate of printing accelerated.

To appreciate this, we have only to consider some revealing statistics on Haggadah printing through the ages. If we take as our comparative base the figures that emerge from the most comprehensive single bibliography available, the following pattern develops. For the entire sixteenth century only 25 Haggadahs are listed. In the seventeenth century the figure increases slightly, to 37. In the eighteenth century it leaps to 234; in the nineteenth, to 1,269. As for the twentieth century, over 1,100 editions were printed in the first six decades alone!

Patently the printed Haggadah had won only partial victories before the eighteenth century, and it may not have been until the nineteenth that it became common for every person at a Seder table to hold his own copy. Prior to that the text was probably available only to the head of the house and occasionally to one or two others present. One is also intrigued to discover that in the eighteenth century, the very period in which the pace of publication so noticeably increased, there took place in Europe a minor revival of handwritten and illuminated Haggadahs, which, ironically, were often copied from printed editions. In the East, manuscript Haggadahs continue to be written even in modern times and, together with printed copies, still circulate among oriental Jews.

These details, however, cannot obscure the overall impact of the printed Haggadah itself. It has made the text more widely accessible than was ever dreamed possible. Through its illustrations it has helped to shape the image of the Passover holiday and the events it commemorates in the minds of many generations of Jews. It has interacted with major developments in Jewish history at vital junctures. And, not least, it has by now a richly varied history of its own.

Haggadah Illustration: Debuts, Milestones, and Archetypes

THE HAGGADAH was already a favorite subject for illustrators prior to the invention of printing. The various Passover symbols, the Seder itself, the biblical events and midrashic motifs recorded in the Haggadah all lend themselves as natural themes for pictorial representation. Beautifully illuminated Hebrew manuscripts were produced in the Middle Ages in many genres of Jewish literature. In the case of the Haggadah, however, there was an added pedagogic value. Illustrations were pleasing not only to the adult eye; like other elements in the Seder service, they also stimulated the curiosity of the children and served as a lively medium of visual instruction, much like today's picture books.

As in other respects, the beginnings of printed Haggadah illustrations remain a riddle for whose ultimate solution only tantalizing hints are available.

Apparently the earliest printed illustrations on a Passover theme to have survived are two woodcut pages, with no text whatever, discovered and described in 1925. Each of the leaves is divided into two frames, yielding a total of four pictures. They show: (a) Jews smearing lambs' blood on the doorposts of their houses in Egypt (Exodus 12:7); (b) the Passover meal, with the participants standing, rather than seated, around the table; (c) the plague of darkness; and (d) the slaying of the firstborn. Technically these are wood-block prints, recalling the primitive block books which, in the Low Countries, Germany, and Italy, antedated printing from movable type. Because of certain stylistic affinities with known Venetian examples, the Passover prints have plausibly been ascribed to that city, and dated sometime in the 1480s. Even so, questions remain. We do not know if they were drawn by a Jew or, as seems more probable, by a Christian who was perhaps commissioned by Jews. Nor can we determine whether these were illustrations intended for a Haggadah. They may have been part of an album of wood-block prints, or perhaps they were merely produced and sold as separate sheets on the occasion of the holiday. Even if the artist was a gentile, some of the elements in the Seder scene are recognizably Jewish, and the Jews themselves are shown with heads covered.

Much more important, but equally enigmatic, are the three printed leaves discovered accidentally by the noted Anglo-Jewish bibliophile Elkan N. Adler within the binding of a manuscript and now in the possession of the Jewish Theological Seminary. These leaves, six printed sides in all, contain two different woodcut illustrations, one of the Seder (Plate 1), the other showing Moses before Pharaoh as he summons the plague of lice. Here, at least, we know for certain that these are parts of an actual Haggadah, since the text is present on every page. It is also clear that these are the oldest remnants of an illustrated printed Haggadah that have thus far been found. The rest remains a matter of speculation. Experts are still divided as to the place and date of publication, some proposing that it was printed in Constantinople or Salonika around 1503 or 1515, while others would assign it to Spain or Portugal before the Expulsion (an opinion to which I personally incline).

There is yet another possibility to be considered. This Haggadah may well have been printed in the Ottoman Empire, but from types and blocks taken there by Iberian exiles. Since the blocks from which the illustrations were pressed onto the paper seem to have been somewhat worn, this may be a Turkish second edition of a Haggadah first printed in the Iberian peninsula. No definitive answer to any of these questions will emerge unless a complete copy is someday found, or at least a final page with a colophon. An encouraging recent development has raised such hopes. Six leaves of this Haggadah, five of them entirely new, have been discovered within the past decade in the Genizah collection of Cambridge University in England. These contain six illustrations and cuts that do not duplicate the ones already known.

The earliest illustrated Haggadah that can be consulted today in complete copies is not, strange to say, a Jewish publication at all, but a Latin translation produced entirely under Christian auspices. This is precisely the reason for its excellent state of preservation. Never in actual circulation among Jews, it was not subject to the deterioration that derives from constant use. It comes to us out of the famous "Battle of the Books," the great Christian controversy over Hebrew literature in Germany that, in the early sixteenth century, helped pave the way for the advent of the Protestant Reformation.

As had happened before, the attack against Hebrew books was launched by a Jewish apostate. In 1507 Johann Pfefferkorn, a recently baptized Moravian Jew of mediocre erudition and a violent hatred for his former coreligionists, began to trouble the life of German Jewry. Sponsored by the bigoted Dominicans of Cologne, he began a vitriolic campaign to induce the Emperor and the German princes to order the destruction of Hebrew books, especially the Talmud, and to persecute the Jews in other ways as well. In a series of anti-Semitic pamphlets he ridiculed every aspect of Jewish belief, presented the Jews as a sinister threat to Christendom, and called for drastic measures to cope with both Jews and their pernicious literature. Soon, however, the issue began to transcend the problem of the Jews alone, widening into a debate that affected German and other European intellectuals generally, as well as the Church itself. The right of the Jews to retain their books shifted into a question of the intrinsic validity and legitimacy of Hebrew studies among Christians, just at a time when Hebraic scholarship in Germany was making its first important strides. In the ensuing battle the field was taken by humanists, on one side, and by the Dominicans and their fellow travelers, on the other. Johann Reuchlin, the greatest German humanist and Hebraist of his day, staked his own enormous prestige in the balance to champion both Hebrew studies and the Jews against their attackers. The struggle took place on many levels, and though the Latin Haggadah represents but one of the minor skirmishes, our interest in it is not thereby diminished.

In 1509 Pfefferkorn had received permission from the Emperor Maximilian for the destruction of Hebrew books, and had come to Frankfurt am Main to order their confiscation. Resistance by the local Jews and some of the authorities resulted in an appeal. Reuchlin was requested to give his opinion. In 1510 he submitted a report that was highly favorable to Hebrew studies, and the Emperor's order was revoked. This development further inflamed the conflict. In 1511 Pfefferkorn published a personal attack against Reuchlin entitled the *Handspiegel*, the latter replying with his famous *Augenspiegel*.

Thomas Murner's Latin Haggadah, published in Frankfurt in 1512, should be seen against this immediate background. Murner was a Franciscan friar from Alsace who achieved fame in Germany as a scholar, preacher, and satirist of contemporary affairs. Though he was later to oppose the Reformation, at this time he seems to have sided with Reuchlin's camp. Like his German translation of the Hebrew Grace after Meals, which appeared in the same year, the contribution made by Murner's Haggadah to the humanist cause was readily apparent. In his report, Reuchlin had discussed and described Hebrew books generally; Murner offered in translation an actual sample of a Hebrew work for all to see. The specific choice of the Haggadah seems not to have been made at random, for in 1509 Pfefferkorn had published a vicious pamphlet on the Jewish Passover that appeared simultaneously in one Latin and two German editions. It should be emphasized that Murner does not seem to have harbored any particular affection for Jews. His motives were probably directed more against the Dominicans than in favor of the Jews, "not for love of Mordecai but out of hatred for Haman," as the Jewish adage would have it. Still, the Jews of Frankfurt must have welcomed its appearance as a useful, if unintended, weapon in their own cause.

The Haggadah itself (Plates 6–8) was printed at the press of Thomas' brother, Beatus Murner, who may also be responsible for the illustrations. Hebrew appears only on the title and one other page, the rest being entirely in Latin. The translation strives to be accurate without always succeeding. Murner himself admitted that Hebrew was for him a relatively late and imperfect acquisition, and he may well have consulted some Frankfurt Jews who would first translate passages for him into German. The six woodcuts that appear with the text are somewhat curious specimens as Haggadah illustrations. All purport to show phases of the Seder meal, and it has been suggested that the illustrator may have had some Jewish Haggadah as his model. The assumption is a tenuous one, however, and it would seem that the figures, at least, were copied from non-Jewish specimens. Crudely drawn, to the modern eye the portraits do not seem very flattering. But at the same time they are certainly not anti-Jewish caricatures, nor are the Jews shown blindfolded, as they are in the woodcuts that embellish some of the works of Johann Pfefferkorn.

These, then, are the meager relics of what may once have been a larger patrimony: two woodcuts, possibly Venetian; some leaves of a Haggadah, perhaps from Spain or Turkey; and a complete Haggadah, printed by a Christian for Christian purposes. Together they represent the entire extant "prehistory" of the illustrated printed Haggadah, whose real development commences only in the second quarter of the sixteenth century. From then on it can be traced consecutively to modern times.

The crucial links were forged, in essence, by four "archetypal" illustrated Haggadahs: Prague, 1526; Mantua, 1560; Venice, 1609; and Amsterdam, 1695. These influenced almost all Haggadah illustration prior to the twentieth century. We shall consider each in turn, along with its derivatives.

In 1526 a group of Jewish printers in Prague set to work and produced—a masterpiece. The Bohemian capital was then one of the major cities of Central Europe and the seat of a considerable Jewish community. The Prague Haggadah, some insist, is the greatest single Haggadah ever printed, and so it may well be. Certainly it is one of the chief glories in the annals of Hebrew printing as a whole and, for that matter, in the history of typography in any language.

Printing had come to Prague in 1487, and a Hebrew press was established in 1512. Its first production was a prayer book, and in the next decade other liturgical works appeared, as well as a magnificent multivolume Pentateuch, completed in 1518. Most of these early works were printed by a consortium that subsequently dissolved. Thereupon one of the partners, Gershom ben Solomon Ha-Cohen, decided to strike out on his own. It was this same Gershom Cohen who, together with his brother Gronem, published the illustrated Haggadah that was completed on December 30, 1526. A lavishly illustrated volume in small folio, it is one of the most sumptuous of all Hebrew books. Moreover, in its superbly cut letters, the layout of its lines, the relation of text to illustrations, and the harmony of the pages, the result is an aesthetic achievement of the first order. While there is hardly an aspect of the Prague Haggadah that does not merit extensive discussion, we shall content ourselves with some of the highlights.

In the typography itself, with its dramatic alternation of huge and smaller letters, the printer was influenced not only by the contemporary German "black-letter" style of non-Jewish books, but even more by the manuscript style with which he was familiar—in this case, the Hebrew manuscript tradition of Central Europe. If any proof were needed of the continuing vitality of the written text even after the invention of printing, it is here. Not only are the letters modeled faithfully after those found in Ashkenazic manuscripts, but also the technical features of a manuscript are preserved in print, even though they are no longer really necessary. For example, the attentive reader with a knowledge of Hebrew will immediately notice that there are no dots for those vowels that require them; instead there are only long and short thin lines under the letters. This is perplexing only until one realizes that this was, for purely technical reasons, the earlier practice in Ashkenazic calligraphy. Jewish scribes used an implement that ended, not in a point, which could produce a dot, but in a straight edge, which produced lines of various thickness. The convention was now carried forth into the printed Haggadah on its own momentum. Of similar manuscript derivation is the practice whereby the end of a line of text is often filled in with an inverted letter, such as the *nun*, or with the opening letters of the first word on the next line, so that no space is left to break the symmetry of the column. This, of course, only makes sense where a scribe, approaching the end of a line, has already committed himself irrevocably and must fill the remaining space as best he can. Some time would elapse before the printed book would free itself from such essentially archaic influences and achieve its full autonomy.

No less than sixty woodcut illustrations accompany the text of the Prague Haggadah, an enormous number for a Hebrew book of the time. In non-Jewish Prague imprints, woodcuts had appeared continuously since 1488. But only three or four Hebrew books with illustrations are known to have been printed in any country prior to 1526. Gershom Cohen's decision to have his Haggadah illustrated so profusely was thus a bold one. There was, however, one direct antecedent of considerable importance. In 1514 Gershom had participated in the printing of a little booklet entitled *Zemirot u-birkat ha-mazon* ("Hymns, and the Grace after Meals"), which contained two woodcuts. One, which accompanies the *Kiddush* over the wine on the eve of the Shavuot festival, shows a family at the table, with the father holding a cup. In the other, a hunter and his hounds are chasing some hares. What is striking is the fact that both themes are invariably to be found together in illuminated German manuscript Haggadahs, and are thus closely linked, not to Shavuot, but to Passover. The hare hunt in particular, though originally not a Jewish motif, had already been long subsumed to Jewish needs by a curious association. The Hebrew words for the sequence to be followed at the beginning of a Saturday night Seder were usually committed to memory by combining the initial Hebrew letters into an acronym pronounced *YaKeNHaZ* (or *YaKNeHaZ*). For Ashkenazic Jews it was easy and natural to transform this artificial word into the German word *Jagen-has*, literally, a "hare hunt." As a result of this coincidence, illustrations of such hunts proliferated in manuscript Haggadahs, and one also appears in the Prague Haggadah of 1526. Given the intrinsic link of both woodcuts in the 1514 publication with the Passover holiday, it would seem that they were originally prepared for a projected Haggadah that was later abandoned.

The crowning glory of the Prague Haggadah (which, like many other early books, bears no title page), consists of three noble pages with magnificent woodcut borders surrounding the text. The first of these (Plate 9) occurs at the very outset, where the instructions for the preliminary search for leaven are illustrated by a woodcut of a Jew with a candle, feather, and bowl, the implements used for that purpose. Both text and woodcut are framed by a border containing a richly floriated design with classical urns, ox skulls, and stylized parts of the female torso. The second (Plate 10) introduces the main text of the Haggadah proper. Here the illustrations appear within the border itself, and include Gershom Cohen's printer's emblem: two hands raised in the priestly benediction with his name inscribed alongside and flanked by two angels. In the vertical borders are the figures of David and Goliath, and on the very bottom is a scene showing the biblical Judgment of Solomon (1 Kings 3:16–28). The third (Plate 13) comes after the text of the Grace which ends the meal, and thus it opens the final section of the Haggadah. Framed here within the border is the great cry of an anguished people, the verse in the Book of Psalms (79:6) beginning *Shefokh ḥamatkha*—"Pour out Thy wrath upon the nations that know Thee not, and on the kingdoms that call not upon Thy name," followed by Lamentations 3:66. Sometime in the Middle Ages, perhaps in the aftermath of the massacres of the First Crusade, it had become customary to recite these verses and to open the door in symbolic welcome to the prophet Elijah, harbinger and herald of the Messiah. Indeed, within the rectangular box that contains the text, there is a small woodcut of the Messiah himself riding on a donkey, in consonance with Zechariah 9:9 ("triumphant and victorious, lowly, and riding upon an ass"). The border itself includes the figures of Adam and Eve, Samson carrying the gates of Gaza, and two savages holding a shield emblazoned with a lion, which served as the arms of Prague.

The most enduring subsequent influence of the Prague Haggadah lay in the iconographic genres that it firmly established. The individual cuts adorning almost every page can be grouped under three general rubrics: scenes and symbols of the Passover ritual; illustrations of the biblical and rabbinic elements that actually appear in the Haggadah text; and scenes and figures from biblical or other sources that play no role in the Haggadah itself, but have either past or future redemptive associations. While similar elements were already present in illuminated manuscripts, it is in the Prague Haggadah that they were first stabilized in print. In subsequent centuries the individual pictures may change, but the basic pattern will remain fairly constant.

This Haggadah also established enduring pictorial traditions in some of its details. Pharaoh, who, according to midrashic legend, bathed in the blood of Jewish children in order to cure himself of disease, is shown in a tub. He will bathe in a host of other tubs during the next four centuries, just as the Egyptians will drown in many other seas and the Messiah will ride upon other asses through the gates of Jerusalem. One other Prague woodcut is especially prophetic: the Wicked Son is represented as a *soldier*, a typical *Lanzknecht* of the time (Plate 11), and, though in different garb and uniform, he will continue to appear in the same role until well into the twentieth century. This Jewish equation of wickedness and war is sufficiently eloquent to speak for itself. In general, one need only add that most of the woodcuts in the Haggadah are essentially, and often delightfully, anachronistic. Biblical characters are clothed in contemporary fashions; ancient Egyptian cities have the architecture of sixteenth-century Prague (Plate 12). But this is a feature that the Haggadah shares with all European art in this and even later periods.

Who was the artist responsible for the illustrations in the Prague Haggadah? Was he Jew or gentile? Was there indeed only one artist at work here? These and similar questions have taxed the ingenuity of specialists in the field and are still far from settled. In all probability the first of the three borders was taken over intact from an available wood frame used previously by some Christian printer, it being the common practice at the time for printers to trade or sell borders to one another. But even if the other two borders had the same origins, the second, at least, was modified to incorporate specifically Jewish elements. Some of the figures in the individual cuts (a man pouring wine, for example) could easily have been lifted from a non-Jewish source. Others, such as the Jew with the taper searching for leaven, have an exclusively Jewish meaning and must have been executed expressly for this Haggadah.

Most mysterious is the appearance of the Hebrew letter *shin* within the bottom of the third border (to the left of the shield), as well as in three of the small marginal woodcuts on other pages. The regnant hypothesis proposes that this letter is an initial connoting Ḥayyim Shaḥor (or Schwarz), who was active in the Prague press since 1514, and that he was the artist, at least in these instances.

The great Prague Haggadah was destined to take its place as the first archetype in a long line of illustrated editions. Its direct influence may be followed, to begin with, in Prague itself. Regrettably, however, masterpieces are never really susceptible of duplication. The new edition printed in 1556 by Gershom Cohen's sons already marks a decline from the original. The three magnificent borders are absent here, and a new one that is substituted for the last of them is hardly its equal. For the next two centuries Prague Haggadahs appeared sporadically in various formats, the progeny, in varying degrees of legitimacy, of the edition of 1526. These occasionally employ some of the original woodcut blocks or clumsily redraw them. Though some are more successful than others, the trend is one of general deterioration.

Only beyond Prague did Gershom Cohen's Haggadah influence two later editions, which, though not its equals, are notable productions in their own right.

In 1534 an illustrated Haggadah was printed in Augsburg, Germany, by the same Ḥayyim ben David Shaḥor who had earlier worked as a printer in Prague and may have been the artist of the 1526 Haggadah. He probably went to Germany in 1527, for in April of that year Gershom Cohen received a royal privilege granting him the exclusive right to print and distribute books in Bohemia, thus excluding all potential competitors. The Augsburg Haggadah is much more modest than that of Prague, to which it is nevertheless linked. In size it is a quarto, the largest grades of Prague letters are absent, and it contains only eight different woodcuts (four large and four small), several of them repeated. However, invidious comparisons are both unfair and irrelevant. Augsburg harbored a much smaller community than did Prague, and Ḥayyim Shaḥor's financial resources were obviously limited.

Still, he produced a very handsome book. The typography, though of the smaller size, is quite as lovely as its Prague counterparts. The two Seder scenes, one with four and the other with six participants (Plate 14), are more finely executed and lifelike. Furthermore, there are some innovations. For the first time in a printed Haggadah we find a title page, framed by a typical German Renaissance border, and where the Prague Haggadah had one woodcut for the *Jagen-has*, here it appears twice. These, however, do not represent a repetition, but a consecutive development of the same theme. In the first, the dogs have driven the hares into a net (Plate 15), just as in Gershom Cohen's Haggadah and in the earlier Prague booklet of 1514 (of which Ḥayyim Shaḥor had been one of the printers). But in the second of the Augsburg hare-hunt scenes we have something significantly new: the hares have *escaped* to the other side of the net and are looking back at their pursuers (Plate 16). We can hardly avoid the impression that by now the hare hunt has passed beyond its prosaic and accidental link to the mnemonic *YaKeNHaZ* and has become a dramatic allegory. The hares could easily represent the Jewish people; the dogs, their oppressors. The successful escape of the former would perfectly suit the theme of salvation so prominent in the Haggadah as a whole.

To open the Haggadah published in Mantua, Italy, in 1560 is to be struck at once by a baffling sense of *déjà vu*, combined with an immediate perception that one has at the same time entered a new world. Leafing through, one easily discovers the reason for the apparent confusion. Except for the preliminary pages of instructions and blessings, the Grace, and the colophon at the end, the text of every page is typographically *identical* with the Prague Haggadah of 1526. From the various sizes of the types, down to the exact disposition and layout of the lines, the Mantua edition is almost an exact facsimile of the other, the only perceptible difference being that the ends of the lines are no longer filled in with inverted letters. The technique employed is clear. The printer had the Prague Haggadah before him, from which he traced the text of each page, letter for letter, and transferred the entire page to a block of wood which he then incised for printing. As a result, this Haggadah has the strange distinction of being the only Hebrew book to be printed from wood blocks rather than from movable type.

Unlike the text, the borders and the illustrations of the Prague Haggadah were entirely ignored in Mantua. In lieu of the three borders of the former, *all* the pages were now surrounded by new borders taken from existing frames used in Italian books of the period. The rather stern Teutonic borders of the Prague Haggadah had readily suited its austere Ashkenazic types. The Italian Renaissance borders of the Mantua Haggadah, with their florid undulations and pudgy naked cherubs (*putti*) playing musical instruments or carousing in the foliage, have a sensuousness that is incongruous with the alien typography they now enclose. They are also sometimes cut down to fit the dimensions of the text, and thus mutilated in the process. Only on one page is this marriage between north and south truly successful, and that is in the

Shefokh ḥamatkha (Plate 26). Here the great initial word, first cut in Prague, has been placed directly against a decorative background, with two tasseled clusters of fruit surrounding the rest of the verse. Only one vertical border panel flanks the right side of the page. Above all, the little Prague cut of the Messiah on the donkey has been abandoned in favor of a large and expressive tableau, which now also includes the prophet Elijah. Through all this the entire page has somehow emerged as a new creation.

Not only the borders of the Haggadah were Italianized in Mantua, but the marginal woodcuts as well. These were now entirely redrawn, and the number of large illustrations at the bottom of the pages increased. The Simple Son is now decked out as an Italian buffoon. Abraham, who was depicted in Prague in a rowboat to illustrate the verse "Your fathers dwelt of old time beyond the river" (Joshua 24:2), now traverses the Euphrates in a gondola, with the gondolier standing on the prow, oar in hand (Plate 24). The Wicked Son, formerly a German *Lanzknecht*, has now changed allegiance and become an Italian *condottiere*. Most revealing of the traditional openness of Italian Jewry to the surrounding culture is the figure of the Wise Son (Plate 23). But for the head and cap, he is an obvious replica of Michelangelo's painting of the prophet Jeremiah in the Sistine Chapel fresco. Our surprise at this diminishes somewhat when we take into account the eyewitness report of Giorgio Vasari, in his *Lives of the Painters*, that, when Michelangelo was at work on his great statue of Moses, the Jews of Rome would flock to gaze in admiration at his progress.

Typographically the direct offspring of Prague, the Mantua Haggadah now became in turn the progenitor of Italian illuminated Haggadahs that were to move ever farther away from the Bohemian archetype. The edition of 1560 was reprinted in Mantua in 1568 (Plates 28–31) but the insertion in the margins of a commentary by Joseph Ashkenazi of Padua entailed a radical rearrangement of the entire format. The small cuts were randomly omitted, bunched together, or moved into other contexts. Everything suddenly becomes fluid. The "Sistine" Wise Son can now serve as a representation of Rabbi Akiba, then as Rabbi Eleazar, and even as a father replying to his son's questions (Plate 31).

From Mantua—to Venice.

At the very end of the sixteenth century four Venetian editions appeared within the brief span of five years (1599, 1601, 1603, 1604). Extremely rare, and largely ignored, these nonetheless served a vital transitional purpose in the history of the illustrated Haggadah (Plates 34–43).

The marginal cuts of the Mantua editions are repeated in these Haggadahs, as are many of the ornaments. But the folio size is reduced to quarto or octavo and, more important, the Prague typography is abandoned—finally and irrevocably. The text is now set in native Italian Hebrew types, uniformly large (though not as large as in the Prague Haggadah) in the 1601 edition, and of various sizes in the other three. The larger illustrations at the bottom of the pages are supplemented with some that are entirely new. Though the text is completely in Hebrew, each of these Venetian editions contains an introductory page with the order of the Passover service explained in three parallel columns. These are in Judeo-Italian, Judeo-German (Yiddish), and Judeo-Spanish (Ladino), all printed in Hebrew characters (Plate 34). In this they adumbrate the next great development in the Haggadah, which would follow only five years later.

Venice in the early seventeenth century harbored one of the largest and most influential Jewish communities in the entire world. Though forced to live in the Ghetto (the first to have been established in Europe), the Jews had long adjusted to this inexorable aspect of their existence, and within its walls a remarkably rich and vibrant Jewish culture was able to flourish. For almost a century the Hebrew presses in the city had made it the greatest center of Hebrew printing on the continent.

Nor did it matter that the Venetian authorities, like those in other Italian cities, did not allow Jews to own a press. The pioneer of Hebrew printing in Venice early in the sixteenth century had been a Christian with a love of Hebrew books, Daniel Bomberg of Antwerp, who had produced, among other important works, the first complete edition of the Babylonian Talmud. Since then various Christian families, most of them Venetian nobles and patricians, had seen the lucrative possibilities of Hebrew printing and had set up their own presses. Though these were owned by gentiles, it was Jews who decided which works should be printed and who were employed in most of the actual printing process, from typesetting to proofreading. With so long and eminent a tradition, and with the experience of the four Haggadah editions of 1599–1604, one might well expect that the Venetian Hebrew press would at some time produce a Haggadah worthy of comparison to its other glories.

And so it was. In 1609 there emerged from the press of Giovanni da Gara an edition that marked a striking new departure in the evolution of the illustrated Haggadah and was to make its influence felt for the next three hundred years and more (Plates 44–48). The man who planned this edition was an Italian Jewish printer, Israel Zifroni, who had participated in the printing of the Talmud in Basel, Switzerland, thirty years before. Together with his co-workers he produced a host of novel features.

Each and every page was placed within a classical architectural border, of a type sometimes encountered on the title pages of Hebrew books but never within a Haggadah. The Hebrew text was set in a uniform bold Italian type, easily legible and pleasing to the eye. The illustrations were entirely new and had been prepared especially for this edition. They were placed at either the top or the foot of almost every page, particularly in the first part of the Haggadah, and depicted the biblical story, beginning with Abraham but focusing on the events around the Exodus. Though indebted to the pictorial themes of earlier Haggadahs, they are generally independent of them in execution and detail. As usual, the artist is not known, and the biblical illustrations may have some non-Jewish Venetian antecedents.

But there are two innovations that are quite unique. For the very first time we encounter, at the beginning of the Haggadah, a page divided into thirteen rectangular woodcuts depicting the various stages of the Seder (see Plate 54). Similarly, in the appropriate place another page is devoted to a group of ten cuts, each illustrating one of the Ten Plagues (Plate 44). Both features, a commonplace by our time, had their origins here.

Another equally lasting innovation was the arrangement and disposition of the pictorial themes, the illustrations for the early part of the Haggadah dealing consistently with the liberation from Egypt and the Passover ritual, while the general biblical motifs and those connected with the messianic era are concentrated in the latter part. Notable in themselves are the lovely large woodcut initial letters scattered throughout the text, each one containing tiny illustrations of the various highlights of the Seder service.

Finally, the sponsors of the Haggadah made an unprecedented decision with regard to the edition itself. They printed it in three separate issues, all identical in format, types, and illustrations, but each accompanied by a different translation set into the vertical columns of the borders. (The significance of this step within the context of the Venetian Jewish milieu will be considered in the section we shall devote to Haggadah translations.)

By the time two decades had elapsed the edition of 1609 was long sold out, and a new one was called for. This was published in Venice in 1629 by Moses ben Gershon Parenzo at the Bragadin press. Again there were three issues, according to the Italian, Ashkenazic, and Sephardic rites, with the corresponding vernacular translations (Plates 49–55). With this edition the Venetian Haggadah reached its definitive form. A commentary was now included: an abridgment of Abravanel's *Zebaḥ Pesaḥ* made by the contemporary Venetian rabbi Leone Modena and entitled *Tzeli Esh*. This was now printed within the architectural columns in place of the translations, which were relocated between the text and the illustrations at the bottom of the pages. The additional material made it necessary to enlarge the size of the pages themselves, as well as their borders. The cuts showing some of the preparations for Passover, which had appeared in 1609 on the title page, were now shifted to enclose the introduction to the commentary (Plate 49), and a new massive architectural title page was added to the whole (Plate 53).

In this final form the Haggadah was to be reprinted in Venice no less than five more times in trilingual issues, down to the very end of the eighteenth century (1664, 1695, 1716, 1758, and 1792), by which time Venetian Hebrew printing all but ceased to exist. Except for the incorporation after 1716 of an illustration from the Amsterdam Haggadah (of which we shall soon speak) showing the Giving of the Law, no further changes were introduced. Blocks were used and reused until they wore out, and then similar ones would be cut.

Such longevity in Venice itself was coupled with an amazing influence abroad. The Venetian Haggadah illustrations became the archetype for most of the Haggadahs published in the Mediterranean lands, especially after Leghorn (Livorno) usurped the place of Venice as printer to the Italian and oriental Jewries. Copied, traced, and imitated, sometimes successfully, often cheaply and primitively, Haggadahs that owe their visual inspiration to Venice have appeared in Italy and in the East down to the present.

In the seventeenth century, however, another great center of Hebrew printing arose in Northern Europe. In 1593, not long after the Dutch had successfully revolted and achieved their independence from Spain, the first group of Sephardic Jews arrived in Amsterdam and established a community. Swelled by constant immigration and the subsequent arrival of German and Polish Jews, Amsterdam Jewry was soon to vie in importance with that of Venice. Its first Hebrew press was established in 1627 by Rabbi Menasseh ben Israel, later to achieve fame for his negotiations with Oliver Cromwell over the readmission of the Jews to England. Unlike Venice, the Dutch capital had no restrictions on Jewish ownership of printing houses, and the Hebrew press proliferated rapidly. Soon the words *Defus Amsterdam* ("Printed in Amsterdam") became a byword for typographic excellence, stateliness of design, and textual reliability.

Yet the first illustrated Amsterdam Haggadah, printed in 1662, was a shabby affair, essentially a loose imitation of the Venetian editions of 1599–1604 but without their charm. More than thirty years were to pass before Amsterdam finally produced a Haggadah with a character all its own.

The Amsterdam Haggadah of 1695, printed with Abravanel's commentary, was novel in several vital respects. It was the first Haggadah ever to be illustrated by copperplates rather than woodcuts. It established a new iconography which, as we shall see, would have the most pervasive impact of any single Haggadah in history. It contained an engraved map of Palestine, with the route of the Exodus and the tribal boundaries of the Land (Plate 69), the earliest complete printed map entirely in Hebrew characters. And for the first time we know for certain who the artist was and how he worked.

He is recorded on the title page as Abraham ben Jacob "of the family of Abraham our father," a phrase which among Jews can only designate a proselyte. In fact, he was a former Christian pastor from the Rhineland who had converted to Judaism in Amsterdam, one of the very few cities in Europe where such an otherwise dangerous step could be taken with relative impunity. There he is known to have worked as an engraver of pictures and portraits, some of which are extant.

For the Haggadah of 1695 Abraham ben Jacob provided an engraved frontispiece (Plate 59) which precedes the title page. On its sides stand the large figures of Moses and Aaron. Arranged above them in small circles are five medallionlike vignettes of biblical scenes. Within the pages of the Haggadah he inserted fourteen illustrations of fairly large size, all copper engraved and all of competent if not inspired execution.

A close scrutiny, however, shows one recurring detail that is always revealing to the connoisseur. Implements, where they appear, are generally held in the left rather than the right hand, and when a hand is raised it is also the left. Now, such "left-handedness" is almost always a sign that an engraving is not original. Unless an extra step is taken to avoid it, when a printed engraving is copied by tracing and then directly retraced and etched into a new plate, the new printed impressions will be reversed, as in a mirror. Abraham ben Jacob must therefore have copied his illustrations from somewhere, and in this case the source has been discovered. Between 1625 and 1630 Matthaeus Merian of Basel had printed a large series of biblical engravings, some of them ultimately derived from Hans Holbein. They became extremely popular and were reprinted several times, including an edition that appeared in Amsterdam in 1655–62. Rachel Wischnitzer, the eminent historian of Jewish art, compared Merian's pictures with the illustrations in the Amsterdam Haggadah and proved conclusively that the latter are essentially faithful copies—with the directions reversed.

Here the fact that our artist was a proselyte assumes special significance. We need not doubt that after his conversion he lived as a believing and committed Jew. But as a former Christian he could hardly escape the pictorial memories of his past. Indeed, he used not only Merian's biblical cycle, but also other pictures by the same artist. Only with this in mind can we understand, for example, the illustration in the *Hallel*, or psalms of praise, where the Amsterdam Haggadah shows King David kneeling before a mysterious glow of light (Plate 61), identified in Hebrew as *Ruaḥ Ha-Kodesh* ("the Holy Spirit"). Entirely Christian in tone and atmosphere, with no precedents in Jewish art, it was inspired by Matthaeus Merian. Even more interesting, now that comparisons are feasible, are the occasional modifications, juxtapositions, and especially the transformations that Merian's figures underwent as they passed into the Haggadah. For the first time the Four Sons appear, not separately, but together (Plate 60). Who were they originally? The Wise Son and he "who knows not what to ask" were lifted from a Merian engraving of Hannibal before an altar. The Simple Son is Merian's Saul, being anointed by the prophet Samuel. The Wicked Son is simply one of Merian's soldiers from a battle scene (but the basic Prague tradition is still alive!). In the scene accompanying the part about the five talmudic sages who discussed the Exodus throughout the night, we have approximately *ten* figures seated at the table. The reason is that the entire tableau is a reproduction of Merian's engraving of the feast given by Joseph to his brothers, with only the dogs in the foreground of the original eliminated, and the time changed to night.

The Amsterdam Haggadah achieved immediate popularity, and before long its illustrations were being reproduced elsewhere: in Frankfurt in 1710 and in Sulzbach in 1711 (Plates 64–65). In short, it had already embarked upon what was to prove an extraordinary career.

In 1712 a second edition was published in Amsterdam, different in some respects from the first. The frontispiece (Plate 66) now contained, instead of the five medallions, a single large engraving of Moses at the Burning Bush. Within, two new illustrations were added. But the most important additions came directly from the Venice Haggadah: the representations of the order of the Seder, as well as the Ten Plagues (Plate 68), each series now engraved from a single copperplate. Also inserted were the Venetian initial letters, with their enclosed miniatures. Perhaps because of these changes, the name of Abraham ben Jacob no longer figures on the title page, though he was still alive at the time.

As with the Venetian Haggadah of 1629, so now the Amsterdam Haggadah reached its own definitive and archetypal form. It was, in fact, to exceed even the former in pictorial influence. For better or worse, since the eighteenth century the Amsterdam illustrations have found their way into countless Haggadahs printed in Northern, Central, and Eastern Europe, in England, and in the United States. The influence is to be felt to this very day, even in the cheap Haggadahs issued by charitable organizations and manufacturers of Passover products.

In general, few of the Haggadahs based on the Amsterdam edition approached the technical quality of their model, though some have a certain historic importance of their own. For example, the edition that appeared in Ostrog, Russia, in 1819, incorporates the Amsterdam illustrations in only fair copies, but at least it has the distinction of being the first illustrated Haggadah to be printed in Eastern Europe (Plates 88–89). I would propose, however, that in one Haggadah with Amsterdam pictures something was produced that can not only stand on its own, but I personally prefer it to the original. I refer to the Haggadah printed in 1722 in Offenbach, Germany (Plates 70–72). Here, it seems to me, whoever was responsible succeeded quite by chance or perhaps, ironically, out of sheer lack of "artistic" training. The engravings were copied, not traced, onto wood blocks and printed as woodcut illustrations. In the process the Amsterdam originals were simplified and "paraphrased," as it were. As a result, instead of the rather slick baroque of Merian and Abraham ben Jacob, we have here a woodcut series with all the crude power of which naive folk art is sometimes capable.

The bleakest period in the history of the illustrated Haggadah extends from the late eighteenth century through the nineteenth century. The Amsterdam and Venetian archetypes become stereotypes, repeated in endless and often tasteless variations. Innovations sometimes occur, but they do not really constitute a further development in the art of the Haggadah; they merely copy from a source that was not used before. Some London Haggadahs of the early nineteenth century are adorned with pictures of Egypt and Palestine taken from contemporary English archaeological and geographical works, or maps of Palestine and the Sinai peninsula that appeared in travelers' accounts. In the Basel edition of 1816 (Plates 86–87), there are twenty-four pleasing new woodcuts on biblical themes which, though often regarded as originals, are actually copies of Christian biblical illustrations (including one modeled after the Last Supper!).

Of all nineteenth-century pictorial Haggadahs, perhaps only three are remarkable enough to deserve special mention.

The most important is undoubtedly the Trieste Haggadah, produced in 1864 by Abraham Vita Morpurgo in two issues, one entirely in Hebrew (Plates 102–105), the other with an Italian translation. Large in format, with beautiful typography, almost every page is headed by a copper engraving made by K. Kirchmayr, a total of fifty-eight in all. Regrettably, the Trieste Haggadah was of no subsequent influence, and the tide of Venetian and Amsterdam imitations continued unabated.

Most unusual is the Haggadah published in Poona, India, in 1874 (Plates 107–110). While an earlier Bombay Haggadah of 1846 (Plates 97–98) had included three preliminary pages depicting the preparations for Passover in multiple cuts, here the number of illustrations is expanded, with the main focus on the Seder itself. But these are preceded by a full-page illustration of the preparation and baking of the matzah, with the women decked out in saris, oriental necklaces, and flowers in their hair (Plate 107). The entire scene is suffused with an authentic Indian feeling. Even the somewhat repetitive cycle illustrating the Seder is effective as exotic folk art.

Finally, mention must be made of the Prague Haggadah of 1889, with a German translation by Rabbi Alexander Kisch. This edition is unusual in that its illustrations were made by a gentile, the Slovak artist Cyril Kutlik (Plate 118). Done in a romantic style, their effect is unfortunately dimmed by rather poor reproduction in the book itself.

Not until the twentieth century was there another renaissance in the art of Haggadah illustration, a development with specific causes and characteristics. It was made possible, to begin with, by the entry of Jews into the mainstream of the arts, a thoroughly modern phenomenon. More immediately, it depended upon the emergence, not merely of artists who happened to be Jews, but of some who regarded themselves as "Jewish artists," or who at least evinced an interest in Jewish themes as part of their general artistic endeavor. These being the preconditions, we are obviously dealing with a narrow circle, though there is every sign that it may expand in the future.

The hallmark of twentieth-century Haggadah illustration, as opposed to that of the past, is its departure from established conventions. This is not only a reflection of the individuality of the modern artist, but a welcome reaction against the clichés of the previous century. It is therefore all the more intriguing to find that in many instances the venerable iconographic traditions reassert themselves, though in new guises. For all his freedom, the artist who illustrates a Haggadah is still circumscribed by the subjects of the book itself, and perhaps also conditioned by the Haggadahs he may have seen as a child. Whatever the interplay of old and new, the art of the illustrated Haggadah in this century can claim some impressive achievements.

New pictorial themes have been discovered within the Haggadah, texts and motifs that were never illustrated before but have now become favorite subjects. Such, for example, are the *Dayyenu* ("It would have sufficed us") in the first section, and the songs *Eḥad mi yode'a* ("Who Knows One?") and *Ḥad gadya* ("One Kid") in the last. Whereas the illustrations of past centuries were often doubly anachronistic, displaying ancient historical scenes in contemporary style and, conversely, not bothering to update the figures in the Seder scenes, these trends are now generally reversed. Above all, the artist brings his own unique style to bear upon each motif he draws or paints, with the result that twentieth-century Haggadahs offer a variety rarely possible in earlier times. It should also be remarked that such Haggadahs have at times provided the occasion for some of the most original and exciting experiments in Hebrew typography in modern times.

Samples from some of the most significant illustrated contemporary Haggadahs are presented in the latter part of the present volume, their features and background being noted in the descriptions that accompany the plates. Three well-known editions that are not included should be mentioned. They are the Haggadahs of Arthur Szyk (London, 1941; Tel Aviv, 1956), "Kafra" [M. Kahan-Frankel] (New York, 1949), and Ben Shahn (Boston and Paris, 1965). All three are essentially illuminated calligraphic manuscripts rather than printed books, though they have been reproduced in book form. On the other hand, the reader's attention is drawn to yet another interesting genre represented here, that of the Israeli kibbutz Haggadahs, whose illustrations are often as original as their contents.

The Gates of Interpretation

NOW THAT we have surveyed the pictorial evolution of the printed Haggadah, we should pause to consider some of its wider implications.

It would be myopic indeed not to recognize the obvious but not often acknowledged fact that the current growing preoccupation of Jews with "Jewish art," however legitimate or inevitable in itself, does not really reflect a primary concern of their forebears. This is not to say that the Jews of the past were any whit less sensitive to beauty; some of the old Haggadahs reproduced in this volume will suffice to discredit such a presumption. It does suggest, however, that their priorities may well have been different from ours.

For Jews in premodern times, the visual image was always ancillary to the word it sometimes adorned. This had nothing to do with the alleged effects of biblical iconoclasm, which, in any case, did not apply to the printed Haggadah. It was simply a natural consequence of the absolute primacy of the word among the Jewish people. The most telling proof is to be found in the history of the most illustrated of Jewish books—the Haggadah itself. Enthusiasm for some of the aesthetic accomplishments we have described must not be allowed to obscure the essential data. Most of the Haggadahs that have appeared since the invention of printing have contained no illustrations at all.

Yet many of these have their own intrinsic or historical importance, and have been no less cherished by their owners. That, of course, still leaves almost a thousand editions that *were* illustrated. But in one sense the figure is misleading. We have seen that, with some exceptions, most Haggadah illustrations prior to the twentieth century were variations of perhaps a total of four archetypes (Prague, Mantua, Venice, and Amsterdam), of which one was definitely copied from Christian models. Yet the hundreds of later plagiarisms of the Venice and Amsterdam illustrations apparently disturbed neither their printers nor their purchasers sufficiently to create demands for change. What is revealed here is not merely a certain innate conservatism, but the relative unimportance of illustration as compared to the text proper.

The text of the Haggadah is susceptible of yet another kind of adornment: the commentaries that have surrounded it even more often than woodcuts, engravings, or ornamental borders.

No important Jewish work of the past could long remain without a commentary—frequently, a host of commentaries. It is always a sure sign of the vitality of both the text and its bearers that this should be so. Any great work of law or religion requires explanation almost immediately if it is to be assimilated into the lives of multitudes. Those that have endured through the ages have opened themselves to a variety of ever-shifting interpretations which have uncovered different and even unsuspected layers of latent meaning, now suddenly become relevant. Only the text itself, at some point in its development, is fixed and canonized, but "the gates of interpretation have never been closed." This has been as true of the Haggadah as of the Bible, and he who would appreciate the history of the Haggadah in all its dimensions must take Maimonides' well-known dictum into account. In modern times, as we shall yet observe, the text of the Haggadah has been altered occasionally by those who found that it no longer spoke to them in its transmitted form. But the generations of the past did not dream of tampering with the revered text. Instead, they reinterpreted it in light of their own concerns, and in the most diverse ways.

From the Middle Ages to the modern era a galaxy of noted rabbis and scholars have written commentaries to the Haggadah, of which no less than 437 have appeared in print, usually accompanying the text. Some of these have been reprinted many times. Isaac Abravanel's *Zebaḥ Pesaḥ* alone has gone through at least 120 editions since it was first printed in 1506. Since then, there has been a constant demand for more commentaries, and many of the greatest Jewish luminaries have addressed themselves to the task. Some, in fact, found the Haggadah commentary a particularly congenial form for the expression of their deepest thoughts, and as a result their commentaries stand as major works in their own right. As but one example we may cite the *Geburot Ha-Shem* ("The Mighty Deeds of the Lord") of Rabbi Judah Loew ben Bezalel of Prague, known as the MaHaRaL, famous in later Jewish folklore as the hero of the Golem legend, and one of the most original thinkers of the sixteenth century. The work is not only a commentary upon the Passover Haggadah, but a full-fledged treatise on the Exodus, and on the meaning of Exile and Redemption.

It would be futile to attempt here a detailed discussion of Haggadah exegesis, a subject that requires a book in itself and for which this introduction is not the proper forum. But one overriding point must be stressed. Nothing can attest more eloquently to the ever-renewed vigor of the Passover Haggadah down through the ages than the rich diversity of meaning that it has yielded to different men at different times. Some commentaries are sober attempts to understand the literal sense of the text, its relation to its sources, or questions of Jewish law involved in its rituals. Others have gone far beyond that. The Haggadah has offered itself equally to all varieties of philosophic and kabbalistic speculation, to Hassidic rabbis and Lithuanian Talmudists, and to incipient secularists of the late eighteenth and early nineteenth centuries. More recently a new type of commentary has come to the fore, focusing on a purely historical examination of the development of the Haggadah, in line with the general thrust of modern critical scholarship. In sum, it is the innate quality of Haggadah commentaries that they not only illumine the text to which they are addressed, but also often reflect faithfully the changing religious and ideological concerns of Jews through the centuries. As such, they are a prime source for the intellectual history of the Jewish people.

Inevitably, many of the Haggadahs selected for facsimile reproduction here, whether illustrated or not, contain commentaries, sometimes several together. The peak is reached, symbolically at least, in a Haggadah issued in 1905 by an unusually enterprising publisher in Podgórze, Galicia, "with 238 commentaries and additions" (Plate 125). Needless to say, all the commentaries do not appear on the same page, and most are only fragments relating to a single line or word in the text.

The Many Tents of Jacob

WHAT MAY PROPERLY be termed the "geography" of the printed Haggadah contains historical implications all its own. It is of considerable importance to the study of the worldwide progress of Hebrew typography. It can reflect the changing patterns of Jewish migrations, and the rise and decline of major Jewish centers. Not least, it offers a particularly telling example of the impact of liturgy and ritual in maintaining the unity of a people physically scattered around the globe.

To date, Haggadahs have been printed in some 175 different locations. These include, besides the familiar foci of Jewish residence, a host of small, even exotic places, seemingly far removed from the main highways of Jewish history. But of course that characterization may derive more from our own parochialism than from the realities of the Jewish dispersion. For Westerners, a perusal of the oriental Haggadahs must bring a salutory revision in conventional stereotypes concerning the nature of Jewry. We have thus made a special effort to include examples from such places as Bombay and Poona in India, Aleppo in Syria, Baghdad in Iraq, as well as Istanbul, Cairo, various towns in Morocco, Tunis, and even the island of Djerba, off the Tunisian coast, which boasts one of the most ancient ongoing Jewish communities anywhere.

The geography of printing has other interesting facets. It can show quite clearly that the "Jewish map" of a particular country may not at all coincide with the familiar one in the atlas. Cities of major general population or of central significance in European history may be peripheral in terms of Jewish history. Thus, in eighteenth-century France a Haggadah could appear in the city of Metz by 1762, but not in Paris itself, which did not officially allow Jewish residence until the French Revolution. Conversely, small towns of no particular distinction sometimes became famous and important in Jewish life. This can be seen especially in Poland and Russia, where in many localities Hebrew books, including the Haggadah, often preceded the advent of non-Jewish printing in the national language. Towns like Sudzilkow, Żolkiew, and Piotrków produced five, fifteen, and twenty-three Haggadah editions respectively. Only one was ever published in Moscow, and one in St. Petersburg.

Great international centers of Hebrew printing always produced a surplus of Haggadahs for export. But at times they also printed editions expressly prepared according to the special rite of a distant Jewish community, and we are thus able to trace some interesting lines of cultural and commercial contact. A prime example is Leghorn, Italy, which in the nineteenth century became the printer for Jewries across the whole of North Africa (Plates 91–92, 106, 111–113, 123). An affecting example elsewhere is the Haggadah that appeared in Jerusalem in 1905 in Hebrew, Arabic, and English (Plate 124), a linguistic combination that does not reflect the actual needs of any one local group in the Holy City at that time. It was commissioned by an Indian Jew in Calcutta, where the Jewish community, originally from the Arabic-speaking lands, had by now learned English under the British raj.

The more meaningful patterns take shape only when we correlate geography with chronology.

We have already traced the origins of the printed Haggadah to the Iberian peninsula and to Italy, as well as its eastward migration in the early sixteenth century as a consequence of the Spanish Expulsion. By mid-century, Salonika in Greece surpassed even Constantinople as the greatest Jewish community in the Ottoman Empire, and the first Haggadah was printed there in 1569 (Plate 32). Both cities continued to produce editions well into our own century, the latest Salonika imprint appearing as recently as 1970 (Plates 198–199).

In Central Europe the Prague Haggadah of 1526 and the Augsburg edition of 1534 were, as we have seen, the pioneers. Prague remained in a dominant position in the area until the eighteenth century, and Haggadahs were printed there until 1927.

By the end of the sixteenth century the printed Haggadah had appeared in Eastern Europe as well. The first extant edition (others may have perished) was printed in 1592 in the village of Bistrowitz, near the

Polish city of Lublin. It has the further distinction of being the only Hebrew book ever to be printed in that place (Plate 33). There is a reason for this anomaly. The printer, originally from Lublin, went to Bistrowitz only to escape the plague, and produced the Haggadah during his temporary sojourn. No other East European edition was to appear until the end of the eighteenth century. Though the Haggadah was printed in many towns in Poland and Russia in the nineteenth and twentieth centuries, the greatest suppliers by far were the Hebrew presses of Warsaw and Vilna.

The very first Amsterdam Haggadah appeared, not in Hebrew, but in Spanish. It was produced in 1622, some five years before the introduction of Hebrew printing in the city. (The significance of this development will be analyzed in the next section.) Toward the end of the century the impact of the great illustrated Haggadah of 1695 may have contributed to the spread of Haggadah printing in Germany and Austria. Whereas only one edition had appeared there before (Frankfurt am Main, 1678), in the eighteenth century the Haggadah began to proliferate in Frankfurt itself and in such cities as Sulzbach, Berlin, Wilhermsdorf, Offenbach, Fürth, and Karlsruhe (for some examples, see Plates 64–65, 70–72, 80, 81, 83, 84). Vienna, whose first Haggadah is dated 1791, was to become, at least in terms of quantity, one of the most important centers of Haggadah printing in modern times, some 260 separate editions bearing its imprint. The first Haggadah in England came off the press in London in 1770 (Plate 74). Leghorn, heir to Venice as printer to the rest of Italy and the East, produced its first Hebrew Haggadah in 1782 (Plate 76).

No permanent Hebrew press arose in Asia until almost the middle of the nineteenth century, though there had been some abortive attempts to establish one earlier. In the sixteenth century Safed in Palestine had a press for about a decade, and in the seventeenth century one

Hebrew book was printed in Damascus. None of these productions were Haggadahs. In 1841, however, a Hebrew press was established in Calcutta and another, coincidentally, in Jerusalem. The first Indian Haggadah appeared in that same year, and the first in the Holy City came out a year later. In Africa, Algiers lays claim to a first in the field (1855), while in Australia the Haggadah was not printed until 1945 (Plate 168).

In the Western Hemisphere, the first edition of the Haggadah in the United States was printed in New York City in 1837, in Hebrew and English (Plate 93). The overwhelming majority of Haggadahs in this country have continued to appear in New York ever since, a token of its absolute primacy in the cultural and religious life of American Jewry. In Mexico City the Haggadah was first published in 1946, with a Spanish translation and interesting illustrations (Plate 171). The first South American Haggadah was hitherto believed to be that of Buenos Aires, in 1934 (Plate 154), but recent information reveals that one had already appeared there in 1919, a copy of which is preserved in the YIVO Institute for Jewish Research in New York.

Through all these peregrinations, one fact stands out: the main body of the Haggadah text remained virtually constant. The various liturgical traditions followed by Jews in different parts of the world affected only occasional phrases or the interpolation of some festival poems hallowed by local usage. This fundamental unity of world Jewry has been breached to some extent only since the last century, of which more will be said later.

Otherwise, one can point to but two exceptions to the rule, if such they may be called. These involve the only two significant Jewish sects to have survived until the present day: the Samaritans and the Karaites.

The Samaritans are an ancient sect that broke off from the main body of the Jewish people in late biblical times. By now only a pathetically reduced remnant lives in the State of Israel. They do not actually have a Haggadah, since they do not really have a Seder. Instead, they still cling to the ancient rite of actually sacrificing the paschal lamb in a collective celebration at their holy place on Mount Gerizim. A book devoted to the Samaritan Passover, published in Tel Aviv in 1962, includes the liturgical hymns intoned on the occasion. Though technically not a Haggadah, we have deemed it proper to include a sample page (Plate 194), both for its historic interest and as an example of the Samaritan script, the only one still in use that preserves the characters of the ancient Hebrew alphabet.

The Karaites, on the other hand, have played a major role in Jewish history and, though they are a sect, have never been completely isolated from the mainstream. Karaism first arose in Iraq in the eighth century in reaction to the dominance of Babylonian Talmudic Judaism. Rejecting the authority of both the Talmud and its rabbinic representatives, Karaites went on to elaborate their own traditions on the same biblical base. Never really powerful enough to pose a decisive threat, they interacted with the majority on many, often polemically stimulating, levels. Through the ages a series of Karaite centers arose in different places. By the nineteenth century European Karaites were concentrated in the Balkans, Poland, and the south of Russia. In 1879 the Karaite Haggadah was published separately for the first time in Pressburg, Hungary, with an Arabic translation intended for the Karaites of Cairo. Four years later, in 1883, it appeared again in Odessa, this time in Hebrew and Russian, for use in the Crimea (Plate 114). We need hardly add that the Karaite Haggadah is composed solely of selections from the Bible, all the classical Rabbinic passages so familiar to most Jews being completely excluded.

The Many Tongues of Exile

TO DATE the printed translations of the Haggadah have included the following languages (in alphabetical order): Afrikaans, Arabic, (Kurdish)-Aramaic, Czech, Danish, Dutch, English, French, German, Greek, Hungarian, Italian, Japanese, Judeo-Arabic, Judeo-German (Yiddish), Judeo-Italian, Judeo-Persian, Judeo-Spanish (Ladino), Judeo-Tatar, Latin, Marathi, Polish, Portuguese, Romanian, Russian, Slovak, Spanish, and Swedish. An impressive list, its inner meaning unfolds only when we examine the larger cultural and historic phenomena that it epitomizes. But first we must understand the significance of the "hyphenated" Jewish languages in the roster.

In daily life throughout the Middle Ages Jews generally spoke the language of their non-Jewish neighbors. Gradually and in varying degrees, however, a number of these vernaculars tended to become Judaized, as it were, and to develop special characteristics of their own. Two factors were primarily responsible for this. Jews learned to read and write only Hebrew in their schools. As a result, they would write even the vernacular tongue in Hebrew characters, and this in turn tended to modify their pronunciation and perception of the language. In addition, they were also inclined to introduce certain Jewish turns of phrase or actual Hebrew words into their vernacular speech. As time went by, the vernacular used by Jews in a particular country or area sometimes developed a specific dialect, recognizably Jewish and varying from that of the gentile majority. In some cases the development transcended the bounds of dialect, and a full-fledged language was the result. It was all a matter of degree and historical circumstance.

The two most famous Jewish vernaculars are those that drifted farthest away from their points of origin. These are Judeo-German, which evolved into Yiddish, and Judeo-Spanish, which became Ladino. Both have a common denominator in that they were first carried out of their native habitats and transplanted into new and alien linguistic environments. Thus, as a result of persecutions and economic pressures, Ashkenazic Jews migrated from the Germanic lands to Poland in the thirteenth and fourteenth centuries, bearing with them their Judeo-German dialect. In Poland both they and their descendents continued to speak it in subsequent centuries. Cut off now from the development of the German language in Germany itself, their speech underwent a further evolution of its own, to become eventually—Yiddish. Similarly, as a result of the Spanish Expulsion, many thousands of Jews made their way to the Near East. But they and later generations continued to speak and write the Castilian dialect they had brought with them in 1492, and which now, like Yiddish in Poland, underwent an autonomous evolution in the Balkans, Turkey, and North Africa. Ladino, indeed, remained somewhat closer to Spanish than Yiddish did to German, but both are distinct languages with rich and significant literatures. Judeo-Arabic, which developed indigenously in the Muslim lands, was the first Jewish vernacular to create an important literary corpus, which includes the bulk of medieval Jewish philosophic and scientific works. Like Arabic itself, Judeo-Arabic exists in many different dialects, depending on the place. All Jewish languages are written in the Hebrew alphabet. And all of them, whatever their origins, have played a major role in Jewish life in the Diaspora. Despite declines in this century, they remain the living speech of Jews in many parts of the world.

The practice of translating the Haggadah into the local vernacular must be very old. It derives from the central purpose of the Haggadah itself: to relate the story of the redemption from Egypt to the son, in fulfillment of the biblical injunction (Exodus 13:8): "And thou shalt tell thy son in that day, saying: it is done because of that which the Lord did for me when I came forth out of Egypt." For this to be accomplished meaningfully, the Haggadah (which means, literally, "the Telling") must also be rendered in a language that the child, as well as adults who do not know Hebrew, will comprehend. It would seem that when such translating took place at the Seder table, however, it was done orally by the head of the house, and that for a long time it was not deemed necessary to provide translations in manuscripts or in books.

The first printed translation of the Haggadah (Murner's Latin version of 1512) was not, as we have observed, the work of Jews. In any case, Latin was inaccessible to all but a few Jewish scholars. The only other Latin translation of the Haggadah, which appeared in Königsberg, Germany, in 1644 (Plates 56–57), was the work of the Christian Hebraist Johann Stephanus Rittangel. (This edition is notable for being the earliest Haggadah to be published with musical notation for some of the hymns.)

The earliest portion of the Haggadah actually to emerge in a Jewish vernacular was the hymn *Adir hu*. It is in old Yiddish, or Judeo-German, and begins with the words *Almekhtiger Got*. In this form it is already found in some fifteenth-century manuscripts. It was printed at the end of the Prague Haggadah of 1526, and thereafter it was carried over into later editions in many places (see, e.g., Plate 37). Other parts of the Haggadah, especially its rules and instructions, were printed in Judeo-German in two Ashkenazic prayer books published in Venice in 1545 and 1549 (Plates 19–20).

Not until the seventeenth century did the first complete Jewish translations appear, with the simultaneous printing of the three issues of the illustrated Venice Haggadah of 1609. The languages (Judeo-Italian, Judeo-German, and Judeo-Spanish) were a reflection of the composite character of Venetian Jewry. In addition to its native Italian Jews, the great city of the lagoons had long contained an Ashkenazic community formed originally by German Jewish immigrants, and since the sixteenth century a Sephardic community as well. Each had its own synagogue and customs, and each perpetuated its own Jewish vernacular. In the revised Haggadah of 1629 (Plates 49–55) the trilingual pattern was maintained, and so it continued in all the Venetian editions to the end of the eighteenth century. Later editions published in Leghorn in the nineteenth century generally preserved only the Judeo-Spanish translation, since they were destined for the Ladino-speaking Sephardim of the Levant (Plates 91, 106).

The first translations printed by Jews in a standard European language appeared in Venice in 1620 and in Amsterdam in 1622. Both were entirely in Spanish, that is, in the Castilian then in use in Spain itself, printed in the Roman alphabet. Another such translation was subsequently published in Leghorn, in 1654 (Plate 58). The very fact that these editions are in contemporary Spanish rather than Ladino, coupled with the complete omission of the Hebrew text, is a clear indication of their historical background. Such Haggadah translations were prepared for those Marranos, or crypto-Jews, who continued to flee from the Iberian peninsula in the sixteenth and seventeenth centuries in order to return elsewhere to the full and open practice of Judaism. Having grown up in post-Expulsion Spain and Portugal, they had received no Hebrew education; if they were to be integrated rapidly into the Jewish community, they would have to use liturgical and other religious works rendered into Spanish. That the first three Spanish editions of the Haggadah were printed in these particular places is by no means accidental. In the seventeenth century Venice, Amsterdam, and Leghorn were the most important centers in the whole of Europe for the reception of Marrano immigrants.

With the English language it was an entirely different matter. English had never really had a chance to develop a significant Jewish offshoot, the Jews of England having suffered, in 1290, the very first of European expulsions. Only in the mid-seventeenth century were Jews again admitted and officially tolerated. For the next century or so, Spanish and Portuguese among the Sephardic community, and Yiddish among the Ashkenazim, were the regnant tongues. However, after the middle of the eighteenth century many Jews were sufficiently rooted to feel the need for translations into the language of the land. The very first Haggadah to be printed in London appeared, as we saw, in 1770, and this was also the first edition anywhere to be accompanied by an English translation (Plate 74). Later London editions would provide the English text for the first American Haggadah of 1837. In London itself, Haggadahs still continued to be produced in Spanish translation into the nineteenth century (Plate 85). In New York, on the other hand, a fair number of mid-nineteenth-century Haggadahs were translations into German, a result of the German Jewish immigration of the 1840s (Plate 101).

Haggadah translations from Germany and the Austrian Empire in the late eighteenth century are sometimes a barometer of the new winds of modernization and change that were then blowing strongly in various Jewish communities. Up to that time the translations had been into Yiddish. But under the influence of the movement for modern enlightenment known as the Haskalah, they began to shift from Judeo-German, or Yiddish, to pure German, though still printed in Hebrew characters (Plates 80–81, 84). The final step was taken in the nineteenth century, when the translations began to be printed in the German alphabet (Plate 94).

Except for the "Marrano" Haggadahs mentioned above, all translations prior to the nineteenth century were published together with the Hebrew text. Only later was Hebrew dispensed with, a sign of the decline of Hebrew literacy among modern Jews. A similar process has occurred also with the progressive abandonment of Jewish vernaculars in favor of the contemporary language of the non-Jewish environment. In certain instances the Jewish vernacular has been kept but the Hebrew alphabet has been dropped. This has sometimes led to curious results. In Bulgaria Haggadahs have been published in which the language itself is Ladino, but the characters in which it is printed are the Cyrillic alphabet used in Bulgarian and Russian. In a Haggadah that appeared in Istanbul in 1932, the Ladino is printed in the Roman alphabet, according to the rules of modern Turkish orthography (Plate 153).

The need of Jews for translations into non-Jewish idioms, and the time these make their appearance, are usually also a fairly reliable index of cultural assimilation into the environment. It is therefore not coincidental that such translations appear earlier in Western than in Eastern Europe. Inevitably, however, the same historical processes created also a desire for Polish, Russian, and other Slavic translations (Plates 145, 146, 156).

Among the oriental Jewries, the linguistic situation was more stable, at least until recently. To this day Judeo-Arabic and Judeo-Persian still enjoy a considerable vogue. But even here there have been inroads, the use of French by educated North African Jews being one major instance, the use of Arabic script, another (Plates 133, 152). In India there were essentially two different Jewish communities. One, derived from Baghdadi and other Arabic-speaking Jews, employed Judeo-Arabic for its books. The other is composed of the so-called Bene Israel, native Indian Jews who managed to maintain their Jewish identity for centuries in the midst of a sea of Hindu religions. Their language is Marathi, one of the major languages of the Indian subcontinent, and is written in Marathi script. Both groups have published Haggadahs in their respective vernaculars (Plates 97–98, 107–110, 120, 124).

Of the many Haggadah translations that might be discussed with profit, one deserves special mention because of the unusual circumstances which gave birth to it. In 1928 a Haggadah was printed in the northern Portuguese city of Pôrto (Plate 151). It was the first Portuguese translation ever published, and thereby hangs a tale.

After centuries of persecution by the Inquisition, it seemed, at the end of the eighteenth century, that the Marrano problem had finally been solved in Portugal and that the Marranos had completely assimilated and disappeared. In reality, however, they had only disappeared from view. In 1917 Samuel Schwarz, a Polish Jewish engineer residing in Lisbon, went on a trip to the north of Portugal, where he began to hear rumors of the continued existence of Marranos in the isolated towns and tiny hamlets of the region. A determined gentleman, he succeeded in making contact with them, and published a book announcing his rather sensational discovery. In Lisbon, Amsterdam, London, and New York, committees were organized to aid the Portuguese Marranos to return to Judaism after an underground existence that had endured for more than four hundred years. Remarkably, a leader arose from among the Marranos themselves, a Portuguese army captain named Arthur Carlos de Barros-Basto. After some Jewish study, with great energy he began a movement of return among his fellow Marranos which, for several decades, had considerable success. A Jewish school was opened in Pôrto, and a synagogue was built with help from abroad. A journal was also published regularly, directed specifically at informing the Marranos of traditional Judaism and encouraging them to declare themselves as Jews. Barros-Basto also undertook to translate some of the more vital Jewish religious literature, with special emphasis on liturgy and ritual. One of these publications was the Pôrto Haggadah of 1928, the only Marrano Haggadah of the twentieth century.

Modern Visions and Revisions

OUR DISCUSSIONS thus far have centered around the traditional Haggadah in its various dimensions, and the translations we have considered have themselves been faithful to the accepted text. Since the last century, however, there have been a number of conscious attempts to depart from the traditional text, now regarded by some segments of Jewry as no longer expressing their deepest religious feelings nor their understanding of the Passover festival itself. For these Jews a new interpretive commentary could no longer suffice as it had in the past; the text itself had to be altered. Such changes neither began nor ended with the Haggadah. They have always been a microcosm of more fundamental changes in the relation of Jews to Jewish tradition.

The Reform movement in Judaism began in Germany in the early nineteenth century and spread from there to other countries on both sides of the Atlantic. Though the earliest Reform prayer book was published in Hamburg in 1818, the first separate edition of a Reform Haggadah appeared, not in Germany, but in England. In 1836 and again in 1839 some members of the Ancient Synagogue of Spanish and Portuguese Jews (Bevis Marks) in London petitioned to introduce some of the Hamburg reforms. Rebuffed on both occasions and unsuccessful in their attempt to form a branch synagogue in the West End, they incorporated in 1840 as an independent Reform congregation, to be called the West London Synagogue of British Jews. In 1841 they issued their first prayer book and, in the following year, their first Haggadah (Plate 96).

Reform Judaism in the United States had its formal beginnings in

Charleston, South Carolina, in 1825, and for a long while pursued a more radical course than its European counterpart. Reform prayer books in America began to appear in the 1850s, and were compiled by individual rabbis until the standardized *Union Prayerbook* was published in 1895. Twelve years later, in 1907, the *Union Haggadah* appeared (Plate 126), and it has since been reprinted often. A thoroughly new and revised Haggadah is to be published shortly, and I am informed that many traditional elements will be restored. Both the other mainstream religious movements in American Jewish life, Conservative and Orthodox, have continued to maintain the traditional text throughout. Only Reconstructionism, originally an offshoot of the Conservative movement founded by Mordecai Kaplan, has produced a new version of its own, published in 1942. In the past decade or so, several new experimental Haggadahs have been published in the United States. These derive, not from any organized religious body, but from individuals or small groups involved in some of the New Left or radical Jewish youth movements that arose in the 1960s. Time alone will tell whether they herald a new trend or are merely ephemeral expressions of the turbulent period in which they were produced.

There remains one entire class of "modern Haggadahs" which, though little known in the Jewish Diaspora, is by now a well-established genre and marks one of the most significant phases in the long history of the Haggadah. I refer to the Haggadahs of the Israeli kibbutz.

The pioneers who went to Palestine in modern times to rebuild the Jewish national home transformed not only the Land but also themselves. It was one of their cardinal tenets that the return to Zion, to farming and manual labor, must necessarily effect profound changes in the ethos and outlook of those who participated in the task and in the structure of the new Jewish society that would arise out of their efforts. Nowhere were these transformations more concretely enshrined than in the kibbutz collectives that they established. But the kibbutz has been more than a daring experiment in social organization. It also represented and represents today a continuing quest for new and viable forms of Jewish life and expression. However secular in orientation most may be, the members of the kibbutzim are Jews living for the first time since antiquity on Jewish soil. The festivals bequeathed by tradition are still the festivals of the kibbutz. But in the "Old-New Land" (Theodor Herzl's apt phrase) it was to be expected that the old festivals would find new forms.

Among these, Passover has retained a preeminent position, and two new elements in the manner of its celebration stand out. While still very much a historical holiday, in an agricultural setting it has also become a celebration of spring. At its core this is not so much an innovation as it is a reassertion of one of the ancient elements in Passover, echoes of which remained even in the liturgy and ritual of the synagogue. The other major change is also a consequence of the kibbutz way of life. The Seder is celebrated, not by the individual family, but by all the members of the kibbutz together, young and old, in the communal dining hall. However secularized, the pioneers of the kibbutzim may be said to have tried to emphasize in Passover that which was most sacred to them: Nature and History, the revival of earth and seasons, the renewal of the nation after its long travail in exile.

Though the Jewish prayer book was largely abandoned, the Haggadah, even if reedited and rewritten, was retained. The first kibbutz Haggadah was issued in Giv'at Brenner in 1935. It will come as a surprise to many that since then at least a thousand different editions have appeared in the various settlements across the land. The early Haggadahs, especially, were primitive in format and usually consisted of mimeographed pages. Later ones have tended to be more elaborate and are often printed with illustrations of considerable originality and beauty. Taken together they constitute a virtually untapped mine of material for the history, attitudes, and folklore of the Israeli kibbutz.

Although recently some of the sponsoring ideological movements have issued some standardized editions for those kibbutzim that are affiliated with them, there is no "authorized version" of the kibbutz Haggadah, and in earlier decades each settlement pursued its own individual course in the matter. Nevertheless, some common features can be perceived in most of them.

Recurring thematic patterns tend to revolve around spring, the Exodus, peace, and the ingathering of the Jewish people to the Land of Israel. The opening text will often consist of verses from the Song of Songs (e.g., 2:11–12: "For lo, the winter is past, the rain is over and gone; the flowers appear on the earth; the time of singing is come . . ."). Some biblical and postbiblical elements from the traditional Haggadah are usually preserved, such as verses from the Book of Exodus and from the Psalms, *Ha laḥma anya* ("This is the bread of affliction"), *Abadim hayyinu* ("We were slaves unto Pharaoh in Egypt"), the *Shefokh ḥamatkha*, and others; but they alternate with passages and poems either written by members of the kibbutz or culled from modern Hebrew literature. The Four Questions figure prominently, but often with an entirely new text addressed to contemporary issues (Plates 166, 182). *Ḥad gadya* appears, both in Aramaic and in Hebrew translation. Curiously, the Four Sons are rarely if ever present, and the same is true of the Ten Plagues. An exception to the latter is a Haggadah issued in Hanita after the War of Independence, in which the plagues are reinterpreted in terms of ten major campaigns that brought victory over the enemy. Indeed, a pervasive feature of almost all kibbutz Haggadahs is their tendency to give immediate expression to historical events. The early Haggadahs, especially, would recite the history of the settlement itself, its struggles, failures, and successes. As we shall yet have occasion to observe, the kibbutz Haggadah also absorbed into itself all the great events that befell the Jewish people both in the Land and in the Diaspora.

In specific details, though, kibbutz Haggadahs have varied widely, each bearing its particular stamp of place, time, and ideology. They can run the gamut from only slight shifts away from tradition to the most radical departures. In a 1938 Haggadah, Passover and the Egyptian Exodus play no role whatever, and the texts and songs revolve entirely around the theme of working the soil. Such neopaganism is, however, rarely to be encountered. The pioneers may have been far removed from the traditional faith of their fathers, but theirs was no less passionate and absolute.

As a matter of fact, even the Lord has not quite disappeared from the kibbutz Haggadah, and He often continues to figure in one way or another, at least between the lines. To be sure, systematic attempts to exclude Him have occasionally been made, by abbreviating biblical verses or changing the words of traditional songs. But it is no easy task. As one scholar has noted wryly in commenting on the phenomenon, the Holy One, blessed be He, is, after all, the hero and main protagonist of the Exodus, and it is difficult to tell the story without encountering Him somewhere. We might add that the gravitational pull of several millennia of Jewish tradition is evident also in other respects. In the latter part of the kibbutz Haggadah some psalms may be deleted and new texts introduced. But such Haggadahs rise to no less a crescendo of messianic hope and expectation for absolute social justice among all men, an end to war, and the return of the Jewish people to a land at peace in a peaceful world. Despite its novelties, the kibbutz Haggadah remains, like its predecessors, a book of remembrance and—a book of redemption . . .

Parodies—Satiric, Esoteric, and Blasphemous

OUR FINAL CATEGORY is an ambiguous one. It includes works that are technically not Haggadahs at all, but rather parodies of the original. Never intended for use at any Seder, they are linked nonetheless to the genuine Haggadah which lies at their base, and testify in yet another way to its enduring influence. Ironically, parodies are almost always an inverted tribute to the very texts they propose to ape, since only the famous and instantly recognizable text can be parodied without becoming a private joke. From this point of view the Haggadah is more than capable of serving as an ideal vehicle.

Parodies of various kinds have long enjoyed a certain popularity among Jews. Some were produced in the Middle Ages. But it was especially in the nineteenth and twentieth centuries that a widespread revival took place, not only in Hebrew, but also in Yiddish and other languages. Among these a considerable number have been written in the guise of a Haggadah, or some portion of it. Some have been geared to historical or political events. Most have provided a biting commentary on a variety of social, economic, or cultural ills, both Jewish and general, major and minor. Several examples will be found in this volume, one of which, a "Teachers' Haggadah" published in Odessa in 1885 (Plate 116), compares the lot of the East European instructors of Jewish children to that of the oppressed slaves in ancient Egypt. Another is the curious species known as the "Purim Haggadah," in which the levity of the Purim holiday is conveyed in the form of a Haggadah (Plate 128). Among the many more that could not be included are "Haggadahs" deploring the poverty of Hebrew authors in Poland (Cracow, 1890) and the sufferings of Russian yeshiva students (Warsaw, 1899). A Yiddish "Passover Haggadah in a New Version," which went through several editions in England and America, was a satire against capitalism produced by a Jewish socialist in 1887. A parody of the *Ḥad gadya* in 1880 aimed its barbs at the burdensome meat tax in Russia. In 1905 a "War Haggadah" satirized the recent Russo-Japanese conflict, and in the same year a parody entitled "Nicolas's Seder" ridiculed the Tsar and the Russian bureaucracy. Out of the East European immigrant milieu in New York came a number of Haggadahs satirizing aspects of American Jewish life. While some of these parodies detailed a litany of abuses, others pursued a special target. Thus in 1883 a "Haggadah" made sport of Galician Hasidim in New York who had recently brought their rabbi to the New World, and another, published in 1900, was single-mindedly concerned with the perils of Jewish boardinghouses. American readers may be intrigued to discover that in the New York election campaign of 1904, a Yiddish parody entitled "The Ten Plagues of Tammany" attempted to expose the evils of Tammany Hall politicians to the Jewish voter.

None of these or similar parodies were aimed at the traditional Haggadah itself, which was for them an object of neither mockery nor attack, but simply a congenial form through which to assail some other target. However, there exist some items of a darker—some would say more insidious—character.

In the Harvard University Library there is to be found a volume which, though some other copies exist (one is at the British Museum in London), is probably unique in its style and content. Fitting into no available category, it may somehow be considered a parody. It is, in effect, a Christian missionary "Haggadah," published in Berlin in 1830 and intended for the conversion of Jews (Plate 90). The Hebrew title ingenuously proclaims it a "Children's Haggadah" (*Haggadat Pesaḥ le-tinokot Yisrael*); the text is entirely in Yiddish. From its language and its allusions to rabbinic literature, we may confidently assume that it was written by a Jewish apostate, perhaps under the sponsorship of the Berlin missionary society for the promotion of Christianity among the Jews. Of course no such attribution is offered explicitly anywhere in the book, nor is the real name of the author recorded. Instead, it blandly palms itself off as a Jewish work, written by a Jew for Jewish youth merely to explain the "inner meaning" of the paschal sacrifice. Structurally, it consists of a series of dialogues that take place around the table on three Passover nights. The main protagonists are a pious Jewish father, called "Reb Shelomo bar Menahem the Preacher," and his inquiring son, Samuel. What distinguishes the work as a whole, besides its unique form, is its relative subtlety of approach. Direct Christian allusions are so minimal as to pass almost unnoticed. The core of the dialogues consists of a progressive uncovering of the alleged problematics of Jewish belief, first by the father and then, more radically, by the son. The technique is one of constantly raising doubts, rather than direct Christian preaching, of erosion rather than frontal attack. The "Haggadah" does not even end with the proclamation of a Christian victory or with an actual conversion, both so common in missionary literature aimed at Jews. Unable to reply satisfactorily to his son's final questions, the father directs him to take them before a rabbi. However, it requires little sophistication to realize that by now the son is well on his way, not to a rabbi, but to the baptismal font.

If the missionary "Haggadah" of 1830 represents a classic Christian effort to subvert Judaism from without, in our own century at least two parodies of the Haggadah appeared as part of an unprecedented campaign to uproot Judaism from within. These were composed by Jews, in the interests not of Christianity but of Communism.

The antireligious campaign that was launched in the Soviet Union in the years following the Bolshevik Revolution was directed against religion generally. Yet like so many other aspects of Soviet policy, it had particular ramifications and nuances for Jews, whose peoplehood and religion are so much more intimately fused than are those of others. More ominous still was the fact that the attack against Judaism as a religion was entrusted to the *Yevsektziia*, the Jewish section of the Commissariat of Nationalities. It undertook the task with an enthusiasm exceeded only by its zealous and successful eradication of all open manifestations of Hebrew culture in the country, Yiddish alone being officially blessed as a Jewish language.

Both antireligious parodies of the Haggadah known to have been printed in the Soviet Union appeared in Yiddish. One, published in Moscow in 1927, is designated as a second edition (Plate 144). Its Yiddish title speaks for itself: *Hagodeh far Gloiber un Apikorsim* ("Haggadah for Believers and Atheists"). In the cover illustration, naive-looking Jews seated at a table are surrounded by the dark outlines of devils and other diabolic creatures. The other parody was published in Kharkov around 1930 and is entitled *Komsomolishe Hagodeh*. It was apparently compiled for the edification of the Jewish members of the Komsomol, the youth organization of the Communist party, as part of a series of atheist tracts called *Kegn Shiml fun Doires* ("Against the Mildew of the Ages").

Atheism among modern Jews is, of course, hardly an unfamiliar phenomenon. Atheism under ideological coercion is an entirely different matter. Unlike the Berlin "Haggadah" of 1830, these are no mere curiosities. They are documents, small but vivid, of an episode in one of the major Jewish tragedies of the twentieth century.

In the Midst of History

THE TITLE of this volume—*Haggadah and History*—implies a dual theme whose nature is now perhaps clearer than it was at the outset. Briefly, it proposes that the history of the Haggadah as a book is, time and again, inseparable from its role as a mirror of history itself. We have already seen that no matter from which angle the printed Haggadah is approached, sooner or later we confront some significant development of the last five hundred years. It remains for us now to enlarge our view and to contemplate how truly faithful a mirror of Jewish history the Haggadah has been.

To the uninitiated, some Haggadahs seem at first to betray no particular historical features at all. Yet as soon as we bring to bear some modicum of knowledge concerning the time and place in which they were printed, their seemingly bland title pages come alive with historical drama. One such instance from among the Haggadahs reproduced in the plates will suffice to demonstrate the point.

In Italy a Haggadah was printed in the city of Cremona in 1557 (Plate 21) and another in 1561 in Riva di Trento (Plate 27). Their title pages bear the usual information, and there is nothing to indicate that they bear any relationship to one another. Yet not only are they historically linked, but they both emerge out of a particularly eventful episode in Italian Jewish history. In the wake of the Catholic Counter-Reformation of the mid-sixteenth century, the Papacy and the Church began to implement an ever more oppressive policy against the Jews. Nowhere were the effects felt more drastically than in Italy itself. Beyond the actual physical and economic restrictions against Jews, their books also came under attack by the recently established Roman Inquisition. As a result, the Talmud was condemned and its confiscation decreed. On September 9, 1553, the Talmud was burned in a great pyre in the Campo di Fiori in Rome, together with many other Hebrew books that had been taken indiscriminately from their owners. Similar burnings soon followed in Bologna, Venice, and other Italian cities.

Fortunately, the decree was not yet obeyed in northern Italy, especially in the Duchy of Milan, which was then under the rule of Spain, itself in conflict with the papacy. Cremona, one of the towns in the duchy, now became a seat of Jewish learning transplanted from other places. With the temporary cessation of the Hebrew presses in Venice, a new one was established in Cremona which, as usual, was owned by a Christian, Vicenzo Conti. It was at the Conti press that the Haggadah of 1557 was printed. However, only two years later, in the summer of 1559, the Talmud was burned in Cremona as well. The many Hebrew books in Conti's shop were also destroyed, and his press was heavily damaged.

A new outlet was now to be found in the small town of Riva di Trento in the Italian Tyrol. A Hebrew press set up there as recently as 1558, having begun as a competitor to Cremona, now became its heir. For a considerable fee the ruler of the town, Cardinal Christophoro Madruzzi of Trent, allowed Hebrew printing to continue. His name appears on the title page of the Haggadah of 1561, along with that of Dr. Jacob Marcaria, a distinguished Jewish physician who was the guiding spirit of the press. In the very next year (1562) the Riva press was also discontinued. There are indications that the Haggadah of 1561, which contained Abravanel's commentary, was planned as part of the usual trilogy of his works, and that the types for the other two had already been set. These were now transported to Venice, where printing had meanwhile resumed, and printed there. The Haggadahs of

Cremona and Riva di Trento are rare and valuable books in themselves. They are also silent yet eloquent witnesses to the desperate attempt to find a haven for the persecuted Hebrew book in a time of travail.

Such examples from the past could be multiplied. It is, however, particularly in the modern era that the Haggadah has become more sensitive than ever to historical events.

One of the most unusual publications of the Haggadah text is that which must be called, for want of a real title, "The Haggadah of the London *Times*" (Plate 95). It consists of a complete English translation printed in that prestigious newspaper in the issue of Monday, August 17, 1840. The circumstances of its appearance are given explicitly in the preamble:

CELEBRATION OF PASSOVER BY THE JEWS

A correspondent has furnished the annexed very minute account of this ceremony, which will be exceedingly curious in itself to most of our readers, and has at the same time an evident bearing on the Damascus case. It repels strongly the barbarous notion that human blood, or blood of any kind, is essential to its celebration.

The Damascus blood libel that had erupted in the Syrian city in 1840 had caused an immediate sensation everywhere. Father Thomas, the head of the local Franciscan convent, was found murdered. At the instigation of an anti-Semitic French consul, the pasha of Damascus had eight leaders of the Jewish community imprisoned and tortured in order to extract from them a confession of ritual murder. In an age perhaps more easily shocked than our own by such outrages, the revival of the medieval slander that Jews require Christian blood for Passover aroused around the world a storm of protest by both Jews and gentiles. The most important protest meeting was held in London on July 3. Ultimately, as a result of the personal intervention of Sir Moses Montefiore in Alexandria, the Egyptian khedive Mohammed Ali, who also controlled Syria, ordered the release of the remaining prisoners (one had died of the torture, and another had converted to Islam).

The Damascus Affair was a cause célèbre, and it was natural that throughout this period the London *Times* should report the latest news, as well as the opinions of its readers. The latter, incidentally, were by no means unanimous as to the innocence of the Jews of Damascus, and letters to the editor argued both sides of the question. Indeed, the column to the immediate left of the Haggadah translation contains a letter signed "Sigma," which sets out to prove that human sacrifice is condoned by the Hebrew Scriptures. The anonymous writer was prepared, however, to give the benefit of the doubt to British Jews, or at least to their middle and upper classes:

> There is a difference in the Christianity of the Archbishop of Canterbury and a follower of Joanna Southcote. May there not be a similar difference between the Judaism of Sir Moses Montefiore and an old rag-broker in the purlieus of Harrow-alley? And what would be according to the law and the prophets in the mind of an ignorant and fanatic Jew, in the dead of night, in a by-lane of Damascus, would be loathsome and horrible to the cultivated mind and polished intellect of the London merchant.

A reply to this came the next day in a letter signed "A Christian," which pointed out that by distorting the biblical view of human sacrifice, "Sigma" had slandered not only Judaism but also Christianity itself. The *Times*'s own stand on the matter is revealed in its long editorial of August 17. Despite a few equivocal phrases, the sympathies of the editors were quite clearly on the Jewish side. In fact, after reviewing the larger issues raised by the Damascus Affair, the editorial goes on to speak of the possibilities of a restoration of the Jews to Palestine, ending in a rather remarkable proto-Zionist flourish:

> All who have paid any attention to the history of modern Judaism know that especially in recent years the minds of Jews have been earnestly directed toward Palestine, and that in anticipation of a reconstruction of the Jewish state, many are

prepared to avail themselves of the facilities which events may afford to return to the land of their fathers. . . .

The Jews, although bereft of their Temple, their city, and their country, have never ceased to be a people. In the East they are found scattered, wandering, oppressed, despising and despised, cultivating a peculiar literature, divided into hostile sects, cherishing hopes ever disappointed and never abandoned. In Europe, an Asiatic people, they partake largely of European civilization; but amidst the diversities of language, of custom, of occupation, and of opinion, they seem with invincible tenacity to adhere to all essential national characteristics. It is for the Christian philanthropists and enlightened statesmen of Europe to consider whether this remarkable people does not present materials which, when collected and brought into fusion under national institutions, might not be advantageously employed for the interests of civilization in the East.

Uncanny forecasts these, consciously or inadvertently, and we marvel in retrospect. Within our own lifetime the term "Asiatic people," innocuously applied in the editorial, would become one of the slogans to sanction the murder of a third of the Jewish people. The Jewish state would indeed be achieved, though not as a benevolent gift but as a hard-earned prize, won after long and bitter struggle. And much else besides, of which not even the omniscient *Times* could as yet conceive.

For Jewry, the past four decades alone have compressed more trauma and triumph than it had experienced in whole centuries. Precisely in this period the Haggadah accompanies every change in Jewish fortunes. Those Haggadahs we have culled for the latter part of this book are by no means all that exist. But they are sufficient to represent the rest and to serve as memorials to an entire epoch.

By the time Hitler came to power in 1933 it had already become clear to Jews in Palestine, as well as those in the Diaspora, that Britain was reneging on the promises of the Balfour Declaration and the specific terms of the Mandate. Three government reports in 1930 had called for restrictions on Jewish immigration to Palestine, and on the acquisition of land for Jewish settlement. The mood of Jewry is caught in a Yiddish parody of the Haggadah that appeared in Warsaw in 1934 (Plate 155). In the caricature on the cover, Pharaoh is King George V of England. Before him stands the "modern Moses," Vladimir (Ze'ev) Jabotinsky, the leader of the Zionist revisionists, pleading: "Let my people *in*. . . ."

France capitulated to Nazi Germany in 1940, and was divided between a German-occupied zone and the puppet Vichy regime. In the south of France, where thousands of Jews had fled from the German invasion, the Vichy government also maintained internment camps. Here were packed all sorts of Jewish "undesirables," including those with no passports or identity papers, aliens resident in France, as well as Jews expelled by the Germans from Alsace-Lorraine and, more recently, from Baden and other areas of Germany, all cramped together under miserable conditions.

In this harrowing time no less than three different Haggadahs were produced. Though published as recently as 1941, they are today among the rarest of all Haggadahs. Until now, only two of them were known, in copies at the National Library in Jerusalem thought to be unique. While all three are also to be found in the library of the Jewish Theological Seminary of America, it is doubtful that many more can have survived. The reason lies not only in the circumstances under which they were created, but also in their very format. They all consist merely of several sheets of paper written by hand and then mimeographed. Whatever they may lack in aesthetics is more than compensated for by historic interest and sheer poignancy.

One Haggadah was produced in the internment camp near Gurs, at the foot of the Pyrenees (Plates 158–159). It opens with a sketch of the Seder dish and gives the entire text in Hebrew. At the end, the songs *Eḥad mi yode'a* and *Ḥad gadya* are transliterated into Roman letters produced on a typewriter. A one-line colophon notes that it was prepared by Rabbi Leo Ansbacher; it is dated Nisan, 5701 (1941).

Another Haggadah was issued in Nice (Plates 160–161). It was produced by three members of the Parisian rabbinate who had fled there and were installed in the Hotel Roosevelt. Its most interesting and moving feature is the appendix at the end. It consists of one page of special instructions relieving some of the normal requirements with regard to certain Passover foods, beverages, and cooking utensils, in view of the prevailing shortages. In one of its provisions it grants permission to substitute tea for the wine of the Four Cups, though with a different blessing.

The third Haggadah was mimeographed in Toulouse by S. R. Kapel, formerly rabbi of Mülhausen in Alsace but now describing himself as "Chaplain to the Camps." At the end (Plate 162) the traditional words *Le-shanah ha-ba'ah bi-Yerushalayim* are writ large. But they are followed by an additional line in Yiddish: *Die Hagodeh zol zayn die letzte in Goles!*—"This Haggadah should be the final one in exile!"

In Budapest it was still possible to print the Haggadah in 1942, and two editions appeared in that year, when the rest of Europe was already in flames (Plates 163–164). They were among the last Haggadahs to be published in the Hungarian capital. Large, richly illustrated folios, they were beautifully printed in signed limited issues, and differed from each other only in that one contained a series of historical introductions written in Hungarian. That so lavish a book should have been undertaken at that time is perhaps to be seen in the light of the opening words of the Hebrew preface:

> The Hungarian Jewish Relief Society is publishing this Haggadah in the year 5702 since the creation of the world, which is the year 1942 according to their reckoning, so that it may encourage this generation with the signs and wonders of the Exodus from Egypt, and in order to show it the way toward the ultimate Redemption.

In less than two years Adolf Eichmann was to arrive in Budapest to begin the deportations to the death camps.

Out of the very midst of World War II comes an unlikely "Haggadah" produced in an unlikely place. A bizarre parody, it is a satire against Nazism published in Rabat, Morocco, in 1943. Written in Judeo-Arabic, it bears the title *Haggadah de Hitler*—"Hitler's Haggadah" (Plate 167).

Of all the Jewish communities in the world, the Palestinian *yishuv* was the most vigilantly aware of the unfolding fate of European Jewry, having been the most directly involved in rescue efforts ever since the advent of Nazism. The kibbutzim, in particular, were at the very center of the repeated attempts to bring "illegal" immigrants into the country. It is therefore not surprising that the European Jewish tragedy, and the Holocaust itself, should have found some of their most piercing echoes in innumerable kibbutz Haggadahs published during and after World War II (Plates 175, 190).

The war also generated another species of Haggadah, produced to meet the needs of the many thousands of Jewish soldiers serving in the various armies of the Allies. Precedent for this was established during the First World War, when Jews had fought on both sides of the conflict. In 1915 an edition was published in Vienna entitled *Kriegs-Haggadah* ("War Haggadah"), for Jewish soldiers in the armies of the Central Powers, and was embellished with portraits of Emperor Franz-Joseph and Kaiser Wilhelm. Simultaneously, an English Haggadah appeared in London, "for Jewish soldiers and sailors on active duty," and another in 1918 in Calcutta, for Jewish soldiers in the British army in India.

During World War II, needless to say, Jews fought on one side only. For some of the armies, standardized Haggadahs were printed by Jewish organizations at home and then distributed in the field. Many Haggadahs for the American armed forces were produced by the

National Jewish Welfare Board, which in 1943 alone produced 145,000, and a similar number the following year. One edition, published in Melbourne for Australian soldiers, is the only one ever printed on that continent (Plate 168). In rarer instances, Haggadahs were sometimes produced by soldiers in one of the theaters of war. Such are the editions printed in Casablanca in 1943, in the Mariana Islands in 1945 for Jewish marines in the Pacific, and by the Rainbow Division of the United States Infantry in Germany in the same year (Plate 169).

In a special category are the Haggadahs produced in the field by members of the Palestinian Jewish Brigade. Despite their intense resentment of the British Mandatory government, thousands of young men in Palestine volunteered for active service in the British Army, recognizing that the general war effort must temporarily override all other considerations. The British managed to put every obstacle in their way. Only after considerable struggle did the Palestinians win the right to see active duty as a unit under its own flag, and went on to fight with great distinction on various fronts. One Brigade Haggadah, mimeographed "in the field" in 1942, is reproduced in this volume (Plate 165).

When the war had finally ended in victory, a new era of anxiety began for Jews, that of the DP's, the so-called "Displaced Persons." Denied entry into Palestine by the British, often turned back to Europe in ships that had already touched the Palestinian coast, the "saved remnant" of the Holocaust were forced to languish in camps and other refugee centers in Germany. In these camps new Haggadahs were now produced, some printed by the Joint Distribution Committee, others by the survivors themselves (Plates 172–173, 176–181). Fruits of their time, these Haggadahs are suffused not with despair but with defiance, a burning hope and fierce determination to make their way to the Promised Land. As it turned out, that time was not far off.

The State of Israel, the third Jewish commonwealth in history, was proclaimed in May 1948. Invaded immediately from all sides, it fought its first and most difficult war. The first Passover following independence was celebrated in 1949, and once more it is in the kibbutz Haggadah that we find the best reflection of what had taken place (Plates 182–185). Joy and exhilaration over the newfound freedom from alien masters are constantly intermingled with grief over the heavy price with which it had been won. The kibbutz rejoices in the independence of the Jewish nation and mourns its own sons, fallen in battle.

The Holocaust and the State of Israel have found various expressions elsewhere. An increasingly widespread custom inserts a "Ritual of Remembrance" for the Six Million immediately before the recitation of *Shefokh ḥamatkha*, and many Haggadahs now include it in their text. A Haggadah printed in New York in 1949 includes the text of Israel's proclamation of independence, a feature found in other editions as well. In Israel, where it is somewhat anachronistic merely to declare "Next year in Jerusalem," it became the custom to add: "in a *rebuilt* Jerusalem" (Plate 187).

Every subsequent milestone in the Jewish state has left an appropriate mark in some of its Haggadahs. In 1956, the year of the Sinai Campaign, the Chaplaincy of the Israel Defense Forces issued for the army a Haggadah that is a major development in itself. It is, for the first time, a Haggadah with a "unified version," that is, with an eclectic text combining elements from the traditions of all the major rites, western and oriental (Plate 188). As might be expected, the Six-Day War of June 1967 did not fail to leave its own imprint, not only in the army Haggadah (Plate 196), but also in a splendid "Jerusalem Haggadah" published in Haifa (Plate 197). Here the central theme is the recovery of the Old City and the unification of the capital. In one illustration an Israeli paratrooper stands at the Tower of David, and the legend reads: *Le-ḥerut Yisrael, u-ge'ulat Yerushalayim*—"[In the year of] Israel's freedom, and the redemption of Jerusalem."

But this is not the final reproduction in our book. That place is reserved for a Haggadah deriving from a still more recent phenomenon, long awaited, yet quite unanticipated.

In the past few years the gates of the Soviet Union have at last been opened slightly to allow the emigration of some of its Jews. Thousands have already emerged; multitudes who aspire to leave still remain. The details are too current and well known to require elaboration. For our central theme only one fact is relevant. Several new Haggadahs in Russian translation have already made their appearance.

Our last plate is from a bilingual Haggadah in Hebrew and Russian, published in Israel in 1972 for the Soviet immigrants, a new Exodus out of a latter-day servitude.

We are left—at the crossroads.

Many more Haggadahs will yet be published before the "ultimate" edition appears. And that will only be if, and when, history itself shall be fulfilled.

ABBREVIATIONS

I. *Bibliographical References* (for full entries see the bibliography at the end of this volume)

Yaari	Abraham Yaari, *Bibliografiah shel Haggadot Pesaḥ.*
Ben-Menahem[1]	Naphtali Ben-Menahem [Additions and corrections to Yaari] in: *Areshet,* III.
Ben-Menahem[2]	Naphtali Ben-Menahem [Additions and corrections to Yaari] in: *Areshet,* IV.
T. Wiener[1]	Theodore Wiener [Addenda to Yaari] in: *Studies in Bibliography and Booklore,* VII.
T. Wiener[2]	Theodore Wiener [Addenda to Yaari] in: *Studies in Jewish Bibliography, History and Literature, in Honor of I. Edward Kiev.*

II. *Location*

HARVARD	Harvard College Library
JTSA	Library of the Jewish Theological Seminary of America

Note: Dimensions are recorded in centimeters, length by width.

(v)	Copy is printed on vellum

Plates and Plate Descriptions

PLACE AND DATE UNKNOWN

The Earliest Illustrated Haggadah

Only eight leaves have been recovered so far from what seems to be the oldest extant Haggadah printed with illustrations. Because of its incomplete state the place and date can only be surmised on stylistic grounds, and scholarly opinions have therefore varied. The Haggadah may have been printed in Spain before the Expulsion of 1492, in Portugal before 1496, or by Sephardic exiles in Salonika or Constantinople in the early sixteenth century, sometime between 1503 and 1515. If it did indeed appear in the Ottoman Empire, it may well have been printed from types and woodcut blocks brought from the Iberian Peninsula, and used there earlier for an edition of which nothing has survived.

Shown here is a Seder scene. The Hebrew text is the beginning of the passage concerning the Four Sons. However, though the woodcut portrays four figures around the table, it is not a representation of the Sons, but merely of guests at the Passover meal. The same illustration is repeated on another page of this Haggadah with a different text.

YAARI NO. 5 JTSA 18.5:12

הַזֶּה כָּל יְמֵי חַיֶּיךָ לְהָבִיא לִימוֹת הַמָּשִׁיחַ

בָּרוּךְ הַמָּקוֹם שֶׁנָּתַן תּוֹרָה לְיִשְׂרָאֵל
בָּרוּךְ הוּא כְּנֶגֶד אַרְבָּעָה בָּנִים
דִּבְּרָה תוֹרָה אֶחָד חָכָם וְאֶחָד רָשָׁע וְאֶחָד
תָּם וְאֶחָד שֶׁאֵינוֹ יוֹדֵעַ לִשְׁאֹל :

חכם מָה הוּא אוֹמֵר מָה הָעֵדוֹת וְהַחֻקִּים
וְהַמִּשְׁפָּטִים אֲשֶׁר צִוָּה
אֱלֹהֵינוּ אֶתְכֶם אַף :

PLATE 2

SONCINO · ITALY · 1486

The Haggadah and the Sidorello

The most notable of early Jewish printers, and perhaps the most famous of all time, were the members of the Soncino family. In 1486, in the town of Soncino, they published a small Hebrew prayer book to which they referred in the colophon as *Sidorello*. At the same time they also printed a Haggadah in exactly the same format, of which only one copy is known today. It is bound in after the prayer book itself in the volume owned by the Jewish Theological Seminary of America. Though it contains no illustrations, its typography and woodcut initial words are choice examples of Soncino craftsmanship.

Above: Preliminary instructions for the searching out and burning of leaven.

Below: *Ha laḥma anya* ("This is the bread of affliction"), and the beginning of the Four Questions.

YAARI NO. 2 JTSA 14:9

אור לארבעה עשר בודקין את החמץ לאור הנר מפני שהנר יפה לבדיקה ומנוה לבדוק כן שנאמר כי נר מצוה ותורה אור ובשעת הבדיקה מברך

ברוך אתה יי אלהינו מלך העולם אשר קדשנו במצותיו וצונו על בעור חמץ

ובודק בכל מקום שהוא צריך לבדוק ואחר כך מבטלו ואומר

כל חמירא דאיכא ברשותי דלא חזיתיה ודלא ידענא ביה לבטיל ולהוי כעפרא ד

ולמחר יבער החמץ בתחילת שש כמו שאמרו רז״ל אוכלין כל ד׳ ותולין כל ה׳ ושורפין בתחלת שש ובשעת הבעור אומר

כל חמירא דאיכא ברשותי דחמתיה ודלא חמתיה דבערתיה ודלא בערתיה לבטיל וליהוי כעפרא

לחמא עניא די אכלו אבהתנא בארעא דמצרים כל דכפין ייתי ויכול כל דצריך ייתי ויפסח הא שתא הכא לשנה הבאה בארעא דישראל הא שתא עבדי לשנה הבאה בני חורין :

מה נשתנה הלילה הזה מכל הלילות שבכל הלילות אנו אוכלין חמץ ומצה : הלילה הזה כלו מצה שבכל הלילות אנו אוכלין שאר ירקות הלילה הזה מרור : שבכל הלילות

PLATE 3

SONCINO · 1486
[CONTINUED]

Matzah and Bitter Herbs

On these pages from the Soncino Haggadah the words *Matzah zo* ("This unleavened bread") and *Maror zeh* ("This bitter herb") are set into woodcut backgrounds. The variety created by the use of square and circle is a pleasing touch. Note also the absolute symmetry of the type margins, achieved by filling the gaps at the ends of certain lines with the first letters of the opening word on the line that follows.

הציל ויקד העם וישתחו

שאנו אוכלין על שום מה על שום שלא ה
הספיק בצקת של אבותנו להחמיץ עד ש
שנגלה עליהם מלך מלכי המלכים הקב״ה
וגאלם שנאמר ויאפו את הבצק אשר הו
הוציאו ממצרים עוגות מצות כי לא חמץ
כי גורשו ממצרים ולא יכלו להתמהמה
וגם צדה לא עשו להם

שאנו אוכלין על שום מה על שום שמ
שמררו המצריים את חיי אבותינו במ
במצרים שנאמר וימררו את חייהם בעב
בעבודה קשה בחומר ובלבנים ובכל עב
עבודה בשדה את כל עבודתם אשר עב
עבדו בהם בפרך

CASALMAGGIORE · ITALY · 1486

From the Roman Maḥzor

The text of the Haggadah has often been printed not only as a separate book, but as part of the festival prayer book (Maḥzor). Indeed, some Jews would have regarded an edition of the latter as incomplete if it did not contain the Haggadah as well as the synagogue services for Passover.

One of the most important and interesting of all Jewish liturgical traditions is the so-called Roman rite (*Minhag Roma*) of the Italian Jews. In 1485–86 the Soncinos began to print their great edition of the Roman Maḥzor, the first ever to be published. One volume was printed at Soncino itself; the second was completed in Casalmaggiore. At the beginning of the Passover section we find the Haggadah.

The page reproduced here is noteworthy for the lovely woodcut strip, actually composed of five separate pieces, which encloses the word *matzah*. The two rabbits at the sides do not derive from the gentile folklore of Easter, but are merely a decorative motif that the Soncinos also employed in other books.

HARVARD 26:17

זו שאנו אוכלים על שום מה על שום שלא הגיחו בצקן של אבותינו להחמיץ עד שנגלה עליהם מלך מלכי המלכים הקב״ה וגאלם שנאמר ויאפו את הבצק אשר הוציאו ממצרים עגות מצות כי לא חמץ כי גורשו ממצרים ולא יכלו להתמהמה וגם צדה לא עשו להם:

ואוחז מרור בידו ואומר

מרור זה שאנו אוכלין על שום מה על שום שמררו המצריים את חיי אבותינו במצרים שנאמר וימררו את חייהם בעבודה קשה בחומר ובלבנים ובכל עבודה בשדה את כל עבודתם אשר עבדו בהם בפרך: בכל דור ודור חייב אדם לראות את עצמו כאילו הוא יצא ממצרים שלא את אבותינו בלבד גאל הקב״ה אלא אף אותנו גאל שנאמר ואותנו הוציא משם למען הביא אותנו לתת לנו את הארץ אשר נשבע לאבותינו:

לפיכך אנו חייבים להודות להלל לשבח לפאר לרומם ולהדר ולקדש למי שעשה לנו ולאבותינו את כל האותות והמופתים והנסים האלה והוציאנו מעבדות לחרות ומיגון לשמחה ומאבל ליום טוב ומאפלה לאור גדול ונאמר לפניו הללויה

הללויה הללו עבדי יי הללו את שם יי יהי שם יי מבורך מעתה ועד עולם ממזרח שמש ועד מבואו מהולל שם יי רם על כל גוים יי על השמים כבודו: מי כיי אלהינו המגביהי לשבת המשפילי לראות בשמים ובארץ מקימי מעפר דל מאשפות ירים אביון להושיבי עם נדיבים עם נדיבי עמו מושיבי עקרת הבית אם הבנים שמחה הללויה:

בצאת ישראל ממצרים בית יעקב מעם לועז: היתה יהודה לקדשו ישראל ממשלותיו: הים ראה וינס הירדן יסוב לאחור: ההרים רקדו כאילים גבעות כבני צאן מה לך הים כי תנוס הירדן תסוב לאחור: ההרים תרקדו כאילים גבעות כבני צאן: מלפני אדון חולי ארץ מלפני אלוה יעקב: ההופכי הצור אגם מים חלמיש למעינו מים:

ברוך אתה יי אלהינו מלך העולם אשר גאלנו וגאל את אבותינו ממצרים והגיענו הלילה הזה לאכול בו מצה ומרור כן יי אלהינו יגיענו למועדים ולרגלים הבאים לקראתנו לשלום שמחים בבנין עירך ששים בעבודתך ובחדוש בית מקדשך ושם נאכל מן הפסחים ומן הזבחים אשר יגיע דמן על קיר מזבחך לרצון ונודה לך שיר חדש על גאולתינו ועל פדות נפשינו ברוך אתה יי גאל ישראל
ברוך אתה יי אלהינו מלך העולם בורא פרי הגפן

ונוטלין בהסיבת שמאל ואחר כך נוטלין ידיהן ומברכין על נטילת ידים ואף על פי שנטלו ידיהם בטבול ראשון

CONSTANTINOPLE · TURKEY · 1505/6

In the Wake of the Spanish Expulsion

For the generation that had experienced the expulsion from Spain in 1492 the age-old problem of exile and redemption assumed a new immediacy. It was perhaps natural that Don Isaac Abravanel, one of the leading figures among the Spanish exiles, should have found it congenial to write a commentary to the Haggadah, which relates the ancient redemption of the Jewish people and points toward the redemption yet to come. Although completed in 1496 in Monopoli, Italy, one of the way stations in his many wanderings after leaving Spain, his *Zebaḥ Pesaḥ* ("The Passover Sacrifice") was not printed until almost a decade later, in Constantinople. It is the first edition of the Haggadah to be published with a commentary of any kind. The printers, David and Samuel Ibn Naḥmias, themselves Spanish refugees, established the first Hebrew press in the Turkish capital.

In common with other early books, the *Zebaḥ Pesaḥ* has no separate title page. Instead, the first page contains a Hebrew poem in praise of the book and the author. It was written by his eldest son, Judah Abravanel, who had also left Spain in 1492. Judah was to become one of the most influential philosophers of the Italian Renaissance, known in the non-Jewish world as Leone Ebreo, author of the *Dialoghi d'amore* ("Dialogues of Love"). His poem was composed in 1505 when he visited his father in Venice. It begins:

Verses Composed by the Sage Rabbi Judah
Abravanel, Son of the Noble Author, on the Book
Zebaḥ Pesaḥ

May he live eternal years,
May he live forever,
May his name glitter over all,
As the gold plate over the forehead [of the High Priest].

The page is framed in an intricately wrought woodcut border of delicate filigree, in which stags and hounds predominate. Similar borders are found in other Constantinople imprints; they derived ultimately from designs used in Hebrew books in Spain prior to the Expulsion.

YAARI NO. 3 | JTSA | 26.8:19.3

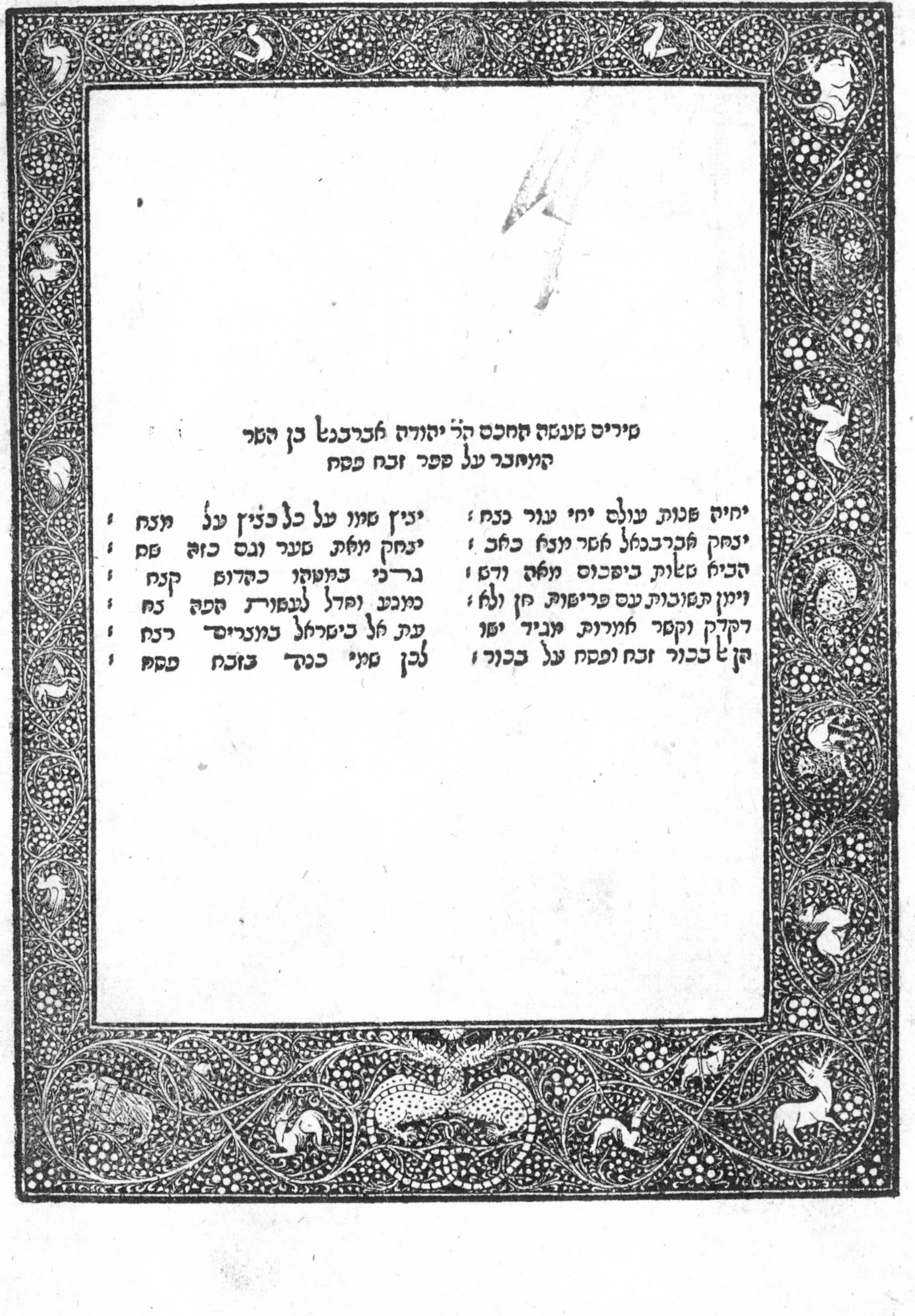

שירים שעשה החכם הר׳ יהודה אברבנאל בן השר
המחבר על ספר זבח פסח

יחיה שנות עולם יחי עוד נצח : יצין שמו על כל נצין על מנצח :
יצחק אברבנאל אשר מצא כאב : יצחק מאת שער וגם כזב שם :
הביא שאלות בישבוס מאה ודם : גרגי במעיו כאדום קנח :
וימן תשובות עם פרישות חן ולא : כמבע ואדל לעמורת הפה נח :
דקדק וקשר אמרות מגיד ישו : עת אל בישראל במצרים רצח :
הן ש בכור זבח ופסח על בכור : לכן שמי כנגד בזבח פסח :

PLATE 6

FRANKFURT AM MAIN · GERMANY · 1512

The Haggadah in the "Battle of the Books"

The tempestuous debate that erupted in early sixteenth-century Germany over the right of the Jews to their books, and the legitimacy of Hebraic studies by Christians, proved to be one of the preludes to the Protestant Reformation. Spearheading the attack against Hebrew literature were the Dominicans of Cologne and the Jewish apostate Johann Pfefferkorn. The defense was led by the scholar Johann Reuchlin, along with other humanists.

Though the Haggadah was not a central issue in the conflict, it became involved in a curious way. In 1509, as part of his campaign to secure the proscription and burning of Hebrew books, Pfefferkorn published a pamphlet deriding the Jewish Passover. It was printed in a Latin and two German editions (see below). Three years later the Franciscan friar Thomas Murner, who was apparently sympathetic to the humanist cause, published a Latin translation of the entire Haggadah. Besides being the first printed Haggadah translation in any language, it served as a specimen of Hebrew literature which, though not intended to vindicate the Jews, might help to advance the cause of Christian Hebraism.

Shown opposite is the title page, headed by the Hebrew words *Ḥukkat ha-Pesaḥ* ("The Rite of Passover"), with a woodcut purporting to show a group of three Jews at the Seder. In a posture prescribed by tradition they are shown reclining on pillows, a vestige of the ancient custom of free men at a feast. Most interesting are the four cups placed before each participant, corresponding to the number of occasions during the Seder when drinking wine is obligatory. Perhaps it did not occur to the artist that one cup per person can suffice if it is filled four times, but more likely he used this device to convey the number in simple visual terms.

YAARI NO. 4 JTSA 19:14

IN disem buchlein vin̄
det Ir ain entlichenn
fürtrag wie die blinden Juden yr Ostern halten vnnd be-
sunderlich wie das Abentmal gessen wirt / Weiter würdt
auß getruckt das die Juden ketzer seyn des alten vnd new
enn testaments / Deßhalb sye schuldig seyn des gerichts
nach dem gesatz Moysi.

Title page of Pfefferkorn's German pamphlet (Augsburg, 1509), beginning: "In this little book you will find a definitive discourse as to how the blind Jews celebrate their Easter." (Houghton Library, Harvard University.)

Ritus et celebratio phase iudeoꝝ/cum orationibus eoꝝ/ ⁊ benedictionibus mense ad litterã interp̄tatis/cum omi obseruatione vti soliti sũt suũ pasca extra terrã ꝓmissionis sine esu agni pascalis celebrare Per egregiũ doctorem. Thomã murner ex hebreo in latinũ traducta eloquium

PLATE 7

FRANKFURT AM MAIN · 1512
[CONTINUED]

Kiddush—*in Latin*

Six of the pages in Murner's Haggadah contain woodcut illustrations, of which one is repeated and the rest vary only slightly from each other. On this page the sanctification over the wine (*Kiddush*) is rendered in a fair Latin translation, with the *Havdalah* ceremony for a Saturday night beginning one line from the bottom. In the woodcut the dish on the table is covered with a cloth. Presumably, underneath one would find the three matzot, which have a special function in the Seder ritual. The dish in the illustration on the title page must therefore represent the same, though the covering is less clearly identifiable.

Bñdcit⁹ tu dñe de⁹ noster rex seculi creās fructū vini.

Benedictus tu domine deus:
rex seculi qui elegisti nos de omni populo/ ⁊ exaltasti
nos de omī ligua/ sanctificans nos in man datis tuis ⁊
dedisti nobis dñe deus noster in liberalitate tēpus ad
gaudendū/festiuādū/ erudiens nos in gaudio die isto
solennitatis asimoꝝ instructionis exitus nostri in dilec
tione/inuocatione/recordatione exitus nostri de egip
to/qꝛ elegisti nos sāctificastiq; nos/de omi populo/sāc
tum sāctitatꝭ tue/in leticia ⁊ in gaudio/ hereditare fe=
cisti Benedictus tu deus/qui sāctificasti israhel ⁊ eru=
ditionē legis tue ¶ Benedictus tu dñe deus noster
rex seculi creās creaturā ignꝭ ¶ Hic accendat̄ cādela

PLATE 8

FRANKFURT AM MAIN · 1512
[CONTINUED]

"Anno Futuro . . . in Hierusalem"

The Latin Haggadah was printed at the press of Beatus Murner, the translator's brother. It has been suggested, though on no substantive grounds, that Beatus may also have designed the woodcuts.

On the very last page the traditional exclamation *Le-shanah ha-ba'ah bi-Yerushalayim* ("Next year in Jerusalem!") is slightly expanded in the Latin to specify the obvious hope that the Passover would be celebrated there. (The word *iherusalem* is, incidentally, a misprint for *hierusalem.*) The hymns and songs that we would expect to follow at this point are not present, since they are only appendices to the Haggadah recital, and some were not even universally sung by Jews at this time.

The lower half of the page is occupied by the printer's emblem, placed there in lieu of a colophon. The word PATIENTIA (patience, or endurance), which figures on the shield, may at first strike one as linked to the hope for a restoration to Jerusalem expressed in the last line of the Haggadah text. However, its appearance here is entirely coincidental. It happened to be Beatus Murner's personal motto.

Quia ad te dulcedo/qꝛ ad te supplices fortis in regno tuo redime regnum tuū/⁊ excercitum tuū ⁊ dicent ei tibi ⁊ tibi/certe tibi tibi/qꝛ tibi tibi deus regnum
Quia ad te dulcedo/ qꝛ tibi supplices Sancte in regno tuo/misericors in regnū tuū expostulator ⁊ dicent oēs ei tibi ⁊ tibi/tibi certe tibi tibi/qꝛ tibi tibi deꝰ regnū.
Quia ad te dulcedo qꝛ tibi supplices fortis ī regno tuo integer ⁊ totus regni tui vniuersi ⁊ dicent oēs ei tibi tibi/tibi certe tibi tibi/qꝛ tibi tibi deus regnum
Pat̄ faīlias accipit cyphū beēdicēs bibit ⁊ cū eo omēs
Postq̄ꝫ singuli biberunt alta voce clamat pater familias exoptans oibꝰ verba sequentia
¶ Anno futuro omēs in iherusalē det scꝫ deus vt tibi pasce celebremus ⁊ respondent omnes amen

45216

PRAGUE · BOHEMIA · 1526

Searching for Leaven

The first page of the great Prague Haggadah printed by Gershom Cohen and his associates, this is also one of three pages in the book framed by woodcut borders. The text here contains the rules and blessings for the searching out and burning of leaven before Passover.

In form and inspiration the Hebrew types seek to duplicate the calligraphy of the Ashkenazic scribes of Central Europe. For the instructions, the blessings, and the initial words, respectively, the letters on this page increase in size. As subsequent plates will show, an even larger, monumental size is achieved elsewhere in the Haggadah.

The border is sufficiently similar in character to known non-Jewish counterparts to warrant the assumption that it was borrowed from a gentile printer. Such exchanges of borders were an accepted and widespread practice.

However, the small cut in the upper right corner was made explicitly for this Haggadah, probably by a Jew. Even if actually drawn by a Christian artist, he was at least guided by Jews, for the illustration makes sense only within the context of the Jewish Passover. It shows a Jew in the costume of the time about to commence the search for leaven in his home. For this specific purpose he carries a candle in his right hand and, in his left, a feather with which to gather the crumbs, and a bowl to contain them.

YAARI NO. 6 JTSA (V) 31:26

Salomon Alperon

אור לארבע עשר בודקין את החמץ ׃ ולא בודקין לאור החמה ולא לאור ה הלבנה ולא לאור האבוקה ׃ אלא בנר של שעוה ׃ ובודקין בחדרין ובסדקין ובכל המקומות שדרכו להשתמש בו שם ׃ ולא יתחיל שום מלאכה עד שיבדוק ואפילו בתלמוד תורה ׃ וקודם שיתחיל לבדוק מברך

ברוך אתה יי אלהינו מלך העולם אשר קד קדשנו במצותיו וצונו על ביעור ח חמץ ׃

ולא ידבר בין הברכה לתחילת הבדיקה כלל ׃ ואחר הבדיקה ישמור החמץ בתיבה או יתלנו באויר מקום שאין עכבר שולט בו שם ויבטלנו ויאמר

כל חמירא וחמיעא דאיכא ברשותי די לא חמיתיה ודי לא ביערתיה לבטל ולהוי פ כעפרא דארעא ׃

PRAGUE · 1526
[CONTINUED]
Biblical Kings and a Priestly Printer's Emblem

The second framed page of the Prague Haggadah introduces the formal recital of the text, in the version that begins *Ke-ha laḥma anya*—"Such as this was the bread of affliction." Here the border is much more elaborate than before and contains four illustrations.

In the horizontal panel above, held by two rather severe-looking angels, we find Gershom Cohen's printer's emblem. It displays two hands raised in the traditional gesture of the priestly benediction, an appropriate symbol since Gershom was of priestly lineage (*kohen*, in Hebrew, literally means "priest"). His name is inscribed in Hebrew on both sides of the shield.

In the lower right panel David is standing on a pedestal; in the lower left is Goliath. The David figure indiscriminately compresses several stages in his life. Though he slew Goliath in his youth (he carries the slingshot and, being a shepherd, is accompanied by a lamb), he is depicted as a mature man with a beard, carrying a sword in his scabbard, and wearing a royal crown.

The horizontal panel at the bottom is devoted to an entire biblical scene, the famous Judgment of Solomon (1 Kings 3:16–28), in which two women bring their infants, one of them dead, before the king, while each claims that the live child is hers. In the illustration Solomon extends his scepter to keep his servant from cutting the child in two. The real mother is on her knees, pleading that the child be given to the other woman rather than killed.

None of the illustrations within the border bear any organic relation to the text on the page, and, indeed, no literal connection need be sought. The practice already existed in some Haggadah manuscripts to portray biblical heroes merely for their intrinsic evocations, even if they played no role whatever in the Haggadah narrative. Gershom Cohen may well have been aware of such antecedents. At any rate, he now established a new precedent that would be followed in later printed Haggadahs.

One other feature on this page demands attention. The first word is printed in large hollow letters interwoven with animal figures and designs. The result is somewhat difficult to read. It is possible, however, that these letters were left hollow in order to allow for subsequent coloring by hand, which, if done, would make them stand out in relief.

כהא

לחמא עניא די
אכלו אבהתנא
בארעא דמצרים
כל דכפין ייתי ויכול
כל דצריך ייתי
ויפסח השתא הכא
לשנה הבאה בארע

PRAGUE · 1526
[CONTINUED]

Wickedness and War

Of the renowned Four Sons in the Passover Haggadah (Wise, Wicked, Simple, and the one "who knows not what to ask"), it is the Wicked and the Simple who appear on the margin of this page.

The Wicked Son (above) is portrayed, significantly, as a German or Bohemian soldier of the early sixteenth century, holding a sword and halberd. This striking equation of wickedness and war harks back to an established iconography in Ashkenazic Haggadah manuscripts, which was itself a reflection of ingrained Jewish attitudes in the Middle Ages. Having now made his debut in print, the Wicked Son will continue to appear as a soldier in innumerable Haggadahs until well into the twentieth century, only changing his uniform as the occasion demands. (For examples, see Plates 60 and 134.) The caption consists of the well-known talmudic dictum (tractate *Sukkah*, 56b): "Woe to the wicked man, woe to his neighbor."

The Simple Son (below) somehow manages to look the part. The curious element here lies in the accompanying biblical verse (Deuteronomy 18:13): "Thou shalt be wholehearted with the Lord thy God." This wedding of caption and illustration has no substantive rationale. It is merely the result of a play on words, *tam* in Hebrew meaning "simple," while *tamim* means "wholehearted."

הפסח אין מפטירין אחר
הפסח אפיקומן׃

אוי לרשע אוי לשכנו

רשע מה הוא אומ
מה העבודה
הזאת לכם׃ לכם ולא לו
ולפי שהוציא את עצמו
מן הכלל כפר בעקר ואף
אתה הקהה את שניו ואמור
לו בעבור זה עשה יי לי
בצאתי ממצרים לי ולא לו
אלו היה שם לא היה נגאל׃

תמים תהיה עם יי אלהיך

תם מה הוא אומר
מה זאת ואמרת

שמעתי הסדר של פסח כנגד הסעודה שאנו מצפים לאכול לעתיד שב
תערוך שלחן נגד צוררי׃ וזה אחד מן הכוסות שנרמז לנו בליל פסח׃
דלעתיד אוכלים שם ג דברים׃ שור הבר׃ ובר יוכני׃ והלויתן׃ ובמשו הבי
לוקחים הזרוע מן הבהמה כנגד שור הבר׃ וביצה כנגד בר יוכני שהוא
עוף׃ והאפיקומן שאוכלין בסוף כנגד הלויתן כי המצות עשויות קגלות
כ מן קשקשת׃ ובתי' אחד באחד יגשו ורוח לא יבא ביניהם׃

PRAGUE · 1526
[CONTINUED]
Bohemian Architecture in Ancient Egypt

"And they afflicted us, as the verse states: '[Therefore they did set over them taskmasters] to afflict them with their burdens. And they built for Pharaoh store-cities, Pithom and Raamses' " (Exodus 1:11).

Relating to this text, illustrations of the two Egyptian cities built by the Israelite slaves are placed in the margin. Above is a section of a city surrounded by a wall, with European roofs and pennants fluttering from the steeples. It is inscribed: THIS IS PITHOM. Below it is a portion of a large tower labeled, with equal aplomb: THIS IS RAAMSES.

The architecture, of course, is neither Egyptian nor ancient, but clearly European, probably Bohemian, and perhaps even that of Prague itself as the artist knew it. In the period in which the Haggadah was printed, historical accuracy in such woodcuts was quite unknown and irrelevant. Similar anachronisms can be found in many early illustrated books and, indeed, in the greatest works of art. The Prague printers had no more hesitation about introducing contemporary buildings into ancient Egypt than did Renaissance painters about clothing biblical figures in Florentine costume.

גם הוא על שונאינו ונלחם
בנו ועלה מן הארץ׃

זה פיתום

ויענונו כמה שנ׳ למען
ענותו בסבלותם ויבן
ערי מסכנות לפרעה את
פיתום ואת רעמסס׃

זה רעמסס

ויתנו עלינו עבודה קשה׃
כמה שנא׳ ויעבידו מצרים
את בני ישראל בפרך׃

ונצעק אל יי׳
אלהי
אבותינו כמה שנאמר ויהי
בימים הרבים ההם מת

PRAGUE · 1526
[CONTINUED]
From Adam to the Messiah

The final full-page border in the Prague Haggadah is the most striking of all. It frames three biblical verses (Psalms 79:6 and 69:25; Lamentations 3:66), the first beginning—*Shefokh ḥamatkha*—"Pour out Thy wrath upon the nations that know Thee not, and upon the kingdoms that call not upon Thy name." Absent is Psalms 79:7 ("For they have devoured Jacob, and laid waste his habitation"), which usually follows in our Haggadahs. The Prague version, however, is found in some German manuscripts.

The custom of reciting these verses before the last section of the Haggadah is medieval in origin. It probably emerged under the impact of the Crusades, which brought the first great wave of massacres to European Jewry. In any event, the nations against whom the wrath of the Lord is invoked were always understood to be those who persecuted and slaughtered the Jewish people. The context is necessarily messianic, an expectation that someday God will surely judge the enemies of Israel, and it is no accident that these verses are said aloud as the door of the house is opened in symbolic welcome of the prophet Elijah, herald of the Messiah.

Within the various panels of the ornamental border the following figures appear:

On either side of the dramatic initial word *Shefokh* (which betrays the influence of the bold black-letter style of some contemporary non-Jewish books) are the figures of Adam (right) and Eve (left).

Below Adam stands Samson, carrying off the gates of the Philistine city of Gaza (Judges 16:3). Below Eve, the apocryphal heroine Judith holds a sword in one hand and the severed head of the Syrian general Holofernes in the other.

In the horizontal panel at the bottom two wild men, covered with hair or fur, hold a shield emblazoned with a lion. To the left of the shield is inscribed the Hebrew letter *shin*, which may stand for Ḥayyim ben David Shaḥor, one of the Prague printers. He may thus have been the artist who designed this frame, as well as three other woodcuts in the Haggadah where the same letter appears.

Finally, within the rectangle containing the text a small cut in the bottom left corner shows the Messiah riding upon an ass, in accordance with Zechariah 9:9: "Behold, thy king cometh unto thee, he is triumphant and victorious, lowly, and riding upon an ass."

While the identity of each particular element is easily established, the symbolism of the border as a whole is sufficiently elusive to offer scope for speculation. It does seem probable that all the illustrations on this page were intended to relate to one another and to the text itself. If so, we have here a progression from Adam and Eve to the Messiah, that is, from the beginning to the end of history. In between, the figures of Samson and Judith would represent the periodic retribution achieved with the help of the Lord against the enemies of Israel in the past, a portent for the final judgment against the nations in the future. The messianic age is conveyed explicitly in the figure of the Messiah himself. But it may be that it is also hinted at in the bottom panel. To be sure, a lion rampant on a shield constituted the arms of Bohemia, and just before the Haggadah appeared Gershom Cohen had received from the king a monopoly on Hebrew printing in the realm. Similarly, savages and wild men were a familiar decorative device. But symbols, by their very nature, are always operative on several levels of meaning, none of them exclusive. To Jewish eyes the lion evoked the tribe of Judah, and could therefore be regarded as a symbol of Jewish sovereignty. The wild men are savage in appearance only. In attitude they sit placidly and uphold the lion-shield. Can this represent the Messianic pacification of the "savage" nations, and their recognition of the ultimate restoration of the Jewish people to the Land of Israel?

שפוך

חמתך על הגוים
אשר לא ידעוך ועל
הממלכות אשר
בשמך לא
קראו׃

שפוך עליהם זעמך וחרון
אפך ישיגם תרדוף באף
ותשמידם מתחת שמי יי׃

PLATE 14

AUGSBURG · GERMANY · 1534

Seder Scene

The Augsburg Haggadah of 1534 was printed by Ḥayyim ben David Shaḥor (in German, Schwarz), already mentioned as the possible designer of some of the woodcuts in the Prague Haggadah of 1526. Though that suggestion has been disputed by some authorities, there is no doubt that he was a master printer in his own right, and that his eventful career embraced some notable pioneering achievements.

Like some of his peers, both Jewish and gentile, Ḥayyim Shaḥor was a wanderer, by necessity rather than by choice. Born in Bohemia, he was involved in the printing of the earliest Hebrew books in Prague, where he undoubtedly learned the craft. Sometime after 1526 he gathered together some types and printing equipment and left Prague in search of a new place in which to establish a press. By 1529 he was in Oels, in Silesia, where he printed a Pentateuch the following year. The troubles then afflicting the Silesian Jews prompted him to move on to Augsburg. There, between 1531 and 1540 he printed nine books, including the Haggadah reproduced here. The Augsburg imprints are among the most beautiful of Hebrew books, and today they are also among the most rare. In 1542–43 Ḥayyim and his sons, who had joined him in his work, found conditions unpropitious and decided to move on once more. Ferrara in Italy was temporarily considered but finally deemed impractical. Instead, the family went to Ichenhausen in Bavaria, where Ḥayyim printed another Pentateuch and a Yiddish prayer book in 1544. From there he went to Heddernheim, near Frankfurt, and produced two more books. In the end, he wandered to Lublin in Poland where, as in all the aforementioned places, he was the first to print in Hebrew. He died shortly afterwards, and his work in Lublin was continued by his sons.

Smaller than the Prague Haggadah in format and typography, the Augsburg Haggadah remains an attractive example of the finest in sixteenth-century Hebrew printing. Of two woodcuts depicting a family seated at the Seder, the second is reproduced on this plate. It is more finely drawn than parallel scenes in the Adler leaves (Plate 1), in Murner's Latin Haggadah (Plates 6–7), or even in the Prague Haggadah itself. The figures are individualized, their positions and gestures more lifelike. The man at the head of the table and the woman at his left are obviously the master and mistress of the house. They are shown performing the ceremony of *karpas*, holding the vegetable before dipping it in salt water and distributing it to the children and the guests.

The text above the woodcut is the Passover *Kiddush* for a Friday night, and the text below it, for a weekday. The letters are very similar to the types of Prague. One detail marks an advance over the Prague Haggadah. Here actual dots begin to appear in the Hebrew vowels that require them, superseding the tiny horizontal slashes of Prague that had been carried over from earlier manuscript practices.

YAARI NO. 9 | JTSA (V) | 20:14

ברוך אתה יי אלהינו מלך העולם אשר בחר בנו מכל עם ׃
ורוממנו מכל לשון וקדשנו במצותיו ותתן לנו יי
אלהינו באהבה שבתות למנוחה ומועדים לשמחה חגים וזמנים
לששון את יום השבת הזה ואת יום חג המצות הזה זמן חרותינו
באהבה מקרא קודש זכר ליציאת מצרים כי בנו בחרת ואותנו
קדשת מכל העמים שבת ומועדי קדשך באהבה וברצון בשמחה
ובששון הנחלתנו ברוך אתה יי מקדש השבת וישראל והזמנים ׃
ברוך אתה יי אלהינו מלך העולם שהחיינו וקיימנו והגיענו
לזמן הזה ׃ ושותין בהסיבת שמאל ׃

ואם יבא פסח בחול מתחיל כאן

ברוך אתה יי אלהינו מלך העולם בורא פרי הגפן ׃
ברוך אתה יי אלהינו מלך העולם אשר בחר בנו מכל עם
ורוממנו מכל לשון וקדשנו במצותיו ותתן לנו יי אלהינו באהבה
מועדים לשמחה חגים וזמנים לששון את יום חג המצות הזה זמן
חרותינו מקרא קודש זכר ליציאת מצרים כי בנו בחרת ואותנו

PLATE 15

AUGSBURG · 1534
[CONTINUED]

Jagen-has—*the Hunting of the Hares*

The hare-hunting scenes that figure in early Haggadah illustrations were the result of a coincidence. The order for beginning a Seder on a Saturday night was memorized by combining the initials of a series of Hebrew catchwords into one artificial word—YaKeNHaZ (sometimes pronounced as *yaknehaz*). The sequence comprises blessings over wine (*yayin*), the sanctification (*kiddush*) of the festival, the candle (*ner*) lit when the Sabbath ends, the separation (*havdalah*) of the Sabbath from weekdays, and the thanksgiving blessing for having reached this festive time (*zeman*). To Ashkenazic Jews, YaKeNHaZ sounded like the German *Jagen-has*, "hare hunt," which thereby came to be illustrated as such in the Haggadah.

Usually (as in the Prague Haggadah, below), the hunter and his hounds are merely shown chasing the hares. In the Augsburg Haggadah for the first time we have *two* scenes. In the first (opposite) the hounds are driving the hares into a net. In the second (Plate 16) the hares escape.

Prague, 1526

קדשת מכל העמים ומועדי קדשך בשמחה ובששון הנחלתנו
ברוך אתה יי מקדש ישראל והזמנים ׃ ברוך אתה יי אלהינו
מלך העולם שהחיינו וקימנו והגיענו לזמן הזה ׃

ואם יבא פסח במוצאי שבת

ברוך אתה יי אלהינו מלך העולם בורא פרי הגפן ׃
ברוך אתה יי אלהינו מלך העולם אשר בחר בנו מכל עם
ורוממנו מכל לשון וקדשנו במצותיו ותתן לנו יי אלהינו באהבה
מועדים לשמחה חגים וזמנים לששון את יום חג המצות הזה
זמן חרותינו באהבה מקרא קודש זכר ליציאת מצרים כי בנו
בחרת ואותנו קדשת מכל העמים ומועדי קדשך בשמחה ובששון
הנחלתנו ׃ ברוך אתה יי מקדש ישראל והזמנים ׃ ברוך אתה
יי אלהינו מלך העולם בורא מאורי האש ׃

ברוך אתה יי אלהינו מלך העולם המבדיל בין קדש לחול בין
אור לחושך בין ישראל לעמים בין יום השביעי לששת
ימי המעשה בין קדשת שבת לקדשת יום טוב הבדלת ואת יום

PLATE 16

AUGSBURG · 1534
[CONTINUED]

Jagen-has—*the Hares Elude Their Pursuers*

Here the hares have succeeded in crawling through to the other side of the net and, in their newfound safety, turn their heads to look back at the hounds.

Although no explanation is offered, it seems plausible to conclude that the two successive representations of the *Jagen-has* are not only an innovation in themselves, but together comprise an allegory of the persecution and salvation of the Jewish people.

הַשְּׁבִיעִי מִשֵּׁשֶׁת יְמֵי הַמַּעֲשֶׂה קִדַּשְׁתָּ ׃ הִבְדַּלְתָּ וְקִדַּשְׁתָּ אֶת עַמְּךָ
יִשְׂרָאֵל בִּקְדֻשָּׁתֶךָ ׃ בָּרוּךְ אַתָּה יְיָ הַמַּבְדִּיל בֵּין קוֹדֶשׁ לְקוֹדֶשׁ ׃

בָּרוּךְ אַתָּה יְיָ אֱלֹהֵינוּ מֶלֶךְ הָעוֹלָם שֶׁהֶחֱיָנוּ וְקִיְּמָנוּ וְהִגִּיעָנוּ
לִזְמַן הַזֶּה ׃ ושותין בהסיבת שמאל ׃

ונוטלין ידיהם ומברכין

בָּרוּךְ אַתָּה יְיָ אֱלֹהֵינוּ מֶלֶךְ הָעוֹלָם אֲשֶׁר קִדְּשָׁנוּ בְּמִצְוֹתָיו וְצִוָּנוּ
עַל נְטִילַת יָדָיִם ׃

ויקח איפך או פטרזיליג ויברך עליו

בָּרוּךְ אַתָּה יְיָ אֱלֹהֵינוּ מֶלֶךְ הָעוֹלָם בּוֹרֵא פְּרִי הָאֲדָמָה ׃ ויטבול
במי מלח ויאכל ויתן לכלם

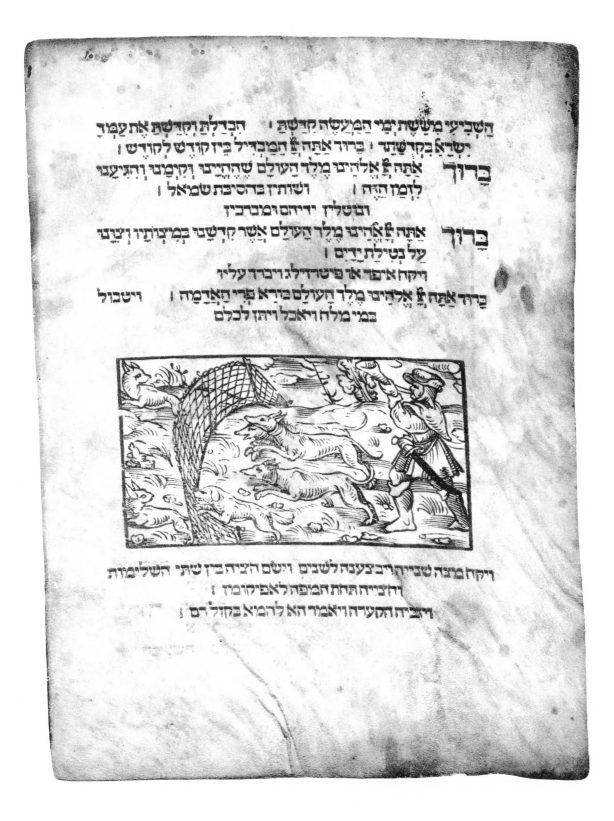

ויקח מצה שנייה ויבצענה לשנים וישם החציה בין שתי השלימות
והחצייה תחת המפה לאפיקומן ׃

ויגביה הקערה ויאמר הא להמא בקול רם ׃

AUGSBURG · 1534
[CONTINUED]

Pouring the Wine

This handsome page of the Augsburg Haggadah offers an example of the largest types employed by Ḥayyim Shaḥor. The cut shows a man pouring wine from a pitcher. It is not placed haphazardly, as sometimes occurs with illustrations in early Haggadahs. The line immediately above is an instruction to pour the second of the Four Cups.

Directly to the left of the cut, the text of the Four Questions begins.

הָא לַחֲמָא עַנְיָא דִיאָכְלוּ

אַבְהָתָנָא בְּאַרְעָא דְמִצְרַיִם · כָּל דִכְפִין יֵתֵי
וְיֵכוֹל · כָּל דִצְרִיךְ יֵתֵי וְיִפְסַח הַשַׁתָּא הָכָא
לְשָׁנָה הַבָּאָה בְּאַרְעָא דְיִשְׂרָאֵל · הַשַׁתָּא
עַבְדֵי לְשָׁנָה הַבָּאָה בְּנֵי חוֹרִין ·
וּמוֹזְגִין כּוֹס שֵׁנִי וְאוֹמְרִין ·

מַה נִשְׁתַּנָּה הַלַּיְלָה
הַזֶּה מִכָּל הַלֵּי
לוֹת שֶׁבְּכָל הַלֵּילוֹת אָנוּ
אוֹכְלִין חָמֵץ וּמַצָּה ה
לַּיְלָה הַזֶּה כֻּלּוֹ מַצָּה
· שֶׁבְּכָל הַלֵּילוֹת אָנוּ א
אוֹכְלִין שְׁאָר יְרָקוֹת ה

הַלַּיְלָה הַזֶּה מָרוֹר · שֶׁבְּכָל הַלֵּילוֹת אֵין אָנוּ
חַיָּיבִים לִטְבּוֹל אֲפִילוּ פַּעַם אַחַת הַלַּיְלָה הַזֶּה
שְׁתֵּי פְּעָמִים · שֶׁבְּכָל הַלֵּילוֹת אָנוּ אוֹכְלִים

VENICE · ITALY · 1545

[ZEBAḤ PESAḤ]

The Temple and the Dome of the Rock

Title page of the second edition of Isaac Abravanel's commentary *Zebaḥ Pesaḥ* (for the first edition, see Plate 5), "printed in Venice, the great and renowned city, which is under the rule of the government, may their glory be exalted and may their empire be magnified and uplifted. Amen. In the year [5]305." Since Jews in Venice were barred from actual ownership of Hebrew presses, the owners were perforce Christians. The bottom line records that this book was produced at the press of Marco Antonio Giustiniani.

As in all Giustiniani publications, the printer's emblem was a fanciful representation of the Temple in Jerusalem. On the dome and below it are the words *Bet ha-mikdash* ("The Holy House"). Furled over it is a banner on which is inscribed the biblical verse: "The glory of this latter house shall be greater than the former, saith the Lord of Hosts" (Haggai 2:9). The verse originally referred to the building of the Second Temple, but was later reinterpreted to point to the future Temple in the time of the Messiah.

For those who have visited Jerusalem, the form in which the Temple is represented here may seem vaguely familiar. Paradoxically, the architecture is that of the great Muslim Mosque of Omar, called the "Dome of the Rock," which stands on the site of the ancient Temple of the Jews. European travelers in the Middle Ages had returned from Jerusalem with drawings of the building, and mosque and Temple were easily fused in the popular imagination. Similar representations of the Temple appear in other books, both Jewish and Christian.

YAARI NO. 10 HARVARD 19.5:14

ספר זבח פסח

המאמר הזה הוא פירוש בהגדות הפסח כולל פרשיות ודרושים׃ וטעמים נכבדים חדשים׃ לא שערום הראשונים מתוקים מדבש ונופת צופים׃

חברו שר וגדול בישראל דון יצחק אברבנאל זצל׃ בן השר דון יהודה אברבנאל זצל ·

נדפס בויניציאה העיר הגדולה המהוללה אשר תחת ממשלת השררה ירה׳ תגדל ותנשא מלכותם׳ אמן׳ בשנת שה לפק׳

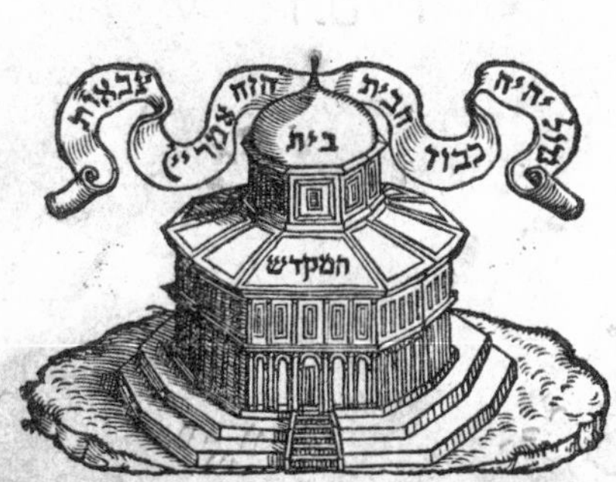

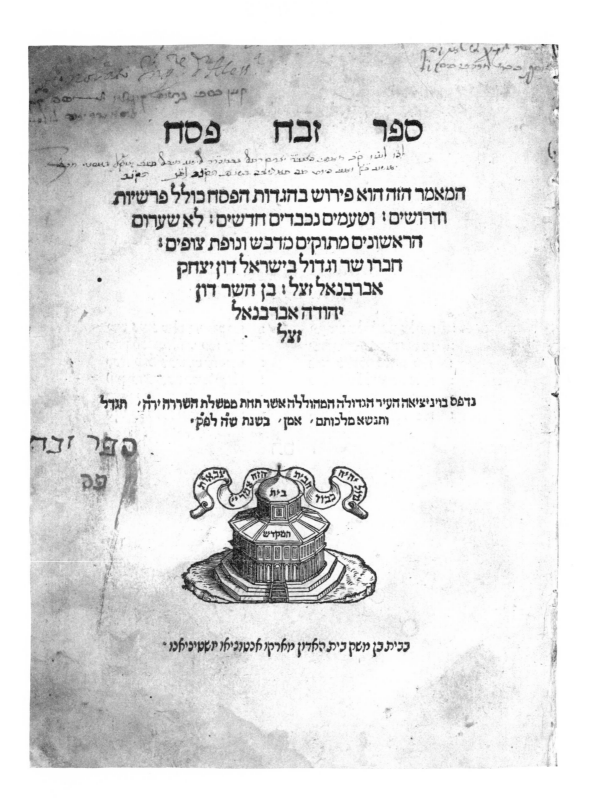

בבית בן משק בית האדון מארקו אנטוניאו יושטיניאנו ·

VENICE · ITALY · 1545
[SEDER TEFILOT]
Yiddish in Venice (I)

Venetian Jewry in the sixteenth century consisted of several distinct and autonomous communities, organized according to their points of origin: native Italian; German (Ashkenazic); and, somewhat later, Ponentine (Spanish-Portuguese) and Levantine (Turkish and other oriental Jews). Each maintained its own liturgical traditions.

German Jews had migrated to Venice since at least the fourteenth century, and their numbers were steadily augmented. They preserved not only their customs but also their Judeo-German language, an early form of Yiddish. In 1545 a prayer book was printed for their use at the Giustiniani press. It contained the entire text of the Haggadah in Hebrew, but many of the instructions were given in Yiddish, in smaller rabbinic or "Rashi" characters. With the exception of the translation of *Adir hu* at the end of the Prague Haggadah of 1526, these are among the earliest examples of Yiddish in a printed Hebrew Haggadah.

Above, right: The Hebrew title page of the prayer book, announcing it as "The Order of Prayers according to the rite of the Germans. Printed in the house of the lord Marco Antonio Giustiniani, in the Rialto, in the year [5]305. . . . Here, in Venice."

Above, left: The Haggadah begins in the middle of the page. The instructions for burning the leaven are in Hebrew.

Bottom, right: The preliminaries to the eating of the meal, with the instructions for washing the hands, breaking the matzah, and so on—all in Yiddish.

Bottom, left: In the small print are the Yiddish instructions for the meal itself, beginning with the injunction: "Then eat and drink, *un los dir gor vol zayn*" (which might be rendered freely as "and enjoy yourself to your heart's content"). In the large type is the beginning of the Grace to be recited after the meal.

JTSA 14.5:9.5

שאו ידיכם קדש וברכו את יי

סדר תפלות

כמנהג האשכנזים נדפס בבית
משק בית האדון מארקו אנטוניו
יוסטיניאנו בריאלטו
בשנת שלש מאות
וחמשה לפ״ק
פה

ויניציאה

קדשת שבת וכבוד מועד והגיגרת הרגל
ותבדילנו יי אלהינו בין קדש לחול בין
אור לחשך ובין ישראל לעמים ובין יום
השביעי לששת ימי המעשה בין קדשת
שבת לקדשת יום טוב הבדלת ואת יום
השביעי מששת ימי המעשה קדשת
הבדלת וקדשת את עמך ישראל ב
בקדשתך: ותתן לנו

הגדה של פסח

אור לארבעה עשר בודקין את החמץ: ולא
בודקין לאור החמה ולא לאור הלבנה
ולא לאור האבוקה אלא בנר של שעוה
ובודקין בחורין ובסדקין ובכל המקומות שדרכו להשתמש
בו שם ולא יתחיל שום מלאכה עד שיבדוק ואפילו בתלמוד
תורה וקודם שיתחיל לבדוק מברך:
ברוך אתה יי אלהינו מלך העולם אשר קדשנו
במצותיו וצונו על בעור חמץ:
ואל ידבר בין הברכה לתחלת הבדיקה כלל ואחר הבדיקה

אונ׳ טריקט · אונ וועשט די הענד אונ׳ זאגט ·
ברוך אתה יי אלהינו מלך העולם אשר קדשנו
במצותיו וצונו על נטילת ידים ·
אונ נימט די אויברשט מצה די גאנץ אונ זאגט
ברוך אתה יי אלהינו מלך העולם המוציא לחם
מן הארץ:
אונ׳ איש ניט דר בון ביז דאז דו נימשט די האלב מצה די
צווישן דען צוואו גנצי מצות אין אונ׳ זאג
ברוך אתה יי אלהינו מלך העולם אשר קדשנו
במצותיו וצונו על אכילת מצה ·
אונ׳ בריך אב בון אין ביידן אונ׳ איש זי מיט אנכדר אונ׳
ניב אין אלי די אס טיש זיצן אזא מיט אנכדר אונ׳ דר נוך ניט
דען לטיך אונ׳ דונק אין אין דעם חרוסת אונ׳ זאג:
ברוך אתה יי אלהינו מלך העולם אשר קדשנו
במצותיו וצונו על אכילת מרור:
אונ׳ איש אונ׳ ניב איררמן אזא דר נוך ביס די דריט מצה
די נוך גאנץ איז אונ׳ בריך דר בון אונ׳ נים איין וויכג לאטיך
אונ׳ טו עז אויף די מצה אונ׳ זאג:
כן עשה הלל בזמן שבית המקדש קיים היה כורך
מצה ומרור ביחד ויאכל כמו שנאמר מצות על

מרורים יאכלהו:
אונ׳ דר נוך איש אונ׳ טריכק אונ׳ לוש דיר גאר וואל זיין
הושטו אנדרש אויפיש גוט בו עשן אונ׳ נוך טיש וועגן מאן
אוף הוירט בו עשן דאז מאן ניט מיין אישט זא ביס די האלב
מצה די אונטר דער צוועהל לינט די אפיקומן הייסט אונ׳
בריך איין שטיק הראב אונ׳ איש אונ׳ ניב אין אלן אויך
די אס טיש זיצן בון דעם אפיקומן אונ׳ דר נוך וועש די
הענד אונ׳ מאך קיין ברכה אונ׳ דר נוך שענק דז גלאז ווידר
בול דז איז דאז דריט מולט אונ׳ בעגש דריף אוף דז זעלביג
גלאז:

ברכת המזון

נברך שאכלנו משלו ובטובו חיינו:
ברוך הוא שאכלנו משלו
ובטובו חיינו: ברוך הוא ברוך שמו:
ברוך אתה יי אלהינו מלך העולם
הזן את העולם כלו בטובו בחן
בחסד וברחמים והוא נותן לחם לכל בשר כי
לעולם חסדו ובטובו הגדול תמיד לא חסר לנו
ואל יחסר לנו מזון לעולם ועד בעבור שמו הגדול
כי הוא זן ומפרנס לכל ומטיב לכל ומכין מזון
לכל

VENICE · ITALY · 1549

Yiddish in Venice (II)

The 1545 prayer book for the Venice Ashkenazim (Plate 19) was apparently a success and sold out quickly. Only four years later another was published, this time by the Adelkind press. In this edition, which also contained the Haggadah, the use of Yiddish was expanded.

Above, right: The title page, this time entirely in Yiddish, stating that it is "The German Prayer Book, more ample than the one printed twenty years ago, with more of all kinds [of material] in it . . . which had not been printed in our prayer books. By Cornelio Adelkind. Venice." The reference is to the Ashkenazic prayer book published in Venice in 1529 by Daniel Bomberg, at whose press Adelkind was then employed. Giustiniani's 1545 edition, being that of a rival press, is ignored.

Above, left: Beginning with the line in large type, the sequence of the Seder is given and then explained in Hebrew.

Bottom, right: The passages in small type are in rhymed Yiddish prose. In the first paragraph are further instructions for searching leaven. All that has been found must be carefully wrapped up until the morning, so that none of it shall be taken away by mice and scattered to some other part of the house.

Bottom, left: More Yiddish instructions for preparing the Passover. Matzah must not be baked until all leaven has been burned. Children should be made to nap in the afternoon, so that they will remain awake at the Seder.

JTSA 14:8.5

אשר קדשנו במצותיו וצונו על מצות עירוב: בדין יהא שרי לנא לאפויי ולבשולי ולאטמוני ולאדלוקי שרגא ולתקנא ולמעבד כל צרכנא מיומא טבא לשבתא לנא ולכל ישראל הדרים בעיר הזאת:

סימן לסדר של פסח

קדש ורחץ· כרפס יחץ· מגיד רחצה·
מוציא מצה· מרור כורך· שלחן עורך·
צפון ברך· הלל נרצה:

בשש עשרה מלות אלו נכלל סדר פסח בכחות רב רבה בקדש ורחץ, שיאמר קדוש ואחר כך יטול ידיו, בכרפס יחץ, שיעשה טבול בכרפס ואחר כך יחלק אחת מהמצות לחצאין, מגיד רחצה, שיאמר ההגדה ואחר כך יטול ידיו לסעודה, מוציא מצה, שיעשה המוציא וברכת על אכילת מצה: מרור כורך, שיעשה טבול שני מרור בחרוסת, ואחריו הכריכ' זכר למקדש כהלל, ובשלחן עורך שיאכל סעודתו ובצפון ברך, שיאכל מחצי המצה הצפונה לאפיקומן, ואחר כך יברך ברכת המזון ויאמר הלל וזה מה שרצה באמרו הלל נרצה:

אונ' דז זעלביג חמץ דז ער וייסט, זול ער אכטן דז ער עז וואל איין ביגט: דאז איז עז ניט ור שלעפן די מוייז, ער מוישט זוישט זוכן אויבר איין נוייז ודאז מאג איין איטליכר וואל דר קענן, בויקש בעות אויף דען טאג זול מאן עז ור ברענן: ווער זיך בוירכט דאז מן אין ור מסיר דער וואוירף עז איבם וואסר: אונ' בויר דעס ור ברענן זול מן דאז חמץ אלז אויז דעס הויז טראגן, אונ' נוך דעס ור ברענן זול מאן אזו זאגן:

כל חמירא דאיכא ברשותי דחזיתיה ודלא חזיתיה דחמתיה ודלא חמתיה דבערתיה ודלא בערתיה לבטיל וליהוי כעפרא דארעא:

וועןּ יום טוב גיבאלט אין דער גיטאלט, דז דער אנדר טאג אס שבת גיבאלט, זא טאר מאן אס יום טוב אויף שבת ניט קוכן נאך באכן, זא מוז מן ערב תבשילין מאכן: מן נימט איין גאנצי מצה זי דארף ניט גרוסר זיין אז איין אייא, אונ' איין כזית ולייש אודר ויש וועלכש ער הוט אייבר לייא: אונ' דז זעלביג אן יום טוב מיט עסן טאר, אונ' אייבר מאג קוכן בויר די אנדרן גאר: אלי די זיך דרויף ור לוסן מויגן ורייא קוכן אונ' באכן אונ' די ברכה מאכן:

ברוך אתה יי אלהינו מלך העולם

מאן טאר בויר דעס חמץ בטלן דיא מצות ניט באכן, אונ' מאן ליגט דיא קינדר בייא טאג אין דר ווארטן דס זיא בו דעס סדר קיינן וואכן: אונ' דס זיא זולן מה נשתנה ורויגן, אז דער פסוק גיט ווען ער ווערט ורויגן דיך דיין זון מורגן בו זאגן: אונ' ווען מן בו נאכט אויז דער שול גיט, זא אכט דס דער טיש גריכט שטיט: אונ' דיא מצות ליגט מאן אובן איינס דיא מיטיל צווייא דיא אויבטר דרייא, דא אראן זער גיווארכט זייא: אונ' מאך דיר איין הסיבה מיט קויסן, אונ' דס חרוסת טאר מאן אס שבת ניט אן מויסן: דרום זול מן עס אס ורייטג גירעכן, אונ' דיא כוסות זולסטו שווענקן: אונ' זול זיא אל בול שענקן איין, די גהושט מצוה איז מיט רוטן ויין: אונ' דער קוישטליכשט גיבט דען סדר אז דא איז דער זיט, דער ווערט זיך אליין אונ' מאכט קיין ברכה אויבר דיא הענד ניט:

ווען פסח גיבאלט אן דען שלעכטן טאגן זא הובט מן קידוש דא אן בו זאגן

ברוך אתה יי אלהינו מלך העולם בורא פרי הגפן:

ברוך אתה יי אלהינו מלך העולם אשר בחר בנו מכל עם ורוממנו מכל לשון וקדשנו במצותיו

ותתן

CREMONA · ITALY · 1557

A Temporary Refuge for the Hebrew Book

The campaign against Hebrew books that began with the burning of the Talmud in Rome in 1553 spread rapidly to other Italian cities. Jews were forced to find new places in which to print, and for a while the press of Vicenzo Conti in Cremona served them well. Among other books, the Haggadah with Abravanel's commentary was published there in 1557. However, it was not long before the Talmud was also burned in Cremona, at which time Conti's printing establishment was all but destroyed and printing had to be transferred elsewhere (see Plate 27).

Shown here is the title page of the Cremona Haggadah. The border is obviously non-Jewish in origin. In the middle of the left vertical panel are the letters S.P.Q.R., the Latin abbreviation for the senate of ancient Rome (*Senatus populusque Romanus*).

YAARI NO. 17 JTSA 21:15

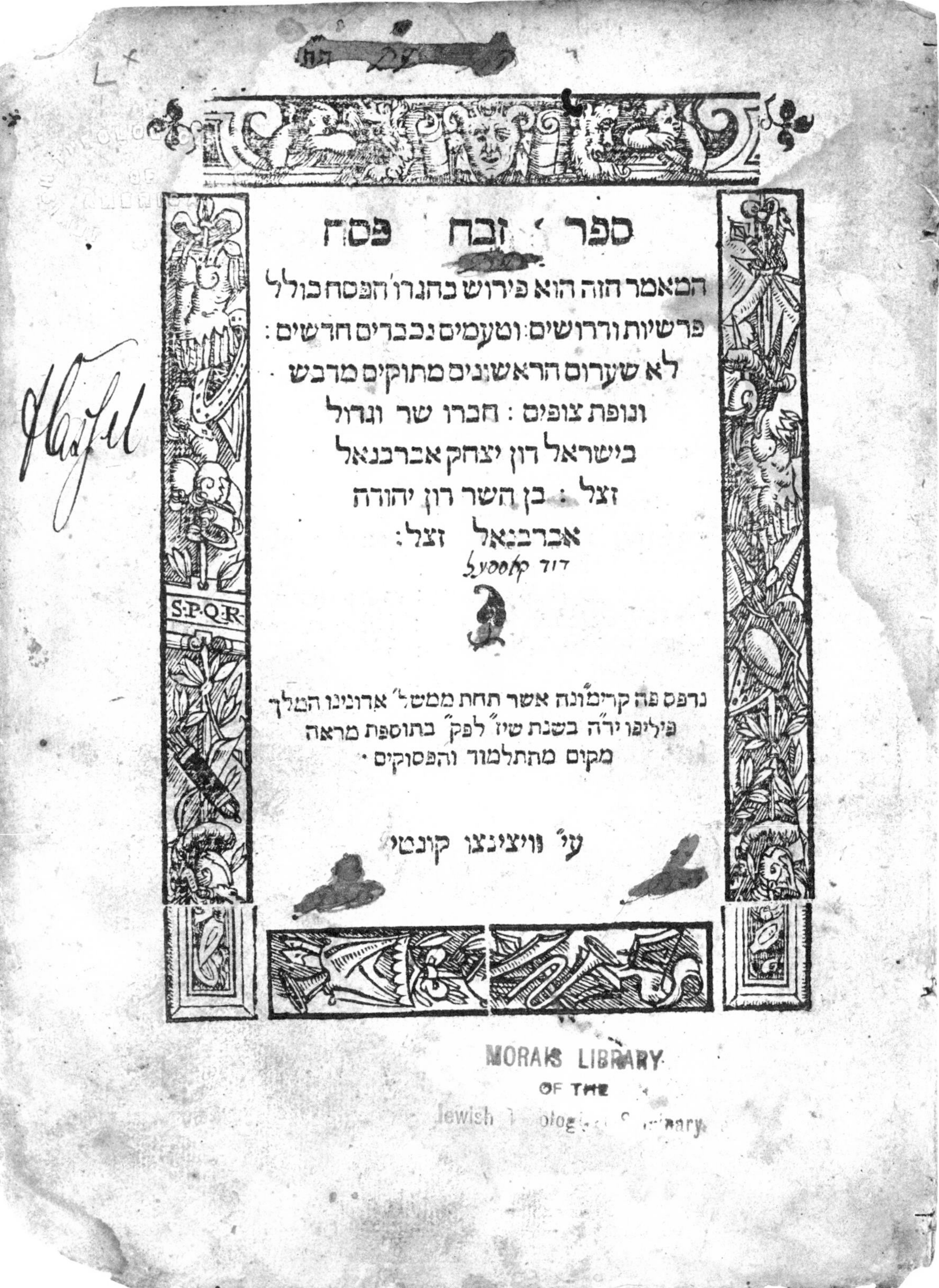

ספר זבח פסח

המאמר הזה הוא פירוש בהגדו׳ הפסח כולל
פרשיות ודרושים: וטעמים נכבדים חדשים:
לא שערום הראשונים מתוקים מדבש·
ונופת צופים: חברו שר וגדול
בישראל דון יצחק אברבנאל
זצל: בן השר דון יהודה
אברבנאל זצל:

נדפס פה קרימ״ונה אשר תחת ממשל׳ אדונינו המלך
פיליפו יר״ה בשנת שיז״ לפק״ בתוספת מראה
מקום מהתלמוד והפסוקים·

ע״ וויצינצו קונטי

MORAIS LIBRARY
OF THE
Jewish Theological Seminary

MANTUA · ITALY · 1560

Passover Preparations

The Mantua Haggadah of 1560 was issued at the press of Giacomo Rufinelli who was, as usual in Italy, a gentile. The actual production was in the hands of a Jew, Isaac ben Solomon Bassan, sexton of one of the Mantuan synagogues.

Except for three preliminary pages (one of which is shown here), a page in the middle containing the Grace, and the very last page, in typography and format the Mantua Haggadah is almost an exact replica of the Prague Haggadah of 1526. Only the illustrations have changed, the three Prague borders have been discarded, and each page is now surrounded by Italian Renaissance borders taken from available woodcut frames.

On this charming page the cut to the right of the text shows a father and his son gathering the leaven with feather and bowl. It is a much more vivid and natural illustration than its parallel in the Prague Haggadah (Plate 9). Starting immediately under the left vertical panel of the frame, and continuing along the bottom, for the first time there appears an illustration of the baking of matzah in its several stages. From left to right we see two men mixing flour and water, a group of men kneading a large mass of dough, women at a table flattening and separating it into circular shapes, two men perforating the dough, and a man and woman placing the cakes into a brick oven.

YAARI NO. 18 JTSA 30:21

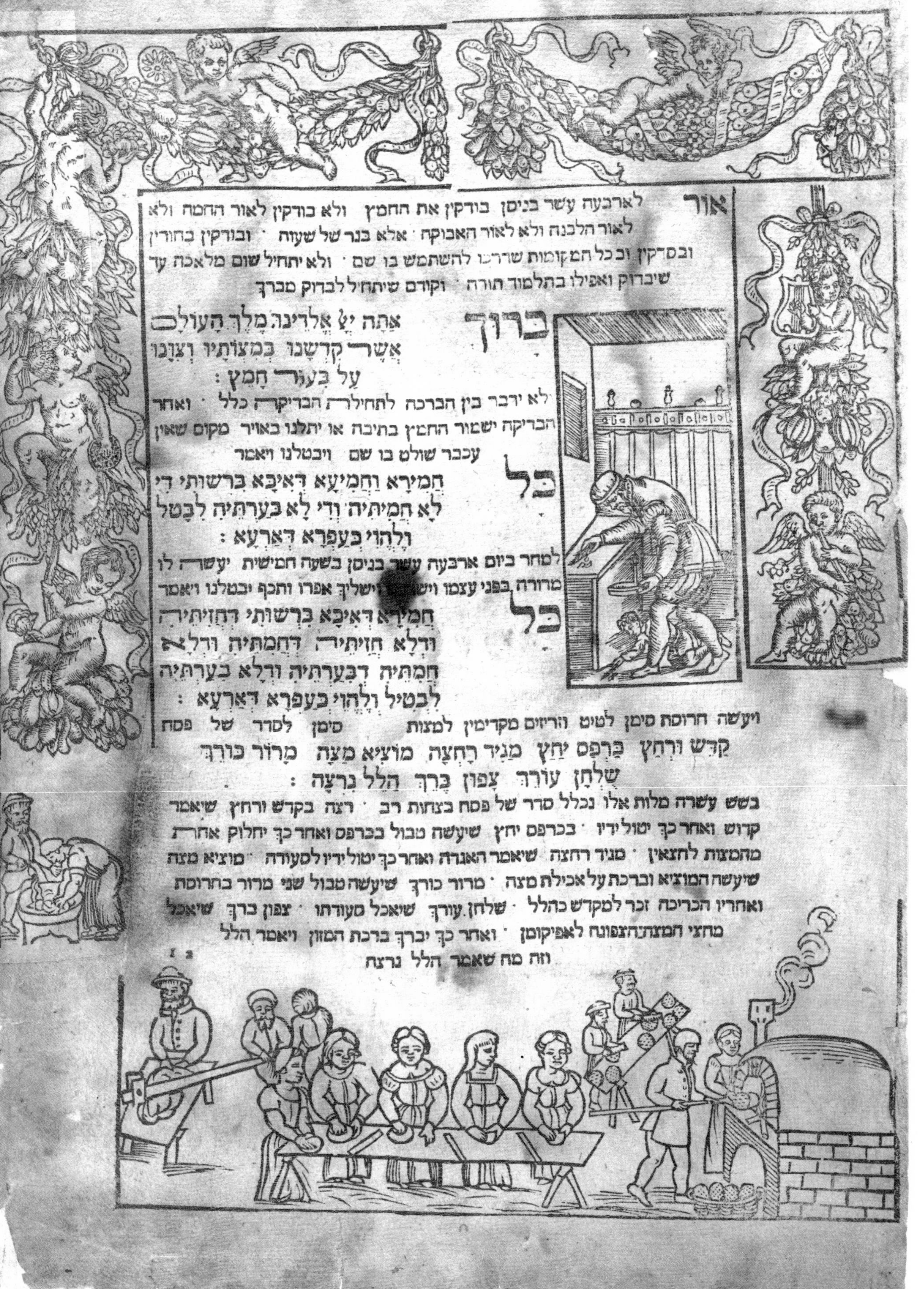

אור לארבעה עשר בניסן בודקין את החמץ ולא בודקין לאור החמה ולא לאור הלבנה ולא לאור האבוקה · אלא בנר של שעוה · ובודקין בחורין ובסדקין ובכל המקומות שדרכו להשתמש בו שם · ולא יתחיל שום מלאכה עד שיבדוק ואפילו בתלמוד תורה · וקודם שיתחיל לבדוק מברך

ברוך אתה יי אלהינו מלך העולם
אשר קדשנו במצותיו וצונו
על בעור חמץ :

לא ידבר בין הברכה לתחלת הבדיקה כלל · ואחר הבדיקה ישמור החמץ בתיבה או יתלנו באויר מקום שאין עכבר שולט בו שם ויבטלנו ויאמר

כל חמירא וחמיעא דאיכא ברשותי די
לא חמיתיה ודי לא בערתיה לבטל
ולהוי כעפרא דארעא :

למחר ביום ארבעה עשר בניסן בשעה חמישית יעשה לו מדורה בפני עצמו וישרפנו וישליך אפרו ותכף יבטלנו ויאמר

כל חמירא דאיכא ברשותי דחזיתיה
ודלא חזיתיה דחמתיה ודלא
חמתיה דבערתיה ודלא בערתיה
לבטיל ולהוי כעפרא דארעא :

ויעשה חרוסת סימן לטיט וזריזים מקדימין למצות סימן לסדר של פסח

קדש ורחץ כרפס יחץ מגיד רחצה מוציא מצה מרור כורך
שלחן עורך צפון ברך הלל נרצה :

בשש עשרה מלות אלו נכלל סדר של פסח בצחות רב · רצה בקדש ורחץ שיאמר קדוש ואחר כך יטול ידיו · בכרפס יחץ שיעשה טבול בכרפס ואחר כך יחלוק אחת מהמצות לחצאין · מגיד רחצה שיאמר האגדה ואחר כך יטול ידיו לסעודה · מוציא מצה שיעשה המוציא וברכת על אכילת מצה · מרור כורך שיעשה טבול שני מרור בחרוסת ואחריו הכריכה זכר למקדש כהלל · שלחן עורך שיאכל סעודתו · צפון ברך שיאכל מחצי המצה הצפונה לאפיקומן · ואחר כך יברך ברכת המזון ויאמר הלל וזה מה שאמר הלל נרצה

MANTUA · 1560
[CONTINUED]

The Wise Son and the Sistine Chapel

In design this page is a typical example of the somewhat uneasy fusion of north and south in the Mantua Haggadah. Typographically, the text is a copy of the corresponding page in the Prague Haggadah of 1526, letter for letter, line by line, almost as though it were a facsimile. The borders, however, are thoroughly Italian and do not quite suit the angular starkness of the Hebrew characters.

The cut over the left border panel shows a Jew with hands raised in a gesture of thanksgiving. It illustrates the opening line of the text, in which the Lord is blessed for having given the Torah to Israel.

This is followed by the passage devoted to the Four Sons, beginning with the Wise Son, who is pictured here in the lower left. In spirit he is descended from older manuscript Haggadah illustrations, in which the wisdom of the son is indicated by a beard. However, in this specific instance there was a more immediate yet alien model. Except for his head and cap, the Mantuan Wise Son is a fairly faithful copy of Michelangelo's Jeremiah in the great fresco of the Sistine Chapel at the Vatican.

Photo Alinari

Michelangelo: The Prophet Jeremiah

ברוך המקום
ברוך הוא
ברוך שנתן תורה לעמו
ישראל׳ ברוך הוא כנגד
ארבעה בנים דברה תורה
אחד חכם ואחד רשע
ואחד תם ואחד שאינו
יודע לשאל
חכם מה הוא
אומר מה
העדות והחקים והמשפטי׳
אשר צוה יי אלהינו אותנו
ואף אתה אמור לו כהלכ

PLATE 24

MANTUA · 1560
[CONTINUED]
Abraham in a Gondola

The verse from the Book of Joshua (24:2) quoted in the Haggadah text states: "Your fathers dwelt of old time beyond the River"—a dim recollection of the Mesopotamian origins of the Jewish people before the Lord commanded Abraham to journey to Canaan. The river is the Euphrates.

In the Prague Haggadah of 1526, Abraham was shown crossing the river alone in a rowboat (see below).

In the Mantua Haggadah the scene, like the borders, has been Italianized. Abraham sits in a gondola, and the oarsman rows while standing in the prow. (Some copies have this woodcut at the bottom of the page.)

Prague, 1526

לַעֲבֵירָתוֹ שֶׁנֶּאֱמַר וַיֹּאמֶר
יְהוֹשֻׁעַ אֶל כָּל הָעָם כֹּה
אָמַר יְיָ אֱלֹהֵי יִשְׂרָאֵל בְּעֵבֶר
הַנָּהָר יָשְׁבוּ אֲבוֹתֵיכֶם
מֵעוֹלָם תֶּרַח אֲבִי אַבְרָהָם
וַאֲבִי נָחוֹר וַיַּעַבְדוּ אֱלֹהִים

אֲחֵרִים

וָאֶקַּח אֶת אֲבִיכֶם

אֶת אַבְרָהָם מֵעֵבֶר הַנָּהָר
וָאוֹלֵךְ אוֹתוֹ בְּכָל אֶרֶץ
כְּנָעַן וָאַרְבֶּה אֶת זַרְעוֹ
וָאֶתֵּן לוֹ אֶת יִצְחָק וְאֶת

MANTUA · 1560
[CONTINUED]
Egypt: The Drowning of the Infants

The text contains the verse "And Pharaoh charged all his people, saying: 'Every son that is born ye shall cast into the river, and every daughter ye shall save alive' " (Exodus 1:22).

In the illustration the Egyptians stand on a bridge and throw the male infants of the Hebrews into the Nile. Along the banks some mothers attempt to save them from drowning, while others lift their hands in anguish and despair. The same theme is present in an illustration in the Prague Haggadah, but on a far smaller scale and in less detail.

Prague, 1526

את ענינו זו פרישות דרך
ארץ כמה שנא׳ וירא אלהים
את בני ישראל וידע אלהים:

ואת עמלינו אלו
הבנים כמה
שנאמ׳ ויצו פרעה לכל עמו
לאמר כל הבן הילוד
היארה תשליכהו וכל הבת
תחיון: ואת לחצנו זה
הדחק כמה שנ׳ וגם ראיתי
את הלחץ אשר מצרים
לוחצים אותם: ויוציאנו יי
ממצרים ביד חזקה ובזרוע

MANTUA · 1560
[CONTINUED]
The Messiah Enters Jerusalem

This is the most striking and successful Mantuan adaptation of one of the pages in the Prague Haggadah. In typography it is, as always, a replica (see Plate 13). But the Prague border has been replaced here by a right-hand panel that is unobtrusive, and the huge initial word has been fixed against a magnificently designed background.

The most important innovation is the substitution, for the small Prague cut of the Messiah, of an entire scene that now occupies almost half the page, depicting not only the Messiah but the prophet Elijah as well. As a result, the entire balance of the page has shifted into a new dimension. Whereas in the Prague Haggadah the page was dominated by the border, in the Mantua edition the Messiah is the focus of attention. As an added touch, a small figure of a soldier holding a pike and shield is inserted at the end of the first part of the text. He would seem to represent the evil nations against whom God's wrath is summoned. In his aggressive, warlike stance he also contrasts vividly with the Messiah, whose advent will usher in the era of universal peace.

שפוך
חמתך על הגוים
אשר לא ידעוך ועל
הממלכות אשר
בשמך לא
קראו
שפוך עליהם זעמך וחרון
אפך ישיגם תרדוף באף
ותשמידם מתחת שמי יי

PLATE 27

RIVA DI TRENTO · ITALY · 1561

At the Press of a Cardinal of the Church

The Haggadah whose title page is reproduced here is linked historically to the Cremona Haggadah of 1557 (Plate 21). When the Cremona press was halted in the summer of 1559, Hebrew printing moved on to Riva di Trento, where a rival press had recently been established. It was owned by the cardinal of Trent, Christophoro Madruzzi, who was also the temporal ruler of the entire area. There is no indication that he allowed the books of the Jews to be printed under his jurisdiction for any reason other than that of potential profits. However, at a time when Hebrew books were being hounded all over Italy, Jews were too grateful for any printing opportunities to inquire into the motives of their sponsors. Madruzzi's fees were paid willingly, and most title pages of Hebrew books printed in Riva di Trento bear his cardinal's coat of arms.

The prime mover of the press was a Jewish physician, Dr. Jacob ben David Marcaria, who had formerly resided in Cremona. The series of books printed within a few years under his dedicated supervision included examples of almost all branches of Hebrew literature. Moreover, some were first editions, especially of philosophical works, to which he was particularly devoted. Marcaria added lucid and erudite prefaces of his own to all the Hebrew books that were printed.

In the realm of liturgy the only work published in Riva di Trento was the Haggadah of 1561, and this must have been issued primarily because it contained the commentary of Abravanel.

The title page has the same frame as the Mantua edition of 1560. The lines within read: "Haggadah, with the commentary of the perfect sage Don Isaac Abravanel, renowned in Judah and Israel, entitled *Zebaḥ Pesaḥ*; and added thereto . . . are the reason and secret [i.e., the mystical interpretation] of the Four Cups, and the reason for the paschal sacrifice, matzah, and bitter herbs, composed by one of the disciples, and Jacob Marcaria is his name; and all the laws which are observed on Passover eve, both by the community of the Sephardim as well as Ashkenazim, with wondrous brevity and pleasant arrangement. Printed and corrected with great care under the rule of the lord Cardinal Christopol Madruz [i.e., Christophoro Madruzzi], may his glory be exalted. . . ."

Only a year later (1562) Hebrew printing in Riva di Trento was also forced to come to an end. Types already set for the other parts of Abravanel's trilogy were taken to Venice. The press in Riva now issued only non-Jewish works. Ironically, Marcaria was entrusted in 1562–63 with the publication of several works in Latin pertaining to the Council of Trent, the great assembly of the Catholic Church which dogmatically consolidated the Counter-Reformation, and was now drawing to a close after meeting over a span of almost two decades.

YAARI NO. 19 JTSA 29:20

הגדה

עם פירוש החכם השלם דון יצחק
אברבנאל הנודע ביודא
וישראל שמו
זבח פסח

ונוסף עליו כי תקראנה
טעם וסוד ארבע כוסות
וטעם פסח מצה ומרור

חובר על יד אחד מן התלמידים ויעקב
פרקריאה שמו

וכל הדינים אשר ינהג בליל פסח הן קהל
הספרדי׳ הן עם האשכנזים · בקצור
מופלא וסדור נאה

נדפס והוגה ברב עיון תחת ממשלת האדון
האומן קריסטופיל מאדרוץ יר״ה

פה ריווה דטרינטו
שנת שכ״א
לפ״ק

MANTUA · ITALY · 1568

Roman Deities on a Hebrew Title Page

Eight years after it first appeared, the Mantua Haggadah of 1560 (Plates 22–26) was reissued in the same city in a revised edition. The printer, Joseph Shalit ben Jacob Ashkenazi, had founded the Hebrew press in the Italian city of Sabionetta in 1551, and came to Mantua in 1555. His printer's emblem, a peacock on a scrolled shield, appears below within the wreath. The Haggadah of 1568 was produced at the Filipponi press.

The major change in this edition was the introduction of a commentary by Rabbi Joseph of Padua into the margins, a step which necessitated a radical reordering of the earlier design. To accommodate the new material, parts of borders were eliminated, illustrations were shifted, and some were thereby assigned new meanings. These and similar alterations seem to have been made arbitrarily, with no overall plan. As a result, the edition of 1568 is visually less coherent than its predecessor.

A new title page, shown here, was also supplied. Whereas the title page of the Haggadah of 1560 had been a frame with two twisted columns at the sides (it appears again in the Riva di Trento edition of 1561 [Plate 27]), here there is an arch covered with vines and fruits, the lower portion being flanked by two figures: Mars (right) and Minerva (left). The entire elaborate frame with its two Roman deities, undoubtedly borrowed from non-Jewish books, had already been used in Hebrew works printed in Sabionetta, and would reappear again in Venice in the early seventeenth century (see Plate 42). Such "pagan" motifs seem hardly to have troubled Jews and were regarded merely as decoration. Parallels easily come to mind. In the Hebrew publications of the Conti press in Cremona and Sabionetta such figures as Neptune and Hercules appear. The 1574 Venice edition of Maimonides' code, the *Mishneh Torah*, has as the printer's emblem a nude Venus standing over a seven-headed dragon.

YAARI NO. 20 JTSA 30:20.5

LC

סדר הגדות

של פסח עם הבריק ז
וברכות וקדוש כחק ז
לאשכנזים ולועזים ולנשיהם ·
למען יל׳ מרון המ״ה ובניהם ·

ועל הנסים ועל הנפלאות מצויירים
עיניכם תחזינה מישרים

גם כל עין בעין יראה ויעמד וישתאה ·
על פירוש ותוספות נמוקי יוסף מפדואה :

נדפס שנית שנת שס״ט לפ״ק במנט בה הבורך ·
עי׳ בני הפילופון בעין כמון ער נמיכה :

בבית ממעלת מעלת ידומין סדוכום
גוליעלמו גוכוליבם ול״ב ·

על יד ובשם

179611

AUG 30 1960

MANTUA · 1568
[CONTINUED]
Displacements in Design

Some insight into the changes that took place in the Mantua Haggadah of 1568 can be gained from this preliminary page, which should be compared directly with the corresponding one in the 1560 edition (Plate 22). The large illustration of the baking of matzah (bottom) has been retained intact, as has the small cut of the search for leaven (right). The latter, however, has been put into the margin, in lieu of the border. The left border of 1560 has been completely replaced by the commentary. Different parts of the former border appear only at the top. The types and their arrangement, including the large framed initial word, are entirely new, and so are the sun and moon which fill the remaining spaces. Another novelty lies in the captions that now accompany each illustration, these being absent in the edition of 1560. The practice of inserting captions (though not the actual wording) reverts to the Prague Haggadah of 1526. It should be emphasized that the types and arrangements of the body of the Haggadah text itself are still the same as in 1560—that is, they are a "facsimile" of the Prague typography (see Plates 30–31).

אור הלבנה

אור החמה

אור

ארבע עשר בניסן בודקין החמץ בכל המקומות שרגילין להכניס בו חמץ אפילו בחורין וסדקין · בנר של שעוה ולא באבוקה · ולא לאור לבנה וחמה · ואין מתחילין שום מלאכה ואפילו ללמוד עד שבדקו : וקודם שמתחילין מברכין

בָּרוּךְ אַתָּה יְיָ אֱלֹהֵינוּ מֶלֶךְ הָעוֹלָם אֲשֶׁר קִדְּשָׁנוּ בְּמִצְוֹתָיו וְצִוָּנוּ עַל בִּעוּר חָמֵץ:

ולא ידבר בין ברכה לבדיקה · וישמר החמץ שבדק בתיבה או יתלנו באויר ויבטל

כָּל חֲמִירָא דְאִיכָּא בִרְשׁוּתִי דְלָא חֲמִתֵּיהּ וּדְלָא בִעַרְתֵּיהּ לִבָּטֵל וְלֶהֱוֵי כְּעַפְרָא דְאַרְעָא

למחר בשעה חמשית ישרפנו במדורה בפני עצמו וישליך עפרו · ויבטלנו ויאמר

כָּל חֲמִירָא דְאִיכָּא בִרְשׁוּתִי דַחֲמִתֵּיהּ וּדְלָא חֲמִתֵּיהּ דְבִעַרְתֵּיהּ וּדְלָא בִעַרְתֵּיהּ לִבָּטֵל וְלֶהֱוֵי כְּעַפְרָא דְאַרְעָא

ועושין החרוכת סימן לטיט · ועושין המצות

בצאת ישראל ממצרים בית יעקב היו לדוגמא אחרי בהמות וגשמות כמנהג הפועלים והקטנים · ולכן הוציא בחדש האביב שאז הדין מתחיל שלימתו ושחיטת הפסח הוא הבהמות · והשבתת החמץ הוא יצר הרע ושאור המביאיש העסה · הכל ב״יד עכבאן ואיך הוא במשך להיותו בו עושין · ולכן הבדיק בלי נהכח דעת בכל סדקי וחדרי הגוף ולאור נר קטן נשמת חיים בהירות האגם · ולא לאור גזירת דבאורות הגדולים ולא באבוקה לשרוף כל החומר הצריך לקיום הגוף · וע״כ נתנו שעיר לעסה וכל פרטי המין יורו וכן ד׳ חלוקי כלים והכשרם נגד ארבע חלוקי כפרה · כפרת מצות עשה בתשובה · ושבוש כלי צונן בשטיפה : לא תעשה נ״כ : וכלי שני בהגעלה : כרת ומיתת בד״ ביסורין · וכלי ראשון בלבון : חלול ה׳ במיתה · וחרס בשבירה ;

כורת לחם לסה ושני מטיל מים בתנוה זו זר לא פכר בכרים :

כורת בעל הבית בודק וחביכו הקטן עמו כדי במנות למככו :

בלילה אין אומרים דחמיתיה ובערתיה דחמץ שראה רוצה בו עוד לשתי סעודות ואינו מבערו עד למחר ·

כורת מנות ותכור וסלופס וסבל לאסר בו קמנות כנפק ·

כורת לכסים סמסרקים ובסוכ עושות חלות : זקנים עם נערים בחורים גם בתולות :

א ב ii i

MANTUA · 1568
[CONTINUED]
A Zodiac and the Work of the Months

In the Mantua Haggadah of 1560 the page containing the beginning of the Four Questions had been framed entirely by its lush Italian border, with no illustrations at all. Here the types alone remain the same; the border has changed almost completely. Only the top and part of the upper left still exhibit vines and cherubs. The middle left is occupied by Joseph of Padua's commentary, printed in small characters. Below it is a cut, clearly portraying a king, which appeared twice in the Prague Haggadah of 1526 and once in the Mantua edition of 1560, representing Pharaoh in each instance. Here, however, the caption above the figure indicates that it is now meant to depict the person who asks the questions at the Seder.

The vertical border on the right had not appeared before. It continues a series showing the occupations of the months of the year, five of which begin on a similar border of an earlier page. Each segment of the border is divided into two unequal parts, one with the sign of the zodiac, the other with the characteristic work of that month. Though signs of the zodiac were used in Hebrew books, there is no relation here to the text. The printer merely had these panels at his disposal, and inserted them to provide some relief from the vines and cherubs that fill the borders on other pages.

דישראל השתא עבדי לשנה
הבאה בני חורין

מה נשתנה
הלילה הזה
מכל הלילות

שבכל הלילות אנו אוכלין
חמץ ומצה הלילה הזה
כלו מצה שבכל הלילות
אנו אוכלין שאר ירקות
הלילה הזה מרור שבכל
הלילות אין אנו מטבילין
אפילו פעם אחת הלילה
הזה שתי פעמים שבכל

חמץ ומצה · פי׳ או מצה : שאר
ירקות · אפי׳ פעם אחת · פי׳ אם
נרצה · הלילה הזה מרור ושני
פעמים דוקא׳ אחת בחומץ וא׳
בחרוסת · והיה למכדר להתום
ב ש״ת שנוי הטבול ולהסמיך
שלשת שאלות שנויי האכילות ·
אבל הפסיק בטבול לעורר אגב
אורחיה ששאלתו ג״כ על שאנו
נ ושין שני הפכים בלילה אחת
שאכיל׳ מצה ומרור לחוד׳ זכר
עבדות · וטבול ואכילת הסיבה
לחוד זכר לחירות : והיגח להם
שהיה להם עבדות : חרות אבל
אנו לא הכרנו לא חרות · והוא
מותיב הארבעה שאלות הללו
באמרו מה נשתנה וכו׳ והוא
מפרק לה באמרו עבדים היינו :

צורת הפסוק כדת וכה לכם ·
למס וקח רקו על ככה ·

4

MANTUA · 1568
[CONTINUED]
The "Sistine" Wise Son Becomes a Father

The Wise Son in the Mantua Haggadah of 1560 had been inspired by Michelangelo's Jeremiah in the Sistine Chapel (Plate 23). The very same figure now appears in the Haggadah of 1568 (upper right), but his role is reversed. The caption reads: "Portrait of an old man who has acquired wisdom, *replying* to the wise [son] with knowledge and deliberation." The figure crops up again on another page as a talmudic rabbi (see Plate 36).

Below: The hard labor of the Hebrew slaves, taken over from the edition of 1560. Two captions are added along the sides. Right: "A picture of the labor with mortar and brick, the work of the fathers a pattern for the sons." Left: "A picture of an Egyptian striking a Hebrew, and he was the husband of Shelomit, daughter of Dibri." This interpretation derives from ancient rabbinic legend. Shelomit, it is told, was the beautiful wife of Datan, one of the Hebrew foremen appointed among the slaves. One day his Egyptian taskmaster ordered him to work, entered his house, and violated Shelomit. Datan discovered what had happened, and thereafter the Egyptian began to persecute him at every turn. It was this Egyptian taskmaster whom Moses killed when he saw him beating a Hebrew slave (Exodus 2:11–12), the latter being identified by the rabbis as Datan.

צורת זקן מקטר מלמה׃
מסיר ׳חכם בדעת ובמזימה׃

הלילות אנו אוכלין בין
יושבין ובין מסבין הלילה
הזה כלנו מסבין׃

עבדים היינו
לפרעה
במצרים ויוציאנו יי אלהינו
משם ביד חזקה ובזרוע
נטויה ואלו לא הוציא הקב׳
את אבותינו ממצרים הרי
אנו ובנינו ובני בנינו משעב
דים היינו לפרעה במצרים
ואפילו כלנו חכמים כלנו
נבונים כלנו זקנים כלנו

עבדים היינו ׳ וזהיא תשובה
לשאלת השני מאכילת מצה
ומרור שהוא זכר לעבדות׃
ויוציאנו יי׳ אלהינו משם ׳ וזהיא
תשובות לשאלת שנוי הטבול
ואכילה בהסיבה שהוא זכרון
לחירות׃ משם ביד חזקה ׳ ר״ל
העבדות והיציאה שניה׳ מש״ם
בפעם אחת ובלילה אחת ׳ וז
היא תשובת למה עושים ש׳
הפכים בלילה אחת׃ ביד חזקה
ובזרוע נטויה ׳ זו ראיה שאנו
ובנינו ובני בנינו משעבדי׳ היינו
ותשובה לשאלת מה לנו לזכרון
העבדות׃ וזה שהוצרך לשדד
המערכה שמצד הטבע לא היה׃
אפי׳ עבד יכול לצאת׳ ואם
בחוקה׃ היתחזק צאן עצום
מול שחל׃ וזהו ולא יתן אתכם
מלך מצרים להלך׳ ר״ל מרצון
ולא ביד חזקה ר״ל גם לא בשבי׳
ידכם חזקה כי אם ושלחתי את
ידי והכתי לשדד המערכ׳ וזהו
בכל אלהי מצרים אעשה שפטי׳
ר״ל אשדד המערכ׳ וע״כ הוצרך
להיות הוא עצמו ולא ע״י שליח
וע״ד זה ארז״ל אין מזל לישראל
שלא עשה כן לכל גוי וע״כ אמר
לאברהם הבט השמימה ׳ שר״ל
מלמעלה למטה שהגביהו על
המערכת השמימיית ואמר לו
כה יהיה זרעך׃

צורת איש מצרי מכה איש עברי
והוא בעלה של שלומית בת דברי׃

בעבודה קשה בחמר ובלבנים׃
ובכל עבודה בשדה.

SALONIKA · GREECE · 1569

In a Sixteenth-Century Jewish Metropolis

In the latter half of the sixteenth century Salonika surpassed even Constantinople as a center of Jewish life in the Ottoman Empire. This is the title page of the first known Salonikan edition of the Haggadah. It contains a commentary by Moses ben Ḥayyim Pisanti entitled *Ḥukkat ha-Pesaḥ* ("The Law of Passover"), as well as other materials. The author, then only twenty-eight years old, was born in Jerusalem and completed the commentary in Gallipoli in 1568.

It was printed, we are informed, "with great care in the house of the young man Joseph, son of my lord the perfect sage our master Rabbi Isaac, son of the pious Rabbi Joseph Yaabetz the Preacher, may the memory of the righteous and pious endure for the life of the world to come." (Joseph Yaabetz, grandfather of the printer, was one of the great homilists of the generation of Spanish exiles.)

Sharing the practice so common in traditional Hebrew books, the work is dated by citing a biblical verse, the numerical value of its letters (or, at other times, of some of the letters) being equal to the date itself. Here we read: "In Salonika, a city of the great king, the realm of our lord the great and mighty king Sultan Selim. . . . The noble and pure labor was [begun] on Thursday, the 27th of the month Adar, in the year *They shall obtain gladness and joy, and sorrow and sighing shall flee away*" (Isaiah 35:10).

YAARI NO. 22 JTSA 20:14

חקת הפסח

סדר חברו הבינו וגם חקרו החכם הותיק פלפלא חריפא כהר״ר משה בכ״ר
חיים בן החכם כה״ר שם טוב פיזאנטי ז״ל והוא פירוש יפה ובאור נחמד
על ההגדה שתקן הרב המגיד לקרות לעת מצא קרא מקרא קדש בכל
ליל חג הפסח ונלוו אליו פירוש גוים רבים משרתי עליון לשרת את פני
ה׳ חדושי הרב רבינו יונה זלה״ה עם נמוקי זיקי מבהיקי הה״ר בנימן אחיו
וחדושי הרב רבינו ישעיה זלה״ה ולהרחבת הביאור נמשכו בעבותות
שיחות אהבת החקירה והעיון כמה פירושי פרשיות ופסוקי דזמרה
והנביאים והכתובים ומאמרים נחמדים מזהב העיון מיוסדים על אדני פז
החקירה התלמודיית ספרי וספרא מכילתא ואגדות בבלי וירושלמי באר
היטב כאשר יראה הרואה את יקר תפארת גדולתו ופרשת אחוזתו וגם כל
הדינים הגלוים כל אותה הלילה בלם נכוחים ובשמן משחת קדש ם
משוחים ואחר כל אלה נמצא פירוש קצר מהחכם השלם הה״ר שלמה
ברוך יצ״ו והובא על שפתו מזה ומזה לזכותו

נדפס בעיון רב בבית הצעיר והקטן יוסף בן לאדוני החכם השלם יצחק
בן הרב החסיד מוהר״ר יוסף יעבץ הדורש זכר צדיקים
וחסידים לחיי העולם הבא

בשאלוניקי

קרית מלך רב ממשלת אדוננו המלך הגדול והאדיר
סולטאן סלים ירום הודו ותנשא מלכותו אמן

היתה התחלה המתחלה זכה וברה יום ה׳
אך לחדש אדר שנת ששון ושמחה יש יגון ונסו
יגון ואנחה

BISTROWITZ · POLAND · 1592

A Printer Flees the Plague

The first Haggadah known to have been printed in Eastern Europe was an edition accompanied by Abravanel's ever-popular commentary, which appeared in Bistrowitz, Poland. It has the further distinction of being the only Hebrew book ever published in that place. The circumstances are explained on the title page where, after praising the book, the printer continues:

> We began the work today, Tuesday the 10th of Elul, in the year *And he stood between the dead and the living; and the plague was stayed* [Numbers 17:13]. Printed in the village of Bistrowitz . . . the royal crown being placed on the head of Sigmund, may his glory be exalted . . . by Kalonymus, son of our master Rabbi Mordecai Jafe of blessed memory.

The biblical verse employed to record the date offers the clue as to what had occurred. Kalonymus ben Mordecai Jafe was a printer in Lublin. When the plague broke out in the city he fled to Bistrowitz and there produced the Haggadah. Afterwards he returned to Lublin.

YAARI NO. 25 HARVARD 20.5:15

זה השער לה׳ צדיקים יבואו בו

ספר

זבח פסח

המאמר הזה הוא פירוש בהגדות
הפסח פרשיות ודרושים וטעמים
ככבדי קדם׳ לא שערום הראשונים
מתוקים מדבש ונופת צופים · חברו
שר וגדול בישראל דון יצחק אברבנאל
זצ״ל · בן השר דון יהודה
אברבנאל זצ״ל

התחלנו המלאכ׳ היום יום ב׳ י׳ אלול
בשנת ויעמוד בין המתים
ובין החיים ותעצר המגפה

נדפס בכפר ביסטרוויץ
תחת השר זאמושקי
והכתר מלכות ריתן ברא״ז יג״ד
ירום הודו ותנשא מלכותו אמן:

על ידי קלונימוס בן הר״ר
מרדכי יפה ז״ל

VENICE · ITALY · 1599

The Multilingual Ghetto of Venice

The four Haggadahs printed in Venice between 1599 and 1604 are of considerable historic importance. They are transitional experiments, occupying a place between the Mantua Haggadahs of 1560 and 1568, on the one hand, and the definitive Venetian editions of 1609 and 1629, on the other. All four were commissioned by the same person, his name appearing on the title pages as Rabbi Solomon Ḥayyim "and his only son," who is later identified as Abraham Ḥaber Tob (see Plate 42). Like the Mantua Haggadah of 1568, these contain the brief commentary of Rabbi Joseph of Padua, but the Prague typography, which was still retained in Mantua, is now abandoned. The Mantuan woodcuts reappear, changing both their locations and their meaning, while new illustrations are introduced along the way which also tend to shift from one edition to the next.

Another feature now emerges that reflects the diversity of Venetian Jewry itself. Besides contemporary Spanish and Portuguese, three "Jewish" languages were current in the Ghetto of Venice, and they were written in Hebrew characters: Judeo-Italian, Yiddish, and Ladino. These were also the languages into which the liturgy would be translated for those who required it. (Portuguese was not written in Hebrew script, nor was it used liturgically. Spanish in the Hebrew alphabet was, in essence, Ladino.)

Reproduced here is a preliminary page from the Haggadah of 1599 where, for the first time, the order of the Seder service is explained in three parallel columns, each in a different Jewish language. Similar pages were to appear in the editions of 1601, 1603, and 1604. The Haggadah text that follows remains entirely in Hebrew. But in this page is already forecast the trilingual translation of the entire text that was to take place exactly a decade later.

Each language on this page is identified by a heading in bold letters. These read, from right to left: *Leshon la'az* ("the vernacular tongue," i.e., Judeo-Italian); *Leshon Sefarad* ("the Spanish tongue," i.e., Ladino); and *Leshon Ashkenaz* ("the German tongue," i.e., Yiddish). The text of the Yiddish column is in rhyme.

YAARI NO. 27 JTSA 23:17

קַדֵּשׁ וּרְחַץ׳ כַּרְפַּס יַחַץ׃ מַגִּיד רָחְצָה׳ מוֹצִיא מַצָּה׃
מָרוֹר כּוֹרֵךְ׳ שֻׁלְחָן עוֹרֵךְ׃ צָפוּן בָּרֵךְ׳ הַלֵּל נִרְצָה׃

לשון לעז לשון ספרד לשון אשכנז

קדש ורחץ סי דיצי לו קדוש אי קון ברכה סי לאוה לי מאני׳

כרפס דדית פוי סי פרה בורא פרי האדמה אי לאפיו קון חרוסת סי מאניין טוטי דוי׃

יחץ סי פרטי לו סיקונדו שמור׳ איט איווי סילאסה אונה פרטי

מגיד סי דיצי לה הגדה פוי קי לאטרו מיזו סיאה פוסטו דה פרטי׃

רחצה סי לאווה לי מאני׳ איט המוציא

מוציא סול פרימו פיאדה דיטו׳

מצה סו לה מיזה אכילת מצה׳ מניינדולי אינסיימי פרה איל סואו דריטו׃

מרור על אכילת מרור סי פרה סופרה איל מרור אין חרוסת אינפוסו׳

כורך איל מירצו שימור קון מרור סינצה ברכה אי איל סואו אוסו׃

שלחן עורך צפון איל ביסוינו סי מנייה פוי אי אין אולטימו לאפיקומן ריסרווטו׳

ברך הלל נרצה סי דיצי ברכה׳ איט הלל׳ אה לאוורי די קי איל טוטו אה קריאטו׃

לי קווטרו כוסות׳ סיני ביווי די ציאסקונו און. רביעית איט אפווייטו אי די לה מצה כזית׳ אי טוחגרלי אדה פר איסנרוסילי דומינמיקטו׃

קדש דירה קידוס׃

ורחץ לאברה לאם מאנוס אי נו דירה ברכה׃

כרפס טומארה דיל אפיו אי איכטיירה איכיל ויכאגרי אי דירה בורא פרי האדמה׃

יחץ פארטירה לה מצה סמורה די איכמידיו אי מיטיר׳ לא מידייה סון לוס מאכטילים׃

מגיד דירה לה הגדה׃

רחצה סי לאואר׳ לאם מאנוס אי דירה על נטילת ידים׳

מוציא הרה המוציא איפלה די איכסימה אי נו קומה אי פארטירה

מצה דילה מידייא די א איכמידיין איקומירה טודו גוכטו אידירה על אכילת מצה׳

מרור איכטיכיירה דילה ליג׳וג׳ איכיל ויכאגרי אי דירה על אכילת מרור׃

כורך טומאר׳ די טודא׳ לאם וירדוראם אי דילה מב׳אי איכטויכיר׳ איכיל חרוסת אי דירה זכר למקדש וכו׳׳

שלחן צפון אורדינארן לה מיזה׃ אי קומיראן קאדה אונו קואכטו אוכה איזייטוכה׃

ברך דירה ברכת המזון׃

הלל דירה הלל׃

נרצה יהי לפני השם לרצון

זען דיך גוט טיט אונ׳ מאך קדוש ביהענדי׳ דר נוך וועט איט ברכה דיא הענד׃

דען נים איפיך אונ׳ אין עסיק טונק איין׳ בורא פרי האדמה זאל זיין ברכה זיין׃

די אנדר מצוה בון אנגדר טפלט איין טייל לוס דורט די אנגדר לו אפיקומן הלט׃

דען ד: איי אונ׳ זרוע׳ אויז דעק בעקן נים׳ אונ׳ זג הא לחמא איט העלר טטים׃

דען טו ד: בעקן נידר אונ׳ טענק ווידר איין׳ אונ׳ עבדים כי: גאל ישראל זאג גר פיין׃

איט די ערשט מצוה אך המוציא׳ אונ׳ די הלכ אכילת מצה אוז צו זאן ביסטו יוצא׃

אכילת מרור אך אונ׳ מרור אין חרוסת טו׳ דר נוך איט דער דריט איט מרור לו׃

אונ׳ טוירן דרויז קיין ברכ׳ אלן דר נוך איז: און זיך איט דער סעודה ביזאכן׃

נוך זעלטן איין כזית אפיקמן זולטטו עסן׃ אונ׳ מזומן בענטשן [illegible] ור גיטן׃

דען זג שפוך אונ׳ [illegible] בולענדן׳ טו אויך די טיר [illegible] גאט ווערט אונ: משיח זענדן׃

PLATE 35

VENICE · 1599
[CONTINUED]
Three Crowns

Like all Venetian Hebrew presses, the one at which the Haggadah of 1599 was printed belonged officially to a Christian, in this case Giovanni da Gara, who also produced the editions of 1603 and 1604. However, the printer's emblem shown here was originally that of another family of Christian printers of Hebrew books in Venice, the Bragadini, whose personal coat of arms consisted of three crowns. When the Bragadini and da Gara presses collaborated for a time, the latter also adopted the device on some of its imprints.

The triple-crown printer's emblem was thus of non-Jewish origin. Nevertheless, there can be little doubt that Jews interpreted it in their own fashion. To any Jew with even a modicum of Jewish knowledge the three crowns were evocative of the passage in the mishnaic tractate *Pirke Abot*, the Chapters of the Fathers (4:13), which declares: "There are three crowns: the crown of the Torah, the crown of the priesthood, and the crown of kingship; but the crown of a good name excels them all." Indeed, in some Bragadini books a tiny fourth crown was placed above the others, probably by one of the Jewish printers who worked at the press, and inscribed: THE CROWN OF A GOOD NAME EXCELS.

The woodcut at the bottom of the page reproduced here is copied from the Mantua Haggadahs of 1560 and 1568. It shows a couple seated with their son at the Seder table. To the left a man, apparently a guest, is about to enter. In the far right a Hebrew caption explains the remaining two figures: "A picture of a servant with a bottle, and a maid with the utensils. This one is bringing water, and that one is cooking. . . ."

ואת יום השביעי מששת ימי המעשה קדשת · הבדלת וקדשת את עמך ישראל בקדשתך ברוך אתה יי המבדיל בין קודש לקודש ·

ברוך אתה יי אלהינו מלך העולם שהחיינו וקיימנו והגיענו לזמן הזה : ושותים ורוחצים ידיהם ומברכים

ברוך אתה יי אלהינו מלך העולם אשר קדשנו במצותיו וצונו על נטילת ידים :

ויקח האפ״יו ויטבל במי מלח או בחומץ ויברך :

ברוך אתה יי אמ״ה בורא פרי האדמה · ויאכל ויתן לכלם

ויבצע מצה שנייה ויניח חצי׳ במקומה והשאר יצפון לאפיקומן ו סיר הביצה והבשר ויתחיל ההגדה :

צורת בעל הבית וקערה וגם ביהו׳ עונה ואומרי ועני דכפין על הפתח שומר

צורת עבד עם קנקן · השפחה עם הכלי ס׳ זה נותן מים וזאת מב של מעור׳ ב עלי

VENICE · 1599
[CONTINUED]
Visual Metamorphoses

The meanings attached to illustrations in sixteenth-century books were fluid, the same woodcut being quite capable of serving several different purposes. This quality, already apparent in the Mantua Haggadah of 1568, is even more evident in the Venetian Haggadah of 1599 and the three subsequent editions.

The cut at the upper right shows a man reading a book. Above him the caption states: "Picture of a wise and understanding man who recounts the Exodus from Egypt at length." As such, it is appropriate to the facing text: "Even were we all wise, all understanding, all of us advanced in years, all endowed with knowledge of the Torah, it would still be our duty to tell the story of the Exodus from Egypt; and the more one tells the story of the Exodus, the more praiseworthy is he." Yet in the edition of 1601, the same man reading his Haggadah will become Pharaoh, king of Egypt. (See Plate 38.)

Below him another man sits in a pensive attitude. He is meant to represent Rabbi Eleazar ben Azariah. Originally, of course, this figure was the "Sistine" Wise Son of the Mantua Haggadah of 1560 (Plate 23). In the 1568 edition he became a father answering his son's questions on one page (Plate 31) and Rabbi Eleazar ben Azariah on another. The background of this woodcut lies in what is told of him in the Talmud:

> They went and said to [Rabbi Eleazar ben Azariah]: "Will your honor consent to become head of the academy?" He replied: "I shall go and consult the members of my family." He went and consulted his wife. . . . She said to him: "You have no white hair." He was eighteen years old that day, and a miracle was wrought for him. Eighteen rows of hair [on his beard] turned white. That is why Rabbi Eleazar said: "Behold, I am about seventy years old" [*Berakhot*, 27b–28a].

The caption states, with disarming naiveté: "A picture of Rabbi Eleazar, astonished at his beard, which grew in one night before its time."

The larger woodcut at the bottom of the page is a telling instance of the undefined state of Venetian Haggadah illustration at this time. It was not drawn for the Haggadah, but must simply have been available, and this is an attempt to have it serve a dual purpose. The second paragraph of the text relates the well-known talmudic tale of the five Palestinian rabbis who sat up all night in Bene Berak, engrossed in expounding the story of the Exodus, until their disciples came to remind them that the time for the morning prayers was at hand. In the woodcut, however, there are seven figures at the table, including, incongruously, two women. To the right, two servants are bearing food on trays. The caption seeks to resolve the difficulties. "This is," we are told, "a picture of desserts being carried in at the end of the meal, *and* the disciples coming to announce the morning prayer."

אֲבוֹתֵינוּ מִמִּצְרַיִם הֲרֵי אָנוּ בָנֵינוּ וּבְנֵי בָנֵינוּ
מְשֻׁעְבָּדִים הָיִינוּ לְפַרְעֹה בְּמִצְרַיִם וַאֲפִלּוּ
כֻּלָּנוּ חֲכָמִים כֻּלָּנוּ נְבוֹנִים כֻּלָּנוּ זְקֵנִים כֻּלָּנוּ
יוֹדְעִים אֶת הַתּוֹרָה מִצְוָה עָלֵינוּ לְסַפֵּר
בִּיצִיאַת מִצְרַיִם שֶׁכָּל הַמְסַפֵּר בִּיצִיאַת
מִצְרַיִם הֲרֵי זֶה מְשֻׁבָּח:

מעשה בְּרַבִּי אֱלִיעֶזֶר וְרַבִּי יְהוֹשֻׁעַ
וְרַבִּי אֶלְעָזָר בֶּן עֲזַרְיָה וְרַבִּי
עֲקִיבָה וְרַבִּי טַרְפוֹן שֶׁהָיוּ מְסֻבִּין בִּבְנֵי
בְרַק וְהָיוּ מְסַפְּרִים בִּיצִיאַת מִצְרַיִם כָּל
אוֹתוֹ הַלַּיְלָה עַד שֶׁבָּאוּ תַלְמִידֵיהֶם וְאָמְרוּ
לָהֶם רַבּוֹתֵינוּ הִגִּיעַ זְמַן קְרִיאַת שְׁמַע שֶׁל
שַׁחֲרִית:

אמר רַבִּי אֶלְעָזָר בֶּן עֲזַרְיָה הֲרֵי אֲנִי
כְּבֶן שִׁבְעִים שָׁנָה וְלֹא זָכִיתִי
שֶׁתֵּאָמֵר יְצִיאַת מִצְרַיִם בַּלֵּילוֹת עַד שֶׁדְּרָשָׁהּ
בֶּן זוֹמָא שֶׁנֶּאֱמַר לְמַעַן תִּזְכֹּר אֶת יוֹם צֵאתְךָ

מארץ

צורת איש חכם ונבון המאריך לספר ביציאת מצרים

צורת רבי אלעזר תמה על זקנו · שבין לילה היה בלא זמנו :

חמץ ומצה פי' או מצה ·
שאר ירקות אפי' פעם אח'
פי' אם כרפס · כל לה הזה
מרור ושני פעמים דוקא
אחת בחומץ' בחרוסת
והיה למסדר לפתוח
משאלת שנוי הטבול
להסמיך שלשת שאלות
שנויי האכילות אבל
הפסיק בטבול לפי ש
אגב אורחיה ששאלתו ג"כ
על שאנו עושין שני הטבי'
בלילה אחת שאכילת מצה
ומרור למוד' זכר עבדות ·
וטבול ואכילת הסיבה
למוד זכר לחירות :
ותירץ להם שהיה להם
עבדות וחרות אבל אבי
לא הכרנו אלא חרות :
והוא מותיב הארבעה
שאלות הללו באמרו מה
נשתנה וכו' והוא מפרש
לה באמרו עבדים היינו :
עבדים היינו : זו
היא התשובה
לשאלת השנוי שאכילת מצה
ומרור שהוא זכר לעבדות
ויוציאנו ה' אלהינו משם ·
זו היא תשובה לשאלת שנוי
הטבול ואכילה בהסיבה
שהוא זכרון החירות משם
ביד חזקה · ר"ל שעבדו
והגאלה שנעשה בפעם א'
ובלילה אחת זו היא
תשובת למה עושים שני
פעמים בלילה אחת כי
חזקה ובזרוע נטויה :
זו ראיה שאנו ובנינו ובני
בנינו משועבדים כי זו
תשובה לשאלת מה נש
לזכרון העבדות · וזה
שהוצרך לסדר שעבוד
מצד הטבע לא היה אפש'
עבד יכול לצאת · ואם
בחזקה · היה זה כאן
עבוד אל מול שאל · וזהו
ולא יתן אתכם מלך מצרי'
להלוך · ר"ל פרעון ולא ביד
חזקה ר"ל גם לא בשביל
ידכם חזק' כי אם ושלחתי
את ידי והכיתי לשרוף ש
המערכה ונזכו בכל אלהי

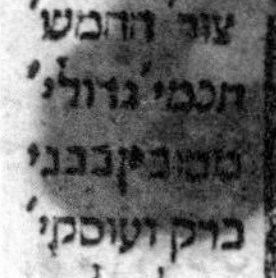

צור' החמש' חכמי גדולי' המסובין בבני ברק ועוסקי' בפלפולים ·

צורת נושאי פרפראות הסעודה ב באחרית ו והתלמידים הבאים על ק"ש של שחרית :

PLATE 37

VENICE · 1599
[CONTINUED]

Adir Hu—*in Yiddish*

The last page of the Haggadah of 1599 concludes with a Yiddish translation of the medieval hymn *Adir hu*. Whereas the original Hebrew is couched in the third person, the Yiddish is in the second person, beginning *Almekhtiger Got, nun boi dayn Tempel shira*—"Almighty God, build Thy Temple soon." The theory occasionally advanced that the hymn was written in Yiddish and then translated into Hebrew is without foundation.

The Yiddish version of *Adir hu* is probably the oldest translation of any part of the Haggadah. It appears in a fifteenth-century manuscript and then in the Prague and Mantua editions. Thereafter it became increasingly popular and was sometimes printed, as here, in editions that were not specifically intended for Ashkenazic Jews. Indeed, it is even placed at the end of the Judeo-Italian issue of the Venice Haggadah of 1609.

At the bottom of the page we find a reduced and crudely simplified copy of the great Mantuan illustration showing the advent of the Messiah (Plate 26). The warrior, who appeared there separately, has now been placed into the picture itself.

אל מעכטינר גאט

נון בויא דיין טעמפיל שירה אלזו שיר אונ׳ אלזו שיר
אין אונזרן טאגן שירה יא שירה ׃ נון בוי נון בויא ׃
נון בויא נון בויא . נון בויא דיין טעמפיל שירה ׃
בארמ האפטיגר גאט ׃ גרושר גוט ׃ דעמוטיגר
גאט ׃ הוהר גאט ׃ ווינר גאט ׃ זיסר גוט יחינער
גוט ׃ טוגליכר גאט ׃ יודישר גאט . נון בוייא דיין
טעמפיל שירה אלזו שיר אלזו שיר אין אונזרן טאגן
שירה יא שירה ׃ נון בויא נון בויא נון בויא נון בויא
נון בויא דיין טעמפיל שירה ׃ כריפטיגר
גאט ׃ לעבריגר גאט ׃ מעכטיגר גאט ׃
נאם האפטיגר גאט ׃ סעגפטר גאט
עיביגר גאט ׃ פורכלואר גאט ׃
ציאליכר גאט ׃ קוניגליכר
גאט ׃ רייכיר גאט ׃ שוינר
גאט ׃ תרויטר גאט ׃
נון בויא דיין טעמפיל
שירה ׃ אלזו שיר
אלזו שיר אין
אונזרן טאגן
שירה יא
שירה ׃ נון בויא נון בויא נון בויא נון בויא
דיין טעמפיל
שירה ׃

תם

ברכת העומר אל תשכח מאומר

72266

VENICE · ITALY · 1601

Experiments on the Title Page

The most immediately perceptible change in the Haggadah published in 1601 at the Venetian press of Daniel Zanetti is its title page, the first to be embellished with woodcut illustrations. Some of these had appeared within earlier editions, but were now reinterpreted once again.

Above: The Hebrew slaves building Pithom and Raamses. The woodcut first appeared in the Mantua Haggadahs of 1560 and 1568.

Right: Standing above, Pharaoh admonishes Moses not to return. This figure appeared in both the Prague and Mantua Haggadahs. Below is Pharaoh on his throne, reading a book of divinations. In the Venice edition of 1599 (Plate 36) the same cut portrayed a Jew reading the Haggadah.

Left: Moses, above, holding a staff, replies to Pharaoh. Below, one of Pharaoh's astrologers counsels him to allow the Jews to leave Egypt. In the Prague and Mantua Haggadahs this figure represented a Jew sanctifying the New Moon.

Bottom: The Exodus, taken from the Mantua Haggadahs of 1560 and 1568.

YAARI NO. 29 JTSA 20:15

פרעה
אל תוסף ראות פני
כי ביום ראותך פני
תמות:

משה
כן דברת לא אוסיף
עוד ראות פניך:

סדר
הגדה של
פסח

ובדיקה וביעור חמץ עם הברכות וקדוש והבדלה
וברכת המזון והניסים והנפלאות שנעשו
לאבותינו במצרי' ועל הים מצויירי'
בצורות יפות:

עם פירוש ותוספות ליקוטי מהר"ר
יוסף מפרוכ"ה ז"ל:

והוספנו בתוספת טובה על הראשונים רמז כוון על קדש ורחץ וכו'
מחדושי הרב הגדול [illegible] תורתו [illegible]
[illegible] כמוהר"ר משה אלשיך זכו"ל
[illegible]
חיים אלשיך [illegible]
הדפוס כדי לזכות בו את
הרבים:

פרעה
יושב על כסאו
והוא מנחש והספר
בידו ואומר ראו כי
רעה נגד פניכם:

ויאמרו אצטגניניו
שלח את האנשים
ויעבדו את ה' אלהיה'
הטרם תדע כי אבד
מצרים:

נדפס [illegible] כה"ר שלמה חיים ובנו
אברהם חבר טוב יצו:

שנת שסא
פה ויניציאה הבירה
בבית דכ"ל והכ"טי

Con licentia de i Superiori.

PLATE 39

VENICE · 1601
[CONTINUED]

The Sun by Day—the Moon by Night

A page from the *Hallel* section of the Haggadah, the psalms of praise. The types are larger and bolder than in the edition of 1599. The text is a continuation, from the previous page, of Psalm 136: "To Him that made great lights, . . . the sun to rule by day, . . . the moon and stars to rule by night." The heavenly bodies appear at the upper right, copied from the Mantua Haggadah of 1568 (Plate 29) where, however, they serve a different purpose. Below them, the same figure who was identified as Pharoah on the title page (Plate 38) is now simply a Jew reading the Haggadah, as in the earlier edition of 1599 (Plate 36). Across the bottom of the page the Egyptians are seen drowning in the Red Sea, relating to verse 13 of the psalm: "To Him who divided the Red Sea in sunder."

את השמש לממשלת

ביום כלח

את הירח וכוכבים

לממשלות בלילה כלח

למכה מצרים

בבכוריהם כלח

ויוצא ישראל מתוכם כל״ח

ביד חזקה ובזרוע

נטויה כי לעולם חסדו

לגוזר ים סוף לגזרים כל״ח

והעביר ישראל בתוכו

כי לעולם חסדו

ונ״ער

VENICE · 1601
[CONTINUED]

The Mantuan Tradition Endures

Citing the verse from the Book of Joshua (24:2), the Haggadah text recalls that Terah, Abraham's father, was an idolator. Accordingly, the small illustration to the right is identified in the caption as "Terah showing the moon to his sons so that they should worship it." It is the same figure that represented a Jew blessing the New Moon in the Prague and Mantua Haggadahs, and an Egyptian astrologer on the title page of this very edition (Plate 38).

At the bottom is a copy of the woodcut showing Abraham in a gondola that first appeared in Mantua in 1560 (Plate 24), and was repeated in the edition of 1568. It is now perhaps doubly appropriate in a Haggadah printed in Venice itself. An added touch is provided by the caption along the sides: "A picture of Abraham our father traveling in a boat, and crossing over so that he shall not be sacrificed to Moloch." Thus, the scene is moved from a biblical context (Abraham's journey to Canaan from "beyond the River") to a midrashic one, the ancient legend of the Babylonian king Nimrod's unsuccessful attempt to kill Abraham by fire.

צירת תרח מראה לבניו הלבנה ולעבודה יתן נפשו לכנה

מעולם תרח אבי אברה
ואבי נחור ויעבדו אלהי
אחרים:
ואקח את אביכם את
אברהם מעבר
הנהר ואולך אותו בכל
ארץ כנען וארבה את
זרעו ואתן לו את יצחק
ואתן ליצחק את יעקב
ואת עשו ואתן לעשו את
הר שעיר לרשת אותו
ויעקב ובניו ירדו מצרים

ברוך

PLATE 41

VENICE · ITALY · 1603

A Touch of Latter-Day Prudery

In an allusion to the rapid increase of the Hebrew population in Egypt, the Haggadah text expounds: "*And populous*, as the verse declares: 'I cause thee to increase, even as the growth of the field. And thou didst increase and grow up, and thou camest to excellent beauty: thy breasts were fashioned, and thy hair was grown; yet thou wast naked and bare' " (Ezekiel 16:7).

Approaching the verse literally and with a total lack of self-consciousness, the Prague and Mantua Haggadahs had shown a nearly naked woman, covered only by a loincloth (see below). However, to those responsible for the Venetian Haggadah of 1603, such a representation of a woman with bared breasts seems to have appeared immodest. More squeamish than their predecessors, yet reluctant to forgo the illustration entirely, they chose a curious compromise. In the page reproduced here (upper left) they transformed the woman into a man, and designated him as such in the caption, in total disregard of the plain meaning of the verse itself.

Bottom: The slaves build Pithom and Raamses. This woodcut already appeared in the Mantua Haggadahs of 1560 and 1568, as well as the Venice Haggadah of 1601, where it was placed on the title page (Plate 38).

YAARI NO. 30 JTSA 19:14

Prague, 1526

צורת איש ערו׳ וערי׳

ורב כמה שנאמר רבבה כצמח
השדה נתתיך ותרבי ותגדלי
ותבואי בעדי עדים שדים נכונו
ושערך צמח ואת ערום ועריה
וירעו אותנו המצרים ויענונו ויתנו
עלינו עבודה קשה: וירעו אותנו
המצרים כמה שנאמר הבה
נתחכמה לו פן ירבה והיה כי
תקראנה מלחמה ונוסף גם הוא על
שונאינו ונלחם בנו ועלה מן הארץ:
ויענונו כמה שנאמר למען ענותו
בסבלותם ויבן ערי מסכנות לפרעה
את פיתום ואת רעמסס: ויתנו עלינו
עבודה קשה כמה שנאמר ויעבידו

רב וגומ׳ · הוא דרש ז׳
והפסוק הראשון מהוידוי ·
גבודה קשה הוא פסוק שני
מהוידוי ומלקו לשש דרשות
דרש ראשון וירעו אותנו
החזיקו אותנו לרעי׳ ושפלי׳
המורדים באדוניהם ומביא
ראיה על מחשבתם זו שהיו
מתחכמים לירא׳תם שילום
גם הוא על שונאינו וגו׳ ·
ומה שהוצ׳ וירעו משמעותו
משום שהוא מיותר לדרשת
רעת המחשבה שעל רעת
הגופים כבר בא בפירו׳ כמו
שמפרש ואזיל :
ויענונו הוא דרש ג׳ מפסוק
ב׳ מהוידוי והביא ראיה
ללשון עינוי שהוא נופל על
סבלות שכן שנאמר למען
ענותו בסבלותם ויבנו הן
קטן הן גדול הבא מאת
המל׳ שמכלכל דבריו במשפט
תמידין כסדרן שנאמר ערי
מסכנות לפרעה ·
ויתנו

מצרים
פיתום

VENICE · 1603
[CONTINUED]

A Separate Frontispiece for Grace

The most unusual aspect of the Haggadah of 1603 lies in the fact that the *birkat ha-mazon*, the Grace after the meal, is preceded by an independent frontispiece, almost as though beginning a separate work. It reads: "The Order of the Grace. The Haggadah was printed at the desire of the honorable Rabbi Solomon Ḥayyim and his son Abraham Ḥaber Tob, may his Rock and Redeemer guard him. Printed a third time in the month of Tammuz, in the year 5363. In the house of Zoan [i.e., Giovanni] da Gara. . . ."

The opulent frame, with the figures of Mars and Minerva, is a reduced replica of the border on the title page of the Mantua Haggadah of 1568 (Plate 28). It also appears in other Venetian Hebrew imprints of this period, for example, in the Ladino abridgment of Joseph Karo's code of Jewish law, published in 1602.

סדר
ברכת המזון
נדפסה ההגדה לתשוקת
הנכבד כמר שלמה חיים · ובנו
אברהם חבר טוב
יצו
נדפס שלישית בחדש תמוז
שנת השסג :
בבית זואן די גארה
בויניציאה
Con Licentia de'
Superiori.

PLATE 43

VENICE · ITALY · 1604

The Venetian Haggadah at a Standstill

No major changes were introduced in the Haggadah of 1604, though the format of the previous year was enlarged, and some of the illustrations were once more rearranged. The title page, shown here, reverts to the design that first appeared in 1599. The commentary is still that of Rabbi Joseph of Padua. It is almost as if, after the experiments of the past five years, no new avenues for genuine innovation suggested themselves.

The reason for this would seem to be implicit in the essentially conservative nature of the Venetian Haggadah enterprise during this period. In retrospect one can only conclude that those who were involved did not really conceive of anything more than a continuation and elaboration of their Mantuan models. The Venice Haggadah of 1599 had been a reworking of the Mantua Haggadah of 1568. In turn, those of 1601 and 1603 were mere variants of the edition of 1599. Now, in 1604, the cycle merely revolved of its own momentum.

Still, something had been accomplished after all. Unlike Mantua, Venice had broken decisively with the Prague archetype. Some new illustrations had been added, and the possibilities still inhering in the Mantuan legacy had been explored—and exhausted. Venice had itself gained the experience of having produced no less than four Haggadahs in a very brief span of time. With this preparation behind it the Venetian Hebrew press would soon strike out boldly on its own.

YAARI NO. 31 JTSA 24:16.5

נדפס רביעית לתשוקת ר׳ שלמה חיים ובנו אברהם

שנת שסד

סדר הגדה
של פסח ובדיקה

וביעור המץ עם הברכות
וקדוש והבדלה ׃

והנסים והנפלאות שנעשו לאבותינו
במצרים ועל הים מצויירים
בצורות יפות דברים
יפים לראות ׃

גם כל עין בעין יראה ויעמוד ויתפלא
פירוש ותוספות מתוקי מהר״ר
יוסף מעלדונס יצו ׃

ויניציאה הבירה

במצות זואן דיגרה ובביתו ׃

Con licentia de' Superiori

PLATE 44

VENICE · ITALY · 1609
[JUDEO-ITALIAN ISSUE]
Debut of the Ten Plagues

In the evolution of Haggadah illustration the edition published in Venice in 1609 marks, after those of Prague and Mantua, the emergence of the third great archetype. Here the Venetian Haggadah finally achieved its full autonomy, and exerted an influence that would be felt for centuries to come.

Among its visual highlights were a magnificent architectural border surrounding every page of text, woodcut initials enclosing miniature figures and scenes, and large woodcut illustrations placed at the top or bottom of almost every page. Not only are these new, but they are arranged into a meaningful biblical cycle that begins with Abraham and later focuses on the narratives actually recalled in the text of the Haggadah.

While many of the themes (though not the organization or execution) had their antecedents, two illustrated pages were novel in every respect. One of these, divided into thirteen rectangular cuts, depicts the entire sequence of the Seder service (see Plate 54). The other, reproduced here, is similarly divided and consists of the Ten Plagues, which had never before been shown together in a printed Haggadah.

The Haggadah of 1609 appeared simultaneously in three issues, identical except for the different vernacular translations that appear in each within the columns that flank the pages. The languages are Judeo-Italian, Judeo-German (Yiddish), and Judeo-Spanish (Ladino), all printed in Hebrew characters.

The page reproduced here (as well as those immediately following) is from the Judeo-Italian issue. Above each cut the plague is labeled in Hebrew. In the marginal columns they are identified in Judeo-Italian as *sangue* (blood), *ranoccie* (frogs), *pidocchi* (lice), and so on, and described in rhymed couplets. For example:

> L'aqua si convierte in sangue;
> Tutto *Mitzrayim* sospira e langue.
>
> [The water is transformed into blood;
> All *Mitzrayim* [Egypt] sighs and faints.]

YAARI NO. 37 JTSA (V) 29:20.5

דם
צפרדע
כנים
ערוב
דבר
שחין
ברד
ארבה
חושך
מכת בכורות :
סאנגוי
ל אקוה סי קונוירטי אין
סאנגוי טוטו מצרים
סוספירה אי לאנגוי :
פידוקיי
גראנדי אירה לה קונטיטה
די פידוקיי גרוסי קומי
גראני די פינוקיי :
פיסטי
ביסטיאמי די אוני סורטי
פוקי סקאמפאנו דה לה
מורטי :
טימפיסטה
טימפיסטה אקומפאניאטה
קון פוקי קונסומאוה
מצרים אין אוני לוקו :
סקורוטו
טוטי גיורני די טיניברה
אי סקורורי אויאנו לי
מצריי אי ישרא ספלינדורי
ראנוקיי
פיר לה גראן קואנטיטה די
ראני נון סי דורמי ני
איפפסה גי קוצי איל פני :
מיסקולייו
לופי אורסי טיגרי אי
ליאוני איראנו אין מצרים
אין טוטי אי קאנטוני :
פיסטולה
משה ספארסי קאליגיני
דינאנצי פאראוני קאסקו
סופרה מצריים אי פיאי
בוניוני :
גרילו
להיירדירה דילי איכורי
אי לי אירביטי :
פירקוסה די פרימי
גייניטי :
פיאנטי סספירי אי גימיטי
סי סינטירה פיר לה מורטי
די פרימי גיניטי :

VENICE · 1609

[JUDEO-ITALIAN ISSUE · CONTINUED]

Scenes from the Life of Abraham

The Hebrew text here speaks of Abraham's progeny and of the Lord's fulfillment of His promises. The Judeo-Italian translation is at both sides of the page.

Above: In the center of the illustration Abraham and Sarah are blessing Isaac. To the right, Keturah stands with her six sons and, to the left, Hagar and Ishmael.

Below: To the right, the angel prevents Abraham from sacrificing Isaac. To the left we see Isaac as a grown man instructing Jacob, who holds a book, and Esau, who has turned his back and blows a hunter's horn. The entire woodcut is flanked by smaller cuts of King David (with his harp) and King Solomon (holding a scepter).

יִצְחָק דָה פָּאדְרֵי אֵי מָאדְרֵי בֵּינְדִיטוֹ׃ אֵי יִשְׁמָעֵאל קוֹן הָגָר וַיָאה נֵי אֵי גֵּייטוֹ׃

ואקח

אֵי פִּילְיָיאֵל פַּדְרֵי
ווּסְטְרוֹ אַבְרָהָם
דַאל פַּאסוֹ דֵיל רִיוֹמֵי
אֵי מֵינָאֵי קְוֵילוֹ פֵּיר
טוֹטָה לַה טֵירָה דֵי
כְּנַעַן אֵי מוֹלְטִפְּלִיקַאֵי
סֵימֵי סוּאוֹ אֵי דֵיידֵי
אַה לוּאֵי יִצְחָק אֵי דֵייְ־
דֵי אַה יִצְחָק יַעֲקֹב אֵי
עֵשָׂו אֵי דֵיידֵי אַה עֵשָׂו
מוֹנְטֵי דֵי שֵׂעִיר פֵּיר
אֵירֵידִימַרְלוֹ אֵי יַעֲקֹב
אֵי לִי פִּילְיוֹלִי סוּאֵי
דֵישֵׁיסֵירוֹ אַה מִצְרָיִם׃

ברוך

וָאֶקַּח אֶת אֲבִיכֶם אֶת אַבְרָהָם מֵעֵבֶר
הַנָּהָר וָאוֹלֵךְ אוֹתוֹ בְּכָל אֶרֶץ
כְּנָעַן וָאַרְבֶּה אֶת זַרְעוֹ וָאֶתֵּן לוֹ אֶת יִצְחָק׃
וָאֶתֵּן לְיִצְחָק אֶת יַעֲקֹב וְאֶת עֵשָׂו וָאֶתֵּן
לְעֵשָׂו אֶת הַר שֵׂעִיר לָרֶשֶׁת אוֹתוֹ וְיַעֲקֹב
וּבָנָיו יָרְדוּ מִצְרָיְמָה׃

ברוך שׁוֹמֵר הַבְטָחָתוֹ
לְיִשְׂרָאֵל בָּרוּךְ הוּא
שֶׁהַקָּבָּ״ה חִשֵּׁב אֶת הַקֵּץ
לַעֲשׂוֹת כְּמָה שֶׁאָמַר
לְאַבְרָהָם אָבִינוּ ב
בִּבְרִית בֵּין הַבְּתָרִים שֶׁנֶּאֱמַר וַיֹּאמֶר
לְאַבְרָם יָדֹעַ תֵּדַע כִּי גֵר יִהְיֶה זַרְעֲךָ בְּאֶרֶץ
לֹא לָהֶם וַעֲבָדוּם וְעִנּוּ אֹתָם אַרְבַּע מֵאוֹת
ב ב 2 2 שׁנה

בֵּינְדִיטוֹ סֵיאַה
קְוֵיל
קֵי אוּסֵירְוַה לַה פְּרוֹ־
מֵיסַה סוּאַה אַה יִשְׂרָאֵל
סֵיאַה בֵּינְדִיטוֹ קֵי
אֵידִיאוֹ בֵּנֵדִיטוֹ קוֹנְטוֹ
אֵל טֵירְמִינֵי פֵּיר פַּארֵי
קוֹמֵי אַוֵיאַה דִיטוֹ אַה
אַבְרָהָם נוּסְטְרוֹ פַּדְרֵי
נֵיל פַּטוֹ טְרַה לִי פַּרְטֵי
קֵי דִיצֵי אֵיל וֵירְסוֹ אֵי
דִיסֵי אַה אַבְרָם סַפִּינְ־
דוֹ סַאפִּירַאֵי קֵי פִּילְיֵי־
גְרִינוֹ סַארַה אֵיל סֵימֵי
טוּאוֹ אֵין טֵירַה נוֹן
לוֹרוֹ אֵי לִי סֵירְוִירַאנוֹ
אֵי לִי אַפְלִיגֵיירַאנוֹ
קוַאטְרוֹ צֵינְטוֹ אַנִי
אֵי

שְׁלֹמֹה אַבְרָהָם קֵי יִצְחָק קַאבְרִיָה אֵי אִימְפַּארָה׃ אֵי פוֹאֵי פֵּיר סַאקְרִיפִיצִיאוֹ דֵי פְּרִיפַּארָה׃ דָּוִד

VENICE · 1609

[JUDEO-ITALIAN ISSUE · CONTINUED]

The Exodus

The illustration shows Pharaoh finally permitting Moses and Aaron to lead the Jews forth from Egypt. In the cuts at the sides Moses holds the tablets and Aaron appears in his priestly robes.

The large woodcut initial in the text opens the word *Halleluyah* in Psalm 113, and therefore appropriately encloses the figure of King David, traditionally regarded as the author of the Book of Psalms.

אה נואי טוטי לי
סיניי אי מאראויליי אי
מיראקולי קויסטי
אי קאוטוצי דה סיר־
ויטו אה ליבירטה דה
מיסטיציאה אה אלי־
גריצה דה טריסטיציה
אה פיסטה דה טיני־
ברי אה לוצי גראנדי
אי דירימו דינאנצי אה
לואי לאודאטי איל
סיניורי׃
לאודטי איל סיניורי
לאודטי סירוי
דיל סיניורי לאודאטי
איל נומי דיל סיניורי׃
סיאה איל נומי דיל
סיניורי בינידיטו דה
אורה אי פיר סימפרי׃
דאל אוריאינטי דיל
סולי סין אל ריפוניר
סואו

ולנו את כל האותות והמופתים והנסים
האלה והוציאנו מעבדות לחרות ומיגון
לשמחה ומאבל ליום טוב ומאפלה
לאור גדול ונאמר לפניו הללויה׃
הללויה הללו עבדי יי
הללו את שם יי׃ יהי
שם יי מבורך מעתה
ועד עולם׃ ממזרח
שמש עד מבואו מהלל

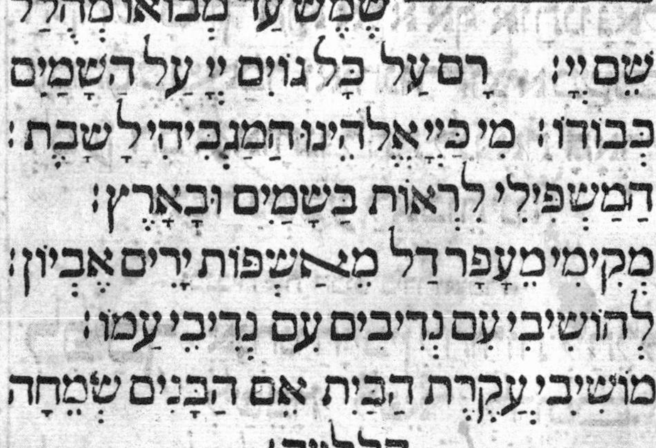

שם יי׃ רם על כל גוים יי על השמים
כבודו׃ מי כיי אלהינו המגביהי לשבת׃
המשפילי לראות בשמים ובארץ׃
מקימי מעפר דל מאשפות ירים אביון׃
להושיבי עם נדיבים עם נדיבי עמו׃
מושיבי עקרת הבית אם הבנים שמחה
הללויה׃

בצאת

סואו אי לודאטו איל
נומי דיל סיניורי׃
אלטו סופרה טוטי לי
גיינטי אי איל סיניורי
סופרה לי צייליאי לו
אונור סואו׃ קי אי
קומי איל סיניור דיאו
נוסטרו קי אינאלצה
אה אביטארי׃ קי סי
אבאסה אה וידירי נילי
צייליאיני לה טירה׃
קי סליוה דלה פול־
וי איל פוירו דאלי
אימונדיציי אינאלצה
איל מיסקינו׃ אה פר
סידירי קון סיניורי קון
סיניורי דיל פופולו
סואו׃ קי פה אביטר
לה סטירילי דילה
קסה מדרי די פיליולי
אינגרה לודטי א סיניורי׃
ניל

PLATE 47

VENICE · 1609

[JUDEO-ITALIAN ISSUE · CONTINUED]

Pharaoh's Magicians

The text begins with *Shefokh ḥamatkha*—"Pour out Thy wrath upon the nations that know Thee not."

In the illustration, the nations that do not know the Lord are represented by the Egyptians themselves. The white figures are sorcerers, standing with a corpse they have raised from the dead. Those wearing turbans are seen literally as "black" magicians, an image evoked by the Italian word *negromanti*. The small figures are demons.

שְׁפֹךְ׃

חֲמָתְךָ עַל הַגּוֹיִם אֲשֶׁר לֹא יְדָעוּךָ וְעַל
מַמְלָכוֹת אֲשֶׁר בְּשִׁמְךָ לֹא קָרָאוּ׃
לא לָנוּ יְיָ לֹא לָנוּ כִּי לְשִׁמְךָ תֵּן כָּבוֹד
עַל חַסְדְּךָ וְעַל אֲמִתֶּךָ׃ לָמָּה
יֹאמְרוּ הַגּוֹיִם אַיֵּה נָא אֱלֹהֵיהֶם וֵאלֹהֵינוּ
בַשָּׁמַיִם כֹּל אֲשֶׁר חָפֵץ עָשָׂה׃ עֲצַבֵּיהֶם
כֶּסֶף וְזָהָב מַעֲשֵׂה יְדֵי אָדָם׃ פֶּה לָהֶם וְלֹא
יְדַבֵּרוּ עֵינַיִם לָהֶם וְלֹא יִרְאוּ׃ אָזְנַיִם לָהֶם
וְלֹא יִשְׁמָעוּ אַף לָהֶם וְלֹא יְרִיחוּן׃ יְדֵיהֶם
וְלֹא יְמִישׁוּן רַגְלֵיהֶם וְלֹא יְהַלֵּכוּ לֹא יֶהְגּוּ
בִּגְרוֹנָם׃ כְּמוֹהֶם יִהְיוּ עֹשֵׂיהֶם כֹּל אֲשֶׁר
בֹּטֵחַ בָּהֶם׃ יִשְׂרָאֵל בְּטַח בַּיְיָ עֶזְרָם
וּמָגִנָּם הוּא׃ בֵּית אַהֲרֹן בִּטְחוּ בַיְיָ

עזרם

שפוך

וירסה לַה אירַה
טואַה
סופרַה לֵי גֵ׳ייֵנטֵי קֵי נון
צַאנו קונושייאוטו טֵי
אֵי סופרַה לֵי אִיכְפֵּירֵ־
יאִי קֵי נֵיל נומֵי טואו
נון אַנו אִינְווֹקַאטו׃
נון אַה נואִי סִינְיוֹרֵי
נון אַה נואִי קֵי צַ
נומֵי טואו דַה אונורֵי
פֵּיר לַה מִיסֵירִיקוֹרְדֵי־
אַה טואַה אֵי פֵּיר לַה
וֵירִיטַה טואַה׃ פֵּיר קֵי
דִירַאנו לֵי גֵ׳ייֵנטֵי דוֵי
אֵי אורַה אִיל דִיאו
לורו׃ אֵי לֵ אִידִיאו
נוֹסְטְרו צַאֵי נֵיל צִ׳יילו
צִ׳יו קֵי וול פַה׃ לִי
אידולי

אִידולִי לורו דִי אַרְגֵ׳ינ־
טו אֵי דֵי אורו אופֵּי־
ירַה דִי מַאנִי דִי
אומו׃ אַנו בוקַה אֵי
נון פַּארְלַאנו צַוקֵיי
אַנו אֵי נון וֵידונו אַנו
אורֵיקְיֵי אֵי נון אודונו
אַנו נַאסו אֵי נון אודו־
רונו׃ לֵי לור מַאנִי אֵי
נון פַּאלְפַּצַנו לֵי לור
פֵּייֵדִי אֵי נון קַאמִינונו
נון רַאגִיונַאנו קון לַה
גולַה לורו׃ קומֵי
אֵיסֵי סִיאַנו לִי פַּאטורִי
דֵי אֵיסִי אונִיי צַונו קֵי
סִי קונְפִּידַה אִין אֵיסִי׃
יִשְׂרָאֵל קונְפִּידַה נֵיל
סִינְיורֵי אַיוטו לורו אֵי
דִיפַרו לורו אֵי קְוֵילו׃
קַצַסַה דִי אַהֲרֹן
קונְפִּידַצַטִיוִי נֵיל
סיניורי

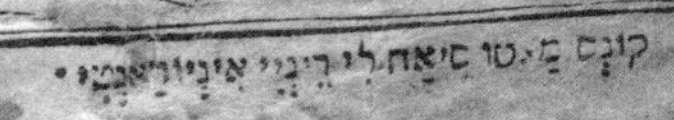

קונס מַטו סִיאַה לִי רֵיגְיי אִינְייורַאנְטִי :
קֵי סֵירְוִינו אַה דֵימונִיי אֵי קְרֵידונו אַה נִיגְרומַאנְטִי :

VENICE · 1609

[JUDEO-ITALIAN ISSUE · CONTINUED]

The Encampment in the Wilderness

The illustration shows one of the camps of the Israelites during their forty-year journey from Egypt to Canaan. In the middle portion are eleven groups, each representing a tribe. The tribe of Levi attends the Ark of the Covenant, placed in the very center.

The portion of the Haggadah text immediately above consists of the opening verses of Psalm 136, thanking the Lord for His goodness, mercy, and wonders. Accordingly, some of the miracles associated with the sojourn in the wilderness of Sinai are compressed into the four corners of the illustration:

Upper right: The descent of the manna (Exodus 16).

Lower right: The quail (ibid.).

Upper left: The water that Moses brought forth by smiting the rock (Exodus 17).

Lower left: The well which, according to midrashic legend, accompanied the Israelites on their wanderings.

ואודך אלהי ארוממך: הודו ליי כי טוב כי לעולם חסדו:

יהללוך יי אלהינו על כל מעשיך וחסידיך צדיקים עושי רצונך וכל עמך בית ישראל ברנה יודו ויברכו וישבחו ויפארו ויעריצו ויקדישו וימליכו את שמך מלכנו כי לך טוב להודות ולשמך נאה לזמר כי מעולם ועד עולם אתה אל:

הודו ליי כי טוב כי לעלם חסדו:
הודו לאלהי האלהים כי לעולם חסדו:
הודו לאדני האדנים כי לעולם חסדו:
לעושה נפלאות גדולות לבדו כי לעולם חסדו:
לעושה

אי טי קונפיסרו מיאו דיאו אי טי איסלטרו: קונפיסאטי אל סיניורי קי אי בונו קי פיר סימפרי אילה מיסיריקורדיאה סואה: לאודאראנו טי סיניורי אידיאו נוסטרו סופרה טוטי לי אופירי טואי אי לי מיס ירדיקורדיאוסי טואי גיוסטי קי פאנו איל וולير טואו אי טוטו איל פופולו טואו לה קאסאטה די ישראל קון קאנטו קונפיסראנו אי בינידיראנו אי לאודאראנו אי גלוריפיקאראנו אי [illegible] אי מאניפיקאראנו אי סאנטיפיקאראנו אי ריקונושיראנו

ריקונושיראנו פיר רינייו איל נומי טואו די נוסטרו קי אדי טי אי בונו די קונפיסארי אי אל נומי טואו אי סיאוי די סאלמיגיירי קי דה סימפרי אי פיר סימפרי טו סיאי דיאו: קונפיסאטי אל סיניורי קי פיר סימפרי אילה מיסיריקורדיאה סואה: קונפיסאטי אל דיאו דילי דיאי קפס למס: קונפיסאטי אל סיניור דילי סיניורי קי פיר סימפרי אי לה מס: אה קויל קי פה מיראוילייי גרנדי סולו לואי קפס למס:
אה

אי ציבי אי לי ביראנדי דיל דיסירטו גוטאטי גילי קאנטוני: אין מיזו איל טבירנאקולו לי סקוארדי אי קונפאלוני:

VENICE · ITALY · 1629
[JUDEO-ITALIAN ISSUE]
Leone Modena Introduces a Commentary

Twenty years after it first appeared, the Venice Haggadah went through a second edition, this time at the Bragadini press. Once again there was a trilingual issue. With some additions and modifications, a definitive format was now achieved.

The basic change—the inclusion of a commentary—dictated all others. It was the work of Leone Modena (1571–1648), the famous Venetian rabbi who had also been responsible for the Judeo-Italian translation of 1609. One of the most captivating personalities that Italian Jewry ever produced, and surely the most versatile, he himself admitted to having practiced twenty-six professions at one time or another in his life. A preacher so gifted that even Christians came to hear him, he was also an inveterate gambler; author of responsa in Jewish law, he also produced comedies in the Venetian Ghetto. For all his polarities, however, his contemporaries recognized his learning, and when a commentary was sought for the Haggadah, his help was enlisted. The circumstances are described in his own introduction, reproduced here.

He states that the earlier edition (of 1609) has proved so popular that no more copies are available. Moses ben Gershon Parenzo has decided to have it reissued, but desires that it now be accompanied by a commentary: "For if it already contains illustrations to entice the bodily eyes, how much better that there should be an explanation to delight the spiritual eye. And if the words are translated into the respective vernaculars for children and people of low understanding, it is only right that there be found within an explanation . . . for the mature and knowledgeable." Leone Modena had himself written a commentary to the Haggadah several years before. But, he continues, "I did not wish to seem to favor myself." And so he prepared a concise abridgment of Isaac Abravanel's well-known *Zebaḥ Pesaḥ* ("The Passover Sacrifice"), which he entitled, somewhat playfully perhaps, *Tzeli Esh* (literally, "Roast with Fire" [Exodus 12:9]), explaining that "since the Passover sacrifice was eaten roasted, it shriveled, diminished, and shrank, but its taste was good."

The commentary was placed in the architectural columns on each page, thus displacing the vernacular translations that had been situated there in the edition of 1609. These were now inserted between the Hebrew text and the illustrations. Even so, there was not quite enough space, and the entire format of the Haggadah was expanded, both the size of the pages and the borders.

Finally, the two large and four small woodcuts of the Passover preparations, which in 1609 had framed the title page, were transferred to enclose Modena's introduction to the commentary, as shown in this plate, with Moses and Aaron added for good measure in the upper corners. A new title page was designed for the Haggadah as a whole (see Plate 53).

YAARI NO. 41 JTSA 35:24

משה

לה בונה דונה קיוה טוטה ויאה׳ בשיריאנדו לה סואה מאסאריאה:

אהרן

קייסטו אלטרה קוי פה פסח אלה קסה׳ אי ניאנטי די חמץ דינטרו צילסה:

יהודה אריה ממודינא בכה״ר יצחק ז״ל

הקדמה לפירוש צלי א״ש:

מיום באת על פני חוץ הגדה זאת תמה וברה ופותר ים אותה׳ בלם דמות תבניתה וצורו׳ לבב כל איש הרחיבו׳ עד כי כל אחד במעוט הסמים הרבה מקנתו ולא נותרה בבת ציון׳ לכן רוח היתה באנוש מאד נעלה היקר כמ׳ גרשון בן כמוא פני ונכבר כמ׳ משה פאריכץ יצ״ו׳ לסוב ולחקוק אותה שנית יראו רבים וישמחו׳ ויען היה עם לבבו להשלים ולא לגרוע חקה׳ מלבד יופי וגודל הבייר וכל הנגרר להדפסה׳ גבי להוסיף מן דיליה פירוש לדברי ההגדה על מתכונתם׳ כי אמר אם כבר באו בה ציורים וכוונים תאוה לעינים הגופניים הנה מה טוב כי יהיו בה ביאורים וכוונות מחמד כל עין רוחני ואם יתראה בתוכה פתרון המלות ללועזים בלעז כל א׳ ללמוכו בגוייהם לתנוקו׳ ולספלי הדעת נכון הדבר לאמבא בה ביאור תם חיים דברי המגיד לזקנים ויודעים׳ ויהיו דבריו עמי ומתני ואלתי בקם לבחור לזה איזה פירוש כפי ראות עיני׳ והנם כי אני בעניי הכינותי זה כמה שני׳ פירוש פלי על ההגדה קראתי שמו גאון יהודה (כי יציאת מצרים תפארת וגאון כל עדתנו היא) אמר באולי אם אדפיסנו לא יהיה לבוז׳ לא רביתי לראות חבה לעצמי׳ ויעצתי אותו להתלות באילן גדול המר הרב אברבנ״אל ז״ל אשר בכל ביאוריו הפליא עצה הגדיל סברא על כל וגם פה בביאור ההגד׳ בספרו זבח פסח לא קם כמהו׳ אמנם כי קוצר היריעה היה קטן מהכיל אחד אחוז מן החמשים מספרו הלז׳ ירדתי לגנו ולקטתי במספיק להבין בפירושו כל פרט וכלל מדברי המגיד ותירוץ קושיותיו אף אם לא כמאלו ומאומה לא הוספתי משלי׳ אשר את פני מבין חכמה תחשב ולא מלאכה להחזיק במעט את המרובה: קראתיו צלי א״ש כי כן קרבן הפסח בתיגתו כאכל צלי היה מתכוין ומתמעט אך מבטמיק ויפה לו בטעם׳ כן זבח פסח אשר קרא חבורו הרב ז״ל הבאתיו בספור של רמוני׳ ואעשהו צלי והכמקתיו אך לטובה וטעם לטבח׳ כי אם כל המרבה לספר ביצ״מ הרי זה משובח כל א׳ בזה יוסף לקח וירבה אמרים הלילה הזה על שטחיות מלות ההגדה ואבלו את הבשר בלילה הזה צלי א״ש זבח פסח הוא לה׳׳ והזוכים במצוה זו עורך מבטל ואוכל יאכלו את חקם לרצון לפני ה׳ עד אשר נזכה נזבחה לאלהינו בירושלם הבנויה מהרה אמן:

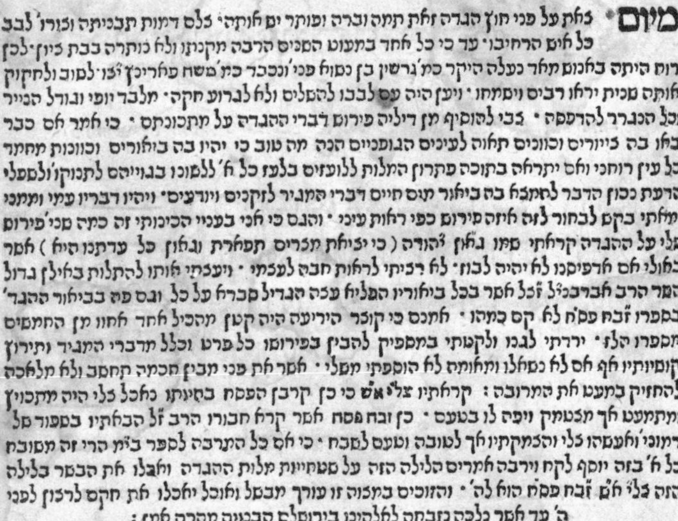

אי קויסטה קי איל סואו ראמי אי פילטרי ויקיו׳ פרינה פיר מועד לוסטרו קומי און ספיקיו:

קויסטה בוראטה לה פארינה׳ אי איל פיורי פיר לי מצות קאוה׳ די טוטו קורי:

1 2 א ב

קי אימפאסטנו איל פיור דילה פארינה׳ איפוי סוטו לה גראמולה סי ריפינה׳

קי פאניטי קי שפולי קי פיציקארי אי פוי ניל פורנו סיפאן קונייאני׳

PLATE 50

VENICE · 1629
[JUDEO-ITALIAN ISSUE · CONTINUED]
Twin Beds in Egypt

The text here speaks of the oppression of the Israelites in Egypt.

Above: The hard labor of the slaves under their Egyptian taskmasters.

Below: Perhaps the most poignant illustration in the Venice Haggadah. Midrashic legend asserted that after Pharaoh ordered that all male children born to the Israelites be drowned, men and women began to sleep apart so as not to conceive children at all. This is the theme of the illustration. In the large panel a man and his wife are asleep in separate beds. To the left, in accordance with Pharaoh's decree, the Egyptians are drowning the male infants.

On this page the architectural column on the right contains Leone Modena's commentary; the one on the left has the Judeo-Italian translation of the text.

לה מולטה אפליציון מוליסטיאה אי סטינטי קי אין מצרים אויאן קון גרן טורמינטי

כמה שנאמר ויעבידו מצרים את בני ישראל בפרך:

ונצעק אל יי׳ אלהי אבותינו כמה שנאמר ויהי בימים הרבים ההם וימת מלך מצרים ויאנחו בני ישראל מן העבודה ויזעקו ותעל שועתם אל האלהים מן העבודה: ונצעק אל יי׳ אלהי אבותינו וישמע יי׳ את קולנו וירא את עניינו ואת עמלינו ואת לחצינו:

וישמע יי׳ את קולנו כמה שנאמר וישמע אלהים את נאקתם ויזכור אלהים את בריתו את אברהם את יצחק ואת יעקב:

וירא את עניינו זו פרישות דרך ארץ כמה שנאמר

וירא ב ג 3 2

מאריטו אי מוליי אונייי און סול נילי פיומי · פיר נון גייטאר לי פיליגאטי אל פיומי:

פירוש צלי אש

כמ״ש ויעבידו מצרים וגו׳ וזו קשה מכלם להיות עבדים לעבדים:

ונצעק אל

רצה מגלה הכתוב בודוי בכורים זה פמ״ס בפסוק ויהי בימי׳ הרבים ההם ויאנחו ויצעקו היתה תפלה לה׳ ולא כמתרע׳ על צער · ולספר טעמו עכ״מ כמספידים ומיללים על מות המלך ולבם נכון לצעוק בתפלה לה׳ יתברך׳ וישמע ה׳ וגו׳ · מה ששמע להם ה׳ לא היה בעדם לבד אלא כמ״ש ויזכור אלהים את בריתו וגו׳ מפני הבטח׳ האבות כי תשובת׳ ותפלתם בלי הברית ההוא לא היתה מספקת לגאולה:

וירא ביאר מהענוי והלחץ הכתו׳ כאן אומרו מ״ש ויענונו ויתנו עלינו וגו׳ שאמר הז״ל וירא את הענוי לנו במצרים שלא אלה הם צרות נסתרות שהיו עושים להם מלבד הנגלות שהוזכרו · ותחלה פרישות דרך ארץ שסבבו שרבים פירשו מנשותיהם לבל ילדו לריק הנקרא ענוי כמו שדרשו ז״ל אם תענה את בנותי מתשמיש · ועז׳ דרש וירא אלהים בעדם ונתן להם כחת רוח שידעו נשותיהם למען יפרו וירבו ובדרך השמכתא פירשו

וירע

דורה קומי דיזי איל וירסו אי פיזירו סירויר מצרים אלי פיליולי די ישראל קון דוריזה:

אי גרידאסימו אל סינייור אידיאו דילי פאדרי נוסטרי קומי דיזי איל וירסו אי פו גילי גיורני מולטי קיילי אי מורסי אל רי די מצרים אי סוספירורונו לי פיליולי די ישראל פירלה סירויטו אי גרידורונו אי סאלי איל גרידו לורו אה אידיאו דאלה סירויטו: אי גרידאסימו אל סינייור אידיאו דילי פאדרי נוסטרי אי אינטיסי איל סינייורי לה ווצי נוסטרה אי וידי לה אפליציון נוסטרה אי לה פאטיקה נוסטרה אי לה מוליסטיאה נוסטרה:

אי אינטיסי איל סינייורי לה ווצי נוסטרה קומי דיזי איל וירסו אי אינטיסי אידיאו איל גיימיטו לורו אי סי ראקורדו אידיאו דיל פטו סואו קון אברהם קון יצחק איקון יעקב: אי וידי לה אפליציאון נוסטרה ציואי לה ספארציוני

דיל

VENICE · ITALY · 1629
[JUDEO-GERMAN ISSUE]
The Finding of the Infant Moses

A page from the Judeo-German (Yiddish) issue of the Venice Haggadah. The translation is directly below the Hebrew text.

At the bottom, flanked by the figures of Moses and Aaron, is a large woodcut showing (from left to right): Pharaoh on his throne addressing the Hebrew midwives Shifrah and Puah (Exodus 1:15); the drowning of the male children; and Pharaoh's daughter holding the infant Moses who has just been retrieved from his hiding place on the bank of the river. She is speaking to a woman and a young girl, apparently Moses' mother Yochebed and his sister Miriam (Exodus 2:7–9).

YAARI NO. 42 JTSA 35:24

וירא אלהים את בני ישראל וידע אלהים׃

ואת עמלינו אלו הבנים כמה שנאמר ויצו פרעה לכל עמו לאמר כל הבן הילוד היאורה תשליכהו וכל הבת תחיון׃ **ואת לחצינו** זה הדחק כמה שנאמר וגם ראיתי את הלחץ אשר מצרים לוחצים אותם׃

ויוציאנו יי ממצרים ביד חזקה ובזרוע נטויה ובמורא גדול ובאותות ובמופתים׃

ויוציאנו יי ממצרים לא על ידי מלאך ולא על ידי שרף ולא על ידי שליח אלא הקב״ה בכבודו ובעצמו שנאמר ועברתי בארץ מצרים בלילה הזה והכיתי כל בכור

בארץ

אז דער פסוק זאגט אונ׳ ער זאך גוט קינדר ישראל אונ׳ ער וואלשט ווימן גוט׃

ואת אונ׳ אונזר ערבייט דז מיינט דיא קינדר אז דער פסוק זאגט אל די זון דיא דא ווערדן גיבורן אין דען וואסער זולט איר זיא ווערפן אונ׳ אל די טעכטר זולט איר לושן לעבן׃

ואת אונ׳ אונזר ביצווענקנים דס מיינט דס גידראנג דס זיא דיא מצריים דראנגן· אז דער פסוק זאגט· אונ׳ אויך איך הון גיזעהן דען צוואנק דס דיא מצריים ביצווינגן זיא׃

ויוציאנו אונ׳ ער הוט אונס אויז גיפוהן גוט פון מצרים מיט מאכט שטארק אונ׳ מיט ארמן גישטרעקט· אונ׳ מיט גרוסר· פורכט אונ׳ מיט צייכן אונ׳ מיט וואונדר׃

ויוציאנו אונ׳ ער הוט אונס אויז גיפוהן גוט פון מצרים ניט דורך איין מלאך אונ׳ ניט דורך איין ברענדיגן מלאך אונ׳ ניט דורך איין שליח נוייערט הקדוש ברוך הוא מיט זייני איר אונ׳ ער זעלברט אז דר פסוק זאגט אונ׳ איך וויל אויבר פארן אים לנד מצרים אין דער נאכט דער דוזיג· אונ׳ איך וויל שלאגן די אירשטן אים לנד מצרים פון

פירוש צלי אש

ויוציאנו יי

לא ע״י מלאך· ומ״ש וישלח מלאך ויוציאנו ממצרים פי׳ שלא משה להתרות בפרעה ואח״כ ויוציאנו ה׳ ממצרים· וכן אומרו ולא יתן המשחית לבא וגו׳ ואומרם ז״ל כיון שנתנה רשות למשחית לחבל אינו מבחין וכו׳ שנראה אם כן שהיה ע״י מלאך יהיה פירוש משחית כח ההשחתה· וזכר שה׳ עשה בעצמו ג׳ דברים לגאולת ישראל הא׳ ועברתי וגו׳ שהמערכ׳ היתה מחייב׳ שלא יצאו ישראל ממצרים והוא העביר וסדר אותו כח שלא היה יכול לעשות זה שום מלאך ומושל אלא רצונו ויכלתו יתברך וזא אני ולא המלאך· הב׳ והכיתי כל בכור וגו׳ סימתנה

פירוש צלי אש

וידע אלהים יוצא מן הקל׳ שלשון והאדם ידע את חוה אשתו· גם כי נכון לדרוש וידע אלהים על תשמיש המטה כי אין אדם יודע מה שבין אדם ואשתו כי אם האלהים·

ואת עמלנו

שצוה בסתר לאנשיו להשליכ׳ ליאור כי חרפה היא לו לעשות מזה דת יפורסם׳ ורא ה׳ העמל שהיו עושים להסתי׳ בניהם ולגדלם שלא ידעו המצרים ואת לחצנו זה הדחק· הכונשים אנ״ש ודוחקים אותם בעבודה· או ירצה שאחר שספר מהענוי הגופני ויענונו ויתנו וגו׳ ספר מהצרות הנפשיית האלה בפרישות ד״א ועל שמירת הבנים ודוחק לואיהם שהבזיון דבק בנפש כי התונות הנפשיות קשות מהגופניות׃

משה

אהרן

וויא די טאכטר פון פרעה אין גאנגן אין וואסר זיך צו טוקן·
אונ׳ הוט משה רבינו אויש דעם וואסר הירויש טון צוקן׃
וויא דיא מצריים האבן די יודן קעמערליך דר טרענקט אין וואסר·
אז ער הוט גיבוטן צו זי פרעה דער בייזוויכט אונ׳ דער אונ׳ גי הווייאר׃

VENICE · 1629

[JUDEO-GERMAN ISSUE · CONTINUED]

The First Matzah

This page of the Haggadah explains the meaning of the matzah and the maror (bitter herbs), each shown as it is held up by a Jew at table within the two woodcut initials of the Hebrew text. They are also sketched independently to the right of the Yiddish translation.

The large illustration at the bottom shows a group of Israelites, just emerged from Egypt, in the process of baking and eating matzah, in accordance with the biblical verse: "And they baked unleavened cakes of the dough which they brought forth out of Egypt, for it was not leavened; because they were thrust out of Egypt, and could not tarry" (Exodus 12:39).

מצה זו שאנו אוכלים על שום מה על שום שלא הספיק בצקם של אבותינו להחמיץ עד שנגלה עליהם מלך מלכי המלכים הקדוש ברוך הוא וגאלם שנאמר ויאפו את הבצק אשר הוציאו ממצרים עגות מצות כי לא חמץ כי גורשו ממצרים ולא יכלו להתמהמה וגם צדה לא עשו להם:

ואוחז מרור בידו ואומר ·

מרור זה שאנו אוכלים על שום מה על שום שמררו המצריים את חיי אבותינו · במצרים שנאמר וימררו את חייהם בעבודה

אוכ׳מן כימט דיא מצות אין הענדן אוכ׳ זאגט :

מצה דיא מצה דיא דוזיג די מיר עסן וואורס עסן מיר זיא דרוס דס ער ניט וויל האט דער טאייג · בון אונזרן בורדרן דז ער קונט אויף בין ביז דז ער זיך דר כייגיט אויף זי דער קוייניג דער דא איז איין קוייניגן אויבר אל דיא קוייניג · הקב״ה אוכ דר לוזט זיא אז דער פסוק זאגט אוכ׳ זיא באכטן דען טאייג דען זיא האטן אויס גיצוהן בון מצרים קוכן מצות דען ער וואר כיט אויף · גאנגן ווען יז וואורדן בור טריבן בון מצרים אוכ זיא קונטן זיך כיט זוויימן אוכ׳ אויך קיין ספייז מאכטן זיא זיך כיט אויף דען וועג :

אוכ מן כימט דען מרור אין הענדן אוכ׳ זאגט :

מרור דס ביטר קרוייט דס דוזיג דז מיר עסן וואורס · עסן מיר עס דרוס דס דיא מצריים ביטרטן דס לעבן אונזרר בורדרן כו מצרים אז דער פסוק זאגט אוכ׳ זי ביטרטן איר

דין טייג דס זי האבן גיבוכט אין איילוכג אויז מצרים · אי כוכדר באכן זי אוכ׳ עסן עז כל ישראל אוכ׳ · אפרים :

פירוש צלי אש

מצה ראה רבן גמליא׳ בסגנון הכתובי׳ · ב׳ טעמים במצות · המצה הא׳ שתהיה הוראתה על הגלות לחם עוני · הב׳ שבעת ימים תאכל עליו מצות לחם עוני כי בחפזון יצאת וגו׳ · והתיר הסתירה הזאת באומרו שהמצה שנצטוו עליה בפסח מצרי׳ לא היו יודעו טעם שנצטוו עליה לדורות כי האח׳ היה זכר לגלו׳ ולעוני והשני׳ זכר לחפזון הגאולה ולז״א מצה זו שאנו אוכלים ולא כמ״ש בפסח שהיו אבותינו אוכלין שהכל יהיה מטעם אחר אבל המצה שאנו אוכלין ר״ל שנצטוינו בה לדורות לא היתה לעיני וכמ״ש בתחלת ההגדה הא לחמא עניא וגו׳ אלא אלא שלא הספיק בצקם של אבותינו להחמיץ לזכר מהירות הגאולה · עד שנגלה וכו׳ · אין עד זה מורה על הגבול כי במכת בכורות נגלה הב״ה עליהם כמ״ש ועברתי בארץ מצרי׳ וגו׳ ומה שלא הספיק בצק׳ להחמיץ היה אחר היציאה לא כאילו אמר שלא הספיק וכו׳ בעוד שנגלה עליהם מלך מלכי המלכים הב״ה וגאלם שהרי אחר כאמם כאמ׳ ויאפו את הבצק וגו׳ כי את למה לא אפו אותה במצרים כי לא יכלו להתמהמה וגם צדה אחר׳ בשר או דגי׳ לא עשו להם כי

פירוש צלי אש

כי לא החמיצו שתהי׳ יציאת׳ כלה בחפזון · ואפשר ג״כ לומר שהגלות הזה היה על עמוד הענן שנאמר בו וה׳ הולך לפניהם יומם ובא אליהם בסוכות כי שם אפו הבצק :

מרור בכל מקום שבות התור׳ על אופן אכילת הפסח הזכירה שאכל עמו המרור על מצות ומרורים יאכלוהו כי המצה רמז לעבדות גופני והמרור למרירות הנפשיי אשר בו הביט ה׳ ונתעורר להכות מצרים בבכוריהם ופסח על בתי בני ישראל · ולכן אמר ר״ג שהוא הרב׳ שגליטי שחייב אדם להזכיר בלילה הזה · וחז״ל אמרו ג׳ שמו׳ נקראו לו מרור חסא חזרת · מרור שמררו חייהם · כמ״ש וימררו את חייהם חסא שחס הב״ה וריחם עליהם · חזרת שאין ישרא׳ מחזרין על הפתחי׳ · ולמדנו מזה המאמר שכל אחד מג׳ אלה יש להם שתי הוראות הפכיות · הפסח מורה על מכת בכורות ולקות מזל טלה ומשפט במצריים ועל הרחמים לישראל אשר פסח על בתיהם · מצה לעניים ולחכם ועל מהירו׳ גאולת׳ כאמור · המרור למרירות חייהם בגלות ושחס עליה׳ הב״ה עליהם וגאלם על כן נקרא חסא :

VENICE · ITALY · 1629
[JUDEO-SPANISH ISSUE]
For the Sephardic Jews

The massive architectural title page shown here was the same for all three issues of the Venice Haggadah of 1629, the only difference being the vernacular language announced for the translation. This is the title page of the Judeo-Spanish (Ladino) issue, beginning: *Seder Haggadah shel Pesaḥ bi-leshon ha-kodesh, u-fitrono bi-leshon Sefaradim*—"The Order of the Passover Haggadah in the Holy Tongue, and Its Translation into the Language of the Spaniards" (i.e., the Sephardic Jews).

The remainder of the page proclaims the quality of the illustrations, and notes the addition of the commentary entitled *Tzeli Esh* (see Plate 49). It is somewhat odd that Leone Modena, who prepared the commentary, is not mentioned by name, though reference is made to other persons (Israel Zifroni, who created the Haggadah of 1609; Moses ben Gershon Parenzo, who commissioned the present edition; the printer, Giovanni Caleoni; and the owners of the press, Pietro, Alvise, and Lorenzo Bragadin).

YAARI NO. 43 JTSA 35:24

סדר

הגדה של פסח

בלשון הקדש ופתרונו בלשון ספרדים׃

עם כמה צורות על כל האותות והמופתים אשר נעשו לאבותינו במצרים ועל הים ובמדבר׃

וכל סדר קדש ורחץ לא תרחק ממנו כי צורה קרובה׃ וכן מכות מצרים ואותיות מצויירות מורות איכות הברכות ודברים אחרים יפים עד מאד׃

המצאה חדשה ערוכ׳ בכל עמוד ועמוד ולכל הנמצא בכתב נעשו צורו׳ זו לזו בכל הכתוב בספר התור׳ ומתוכם יראו דברי׳ נפלאים לא שערום אבותיהם׃

הבינה וגם הקרה זה כמו עשרים שנה זקן שקנה חכמה הח׳ הישיש ונעלה כמ״ר ישראל הזפרוני ז״ל׃

ואלה מוסיף על הראשונים פירוש צלי אש והוא קצור זבח פסח מהרב הגדול השר דון יצחק אברבנאל זצ״ל׃

כדפס לתשוקת הבחור היקר ומשכיל כמ״ר משה בן הנעלה לתהלה כמ״ר גרשון פרינצו יצ״ו׃

בויניציאה

בבית יוואני קאליוני המדפיס

שנת שפט לפ״ק׃

Appresso gli Illustr. Sig. Pietro, Aluise, & Lorenzo Brag.

VENICE · 1629

[JUDEO-SPANISH ISSUE · CONTINUED]

The Order of Passover—in Ladino

The Hebrew word *seder* literally means "order," that is, the sequence to be followed on the night of Passover. It was one of the significant innovations of the Venice Haggadah of 1609 to have illustrated the various stages in a series of thirteen woodcuts joined together on one page. These were reprinted in a somewhat larger dimension in the edition of 1629, reproduced here.

The sequence begins with the column on the right, continues on the left, and ends with the large woodcut at the bottom. Each stage is given its Hebrew designation, with an explanation in Judeo-Spanish (Ladino) printed in smaller Hebrew characters.

With minor variations this entire cycle was to become a familiar feature of illustrated Haggadahs in later centuries.

סימן לסדר של פסח

קַדֵּשׁ

הִינְגִּירָה אֵיל בַּאזוֹ דֵי וִינוֹ
אִי דִּירָה קִדּוּשׁ׃

וּרְחַץ

לַאבָּארָה לַאשׁ מַאנוֹשׁ
אִי נוֹ דִּירָה עַל נְטִילַת
יָדַיִם׃

כַּרְפַּס

טוֹמַארָה דֵיל אַפְּיוֹ אִי
אִינְטִינְגְּרָה אֵינֵל וִין אַגְרֵי
אִי דִּירָה׳ בָּרוּךְ אַתָּה יְיָ
אֱלֹהֵינוּ מֶלֶךְ הָעוֹלָם בּוֹרֵא
פְּרִי הָאֲדָמָה׃

יַחַץ

פַּארְטִירָה לַה מַצָּה דֵי
מֵידְיוֹ׳ אִי פּוֹנְדְּרָה לַה
מֵידְיָיא אֵינְטְרֵי לַשׁ דּוֹשׁ׳
אִי לַה אוֹטְרָה מֵידְיָא
פּוֹנְדְּרָה שׁוֹן לוֹשׁ מַנְטֵילֵישׁ
פַּארָה אֲפִיקוֹמָן׃

מַגִּיד

אִינְגֵּירָה אֵיל בַּאזוֹ אִי טוֹר
נָארָה אֵין׳ שׁוּ מַאנוֹ אֵיל
פְּלַאטוֹ דֵי לַאשׁ מַצּוֹת אִי
דִּירָה לַה הַגָּדָה׃

רָחְצָה

לַאבַּארַאן לַאשׁ מַאנוֹשׁ
אוֹטְרָה וֵיז אִי דִּירָה עַל
נְטִילַת יָדַיִם׃

מוציא מצה

הַלֵּל

אִינְגִּירַאן לוֹשׁ בַּאזוֹשׁ דֵי
וִינוֹ אִי דִּירַאן הַלֵּל׃

מוֹצִיא מַצָּה

טוֹמַארָה לַה מַצָּה דֵי אַרִבָּה
אִי לַה פַּארְטִירָה׳ אִי פַּאר
טִירָה דֵי לַה סָנָה אִי דִּירָה
בָּאִי אֻמָּה הַמּוֹצִיא לֶחֶם
מִן הָאָרֶץ׳ אִי נוֹן קוֹמָה׳ אִי
פַּרְטֵי דֵי לַה פַּארְטִידָה אִי
דִּינָה׳ בָּאִי אֻמָּה אֲשֶׁר קִדְּשָׁנוּ עַל
אֲכִילַת מַצָּה׃ אִי קוֹמָה
טוֹדוֹ נַיינְטוֹ׳ הַמּוֹצִיא אִי
מַצָּה אַרִישְׁקוֹבְדַאדוֹשׁ׃

מָרוֹר

טוֹמַארָה דֵי לַא לֵיגּוּנָה אִי
אִינְטִינְיֵירָה אֵינֵל חֲרוֹסֶת
אִי דִּירָה׳ בָּאִי אֻמָּה אֲשֶׁר
קִדְּשָׁנוּ בְּמִצְוֹתָיו וְצִוָּנוּ׳
עַל אֲכִילַת מָרוֹר׃

כּוֹרֵךְ

טוֹמַארָה לַה מַצָּה דֵי אַבַּ׳
אשׁוֹ קֵי אֵישְׁטָה שַׁאנָה׳
אִי דֵי לַה לֵיגּוּנָה אִי דַּלַשׁ
וֵירְדוּרַאשׁ אִי אֵינְטִינְיֵירָה
אֵינֵיל חֲרוֹסֶת אִי דִּירָה׳
זֵכֶר לַמִּקְדָּשׁ כְּהִלֵּל
הַזָּקֵן׃

שֻׁלְחָן עוֹרֵךְ

אַפַּארֵיגַּארַן לַה מֵיזָה אִי
סֵינַארַאן׃

צָפוּן

טוֹמַארָה לַה מֵידְיַא מַצָּה
קֵי פּוּשׁוֹ שׁוֹן לוֹשׁ מַאנְטֵי
לֵישׁ אִי דַּארָה אַקַאדַה
אוּנוֹ קוּאַנְטוֹ אוּנָה אַזֵיטוּ
נַה אִי קוֹמֵירַאן אַרִישְׁקוֹ
בְּדַאדוֹשׁ׃

בָּרֵךְ

אִי הֵינְגֵּירַאן לוֹשׁ בַּאזוֹשׁ
דֵי וִינוֹ אִי דִּירַאן בִּרְכַּת
מָזוֹן׃

נִרְצָה׃

יְהִי לְרָצוֹן לִפְנֵי יְיָ אָמֵן׃

VENICE · 1629

[JUDEO-SPANISH ISSUE · CONTINUED]

Toward a Restored Jerusalem

A page from the Grace after the meal. The second paragraph of the familiar text reads:

> Take pity, O Lord our God, upon Israel Thy people,
> And upon Jerusalem, Thy city,
> And upon Zion, the habitation of Thy glory . . .
> And upon the great and holy House
> over which Thy name was called.

In the Ladino translation (lower right margin) this is rendered:

> Apiada, *Adonay* nuestro Dio, sobre nos y sobre *Yisrael* tu pueblo,
> Y sobre *Yerushalayim*, tu sivdad,
> Y sobre Monte de *Tzion*, morada de tu *shekhinah*,
> Y sobre la casa la grande y la santa
> que fue llamado tu nombre sobre él.

(The occasional words placed in italics here are Hebrew. Such incorporation of Hebrew words in their original form is a characteristic of all Jewish vernaculars. Compare Plate 44.)

In the illustration the Messiah, preceded by Elijah the prophet, leads the dispersed Jewish people back to Jerusalem. In the very center stands the rebuilt Temple, visualized in the now traditional form derived from the Dome of the Rock (see Plate 18).

ורחבה ברית ותורה חיים ומזון על שהוצאתנו מארץ מצרים ופדיתנו מבית עבדים על בריתך שחתמת בבשרנו ועל חוקי רצונך שהודעתנו ועל חיים ומזון שאתה זן ומפרנס אותנו ועל הכל יי אלהינו אנו מודים לך ומברכין את שמך כאמור ואכלת ושבעת וברכת את יי אלהיך על הארץ הטובה אשר נתן לך ברוך אתה יי על הארץ ועל המזון:

רחם יי אלהינו עלינו ועל ישראל עמך ועל ירושלם עירך ועל הר ציון משכן כבודך ועל היכלך ועל מעונך ועל דבירך ועל הבית הגדול והקדוש שנקרא שמך עליו אבינו רוענו זוננו פרנסנו כלכלנו הרויחנו הרוח לנו מהרה מכל צרותינו ואל תצריכנו יי אלהינו לידי מתנות בשר ודם ולא לידי הלואתם שמתנתם מעוטה וחרפתם מרובה אלא לידך המלאה והרחבה העשירה והפתוחה שלא נבוש בעולם הזה ולא נכלם לעולם הבא ומלכות בית דוד משיחך תחזירנה למקומה במהרה בימינו:

אלהינו ואלהי אבותינו יעלה ויבא יגיע ויראה וירצה וישמע ויפקד ויזכר זכרוננו וזכרון אבותינו זכרון ירושלם עירך וזכרון משיח בן דוד עבדך וזכרון.

אי אנגה פירממינטו אי ליי וידאש אי מנטינימינטו. אי סובריקי וש סאקאשטיס די טיירה די אגיפטו אי נוש רימישטיש די קאזה די סירווס. שוברי טו פירממיינטו קי סיליסטיש אין נואיסטרה קרני. אי סוברי פאירוס די טו וילונטאד קי נוס פיזישטיס סאבר. אי סוברי וידאש אי מנטנימיינטו קיטו גובירנן אי מאנטיניין אנוש. אי סוברי לו טודו יי נואיסטרו דייו נוש לואנטיש אטי אי בינדיזיינטיש א טו נומברי קומו איש דינו אי קומירס אי פרטריאס אי בינדיזיראש א יי טו דייו סוברי לה טיירה לה בואינה קי דייו א טי. בינדיגו טו יי סוברי לה טיירה אי סוברי איל מאנטינימיינטו:

אפיאדה יי נואיסטרו דייו שוברי נוס אי סוברי ישראל טו פואיבלו אי סוברי ירושלם טו סיבדד אי סוברי מונטי די ציון מורדה די טו שכינה אי סוברי לה קאזה לה גרנדי אי לה סאנטה קי פואי ליאמדו טו נומברי סוברי איל נואיסטרו פאדרי נואיסטרו

נואיסטרו פאסטור נואיסטרו מאנטיניין נואיסטרו גובירנן נואיסטרו רינדור אישפאסייאנוש איספאסייאנוש אאינה די טודש נואישטרס אנגוסטייאש אי נו נושטרייאס אמנסטיר יי נואיסטרו דייו אדדיבס די אומברי אי נו א מיניסטיר דישוש אינפריסטוסקי שוש דדיבש פוקה אי שוש ריפודיו מוגו סלווא טו מאנו לה לייניא א לה אנגה נון נוש ארינגיסטרימוש איניל מונדו איל איסטי אי נון נוש אוירגואינסרימוש איניל מונדו איל ויניין אי ריינו די קזה די דוד טו אונטאדו טורנראס אסולונאר א אינה אין נואיסטרוס דיאס:

נואיסטרו דייו אי דייו די נואיסטרוש פאדריס סובה אי ויננה אליינייסי אי סיאה אפריסידו סיאה אינוילונטאדו סיאה אואידו. סיאה ויניטדו אי סיאה מימברדו נואיסטרה מימבראסייון אי מימבראסיון די נואיסטרו פאדריש. מימבראסיון די ירושלם טו סיבדד אי מימברסיון דיל אונטדו פינו די דוד טו סירמו

KÖNIGSBERG · EAST PRUSSIA · 1644

The Haggadah of a Christian Hebraist

The first Latin translation of the Haggadah was printed in 1512 (Plates 6–8). This, the second Latin version (as well as the first in German), also contains a totally unexpected feature. It is the first edition of the Haggadah in any language to be printed with music (see Plate 57).

The translator, Johann Stephanus Rittangel, was professor of oriental languages at Königsberg. He is alleged to have been born a Jew and to have become first a Catholic, then a Calvinist, and finally a Lutheran. Among other Hebrew works, he translated the mystical *Sefer Yetzirah* (1642) and the New Year's liturgy (1652). All his translations and studies of Jewish literature were made for Christian purposes, either to demonstrate the truth of Christianity or to facilitate theological polemics against Judaism by making possible a closer acquaintance with its sources.

In the Haggadah of 1644 the Latin translation of each passage faces the Hebrew text, followed by the German. *Regiomonti*, which appears here on the title page, is simply the Latin equivalent of Königsberg, the place of printing. This Haggadah translation was reprinted in 1698.

YAARI NO. 45 JTSA 19:15

סדר הגדה
של פסח

LIBER RITVVM PASCHALIVM

Wit was für Ceremonien vnd Gebräuchen die Juden das Osterlamb gegessen haben.

Translatus à

JOANNE STEPHANO RITTANGELIO
Ling. Orient. in Electorali Academia Regiomontana Prof. Extr.

REGIOMONTI,

Apud PASCHALEM MENSENIUM,
M. DC. XLIV.

Ad usum Ioh. Schellhammer

PLATE 57

KÖNIGSBERG · 1644
[CONTINUED]

Music for the Seder

Rittangel's Haggadah was the first to contain musical notation. The example reproduced here is the music to *Adir hu* ("Mighty is He"), with the Hebrew text and Latin translation underneath, and the Hebrew words transliterated along the bars. In the German and Latin remarks printed above, we are informed that this hymn is sung on the second night of Passover, in place of *Ki lo na'eh* ("For to Him praise is proper"), which is sung on the first. The music for the latter is also included in this edition.

DJeses Lied wird am andern Osterabend / an stat dessen/welches/also(Dann dir geziembts) anfängt/gesungen.

CAntio hæc secundis ferys Paschalibus, loco ejus; quæ à capite, Ky lo Naeh, Ky lo Jaeh, incipit, canitur,

Adir hu ifne bero be- ka- rub bim hero beio menu bekaruf

El bene bene bene be- ne bet cha be ka- ruf.

MAgnificus (qui est) ille ædificabit domum suam brevi, cito in diebus nostris ocyus; (Ah) ædifica, ædifica, ædifica, ædifica domum tuam brevi:

Electus(qui est)ille ædificabit domum suam brevi, cito in diebusnostris ocyus; (Ah) ædifica,ædifica, ædifica, ædifica domnm tuam brevi:

אדיר הוא יבנה ב
ביתו בקרוב במהרה בימינו
בקרוב אל בנה בנה בנה
בנה ביתך בקרוב:

בחור הוא יבנה ביתו
בקרוב במהרה בימינו בק
בקרוב אל בנה בנה בנה
בנה ביתך בקרוב:

PLATE 58

LEGHORN · ITALY · 1654

For Former Marranos—a Recipe for Ḥaroset

A Haggadah printed entirely in Spanish for the use of Marranos, or crypto-Jews, after their return to the Jewish community.

The Marrano phenomenon had its origins in the periodic waves of conversion that engulfed masses of Jews in the Iberian peninsula during the fifteenth century. It began with the pogroms of 1391, when thousands of Spanish Jews chose baptism in order to save their lives, and culminated in 1497 with the forced conversion of all the Jews of Portugal. Some of the converts became sincere Catholics, but many others still regarded themselves as Jews despite their baptism. These managed to practice a clandestine Judaism, which they transmitted to their descendants, a Judaism that even the Inquisition could not eradicate.

As late as the seventeenth and eighteenth centuries, Marranos would risk their lives to flee from the peninsula and settle in Jewish communities where they could live openly as Jews. Born and raised in lands where all Jewish schools and synagogues had long been suppressed, cut off from the rest of Jewry, they were often ignorant of much of the Jewish knowledge common even to ordinary Jews elsewhere. When they finally arrived in a Jewish community they had to be educated as quickly as possible in the rudiments of normative Jewish practice, so that their integration might be accelerated and eased. Since they generally did not know Hebrew, Jewish sources had to be made available to them in Spanish or Portuguese translations. Of an entire literature created for such purposes, the Haggadah of 1654 is an instructive example. Together with Venice and Amsterdam, where Spanish Haggadahs appeared in 1620 and 1622, Leghorn (Livorno) in Italy was one of the major European centers in the seventeenth century for the absorption of former Marranos.

Left: The title page of the Haggadah—"Order of the Haggadah for the night of the festival of Passover, translated from the original Hebrew, conforming to that which our sages ordained . . . printed at the request and expense of David [son] of Jacob Valençin."

Right: The final page, with a recipe for preparing *ḥaroset*, the paste of fruits and nuts which, at the Seder, recalls the mortar used by the Hebrew slaves in their labor in Egypt. It reads:

> Take apples or pears, cooked in water; hazelnuts or almonds; shelled chestnuts or walnuts; figs or raisins; and after cooking, grind them thoroughly and dissolve them in the strongest wine vinegar that can be found. Then mix in a bit of brick dust, in memory of the bricks which our fathers made in Egypt. For the eating, a little cinnamon powder is sprinkled above.
>
> Those who wish to add other fruits and spices into the concoction may do so.

JTSA 17:11

ORDEN
DELA HAGADAH
DE NOCHE
DE PASCOA DE PESAH.

TRADVSIDA

Dela original Hebraica conforme la ordenaron nueſtros Sabios y las Bendiçiones, y modo de Baldar el leudo con todas las particularidades que ſedeuen hazer en las dos primeras noches de Peſah, por muy claro, y inteligible modo, todo ſigido con ſu bendiçion dela meſa.

Ordenado, y Imprimido, a requiſicion, y deſpeza de Dauid de Iacob Valençin.

IN LIVORNO.

Nella Stamperia di Gio. Vincenzo Bonfigli, per gl'Eredi del Minaſchi. *Con Licenza de Sup.* 5414.

ORDEN

De hazer el Aroſſet.

TOmaran manſanas, o peras, cozidas en agua: auellanas, o almendras: caſtañas piladas, o nuezes: higos, o paſſas: y deſpues de cozido, molerloan mucho, y deſtemplarloan con vinagre de vino el mas fuerte que hallaren. Y deſpues meſclarlean vn poco de poluo de ladrillo, por memoria de los ladrillos que nueſtros padres hizieron en Egipto. Y para ſe comer, ſe echa vn poco de poluo de canela por en ſima.
Y queriendo poner mas de otras frutas y eſpeſias dentro del coſimiento, lo pueden azer.

71323

PLATE 59

AMSTERDAM · NETHERLANDS · 1695

A Proselyte Illustrates the Haggadah

The Amsterdam Haggadah of 1695 was the first ever to be illustrated with copperplate engravings rather than woodcuts. These were the work of a proselyte who had come to Amsterdam from Germany and who, upon his conversion to Judaism, adopted the name Abraham ben Jacob.

It is somewhat ironic that these illustrations, which were destined to be copied and imitated more than those of any Haggadah in history, were themselves borrowed from a Christian source: the biblical engravings published by the Swiss artist Matthaeus Merian in 1625–30, and reprinted several times thereafter. Most of the pictures in the Haggadah were copied almost slavishly from Merian. Others were somewhat altered and rearranged to suit the Haggadah text, and were necessarily "Judaized" in the process. In addition to Merian's biblical cycle, use was also made of his illustrations to the history of ancient Rome.

Shown here is the engraved frontispiece that precedes the title page of the Amsterdam Haggadah. Above the large figures of Moses and Aaron are six circular vignettes on biblical themes, each of them a greatly reduced miniature of one of Merian's scenes. At the very top is the expulsion from Eden (compare Merian's illustration, reproduced below). Underneath it, from right to left, we see the building of the Tower of Babel, Jacob's dream at Beth-El, Noah and the ark. The lower pair depict Abraham and Melchizedek (right), and Lot and his daughters (left).

The text of the frontispiece reads:

> The Order of the Passover Haggadah, with a pleasant commentary [by Isaac Abravanel] and lovely illustrations of the signs and wonders which the Holy One, blessed be He, performed for our fathers. Added to this are the travels in the wilderness until the division of the Land among the tribes of Israel, and the form of the Temple, may it be restored and rebuilt in our time, Amen. . . . Engraved upon copper tablets by . . . Abraham ben Jacob of the family of Abraham our father, in the house and at the command of the distinguished man, his honor Rabbi Moses Wiesel. . . . Printed in Amsterdam, in the year *Blessed be Abram of God Most High, Maker of heaven and earth* [Genesis 14:19].

The reference to the travels in the wilderness and the division of the Land alludes to the large folding map included in the Haggadah (see Plate 69).

YAARI NO. 59 | JTSA | 32:19

Matthaeus Merian: The Expulsion from Eden

אדם וחוה
סדר
הגדה של פסח
עם פירוש יפה וציורים נאים מהאותות
והמופתים שעשה הקב״ה לאבותינו
ונוסף
על זה כל המסעת במדבר עד
חלוקת הארץ לכל שבט״ה
ישראל : וצורת בית
המקדש תובב אכי״ר
חרות
על לוחת נחושת ע״י הבחור
כמר אברם בר יעקב
ממשפחת אברהם אבינו
בבית ובמצות האלוף
כהרר משה ווייזל יצו
אשרי אדם מצא חכמה
והורני דרך במלאכת הקודש
נדפס
באמשטרדם
בשנת ברוך אברם לאל עליון קנה שמים וארץ לפ״ק

PLATE 60

AMSTERDAM · 1695
[CONTINUED]
The Four Sons Assembled

While the Four Sons had been a traditional subject for Haggadah illustration, they had always appeared separately. In the Amsterdam Haggadah they are shown together for the first time. This was Abraham ben Jacob's essential contribution to the pictorial development of the theme.

Each individual figure, however, was copied from one which had appeared in totally different contexts in Matthaeus Merian's engravings. Thus, looking at the sons from right to left, we can indicate the source of each.

The Wise Son: Turbaned and bearded, but with a slightly different gesture, he was originally a figure in Merian's illustration of "Hannibal swearing eternal enmity to Rome."

The Wicked Son: A soldier, from one of Merian's battle scenes.

The Simple Son: From Merian's engraving of the young Saul being anointed by the prophet Samuel (see below).

The son "who knows not what to ask": A figure in the Hannibal engraving.

In this form, and in this grouping, the Four Sons were henceforth to appear in countless Haggadahs down to the present day.

Matthaeus Merian: Saul Anointed by the Prophet Samuel

רָשָׁע מה הוא אוֹמֵר מַה הָעֲבוֹדָה הַזֹּאת לָכֶם לָכֶם וְלֹא לוֹ וּלְפִי שֶׁהוֹצִיא אֶת עַצְמוֹ מִן הַכְּלָל כָּפַר בְּעִקָּר וְאַף אַתָּה הַקְהֵה אֶת שִׁנָּיו וֶאֱמוֹר לוֹ בַּעֲבוּר זֶה עָשָׂה יְיָ לִי בְּצֵאתִי מִמִּצְרַיִם לִי וְלֹא לוֹ אִלּוּ הָיָה שָׁם לֹא הָיָה נִגְאָל:

רשע מהו אומר מה העבודה הזאת לכם בפרשת בא והיה כי יאמרו אליכם בניכם מה העבודה הזאת לכם והנה שלשה דברים הביאו למגיד שהמאמר הזה היה מאויב חרף ה' האחד שלא אמר בלשון שאלה כמו שאמר בחכם כי ישאלך בנך מחר ובתם כי ישאלך בנך רק אמיר' כלומר כאשר בניכם שהיה ראוי שישאלו וילמדו מאבותיהם ליראה את ה' יהיו בנים סוררים ולא ידברו בדרך שאלה רק בדרך כפירה וערעור יאמרו אליכם מה העבודה כי כבר נשתמש הכתוב בלשון אמירה במאמרים המגונים כמו שאמרו בני גד ובני ראובן על המזבח אשר בנו בעבר הירדן מחר יאמרו בניכם לבנינו מה לכם ולה' אלהי ישראל וגומר וכן אמר הנביא ישעיה הוי האומרים לרע טוב ולטוב רע האומרים ימהר יחישו מעשהו ושלמה עליו השלום אמר אומר לרשע צדיק אתה יקבוהו עמים כי תמיד יבא הלשון הזה על הקנטור והמאמר המגונה· לא על השאלה בכונה טובה והסבה השני' לפי שלא אמר מה העבודה הזאת אשר צוה ה' אלהינו לכם כמו שאמר הבן החכם כי לא היינו חושבין למלת לכם כמו שלא חששנו על מלת אתכם שאמר החכם אבל הרשע באמת כפר בהיותה מצוה אלהית ולכן לא אמר אשר צוה ה' אלהינו והסבה השלישית שהוא לא קרא המצוה הזאת לא עדות ולא חקים ולא משפטים לפי שלא האמין היות בה עדות יציאת מצרים והיותה משפט וצדק וחק וגזירת מלך אבל אמר מה העבודה הזאת לכם וכיון בו שתי כפירות האחת שלא היתה המצוה אלהית ולא צוה בה השם יתברך אבל הם בעצמן סדרו אותה והוא אומרו מה העבודה הזאת לכם שהוא כפירה בפועל ומצוה אותה מצוה וכפירה שנית בענין התכלית וכאלו אמור אין זו עבודה לגבוה ולא זכר לחסדיו אבל היא עבודה עשויה לתועלתכם שתאכלו כבש בן שנתו רך וטוב בלי אש ותשתו ד' כוסות עליו הלא זאת העבודה היא לכם ולא לשם ולפי שהיו שני כפירות לכן אמר בנים בלשון רבים והיו כי יאמרו אליכם בניכם כאלו היו בכאן בנים סוררים בנים משחיתים בכפירות שונות ולזה השיבה התורה ואמרתם זבח פסח הוא לה' כלומר הש"י צוה בה ולא אנחנו ולכן צוה השם יתברך שלא יאכלו את הפסח כי אם על השבע כדי שלא תמצא באכילתו שום הנאה גשמית כי אם קיום המצוה שהוא לזכר שפסח ה' על בתי בני ישראל ולפי שראה המגיד שכיון הרשע במילת לכם ב' הכפירות האלה · אמר אף אני במלת לכם אדרוש דרשה שלישית ופי כסיל מחתה לו ולכן אמר מה העבודה הזאת לכם להוציא את עצמו מן הכלל שלא יבא בקהל ה' כי הנה המצוה נתנה לטובים ולישרים בלבותם ולא לרשע והנה אמרו לכם ולא לו הוא מדברי המגיד ולזה אמר ולפי שהוציא את עצמו מן הכלל באמונותיו כפר בעיקר שהעקר הוא היות המצוה אלהית ולא אנושית אף אתה הקהה את שיניו כלומר מלבד מה שהשיבתו התורה אף אתה השומע כפירה מפיו ענה כסיל כאולתו ואמור לו בעבור זה וכו' ופירש הקהה שיניו כלומר הכעיסהו ואמור לנו וכו' וזו פי' הקהה את שיניו כמו ושני בנים תקהינה כלומר זה שכפר בעיקר הרי הוא בכלל בן נכר לא יאכל בו שאסור לאכול בפסח ואז שניו תקהינה שרואה לאחרים אוכלים והוא אינו אוכל ואמור לו כלומר וגם אמור לו בעבור זה עשה ה' לי כלומר ראה רשע כי בעבור קיום המצוה והאמונה שהיה לי בהשם יתברך עשה ה' לי חסד גדול בהוציאני ממצרים ואתה רשע אלו היית שם לא היית זוכה להגאל ואף על גב שפסוק בעבור זה עשה ה' לי הוא בפרשת שאינו יודע לשאול אם אינו ענין לשאינו יודע לשאול תנהו לענין רשע:

תם

צורת ארבעה בנים דברי תורה

AMSTERDAM · 1695

[CONTINUED]

King David and the "Holy Spirit"

A page from the section of psalms in the Haggadah. King David kneels before "the Holy Spirit," which is depicted as a glowing halo in the upper left, with the Hebrew words *Ruaḥ Ha-Kodesh* inscribed within. Before him on the table lies the Book of Psalms, identified as *Sefer Tehilim.*

Though there is certainly nothing heterodox in the concept of David having been inspired by the Holy Spirit to write the Psalms, the visual representation is entirely Christian in atmosphere.

In this particular illustration the proselyte engraver did not actually copy any single illustration from Matthaeus Merian, but combined elements from several. Like other Christian artists, Merian was fond of depicting the Divinity as a glow of light, and on several occasions does so even with the name of God inscribed in Hebrew characters. The architectural features here are reproduced from one of Merian's engravings for the Gospel of Luke (18:9–14), which shows the Pharisee and the publican in the Temple (see below). The latter is naturally eliminated from the engraving in the Haggadah. King David himself derives partly from Merian's Pharisee, but also from some of Merian's other kneeling figures, such as King Solomon praying at the dedication of the Temple.

Matthaeus Merian: The Pharisee and the Publican

יְדֵיהֶם וְלֹא יְמִישׁוּן רַגְלֵיהֶם וְלֹא יְהַלֵּכוּ לֹא יֶהְגּוּ
בִּגְרוֹנָם: כְּמוֹהֶם יִהְיוּ עֹשֵׂיהֶם כֹּל אֲשֶׁר בּוֹטֵחַ
בָּהֶם יִשְׂרָאֵל בְּטַח בַּיְיָ עֶזְרָם וּמָגִנָּם הוּא: בֵּית
אַהֲרֹן בִּטְחוּ בַיְיָ עֶזְרָם וּמָגִנָּם הוּא: יִרְאֵי יְיָ בִּטְחוּ
בַיְיָ עֶזְרָם וּמָגִנָּם הוּא:

פירוש אברבנאל

ידיהם ולא ימישון לא יעשו המלות התלויות במעשה רגליהם ולא יהלכו לדבר מצוה ועבודת ה' · יהגו בגרונם בתפלה ושבח הבור' ואומר יהיו רצון שכמו הכסף והזהב הם המשתדלים בהם ומשימים בהם · אבל בית ישראל יבטחו בה' משפחה ומשפחה והוא יעזרם ויגן בעדם:

הנני בבלי שיר דוד איש האלהים

יי זְכָרָנוּ יְבָרֵךְ יְבָרֵךְ אֶת בֵּית יִשְׂרָאֵל יְבָרֵךְ אֶת בֵּית
אַהֲרֹן: יְבָרֵךְ יִרְאֵי יְיָ הַקְּטַנִּים עִם הַגְּדֹלִים: יֹסֵף
יְיָ עֲלֵיכֶם וְעַל בְּנֵיכֶם: בְּרוּכִים אַתֶּם לַיְיָ עֹשֵׂה
שָׁמַיִם וָאָרֶץ: הַשָּׁמַיִם שָׁמַיִם לַיְיָ וְהָאָרֶץ נָתַן לִבְנֵי אָדָם:
לֹא הַמֵּתִים יְהַלְלוּ יָהּ וְלֹא כָּל יֹרְדֵי דוּמָה: וַאֲנַחְנוּ
נְבָרֵךְ יָהּ מֵעַתָּה וְעַד עוֹלָם הַלְלוּיָהּ:

אהבתי

פירוש אברבנאל

יי כנגד הסבה השנית כי אהב את יעקב לאחוז חבלת היותם עמו ונחלתו אמ' ה' זכרנו אשר זכר אותנו במצרים יבר' אותנו ג"כ בגלותינו זה ופיר' המבורכי' בית ישרא' בכללי' בית אהרן כהני' ולוים קדושיו · יראי ה' חסידי דור ודור · הקטנים שאין להם זכו' בזכו' הגדולי' ולפי שבפה אורך הגלו' הטיח בלא יכלו באומרו יוסף ה' עליכ' וגו' ואמר ברוכים אתם לה' עשו ולא חסרי מעלה כי יתעו הגוים וגו' · ואם תראו כי ממלכות הארץ מושלים ומחזיקים בה גזירות לא ימנע תשועת ה' כי השמ' הוא נתן אותה לבני אדם וכשירצ' יקחנה מהם ולמאן דיצבא יתננה · אמנם אנחנו נברך יה בהכירנו גדול נפלאותיו ומעתהועד עולם לרמוז אל זמן הגאולה יהיה מתי שיהיה ·

AMSTERDAM · 1695

[CONTINUED]

A Seventeenth-Century Vision of the Temple

The future Temple and the city of Jerusalem in the messianic era. It is a copy of Matthaeus Merian's engraving of the Temple of Solomon.

Printed below the illustration is the Yiddish version of *Adir hu* (compare Plate 37).

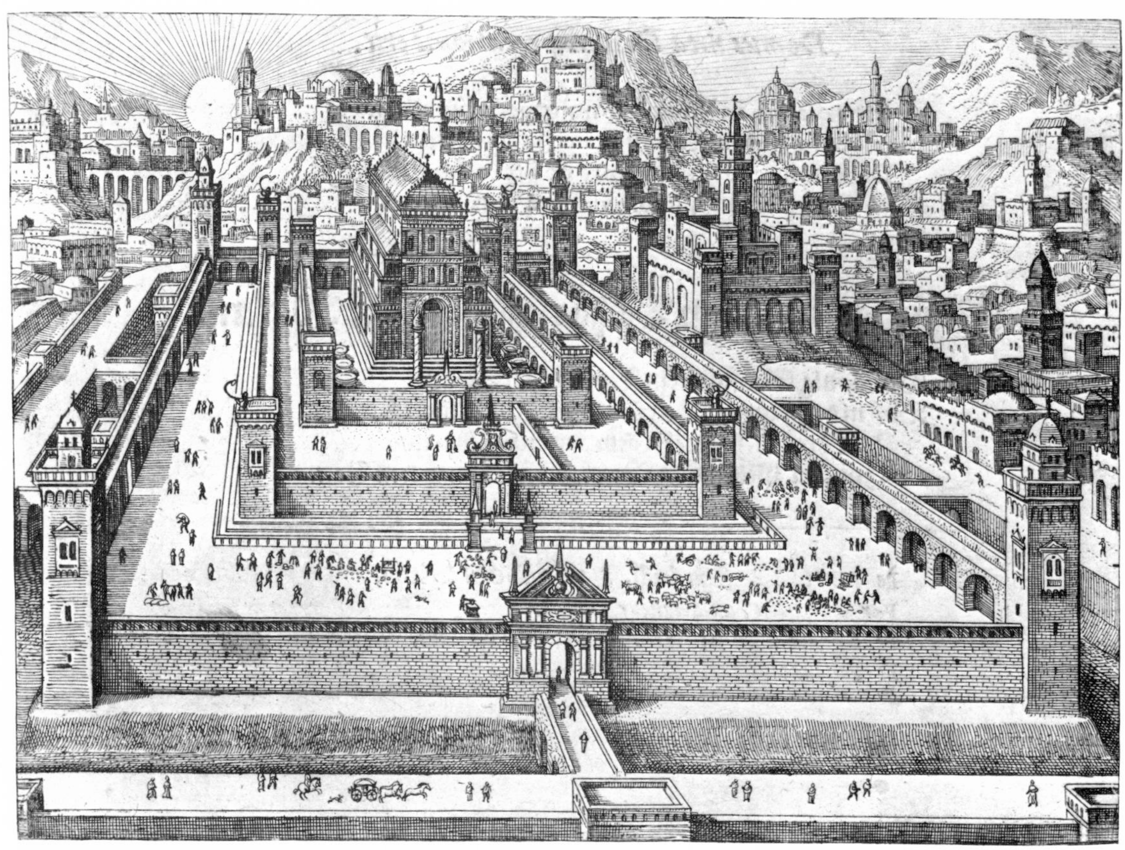

Matthaeus Merian: The Temple of Solomon

בליל שני מתחיל העומר

בָּרוּךְ אַתָּה יְיָ אֱלֹהֵינוּ מֶלֶךְ הָעוֹלָם אֲשֶׁר קִדְּשָׁנוּ בְּמִצְוֹתָיו וְצִוָּנוּ עַל סְפִירַת הָעוֹמֶר׃ שֶׁהַיּוֹם יוֹם אֶחָד בָּעוֹמֶר׃

יְהִי רָצוֹן מִלְּפָנֶיךָ יְיָ אֱלֹהֵינוּ וֵאלֹהֵי אֲבוֹתֵינוּ שֶׁיִּבָּנֶה בֵּית הַמִּקְדָּשׁ בִּמְהֵרָה בְּיָמֵינוּ וְתֵן חֶלְקֵנוּ בְּתוֹרָתֶךָ׃

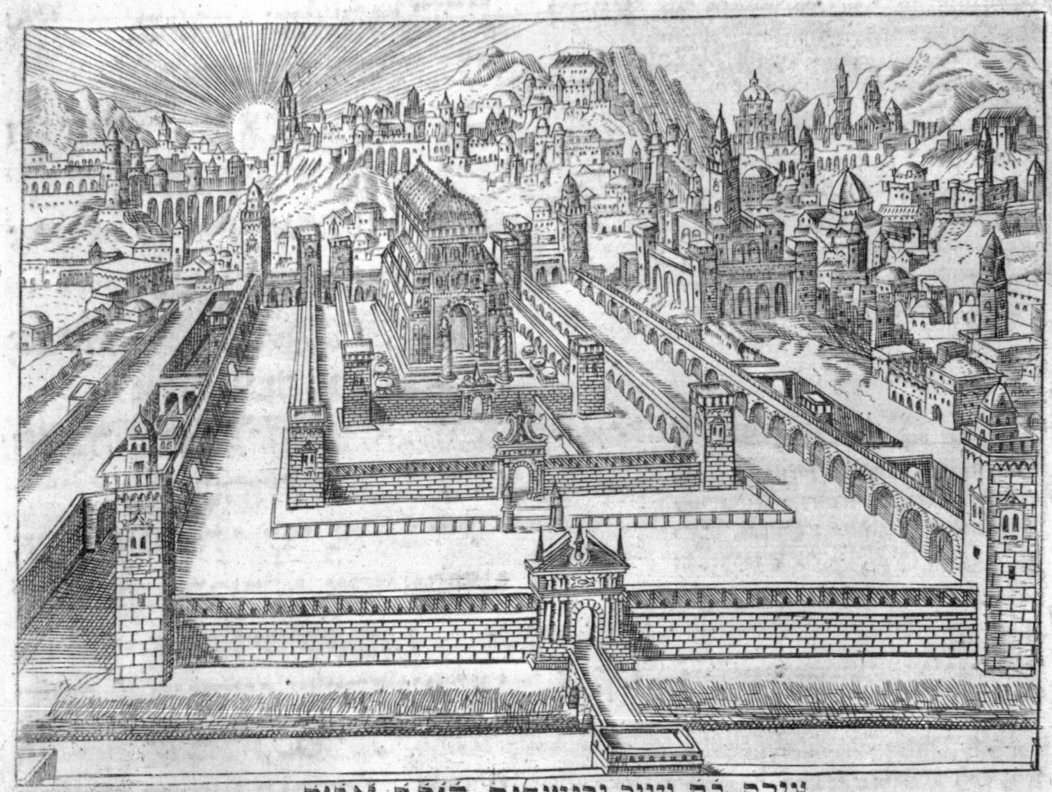

צורת בה ועיר ירושלים תובב אמיר

אלמעכטגר גאט נון בויא דיין טעמפיל שירה׳ אלזו שיר׳ אונ׳ אלזו באלד׳ אין אונזרן טאגן שירה׳ יוא שירה׳ נון בויא׳ נון בויא׳ נון בויא דיין טעמפיל שירה׃ בארים הערציגר גאט נון בויא דיין טעמפיל שירה׳ אלזו שיר׳ אונ׳ אלזו באלד׳ אין אונזרן טאגין שירה׳ יוא שירה׳ נון בויא׳ נון בויא׳ נון בויא דיין טעמפיל שירה׳ גרושר גאט׳ דעמוטיגר גאט׳ נון בויא דיין טעמפיל שירה׳ אלזו שיר׳ אונ׳ אלזו באלד׳ אין אונזרן טאגין שירה׳ יוא שירה׳ נון בויא׳ נון בויא׳ נון בויא דיין טעמפיל שירה׃ הוכיר גאט׳ ויינר גאט׳ זיסר גאט׳ חינטר גאט׳ נון בויא דיין טעמפיל שירה׳ אלזו שיר׳ אונ׳ אלזו באלד׳ אין אונזרן טאגין שירה׳ יוא שירה׳ נון בויא׳ נון בויא׳ נון בויא דיין טעמפיל שירה׃ טוגליכר גאט׳ יודשר גאט׳ נון בויא דיין טעמפיל שירה׳ אלזו שיר׳ אונ׳ אלזו באלד׳ אין אונזרן טאגן שירה׳ יוא שירה׳ נון בויא׳ נון בויא׳ נון בויא דיין טעמפיל שירה׃ כרעפטיגר גאט׳ לעבנדיגר גאט׳ מעכטיגר גאט׳ נאמהאפטיגר גאט׳ סענפטיר גאט׳ עיביגר גאט׳ נון בויא דיין טעמפיל שירה׳ אלזו שיר׳ אונ׳ אלזו באלד׳ אין אונזרן טאגן שירה׳ יוא שירה׳ נוין בויא׳ נון בויא׳ נון בויא דיין טעמפיל שירה׃ פורכצומר גאט׳ צימליכר גאט׳ קינגליכר גאט׳ רייכר גאט׳ נון בויא דיין טעמפיל שירה׳ אלזו שיר׳ אונ׳ אלזו באלד׳ אין אונזרן טאגן שירה׳ יוא שירה׳ נון בויא׳ גון בויא׳ גון בויא דיין טעמפיל שירה׃ שינר גאט׳ תרויטר גאט׳ נון בויא דיין טעמפיל שירה׳ אלזו שיר׳ אונ׳ אלזו באלד׳ אין אונזרן טאגן שירה׳ יוא שידה׳ נון בויא׳ טן בויא׳ נון בויא דיין טעמפיל שירה׃

דוא בישט גאט אונ׳ קיינר מער׳ נון בויא דיין טעמפיל שירה׳ אלזו שיר׳
אונ׳ אלזו באלד׳ אין אונזרן טאגן שירה׳ יוא שירה׳
ען בויא׳ נון בויא׳ נון בויא דיין טעמפיל שירה׃

PLATE 63

MANTUA · ITALY · 1695

The Commentary of a Palestinian Rabbi

Not all printers or their customers were necessarily interested in illustrated Haggadahs. Far more important in the eyes of some were the commentaries which might enrich their understanding of the text.

In 1695, the very year that saw the emergence of the copper-engraved Amsterdam Haggadah, as well as reprints of the trilingual issues of the illustrated Venice Haggadah, an edition without illustrations but with a new commentary was published in Mantua. Entitled *Ḥebel beney Yehudah* ("The Portion of the Sons of Judah"), it had been written by Simon ben Judah Ḥabillo, rabbi of the town of Hebron in Palestine in the middle of the seventeenth century. As the title page records, it was edited and brought to the press by the Mantuan rabbi Judah Brielli, and printed under the reign of the Duke of Mantua, Fernando Carlo Gonzaga.

YAARI NO. 64 HARVARD 22:13.5

בשם יי

ספר
חבל בני יהודה

חברתיו אני הצעיר שמעון חביליו בן
לא"א הרב הכולל הדר גאון לכל חסידיו
יהודה חביליו נר"ו והוא פירוש על
דברי ההגדה לליל פסח והלל ומזמור
ואמרו באלוקים ור' כיצד באתנו ממצרים
וראני נפלאות הוגה בעיון במרן עי'
הרב הכולל כמהר"ר יהודה בריאל
נר"ו ימנת להחיות רוח שפלים סדר
כי הוציא ה' את ישראל ממצרים

נדפס פה מנטובה תחת ממשלת
אדוננו פירדי, אנדו קרלו גונזאגה

בבית האחים בני כמ"ר יהושע
מפירנסה ז"ל

PLATE 64

SULZBACH · BAVARIA · 1711

A Baroque Frontispiece

The success of the Amsterdam Haggadah of 1695 was such that within a relatively short time its illustrations were copied in other places. It was the beginning of a series of peregrinations which, during the next three centuries, would extend around the world.

First among the Amsterdam imitations was an edition published in Frankfurt am Main in 1710. In quality and fineness of reproduction, however, it was surpassed by the Haggadah that appeared in Sulzbach a year later. The Sulzbach illustrations are exactly the same as those of Amsterdam, and are again engraved from copperplates. But while the printer consciously followed his Amsterdam model throughout, he also reserved something for himself. A new frontispiece (shown here) and a new title page (Plate 65) now replace the corresponding leaves in the former.

The frontispiece is among the most imposing to be found in eighteenth-century Hebrew books and has a magnificent sculptured quality. Held by two angels above is a portrait of King David with his harp. Below are Moses and Aaron and, at the very bottom, the Binding of Isaac. Within the central rectangle we read: "The Order of the Passover Haggadah—in the letters of Amsterdam."

YAARI NO. 72 JTSA (V) 33:21.5

סדר
הגדה
של פסח
באותיות אמשטרדם

SULZBACH · 1711
[CONTINUED]

The Printer Proclaims His Praises

The architectural border on the title page of the Sulzbach Haggadah can be found in other Hebrew books of the same printer, Aaron ben Uri Lipmann Fraenkel, whose press functioned between 1699 and 1720.

In the vignettes at the top, the serpent is curled around the Tree of Knowledge, and is approached by what appears to be a unicorn. In the bottom panel is the printer's emblem, a palm tree flanked by two signs of the zodiac: Pisces, the sign for the Hebrew month Adar, and Cancer, the sign for the month Tammuz. While zodiacal emblems, especially Pisces, are quite common among Hebrew printers, the significance of this combination is difficult to ascertain. The two months may have had some personal significance.

The text reads:

> Order of the Passover Haggadah with the fine commentary of Abravanel, as formerly printed in Israel with pleasant form and illustrations etched and designed with a pen in copper . . . and there has remained . . . only one in a city . . . but now the situation has changed for the better, worthy of all praise. And the glory of the last [i.e., the present edition] is greater than the first [the Amsterdam edition] for it has been corrected of all errors and flaws. It has been printed in large characters, in the typography of festival prayer books, and upon lovely paper, as your eyes shall straightway clearly see . . . thus may the Lord quickly vouchsafe us the rebuilding of Ariel [i.e., Jerusalem]. Printed here, in the holy community of Sulzbach, in the year *May the light of Redemption come upon us*, by the printer R. Aaron son of the great and famous rabbi and preacher . . . Uri Lipmann . . . of Vienna.

סדר
הגדה של פסח

עם הפירוש הנחמד אברבנאל : כאשר מלפנים היו בישראל : שנדפסו
בימי קדם בדמות וצורות נאים לחקוק ולצור בחרט בנחושת קליל :
ולא נותרה בבת ציון כי אם אחד בעיר ושנים במשפחה מכל וכל : ועתה
נשתנה הדבר למעליותא בכל שבח והלל : וגדול כבוד האחרון מן הראשון
שנתקנו מכל טעות וקלקול : ונדפסו באותיות גדולות בכתב של המחזורים
וביופי הנייר כאשר תחזנה במישרים בעיניכם כלול :
בזה הגדה מה שאומרים בליל : כן
יזכנו ה׳ במהרה בבניין
אריאל :

נדפס פה ק״ק
זולצבאך

CUM LICENTIA SERENISSIMI.

תחת ממשלת מעלות אדונינו הדוכס המיוחס מאוד דעאיטארום
פפאלץ גראף יר״ה יי׳ יאריך ימיו ושנותיו : לו ולזרעו ולדורותיו :

בשנת תבוא עלינו אור הגאולה לפ״ק :

על ידי המחוקק ר׳ אהרן יצ״ו בן הרב הדרשן הגדול המפורסם הגאון מוהר״ר
אורי ליפמן זצ״ל ה״ה מווין :

AMSTERDAM · NETHERLANDS · 1712

Moses at the Burning Bush

In its second edition, the frontispiece of the Amsterdam Haggadah of 1695 (Plate 59) was redesigned. Gone are the six vignettes across the top. In their place there is one large engraving of Moses kneeling in awe at the Burning Bush. One shoe at his side, he is about to remove the other, in accordance with the verse (Exodus 3:5) "put off thy shoes from off thy feet, for the place whereon thou standest is holy ground."

It is strange that the name of Abraham ben Jacob, responsible for the illustrations in the first edition, no longer figures here, even though all his work has been reprinted. We now read only that the illustrations were made "by the most facile craftsman in the art of etching engraved plates."

Whatever the reason for this sudden anonymity, the proselyte should not be ruled out as having executed the new frontispiece as well. He was still alive when this edition was published. Moreover, the illustration of Moses at the Burning Bush is again taken from Matthaeus Merian (see below), and that was the hallmark of Abraham ben Jacob's work.

YAARI NO. 73 | JTSA | 34:22

Matthaeus Merian: Moses at the Burning Bush

סדר
הגדה של פסח
עם פירוש יפה וציורים נאים
מהאותות והמופתים שעשה
הקב״ה לאבותינו
ונוסף
על זה כל המסעת במדבר עד
חלוקת הארץ לכל שבטי״ה
ישראל וצורת בית המקדש
תו״בב אב״יר
חרות
על לוחת נחשת ע״י אומן
היותר מהיר במלאכת חרש
וחושב לפתח פתוחי חותם
במלואותם וכתבניתם לשמח
עין כל רואהו ולקיים
זה אלי ואנוהו
בדפוס ובבית
כה״רר שלמה בן כה״רר יוסף
כ״ץ זצ״ל פרופס מוכר ספרים
נדפס
באמשטרדם
בשנת הלוואת שם ה׳ לפ״ק

1712

PLATE 67

AMSTERDAM · 1712
[CONTINUED]

Abraham the Iconoclast

The second paragraph of the Haggadah text on this page begins: "In the beginning our fathers were idolaters."

In this engraving, which also appeared in the 1695 edition of the Amsterdam Haggadah, Abraham is seen wielding a hammer and smashing his father's idols in Ur of the Chaldees.

This illustration is of particular interest because Abraham ben Jacob did not copy it from Merian's biblical cycle. Indeed, such a theme would not have been accessible to a Christian artist to begin with, for although it involves the patriarch Abraham, this story does not appear in the Bible at all, but only in postbiblical Jewish legend.

Here at last, then, we have an original illustration. Though some of its components may possibly have been taken from other sources, the whole makes sense only within a Jewish context.

לבלתי שאול אפי' אחר אכילת המצה ומרור · אמנם דרשו ז"ל שאחר שישמע הבן ההגדה וידע הסבה ופרטיה אח"כ יאכל המצה והמרור לשם מצוה · ולפי זה ג"כ הי' עולה על הדעת שיגיד לו מבעוד יום קודם אכילת מצה עד שלזה הוצרך לדרוש יכול מבעוד יום ולא דרש כן בשאר הבנים :

מתחלה ר"ל קודם היותנו עבדים היו אבותינו עובדי' ע"א ועכשיו ר"ל בזמן ההוא שנעשינו עבדים קרבנו המקום לעבודתו שבמה שעשה אותנו עבדים למצרים והוציאנו קרבנו לעבודתו לפי שבירידתנו למצרים נתפרסם אלהותו על ידינו שזו היא עבודתו לפרסם אמיתותו · וזה אמרו שמה שהיינו עבדים אינו גנאי · לפי שמתחלה קודם שהיינו עבדים לא היינו קרובים לעבודתו · וכיון שבמה שנעשינו עבדים קרבנו לעבודתו הרי הוא שבח ואינו גנאי · ומביא ראי' לדבריו שעבדו ע"א ושמגודל אהבתו את אברה' הוריד' למצרי' לעבודתו · כי לענין הע"א כאמר ביהושע ויעבדו אלהים אחרים · ולענין שקירב אותם לעבודתו בירידת מצרים הביא ראי' ממה שנתן הנחלה לעשו שבזה נתפרס' שלא נקרא זרעו של אברה' שנ' עליו גר יהי' זרעך בארץ לא להם ועבדום וגו' ומאחר שעשו נתיישב בארץ נחלתו הרי אינו נקרא זרעו של אברהם אשר הבטיחו הש"י שע"י זרעו תושלם כוונתו בפרסום האלהות : (מעשה ה')

זכרה התור' בו ענין שאלה ולא אמיר' רק אמר' והגדת לבנך ירא' שהבן הזה לא היה יודע לשאול והתורה צוה לאביו שיפתח פיו לאלם ויגיד לו הדברים כמו שהיו ולפי שהת' ושאינו יודע לשאול לא במצא להן עיון כי אם קוצר ידיעה לא בהתפארות החכמ' כבן החכם ולא ברשע ופשע כרש' לכן כשתפ' המגיד להשיב אליהם מה שהשיב' התורה ולא הוסיף לומר עליהם אף אתה כמו שעשה בבן חכם ורשע :

יכול מר"ח שהתחיל' הגאול' ועוד ששואלין בהלכות הפסח קוד' הפסח · תלמוד לומר ביום ההוא כלומר יום הגאולה · יכול מבעו'יום כששוחטין פסחיהן בעבור זה לא אמרתי אלא בשעה שיש מצה ומרור מונחי' לפניך לפי שלבן הנער ובער הזה יצטרך האב להראות' לו באצבע · ויש מפרשי' ז"ה בגימטריא י"ב מצות שאדם עושה בליל פסח ואלו הן ארבע כוסות חרוסת כרפס שתי נטילות ידים המוציא מצה מרור כריכה :

מתחילה עובדי עבודה זרה היו אבותינו עתה מתחיל סדרו של אביי שמפרש מאי גנות · שנאמר ויאמר יהושע וגו'

יָכוֹל מֵרֹאשׁ חֹדֶשׁ · תַּלְמוּד לוֹמַר בַּיּוֹם הַהוּא · אִי בַּיּוֹם הַהוּא · יָכוֹל מִבְּעוֹד יוֹם · תַּלְמוּד לוֹמַר בַּעֲבוּר זֶה · בַּעֲבוּר זֶה לֹא אָמַרְתִּי אֶלָּא בְּשָׁעָה שֶׁיֵּשׁ מַצָּה וּמָרוֹר מֻנָּחִים לְפָנֶיךָ :

מִתְּחִלָּה עוֹבְדֵי עֲבוֹדָה זָרָה הָיוּ אֲבוֹתֵינוּ · וְעַכְשָׁיו קֵרְבָנוּ הַמָּקוֹם לַעֲבוֹדָתוֹ שֶׁנֶּאֱמַר וַיֹּאמֶר יְהוֹשֻׁעַ אֶל כָּל הָעָם כֹּה אָמַר יְיָ אֱלֹהֵי יִשְׂרָאֵל בעבר

מתחלה הטעם שהפך הסדר וספר תחלה עבדים היינו ואח"כ שאבותינו היו עובדי ע"ז · ועוד מה טעם יש בגנות הזה שאנו מדברים על אבותינו · נראה כדי שלא יאמר האומר שילך הוא ג"כ ויתפוש אומנות אבותיו ויעבוד ע"ז ח"ו · לכן אנו מזכירין תחלה חסדיו וגבורותיו ית' המגיע אלינו בלילה הזה אל הגוף הגשמי ואח"כ אל הרוחני שקרבנו לעבודתו · וע"י זה אין שום אדם נמשך אחרי הדעות הנפסדות הנזכרות :

ויאמר יהושעאל כל העם כה אמר יי אלהי ישראל בעבר הנהר ישבו אבותיכם מעולם תרח אבי אברהם ואבי נחור ויעבדו אלהים אחרים

PLATE 68

AMSTERDAM · 1712
[CONTINUED]

Borrowed from Venice—the Ten Plagues

The illustrations of the Amsterdam Haggadah of 1712 were identical with those of 1695 except for the frontispiece (Plate 66) and three other features: woodcut initial letters, a page with thirteen cuts showing the sequence of the Passover Seder; and a page depicting the Ten Plagues. These were taken over from the Venice Haggadah first published in 1609, and reprinted in 1629 and 1695.

A comparison of the Ten Plagues in the Amsterdam edition shown here with those of Venice (Plate 44) reveals only insignificant variations in the individual cuts. The only major changes are in the rearrangement of the rows (three instead of two), and the fact that the entire series was now copper engraved.

לאופתים כאמר כאן ובמופתים וכאמר להלן ונתתי מופתים מה להלן ב' אלה אף כאן ב' אלה מה להלן נקרא דם הכרב והחושך אף כאן כן: ותמרות לפי שהתמ' עץ גבוה וישר ושוה ידמה הדבר הנגבו' והיש' אליו וכן נדברי רז"ל משתעלה העשן תמרותו:

דבר אחר ביד חזקה שתים וכו' לפי שהין המכות י' ויש בפסוק הזה ה' שמות יד חזקה וזרוע נטויה ומורא גדול ואותות ומופתים אמר המגיד שכיון שאילו הה' לשונות כאמרו על כל הי' מכות שיתחייב מזה שכל א' מאלה הה' יורה על שתים מהם ונזה הדרך יוכללו כל המכו' באלה הה' לשונות ומלא סמך לזה לפי שיד חזקה הם ב' מלות ולכן ירמוז ב' מכות וכן ובזרוע נטויה ובמורא גדול ובאותות עם היותו מלה אחת הוא לשון רבים ומיעוט רבים שנים וכן ובמופתים לשון רבים:

אֵלּוּ עֶשֶׂר מַכּוֹת שֶׁהֵבִיא הַקָּדוֹשׁ בָּרוּךְ הוּא עַל הַמִּצְרִים בְּמִצְרַיִם: וְאֵלּוּ הֵן:

דָּם צְפַרְדֵּעַ

כִּנִּים עָרוֹב

דֶּבֶר שְׁחִין

בָּרָד אַרְבֶּה

חוֹשֶׁךְ מַכַּת בְּכוֹרוֹת

בשדה נתחזק לבו אז יותר לאמר שהמכות חוזרות ומתרחקות מן הגוף אח"כ בא השחין שהי' ממש בעורם ובשרם יותר קרוב אל הגוף מן הכנים חזר להתיירא פן יגע בגופו· אחר זאת בא הברד גם הוא בשדה חזר ונתחזק לבו שראה שהמכה מתרחקת· אח"כ בא הארב' שהי' קרוב מזה שעם היות הנזק נמשך בשדה כבר נאמר ותחשך הארץ שהיתה קרובה אל הגוף מן הברד· וזה הי' הסבות כי בהיות המכות מתקרבות הי' מתירא ובהיותם מתרחקות הי' מכביד לבו ולכן נתן ר' יהודה סימנים וחלקם לג' חלקים שלעולם האחרונה מהם קרובה אל הגוף קירוב נוסף על הראשונה לה: (מעשה ה')

רבי

אלו עשר מכות וכו' ר' יהודה הי' נותן בהם סימנים כו'· נ"ל שר"י אתא לאשמועינן דלא תימא הסדר הוא מה שהוזכר בספר תהלי' מזמור ע"ח ולא מה שהוזכר

רבי יהודה היה נותן בהם סימנים רצ"ך עד"ש באח"ב לפי שבספר תהלים לא נמנו כסדר הזה ונאמר אין מוקד' ומאוחר בתורה לכן עשה ר' יהודה זה הסימן להודיענו כי כן היו כסדר הכתובים בתורה· וי"א שדם וצפרדע היו בהתראה וכנים בלא התראה וכן ערוב היה בהתראה ושחין בלא התרא'· וכן ברד וארבה היו בהתרא' וחושך בלא התראה· ולהיותם בזה הדרך

דָּם
צְפַרְדֵּעַ
כִּנִּים
עָרוֹב
דֶּבֶר
שְׁחִין
בָּרָד
אַרְבֶּה
חוֹשֶׁךְ
מַכַּת בְּכוֹרוֹת:
אלו עשר מכות שהביא הקדוש ברוך הוא על המצרים במצרים

AMSTERDAM · 1712
[CONTINUED]

A Second Edition of the First Hebrew Map

The 1712 reprint of the map designed for the Amsterdam Haggadah of 1695 (at the time, the first Hebrew map ever published).

The superscription states: "This is to make known to every understanding person the route of the forty-years journey in the desert, and the breadth and length of the Holy Land from the River of Egypt to the City of Damascus and from the Valley of Arnon to the Great Sea, and within it the territory of each and every tribe. . . ."

In this map, the Land of Israel has been revolved counterclockwise and laid on its side, so that Egypt appears in the bottom right corner, the Jordan across the upper portion, and the Mediterranean (in large Hebrew letters, *Yam ha-Gadol*: "The Great Sea") across the lower.

The table within the scrolled frame lists forty-one way stations of the Israelites during their long journey to the Promised Land. To its left is a ship with a man falling overboard, obviously the prophet Jonah. Immediately underneath we see him once again, emerging from the fish onto dry land.

Continuing to the left, a circular compass gives the directions in Hebrew. The cows and the beehives on the porch of the house at the extreme left are labeled, respectively, "milk" and "honey," another reference to the Land of Israel. Along the coastline is a flotilla of ships and barges, inscribed: "Rafts of cedars of Lebanon sent by Hiram, king of Tyre, on their way to Jaffa, from whence Solomon brought them to Jerusalem" (1 Kings 5:21–25).

The significance of the eagle is explained by the verse inscribed over it: "Ye have seen what I did unto the Egyptians, and how I bore you on eagles' wings, and brought you unto Myself" (Exodus 19:4).

Inscribed in small letters along the margin below the figure of Jonah is the name Abraham ben Jacob.

OFFENBACH · GERMANY · 1722

From Copperplate to Woodcut

The Amsterdam Haggadah of 1695 had marked a new departure, not only in Haggadah illustration but in the history of Hebrew printing. It was the first Hebrew book to be illustrated entirely with copper engravings. The same technique was employed in the derivative editions of Frankfurt (1710) and Sulzbach (1711), as well as in the second Amsterdam edition of 1712.

From this perspective the Offenbach Haggadah of 1722 represents something of an anomaly. It attempts to reproduce all the Amsterdam illustrations—and yet it does so, not by means of engraved plates, but by the venerable method of woodcuts. If some would regard this as a regression technically, aesthetically it results in a new creation. Precisely because the medium is a different one, and because there is no attempt at an exact "facsimile" copy of the Amsterdam illustrations, the Offenbach Haggadah infuses its models with a different spirit. To modern tastes the primitive woodcuts of Offenbach may well appear more forceful than their Amsterdam prototypes.

Recorded on the title page are the pertinent details concerning the text and printing of the new edition. The Haggadah is accompanied by a dual commentary entitled *Abodat ha-gefen* ("The Work of the Vine"), one part of it largely mystical. It was composed by Judah Leb ben Elijah, rabbi of Horodetz, and his son Ze'eb Wolf, rabbi of Pinsk. The book was published by Rabbi Zalman Waltern of Mayence, Rabbi Moses ben Ḥayyim of Tiktin, and Israel ben Moses (who was also the printer), at the press of a gentile, Bonaventura de la Naye.

YAARI NO. 92 JTSA 32:19

הגדה של פסח

עם פירוש עבודת הגפן

עם חידושי דינים מפוסקים ראשונים ואחרונים · אשר על דגליהם חונים · ודרושים נאים והמודים · על מאמרים ומדרשים תמוהים · מיושבים ע"פ פילפול חידודים · ופירש מספיק קצת דרך נסתר והמשכיל יבין בקריאתו · תאוה היא לעיני הקורא · והוא למשיבת נפשו · אשר חברו ויסדו הני שני המאורים הגדולים המפורסמים · האחד המאור הגדול החסיד מהור"ר **יהודה ליב** בן הרב החסיד מוהר"ר אליהו ז"ל שהי' אב"ד ור"מ בק"ק הארדץ · והשני ה"ה בנו ו אי ברא כרעא דאבוה החבל הולך אחר הדלי ה"ה הרב המאור הגדול המפורסם מהור"ר זאב **וואלף** בעל המחבר ספר **גפן יחידית** שהיה אב"ד ור"מ דק"ק לבשוב · ואת"כ היה ר"מ ורישא דריגא בק"ק פינסק יצ"ו :

והובא לבית הדפוס ע"י בנו האלוף התורני המופלא כ"ה מוהר"ר שלמה **זלמן** וואלטירן · דיינא ומ"כ בגליל עליון מנגנ"א : והמשותפי' כ"ה האלוף התורני מהור"ר **משה** במהור"ר חיים מק"ק טיקאטין והאלוף היקר והנעלה הר"ר ישראל בן הר"ר משה יצ"ו : והחוט המשולש במהרה לא ינתק אכי"ר :

בדפוס נאה ומשובח ומוגה מכל טעיות כאשר יראה עיני הקורא בהם :

פה קק אופן באך

לפרט ואמרתם זבח פסח :

על ידי המדפיס האלוף היקר הנעלה הר"ר ישראל בן הר"ר משה יצ"ו :

בדפוס הארון באנע פענטורא רע לא נאיי :

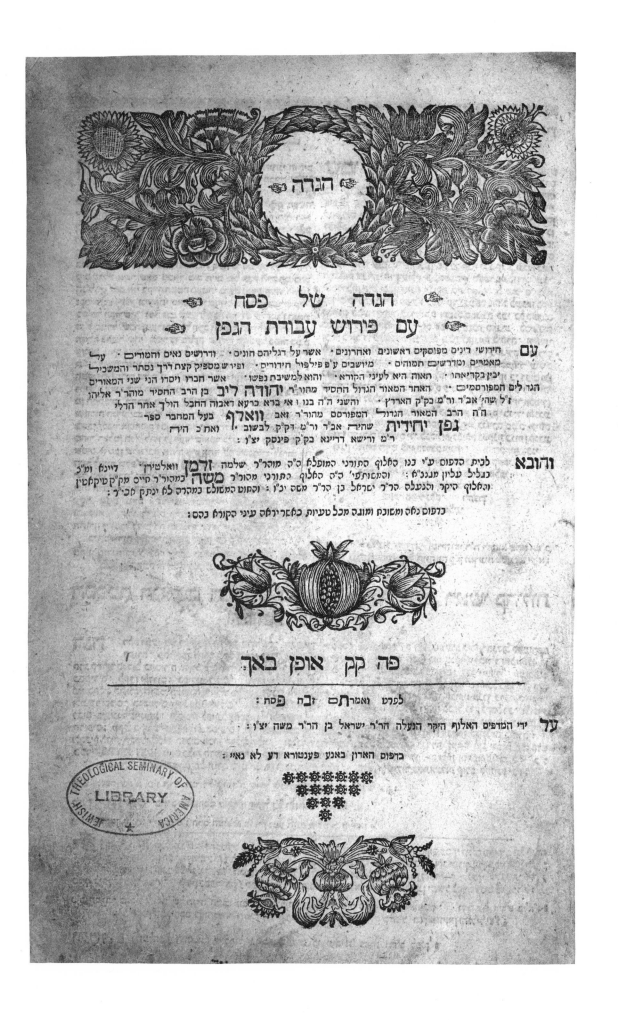

OFFENBACH · 1722
[CONTINUED]

The Angels Visit Abraham

An Offenbach woodcut version of the Amsterdam engraving shows the appearance of the three angels at Abraham's house (Genesis 18). The figure in the boat is Abraham crossing the Euphrates, a motif as old as the Prague Haggadah of 1526.

The layout of the page has the Haggadah text in the upper left. To the right is a literal commentary and below, a kabbalistic one.

מעתה כל בן נכר לא יאכל בו ה"נ בו אינו אוכל אבל אוכל בפסח דורת: אמר קרא ועבדת את העבודה כל העבודות כחדש שוין לכך אותו הרשע קאמר מה העבודה הזאת ר"ל עבודה דייק' מנ"ל לדרוש ועבדת את העבודה וללמוד מיני' שאף בפסח דורת כל בן נכר לא יאכל בו: כי אם לכם ניתן לאכול: לכם ולא לו: ומעתה לפי שהוציא את עצמו מן הכלל ועשה את עצמו לבן נכר כפר בעיקר: ואף אתה הקהה את שיניו ואמור לו שאילו היה שם לא הי' נגאל דאמרינן תו התם בפסחים: אלא מעתה ועצם לא תשברו בו ה"נ בו אי אתה שובר אבל אתה שובר בפסח דורת: ושני ועבדת את העבודה וכו' ואי' כמפרשים טעם על עצם לא תשברו בו: כי לכלבים תשליכון אותו · שאין הקב"ה מקפח שכר כל ברי' ונתן לכלבים לשכר על לא יחרץ כלב לשונו ע"כ: א"כ לפי דברי הרשע שאין ללמוד מעבדת את העבודה על פסח דורת לענין אכילת פסח לבן נכר לפ"ז אף לענין שבירת עצם אין ללמוד מעבדת את העבודה וסבר דמותר לשבור העצם א"כ אף אתה הקהה את שיניו ר"ל לפי סברתו יגרם בעצם שיניו: ואלו הי' שם לא היה נגאל דלסברת הרשע א"ו מקפח הקב"ה שכר ברי' להשיב כגמול איש כראשו והגאולה היתה בשביל שכר מצות פסח א"כ כפי פעלו ודעתו כן הי' משכורתו ולא הי' נגאל וק"ל:

תם מה הוא אומר מה זאת ואמרת וכו' מבית עבדים הנה מצינו פסוק זה בסוף פ' בא אחר אמירת פרשת בכור שסיים וכל בכור תפדה וע"ז נאמר מיד והיה כי יאמר מה זאת נבו' וקשה מה ענין לשאלה מה זאת אחר וכל בכור בניך תפדה:

ועוד

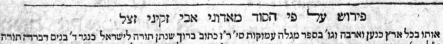

את הר שעיר לרשת אותו ויעקב ובניו ירדו מצרים:

ברוך שומר הבטחתו לישראל ברוך הוא שהקדוש ברוך הוא חשב את הקץ לעשות כמו שאמר לאברהם אבינו בברית בין הבתרים שנאמר ויאמר לאברם ידע תדע כי גר יהיה זרעך בארץ לא להם ועבדום וענו אותם ארבע מאות שנה וגם את הגוי אשר יעבדו דן אנכי ואחרי כן יצאו ברכוש גדול:

והיא שעמדה לאבותינו ולנו שלא אחד בלבד עומד עלינו לכלותינו אלא שבכל דור ודור עומדים עלינו לכלותינו והקדוש ברוך הוא מצילנו מידם:

פירוש על פי הסוד מאדוני אבי זקיני זצל

ואוליך אותו בכל ארץ כנען וארבה וגו' בספר מגלה עמוקות סי' ר"ז כתוב ברוך שנתן תורה לישראל כנגד ד' בנים דברה תורה ר"ל דפי' כן בגמרא יצחק כי תורה אתי מסיטרא דיצחק כמ"ש וידבר אלקים את כל הדברים תורה מפי הגבורה שמענו וכמו יצחק עולה ר"ת ר"ח כוחות הדיני' כו' וע"כ כתוב הרבה ארבה את זרעך הרבה דייקא ר"ת שבעיקרתו המתיק ר"ח כוחות הדינים וכו' עכ"ל · וזה יהיה הפי' מתחילה היו אבותינו עע"ז ומכח זה השליטו הכוחות הדינים שהם בסוד בינה דמיני' דינין מתערין וכמ"ש לעיל ומשום זה בנה במ"ק כמנין אח"ר להורות על אחדות ב"ה שהוא יחיד ומיוחד לאפוקי הרשעים המה העובדי' ע"א ולכן אלישע בן אבוי' נקרא אחר מלשון אלהים אחרים גם אחר בגימ' ר"ח עם א' הוא הכולל ר"ח דינים אשר ימשכו עליו מסוד הבינה וג"כ אבוי' עם הכולל בגימט' ה"ה בינה נ"ל מכח זה הושלט בעולם גם לילית הרשעה עם כל חיילותיהן עד שבא אברהם וכרת הברית שהוא בגימ' סמאל לילית ובזה סילק תפ"א חיילותיה ומכח זה הומתקו הר"ח כוחות של דינים וזה פירש ואוליך אותו בכל ארץ כנען שהוא גימטרי' תפ"א ור"ל שהשליטו הש"י על לילית וחיילותי' שהוא תפ"א וארבה את זרעו ואתן את יצחק שמכח זה המתיק ר"ח דיני' שהוא גימט' של ארבה כמנין יצחק וכמ"ש בשם מגלה עמוקות נ"ל ואוליך אותו וארבה וגו' הרבותא היא כפירש בפ' לך לך רע"פ דדרך ממעט שלשה וחד מנהון מפרי' ורבי' אע"פ כן הרבתי את זרעו ואתן לו את יצחק · דישמעאל לא חשוב זרעו:

וישא עיניו וירא והנה שלשה אנשים נצבים עליו ויעבר אברם בארץ

PLATE 72

OFFENBACH · 1722
[CONTINUED]
The Drowning of the Egyptians

The woodcut on this page offers perhaps the most intriguing example of the manner in which the unknown artist of the Offenbach Haggadah approached his task. In comparison to the crowds of Israelites and Egyptians in the corresponding Amsterdam engraving, there is a close-up focus here on certain key figures (Moses raising his staff, Pharaoh throwing up his hands as the waves engulf him). In fact, the Offenbach woodcut seems so far removed from its Amsterdam counterpart as to arouse the suspicion that in this instance, at least, the artist may have used another model.

And so he did. Not Abraham ben Jacob's Amsterdam engraving, but Matthaeus Merian's illustration on the same theme is the source for the Offenbach woodcut. Pharaoh, Moses with his staff, the woman holding her child—are all there. In other words, the Offenbach artist here bypassed Abraham ben Jacob in favor of the latter's own model (or a copy thereof), and proceeded merely to simplify it in his own fashion.

Matthaeus Merian: The Drowning of the Egyptians

וינער ה' את מצרים בתוך הים ובני ישראל הלכו ביבשה בתוך הים

כַּמָּה מַעֲלוֹת טוֹבוֹת לַמָּקוֹם עָלֵינוּ אִלּוּ הוֹצִיאָנוּ מִמִּצְרַיִם: וְלֹא עָשָׂה בָהֶם שְׁפָטִים דַּיֵּנוּ: אִלּוּ עָשָׂה בָהֶם שְׁפָטִים וְלֹא עָשָׂה בֵאלֹהֵיהֶם דַּיֵּנוּ: אִלּוּ עָשָׂה בֵאלֹהֵיהֶם ולא

נאקתם מכת שהרהרו בתשובה · א"כ ויזכור את בריתו ר"ל זכות אבות דמעתה אבא מוכא כרא ודילג את הקץ וכנאלו וק"ל: במסכתות סמחות וו"ל כתי' ועברתי בלילה וגו' וכתיב ביום הכתי כל בכור וגו' · אמר ר"י הנותן פת לתינוק צריך להודיע לאמו מלמד שהיה נשמתם מפרפרת כל הלילה עד הבקר וראו כל ישראל ע"ש · וואי לפי פשוטי בא לתרץ דלא

פירוש על פי הסוד מאדוני אבי זקיני זצ"ל

ואלהים במלואה הוא ש"ן כזה אל"ף למ"ד ה"א יו"ד מ"ם וה' אותיות וכנודע למבינים וע"כ מביא ראיה אלהים נצב בעדת אל שם אלהים הוא נצב להם לישראל שנקראו עדת אל וזש"ה תהלים סי' ע"ה כי אלהים שופט וגו' כי כוס ביד ה' ויין חמר מל"א מסך וגו' ואית' במדרש שוחר טוב דוה קאי על פרע"ה ע"ש שז"ל רבי יודן ור' נחמי' ור' יצחק אמרו לעתיד לבא אומר הקב"ה לפרעה שתה ניסך והוא אומר רבש"ע ולא שתיתי כוסי בע"הז והוא אומר לו מה שתית כמין אגוזה אחת שנאמ' ויין חמר מלא מסך ויגר מזה אבל עכשיו אך שמרו ימצו ע"כ ועוד שם וז"ל כי כוס ביד ה' יכול ריקן ת"ל מלא מסך וכו' ע"כ וזה יהיה הפירש לפי מ"ש כי אלהים שופט השם של אלקים הוא שופט את העכו"ם כי כוס התרעלה ביד ה' וכוס הוא גימ' פ"ו כמנין אלהי"ם יכול ריקן ת"ל מלא כסך ר"ל השם אלקי"ם במלואי' הוא ש"ן כמנין הזה שפוט לכן כתב מסך הוא בגימטרי' ק"ך כמנין ק"ך צירופי' של אלקי' וק"ל למבין:

כמה מעלות טובות למקום וכו' ט"ו מעלות קחשוב כנגד ט"ו שיר למעלות אמר דוד המע"ה עיי' בפי' כמה גימטרי' ס"ה כמנין שם של אדנ"י שהוא מלכות שמשפיע לנו הטובו' ממעל גם כמה אותיות מכה לרמז שה' אחד הוא הפועל הרע והטוב ולכן נ"ל שמכה במ"ק כמו ברכה במ"ק מטעמא הנ"ל ויש נדרשי' השם למקום ג"כ הוא צירף הוי"ה א' הים כי הקו"ף היא הוי"ה שהוי"ה הוא עשר ספירות כנודע וכל אחד כלול עשרה נמצא הוא ק' ונשאר פ"ו כמנין אלהים ולכן נאמר נגמ' קו"ף הוא שמו של הקב"ה כי קו"ף ג"כ צירף הוי"ה אלהים וכאשר עיניך רואות ולכן קאמר שמו של הקב"ה כי הקב"ה הא בגימט' קי"ג כמנין הוי"ה אלקים ועיי' מ"ש לעיל בשם מ"מ: למקום עלינו ר"ל שהטובות ההם הם עלינו תמיד כש"ח ויש לנו לפרוע הטובות שעשה עמנו: אלו הוציאנו ממצרים ולא עשה באלהיהם לשדר המערכה ולבטל כוחות העליונה מפני התחתונה כ"ה בפי' זהו עשה באלהיהם ר"ת עליון שירד המערכת כנ"ל: ולא הרג בכוריהם כו' מה ראוי' נפש החטאת היא תמות ולא ימותו אבות על בנים ולא נתן ממונם כי מן הדין אין לענוש בממון כי קים לי' בדרבה מיני' בעונש הגוף כ"ה בפי': אלו עשה באלהיהם של עץ נשבר כהנת וכמ"ש לעיל: לא קרע את הים ששנה הקב"ה הטבעו מה שהטבעו ברצונו משש ימי בראשית ולא סיפק צרכינו מ' שנה פי' שיהיה אפשר להולכם דרך ארץ כי קרוב הוא וארץ בישיבת היא למצוא אוכל לנפשם: ואלו האכילנו את המן פירש שהוא חוץ הטבע רק מאכל מלאכי שרת כמ"ש לחם אבירים: ודכריני' מילתא מה ששמעתי מפי אמ"ו ז"ל שאמ' טעם נכון מפני מה כשאכלו את המן הי' נבלע באיברים דהא אין הש"י ב"ה עושה גם נס מה שהוא חוץ לטבע ופי' הנאה דאית' דהענין של אכילה הוא מה שיש באכילה משל הקדוש' נבלע בגוף האדם וממנו הוא כח האדם וחלק הטומאה היא יוצא לחוץ ובגמ' סנהדרין דאין דבר טמא יוצא מן השמי' וא"כ הוי כולה קדושה ע"כ שבלע כולו בגוף ואברים ע"כ והוא פלא: ושמעתי משארי ופארי הגאון הגדול מהור"ר מרדכי כהנא אב"ד ור"מ דק"ק אפשא לך ה' הצדקה במן ולנו בושת הפנים בעגל וה"פ דעל עגל יש תירץ דלמשה צוה ולא לישראל דהא בלשון יחיד · אבל נת המן דגם משה הוי כרבים וא"כ ע"כ לשון יחיד לא הוי דקדוק וא"כ אפשר לישראל ג"כ הי' הצווי' וק"ל ורפת ח:

SALONIKA · GREECE · 1741

A Mystical Commentary

An eighteenth-century Salonika edition of the Haggadah is accompanied by a commentary entitled *Shaarey ratzon* ("The Gates of Grace"). This commentary was ultimately derived from the writings of the sixteenth-century kabbalist Isaac Luria (the "Ari"), founder of the great school of Safed mysticism that was later disseminated throughout the Jewish world. The Haggadah is followed by prayers and laws for other festivals, all of them accompanied by kabbalistic interpretations. "Printed in Salonika . . . which is under the rule of our lord the King Sultan Mahmud . . . in the year *Know the lord God of thy father and serve Him.*"

YAARI NO. 120 HARVARD 18:13

זה השער לה׳

ספר שערי רצון

חבו ממתקים אשר לא היה לעולמים
כאשר עיניכם תחזינה מישרים
וזה מלוקט מכתבי הרב האלהי חיים הכהן
אשר ליקט מכתבי הקודש האלהי
האר״י ז״ל [illegible]

הביאו לבית הדפוס לזכות בו את הרבים
זכות הרבים תלוי בו יהי רצון
מלפני האל ותורה לא תשכח מפי זרעו
אכי״ר

והוגה ע״י החכם הש׳ כמהר״ר בנימין
קמחי נר״ו יאיר אמן

נדפס בשאלוניקי יע״א

אשר תחת ממשלת אדונינו המלך סולטן
מחמוד יר״ה

בשנת דע את אלהי אביך
ועבדהו לפ״ק

LONDON · ENGLAND · 1770

The First English Translation

The modern settlement of the Jews in England dates from the mid-seventeenth century when, for the first time since the expulsion of 1290, professing Jews were permitted to reside there. The first to take advantage of the opportunity were Sephardic Jews, who were later followed by the Ashkenazim. Well into the eighteenth century the vernaculars of the two groups remained Spanish and Portuguese or Judeo-German (Yiddish). Spanish translations of parts of the liturgy had already been printed by 1705 and continued to be published in subsequent years. Yiddish made its appearance in a prayer book of 1770. The same year marked the publication in London of the very first English translation of the Haggadah.

This development is significant not only as a measure of the linguistic acculturation of English Jews by the latter part of the eighteenth century, but also as a break with previous policies. Only five years before, the publication of an English translation of the prayer book prepared by Isaac Pinto had been thwarted by the conservative leaders of the Sephardic community. In their view only Spanish translations, hallowed by the practice of centuries, were to be allowed. Pinto's English prayer book therefore had to be printed across the ocean in New York City.

The Haggadah of 1770 is a bilingual edition, with Hebrew and English on facing pages. At the end, the hymn *Adir hu* and the song *Ḥad gadya* appear in Judeo-German. A separate edition was issued for Sephardic Jews. The translator, Alexander Alexander, was one of the pioneers of the Hebrew press in London, and also produced the Ashkenazic prayer book with English translation that appeared in the same year.

YAARI NO. 167 HARVARD 16.5:10.5

THE

הגדה של פסח

CONTAINING THE

CEREMONIES and PRAYERS

Which are used and read

By all FAMILIES, in all HOUSES

OF THE

ISRAELITES,

THE

Two first Nights of PASSOVER:

Faithfully TRANSLATED from the

ORIGINAL HEBREW.

TO WHICH IS ADDED,

The EXPLANATIONS thereon.

TRANSLATED by *A. ALEXANDER*,

And ASSISTANTS.

LONDON:

P[illegible]d for the TRANSLATOR, by W^m. GILBERT.

A. M. 5530

AMSTERDAM · NETHERLANDS · 1781

Amsterdam Revisited

Toward the end of the eighteenth century the Amsterdam Haggadah was redesigned in a smaller format, being reduced from the folio of 1695 and 1712 to a quarto. Undoubtedly, this size was easier to handle at the Seder table. All the old illustrations reappear, printed as before, from copperplates, as well as the map of the Exodus, of which this is the third edition. Abravanel's commentary is retained, and to it are added the *Geburot Ha-Shem* ("The Mighty Deeds of the Lord") by Rabbi Judah Loew ben Bezalel (the MaHaRaL) of Prague; a commentary attributed to the sixteenth-century Safed exegete and mystic Moses Alshekh; and selections from the *Olelot Ephraim*, a collection of ethical homilies by Ephraim Solomon Luntschitz, rabbi of Prague in the early seventeenth century. The three commentaries first appeared together in Metz, France, in 1767. Like the latter, the Amsterdam edition is entitled *Bet ḥorin* ("The House of Free Men").

Shown here is the engraved frontispiece: "The Passover Haggadah according to the custom of the Ashkenazim and the custom of the Sephardim. In Amsterdam. In the year [5]541. In the house and at the press of the orphans of the deceased . . . Jacob Proops."

The house of Proops, founded in 1704, provided three generations of distinguished Hebrew printers in the Dutch capital. Solomon ben Joseph Proops had printed the Haggadah of 1712. After his death in 1734 the press was directed by his three sons in partnership, but in 1773 the inheritance was divided and each set up his own establishment. One of the three, Jacob ben Solomon, died shortly before the Haggadah of 1781 was issued. Since the family was of priestly lineage, one of their printer's emblems consisted of two hands raised in the attitude of the priestly blessing.

YAARI NO. 199 HARVARD 28:21

בית ישראל
בית חורין
הגדה
של פסח
כמנהג אשכנזים
וכמנהג ספרדים
באמשטרדם
בשנת תקמ״א לפ״ק:
פרופס
בבית ובדפוס
יתמי המחוקק כהר״ר יעקב פרופס כ״ץ ז״ל מ״ס:

LEGHORN · ITALY · 1782

A Palestinian Emissary to the Diaspora

The first Hebrew Haggadah to be published in Leghorn was printed by the partners Abraham Isaac Castello and Eliezer Saadun. A Spanish translation had been printed in the city in 1654 (Plate 58).

This Haggadah is also noteworthy for its commentary, entitled *Simḥat ha-regel* ("The Joy of the Pilgrimage Festival"), composed by Rabbi Ḥayyim Yosef David Azulai (1724–1806), one of the most multifaceted Jewish personalities in early modern times. Born in Jerusalem, Azulai was both scholar and fund-raiser, kabbalist and jurist, bibliographer and diarist. He was also the most distinguished emissary from Jewish Palestine to the Diaspora in the eighteenth century, traveling through many countries to collect funds, especially for the yeshiva of Hebron.

YAARI NO. 202 HARVARD 20:15

חיבור הרב הגאון המקובל האלקי רבינו חיים דוד אזולאי זלה"ה

ספר

שמחת הרגל

הרג"ל מועד"ת ליל התקדש חג הפסח פסח"י רנה והלל להודות לשם ה׳ כנסת הרג"ל מגיד דבריו בפירו׳ ההגדה. ויתהלך חנו"ך לנער כדי שיקלו׳ העי׳ן לספיר׳ דברי׳ מזכירין יציאת מצרים את הכ"ם למיכהו לתורה ולתעודה. במוט"כ תלת׳ מקדימין לשם הכניסה ג׳ לימודים מוס"ר מעי"ר על ראש הצעי"ר ללמד בני יהודה. ואתיא מכללא קצת ביאור ופירוש מגילת רות לילדי ישראל טוב ילד גמול ידו הדה. ושעש"ע יונק תחיל׳ אוכל"א קורא ושונה וירץ הנער ויגד כל שישנו בלמידה. ראה קראתי בשם שמחת הרג"ל נוטריקון

הגדה רות ג׳ לימודים

ממני יבאו הדברים שיחת הילדים אני הצעיר חיים יוסף דוד בכמה"רר יצחק אזולאי זלה"ה ס"ט

בליוורנו

בשנת אמרייה לרו"ר שמ"ח צדקה לפ"ג

כדפו׳ השותפי׳ החכם כמוהר"ר אברהם יצחק קאשטילו נר"ו

והמשכיל כמוהר"ר אליעזר סעדון נר"ו

Con Licenza de Superiori

PLATE 77

AMSTERDAM · NETHERLANDS · 1783

So That All May Know What They Are Saying

Shown here is an example of one of several Yiddish translations of the Haggadah that appeared in Amsterdam in the second half of the eighteenth century. It is a Yiddish version of a Haggadah published simultaneously in Hebrew with the same commentaries.

On the title page the translator, Elhanan ben Moses, declares modestly that "such a translation has never been seen before in the world." The motive for his work is set forth explicitly: "I see most people sit at the Seder reciting the text as it is written, only in the holy tongue, so that the common folk, be they man, wife, or children, do not know what they say." However, he continues, the commandment to recite the story of the Exodus from Egypt is so important that it must be rendered intelligible in order to be fulfilled properly.

YAARI NO. 204 HARVARD 23.5:18

הגדה של פסח

אן מערקונג

איינה הגדה אויף אזלכי ארט אין עט
טייטשי · אייזט נימאלהלין
אין דר וועלט גוועזן · עס ברינגט איר דא
צו · היילין איך זעהי דוב עולם ביים דעם **סדר** געבין ·
זאגין זיא נור ווייא עס שטיט אין לשון הקודש · זא עס
גאיינה פאלק עס זייא אמן אודר וייב אויך קינדרן · ניכט וויסן
וואס זיא זאגין · ווייא זאל דיזיט הייסן דיא פר ציהלונג פון
יציאת מצרים איינה זאלכה גרויסה מצוה וועלכי
גאט געבאטן האט · דא איט יוצא צו
זיין · ניין דיזיט הייסט נור אלז ווייא מצות תהלים זאגין ·
זא האט איר גאט אלמעכטיגר קראפט אונד שטארקונג דא צו
געגעבן · אום זאלכי אין שטאנד צו בריקען · גלויבט אייזט
ער · אונד וייטר הין איך איהם ביטה · ער איר העלפן
זאל · דיא אנדרי צווייא טייהלין · זאלכי ברייטס געשריבן
האבי · אויך אין דיא דרוק בקרב ימים צו פר
פערטיגן · דיא גוטי אונד ליבה פרייסן · מיכט
נור צו דענקן · אין **פסח** זאלכי דורך צו זעהין
ווערדן אלזו טאג דארינן צו לעזין ·
עס ווירט איהנין וואהל נור נוצין זיין ·
אויך ביידי עולמות · זא וואהל
אלס דיזה צווייא · אויך
דיא אנדרי צווייא ·
זעהר נוצליך
זיין ווערדן ·

עז זיינין

ארבע יסודות וארבע עמודי עולם

נעהמליך דיזה ·

יסוד היראה יסוד האהבה ·

דיא אנדרי צווייא

יסוד העבודה יסוד הברכה

גהייסן ווערדן :

נדפס

באמשטרדם

בבית ובדפוס

יוהנן לוי רופא וגיסו ברוך ואחיו

בשנת המוב והישר לפ"ק

PRAGUE · BOHEMIA · 1784

Under Joseph II of Austria

A Prague Haggadah of the late eighteenth century with Yiddish translation, "since it is incumbent to recite [the Haggadah] in a language which women and children understand," was printed "under the rule of our mighty and great lord, whose fame is over all the earth, the merciful and generous Emperor Joseph II." The approbation of Leopold Tirsch, the royal censor of Hebrew books, appears in Latin characters.

Although here the question of the vernacular appears to be merely intramural—the traditional practice of translating from the Hebrew in order to facilitate understanding of the sacred text—in this period the linguistic problem was assuming new and serious dimensions for the Jews of Central Europe. Within the Jewish communities the Maskilim, proponents of secular enlightenment among Jews (see Plate 80), were agitating for the abandonment of the various Jewish dialects in favor of German. Parallel forces were independently at work from without, as the state itself began to interfere increasingly in internal Jewish affairs.

Only two years before this Haggadah appeared, Joseph II issued his famous Edict of Toleration (*Toleranzpatent*) for the Jews of the Austrian Empire, which included also Bohemia, Hungary, and even part of northern Italy. Prompted solely by the desire to make the Jews more "useful" to the state by facilitating economic integration and cultural assimilation, the edict was a combination of progressive and regressive legislation characteristic of the enlightened absolutism of the time. In the cultural sphere two clauses were significant. One opened the Christian primary and secondary schools to Jewish youth or, as an alternative, called for the establishing of modern Jewish schools where German and secular subjects would be taught. Another stated:

> Considering the numerous openings in trades, and the manifold contacts with Christians resulting therefrom, the care for maintaining common confidence requires that the Hebrew and the so-called Jewish language [Yiddish] and writing of Hebrew intermixed with German . . . shall be abolished.

While this clause had specific reference to the abolition of Yiddish in business documents and records, it is an instance of a more general tendency to promote the linguistic fusion of the Jews with the rest of the population.

YAARI NO. 210 | HARVARD | 20:15

סדר

הגדה של פסח

כיון שנוהג לאמרה בלשון שמבינים הנשים וקטנים ולפרש להן הענין • על כן הגהנו לשון אשכנז ז"ל הגדה • וגם קצת דיני הכשר כלים • ובדיקת חמץ • ושאיבת מים למצות • בלשון אשכנז וגם דפסנו פירש הרב הגדול **רשב"ץ** זללה"ה • הנקרא אפיקומן ופירש גבורות ה' שחיבר הגאון **מהר"ל מפראג** בכרך בפני עצמו וכל א' יוכל לברוך אותו אצל הגדה והי' לאחדי' בידו :

וזאת לדעת כי בשעת ההדפסה לא הי' בידינו ספר גבורות ה' ולכן הדפסנו הפי' כמו שנמצא בהגדת דפוס מען ואח"כ בא לידינו ס' גבורו' ה' בעצמו וראינו שהם השמיטו ממנו כמה דברי' ובפרט הפירש של הלל לא הדפיסו כלל • לכן הדפסנו אנחנו גם פי' הלל הנ"ל :

ונוסף על זה עמדנו בכל מקום דיני הסדר בלשון הקודש ובלשון אשכנז על פי דין השולחן ערוך מה שלא מצאנו בשום הגדה עד הנה :

נדפס פה פראג

שנת ויגע בבשר **ובמצות** לפ"ק

תחת ממשלת אדונינו האדיר והגדול שמו בכל הארץ • רחמן וחסיד הקיסר **יאזעף** השני • ירום הודו ויתנשא מלכותו לאריכת ימים ושנים אמן :

Vidi Leop. Tirſch Cæſar. Reg. Reviſ. tranſl. & in hebr.

געדרוקט אין דער ערקויפטע באקישען אונ' קאלישען פריוויליגירטע בוך דרוקריין :

PRAGUE · 1784
[CONTINUED]

Seder Instructions

As may be seen from this preliminary page of the Prague Haggadah of 1784, the use of Yiddish was by no means abandoned among Central European Jews even when pressures to do so began to mount. (Actually, except for the occasional presence of Hebrew words, the Yiddish in which the laws of the Seder are given here is not far removed from German itself.)

Below: A crude woodcut of the prophet Elijah and the Messiah approaching Jerusalem.

דיני ערוב תבשילין

בְּדֵין יְהֵא שָׁרֵא לָנָא לַאֲפוּיֵי וּלְבַשּׁוּלֵי וּלְאַטְמוּנֵי וּלְאַדְלוּקֵי שְׁרָגָא וּלְתַקָּנָא וּלְמֶעְבַּד כָּל־צָרְכָנָא מִיּוֹמָא טָבָא לְשַׁבַּתָּא :

ב און דאמיט ניכט · וואן אן גלייך ערוב תבשילין גמאכט האט · פון דאנרשטאג · זאנדרן פון
פרייטאג אויף שבת קאכין :

ג וואן דאש ערוב תבשילין פור שבת אויף גיגעסין אודר גיווארפן איז אזו מאן איין שאלת חכם
מאכין ::

דיני סדר

א אין אזו דען מדר טיש שאהן פון ערב י״ט בייא טאג צו רעכט מאכין · דא מיט אן קידוש מאכין קאן
זא באלד אז נאכט איזט ·· אבר נאכט מבר דארף אן קיין קידוש מאכין :

ב דיא ארבע כוסות אזו אן אן גלעהנט טרינקן אויף אזו אן דיא אלה אן גלעהנט עסין אן אזו אבר
זיך אויף דיא לינקע זייט ·· אונד ניכט אויף דיא רעכטי זייט אן לעהנין וואן ער גלייך פון נאטור
לינק איזט · נאך בעסר איזט וואן אן איבר דיא גאנצי סעודה אן גלעהנט זיצט :

ג אין גהער זיך איהע געבין אזוא בענשין צו קענין אויף גהער דער בעל הבית · זא ערבט בענשין
שנאמר טוב עין הוא יבורך :

ד וואן איינר פרגעסין האט אפיקומן צו עסין אונד האט זיך ערשט ערמאהנט · נאך דעם ער זיך
שאהן דיא הענד צו בענשין געוואשין האט · אדר נור דאש ער שאהן גזאגט האט · ברינגט הער צום
בענשין · זאל ער דען אפיקומן דאך עסין · וואן ער אבר שאהן געבענשט נור עה ער בורא פרי הגפן
גמאכט ערמאהנט ער זיך דאש ער קיין אפיקומן געסין האט · זאל ער זיך גלייך וואשין אונד אפיקומן
מיט ברכה אכילת מצה וכו׳ עסין · אונד הערנאך כסדר ווידר אן פאנגין צו בענשין :

וואן ער אבר זיך נאך בורא פרי הגפן ערשט ערמאנט · וואן ער קיין אלה מאורה האט אודר האט
בתוך הסעודה פון דער אלה מאורה געסין עסט ער קיין אפיקומן מעהר · וואן אבר אלה
מאורה האט אונד האט בתוך הסעודה ניכט פון דער אלה מאורה געסין עסט ער פון דיזער
אפיקומן אונד וועשט זיך דא צו מאכט אכילה · אונד בענשט אודר פון נייען אונד מאכט בורא פרי הגפן
אונד טרינקט דער ייעניגה אבר דער דארף דען יאהר ניכט מקפיד זייט · אונד פאלגט מנהג בכוס
צו בענשין ·· ברויך אויף דיא · יהן קיין כוס :

BERLIN · PRUSSIA · 1785

In the Heyday of the Berlin Haskalah

The Haggadah whose title page is reproduced here contains, in addition to the Hebrew text, what may properly be considered the first real German translation to be published by Jews, even though the German is itself printed in Hebrew characters. The innovation is already hinted at in the phrase used to describe the translation. Whereas those in Judeo-German or Yiddish were generally referred to as *leshon Ashkenaz* (the Ashkenazic or "German" tongue) or some variant thereof, here we encounter the explicit statement that the Hebrew has been *ins Deutsche übersetzt.*

The publication is a typical product of the Haskalah, the militant movement for the acquisition of general culture which arose among German Jews in the eighteenth century and found its most notable exponent in the philosopher Moses Mendelssohn.

It was one of the central tenets of the Haskalah (literally, "Enlightenment") that if the Jews were to enter the mainstream of German and European society they must first learn the German language. The way and the means had already been demonstrated by Mendelssohn himself. He had begun the translation of the Bible into German, a specimen of which appeared in 1778. The entire Pentateuch was completed by some of his disciples and associates in 1783. Since its purpose was pedagogic, the German translation appeared in Hebrew characters, the only alphabet accessible to most German Jews of the time. The same practice was maintained in the Berlin Haggadah of 1785. For thousands of Jews, such translations were to be the portal through which access to the German language would be gained. Once the language had been learned, Hebrew transliterations were discarded.

The translator of the Haggadah was Joel Brill (1760–1802), one of Mendelssohn's followers who had also been involved in the commentaries to the Bible translation. The Hebrew text was edited by Isaac Halevi Satanow (1733–1805), a scholar, poet, and grammarian from Poland who was also an important figure in the Mendelssohnian circle in Berlin. Brill dedicated the Haggadah to Blumchen Friedländer, the wife of yet another leading personality in the Berlin Haskalah, David Friedländer. She was also the daughter of the wealthy banker Daniel Itzig, the head of the Berlin Jewish community.

A final link to the Haskalah may be found in the place of printing. The Jüdische Freischule (Jewish Free School) in Berlin was founded at Mendelssohn's suggestion in 1781 by Friedländer and his brother-in-law Isaac Daniel Itzig. It was the first modern Jewish school in Germany. Attached to it was a bookstore and a Hebrew press, at which a series of important works of Haskalah literature were printed.

YAARI NO. 212 HARVARD 16:9.5

סדר

הגדה על פסח

עם

תרגום אשכנזי

מדויקת היטיב על ידי המדקדק הרבני
מהו' יצחק לבית לוי מסטנאב נ"י

אדר

פארטראג

אויף

דיא ביידן ערשטן אבנדע פסח

אויפס נייע

אינס דייטשע איברזעצט

אונד

מיט אנמערקונגן פרזעהן

פאן

יואל בר"ל

ברלין

ברפוס חברת חנוך נערים

שנת התקמ"ה לפ"ק

Berlin. 1785
Im Verlag der Jüdischen Freyschule

FÜRTH · BAVARIA · 1786

The Aura of Mendelssohn

In 1786 Joel Brill's Haggadah translation (Plate 80) was reprinted in Fürth, though the name of this city does not appear on the title page. Instead, we are told merely that it is "as it was printed in Berlin." Moreover, this time Brill's name is mentioned, not as the translator, but as the commentator. The translation is ascribed to "the sage, Rabbi Moses of Dessau," that is, to Moses Mendelssohn. However, this attribution is patently false. It may be that the revered name of Mendelssohn was invoked in an effort to enhance the prestige of the Haggadah and increase its sales.

VARIANT OF YAARI NO. 114 HARVARD 20:16

סדר

הגדה על פסח

עם

תרגום אשכנזי

מדויקת היטב על ידי המדקדק הרבני מהו׳ יצחק לבית הלוי מסטנאב נ״יו

אדר

פֿארטראג

אויף

די בײדן ערשטן אבענדע פסח

אויפֿס נײע

אינס דײטשע איבערזעצט

פֿאן

החכם ר׳ משה דעסויא

אונד

מיט אנמערקונגן פֿרזעהן

11336

פֿאן

יואל בריל

בבית ובדפוס המשובח כהר״ר איצק יל״ו: בן המנוח כהר״ר ליב ז״ל:

בשנת שנדפס

בברלין

בשנת ואמרתם זבח פסח הוא לה׳ לפ״ק:

NOWY DWÓR · POLAND · 1790

Prelude to the Warsaw Press

Although such Polish cities as Cracow and Lublin boasted Hebrew presses as early as the sixteenth century, printing did not begin in Warsaw until the very end of the eighteenth century. Indeed, up to that time the Jews were themselves largely excluded from permanent residence in the capital.

In 1780 the king of Poland granted a thirty-year privilege to a Christian printer of Warsaw, Peter Defour, permitting him to print Hebrew books. The royal interest in the matter was to insure that the considerable sums that Polish Jews spent on the purchase of books from abroad would remain at home.

Defour, however, found himself unable to embark on such grandiose printing projects as the king seemed to envision. Accordingly, he sold the royal privilege to a wealthy Polish merchant, Johann Anton Krüger. Throughout these negotiations Jews, whose vital interest was at stake, were also involved. Krüger decided that since he would have to employ Jews in the actual work of printing, it would be impractical to establish his press in the city of Warsaw. Instead, he chose Nowy Dwór (Neuhof), one of the nearby towns. The first Hebrew book appeared there in 1781.

The Haggadah shown here was printed almost a decade later, in 1790. As in other Nowy Dwór imprints, it carries as its emblem Krüger's monogram (JAK). The text of the Haggadah is accompanied by Abravanel's commentary, as well as a Yiddish translation "for women and children." The whole was printed "under the rule of the mighty and gracious duke Stanislaw Poniatowsky" (i.e., Stanislas August Poniatowsky, the last king of Poland).

More than one hundred Hebrew books were published in Nowy Dwór within a relatively short period. In 1795 what was left of the independent kingdom of Poland came to an end as a result of its final partition among the neighboring powers. Warsaw and its provinces now fell to the king of Prussia. In that very year Hebrew printing began in Warsaw itself.

YAARI NO. 228 JTSA 33:19

סדר

הגדה

של פסח

עם פירוש המכונה אברבנאל וגם בלשון אשכנז לאנשים ולקטנים

כאשר מלפנים היו בישראל שנדפס מימי קדם :

ולא נותרת בבת ציון כי אם אחד בעיר ושנים במשפחה מכל וכל :

ועתה נסתבה הדבר למעליותא וגדול כבוד האחרון מן הראשון שנתקנו מכל טעות וקלקול
ונדפסו באותיות גדולות בכתב של המחזורים וביופי הנייר כאשר עיני כל חוזים במישרים :

בנאווי דוואהר

תחת ממשלת הדוכס האדיר והחסיד סטאניסלוב פאניטאווסקי גרויש שאץ מייסטר פון
ליטווא אונד שעף פון דער קרוין נארדע

אין דער פרעווילגירטי דרוקריי פון יאהן אנטאן קריגר

Nro. 41

לפרט יבין ואמיתם זבח פסח

Neuhof bey Warschau, 1791.

Gedruckt in der Koenigl, und der Republique privil, Druckerey Jüdischer Bücher
von
JOHANN ANTHON KRÜGER.

KARLSRUHE · GERMANY · 1791

In Praise of the Ruler

A fairly typical German Haggadah of the late eighteenth century, in Hebrew and Yiddish, this one has some special features. It is the first Haggadah to be printed in Karlsruhe, capital of the Grand Duchy of Baden, "under the rule of our lord the noble and praiseworthy Karl Friedrich, Margrave of Baden . . . may the Lord exalt his glory and may sovereignty be uplifted for him and for his descendants, and may He lengthen their days and years in goodness and pleasantness. Amen."

Similarly effusive praises of rulers may be found in many other Haggadahs and in Hebrew books generally, for elementary diplomacy dictated that he who held power over Jews be lauded, regardless of his merits. In this instance, however, it would seem that the praises were not a mere cliché. In 1783 the margrave Karl Friedrich had issued a decree granting the Jews of Baden permission to settle wherever they wished and freeing them from the *Todfall* tax, which formerly had to be paid to the Christian clergy after every Jewish burial. At the time, special commemorative prayers were composed by the rabbi of Karlsruhe, Yedidiah Tiah Weill, who is also the author of the Haggadah commentary included in this edition.

YAARI NO. 238 HARVARD 23:17

הגדה
של פסח
עם ביאור חדש המרבה לספר

בדברים פשוטים · ולפעמים אף רמזים ודרש ידועות בו נקרטים · עם היות בכמות המה מעוטים · עם כל זה באיכות מרובים וכפרטים · ובתחותם עיני כל משוטטים · והרבה ענינים ממדרשים לקוטים · בעדות חוקים ומשפטים · להסביר לבני ביתו בכללות ופרטים · ולזכיהם לשמוע כותים · ועל לוח לבם חרוטים · בדברים מקושטים · ובזה יובן המרבה לספר בפסחים · הרי זה משובח · ויזכו השומעים לפסחי הנשקטים :

תחת ממשלת אדונינו הדוכס המיוחס המהולל

קאריל פרידריך

מארק גראף צו באדין אונד הויך בעריג השם ירום הודו ויתנשא ארנונתיו לו וגם לזרעותיו ויאריך להם ימיהם ושנותיהם בטוב ובנעימים אמן :

בשנת תקנ"א לפ"ק

בבית ובדפוס המטובה אהו' פילטא בן כהרר משה עפשטיין סג"ל
וגיסו פאר הירש בן כאר משה ווירמייש ז"ל בק"ק

קארלסרוא

OFFENBACH · GERMANY · 1795

An Eighteenth-Century Seder

A reprint of the Haggadah with Joel Brill's German translation in Hebrew characters (see Plates 80–81).

On the title page a stag appears, the printer's emblem of Zebi Hirsch Segal Spitz and his son Abraham. (*Zebi*, in Hebrew, and *Hirsch*, in German, both mean literally "a stag.")

The illustration of the Seder, which is printed in the middle of the Haggadah, is of interest. The members of the family are dressed in eighteenth-century fashion, and the entire scene has a contemporary flavor.

This Haggadah is one of several issues, with minor variations, that were printed in Offenbach in 1795.

VARIANT OF YAARI NO. 265 HARVARD 17:10.5

הגדה של פסח

אויפֿ נייא

אינס דייטש איבערזעצט

אונד

מיט ניטצליכען אנמערקונגן

פערזעהן ·

אפענבאך

HARVARD COLLEGE LIBRARY
GIFT OF
LUCIUS N. LITTAUER
1930

יאכלהו :

מאַן טהוט הלל צו ליט־דאַ דער טעאפעז דעם הייליגטהואם נאָך שטאַנד , ער מוואיקלטע אונגעזייארטען קוכען איט ביטטרע קרייטער אונד מס ביידעס צוזאַמאען· אום צו ערפילזען , וואַז געטריבען שטעהט , איט אונגעזייארטעם קוכען אונד ביטטערן קרייטערן זאָלן מאַן עס עסען : דיא טיטזייטע געניסען דיזעם אויך גלייכערווייסע · וואָרויף נאָך גפּאַזזן געגעסען אונד געטרונקען ווירד :

שלחן עורך :

דיא טיטזייטע געניסען דיזעם אויך גלייכערווייסע · וואָרויף נאָך גפּאַזזן געגעסען אונד געטרונקען ווירד :

צפון :

וען מאַן צו עסען פעזזיג אויפגעהערט · זאָ ניממט דער הויזהערר דיא האַזבע (אזוה) דיא ער בייא׳ם אנפאַנגע (נאָך קידוש) וועג געזעגט האַט , מיסט דמפאָן צו (אפיקואן) , אונד טהיילט איך דען איבריגען טיט זייטען דהאַפאָן איט :

ברך :

וען דאַז געטעהן איזט , טענקט מאַן דען דריטטן בעכר איין אונד שפּריכט איבער דעאזעזבען דען געוועהנליכען טישזעגען , וויא פאָלגט .

LONDON · ENGLAND · 1813

For British Sephardim

This, the only Spanish translation of the Haggadah to be printed in London, is also an example of the survival into the nineteenth century of the Spanish language among the Sephardic Jews of England.

The text is in Hebrew and Spanish. Also included are three biblical maps and various engravings on separate sheets. These were taken from a London Haggadah of 1806 printed by Levi Alexander, which derived from contemporary non-Jewish archaeological and geographic works.

YAARI NO. 381 HARVARD 24:19

ORDEN DE LA

AGADA DE PESAH,

EN HEBRAICO Y ESPAÑOL,

SEGUN UZAN LOS

JUDIOS, ESPANOLES, Y PORTUGUEZES,

TRADUCIDO DEL HEBRAICO Y CALDEO.

Por Senior JACOB MELDULA, de Amsterdam.

London:
PRINTED BY L. ALEXANDER, WHITECHAPEL-ROAD
A.M. 5573.

BASEL · SWITZERLAND · 1816

Handsome—but Derivative

In an age of general decline in the art of the Hebrew book, the Basel Haggadah of 1816 commands attention as one of the more attractive editions published in the nineteenth century. Textually, it is a reprint of Joel Brill's German translation in Hebrew characters which first appeared in 1785 (Plate 80). Printed at the Basel press of Wilhelm Haas, and corrected by the Jew Solomon Coschelsberg, the Haggadah contains twenty-four pleasing and well-executed woodcuts. These, however, are not original. They were copied from Friedrich Battier's illustrations to a German Bible published in Basel in 1710 by Johann Brandmüller, Jr. The woodcut of Moses at the Burning Bush shown here on the title page, was taken from the frontispiece of the Amsterdam Haggadah of 1712 (Plate 66).

YAARI NO. 399 HARVARD 21.5:17

סדר

חגדה של פסח

עם

תרגום אשכנזי

פֿאָרטראַג אויף דיאביידען ערסטען אַבענדע פסח,
אינס דייטשע איבערזעצט אונד מיט אַנמערקונגען פֿערזעהען:

באָסעל

בדפוס ווילהעלם האאס

ע"י ר' שלמה קאשילזבערג ·

בשנת תקע"ו לפ"ק

BASEL · 1816
[CONTINUED]

The Spies Return from Canaan

The text on this page is the *Kiddush* over the fourth cup of wine at the Seder, in Hebrew (above) and German (below). Since the Lord is blessed for having created "the fruit of the vine," the woodcut chosen from the Basel Bible of 1710 is related, albeit somewhat indirectly, to this theme. It shows the spies, who were sent from the wilderness of Sinai to report on the Land of Canaan, as they return from there with a cluster of grapes borne on a pole (Numbers 13:23).

לְשָׁנָה הַבָּאָה בִּירוּשָׁלָיִם

בָּרוּךְ אַתָּה יְיָ אֱלֹהֵינוּ מֶלֶךְ הָעוֹלָם בּוֹרֵא פְּרִי הַגָּפֶן׃

מאן טרינקט, אונד מאכט הערנאך דיזע ברכה: (זעגענשפרוך נאך דעם גענוסע דעס וויינס.)

בָּרוּךְ אַתָּה יְיָ אֱלֹהֵינוּ מֶלֶךְ הָעוֹלָם. עַל־הַגֶּפֶן וְעַל פְּרִי הַגֶּפֶן
וְעַל תְּנוּבַת הַשָּׂדֶה וְעַל אֶרֶץ חֶמְדָּה טוֹבָה וּרְחָבָה שֶׁרָצִיתָ
וְהִנְחַלְתָּ לַאֲבוֹתֵינוּ לֶאֱכוֹל מִפִּרְיָהּ וְלִשְׂבּוֹעַ מִטּוּבָהּ. רַחֵם יְיָ
אֱלֹהֵינוּ עַל יִשְׂרָאֵל עַמֶּךָ. וְעַל יְרוּשָׁלַיִם עִירֶךָ. וְעַל צִיּוֹן מִשְׁכַּן כְּבוֹדֶךָ
וְעַל מִזְבְּחֶךָ. וְעַל הֵיכָלֶךָ וּבְנֵה יְרוּשָׁלַיִם עִיר קָדְשֶׁךָ בִּמְהֵרָה בְיָמֵינוּ.
וְהַעֲלֵנוּ בְּתוֹכָהּ. וְשַׂמְּחֵנוּ בְּבִנְיָנָהּ. בְּיוֹם השבת הזה וביום חַג הַמַּצּוֹת הַזֶּה.

ברוך געלאבט זייאסט דוא עוויגער! אונזער גאטט! הערר דער וועלט! דער דוא דיא פרוכט דעס וויינשטאקס ערשאפען:
(יעדער ישראל מוס, וואוואהל פֿאר, אלס נאך דעם גענוסע יעדער שפייזע, גאטט פיר דעססען גיטע דאנקען:)

ברוך געלאבט זייאסט דוא עוויגער! אונזער גאטט! הערר דער וועלט! פיר דען וויינשטאק, אונד דיא פרוכט דעס וויינשטאקס,
וויא פיר אללע ניבליכען פריכטע דעס פעלדעס, אונד פיר דאס אנגענעהמליכע, גוטע אונד וויטפערברייטעטע לאנד,
דאס דיר געפאללען האט, אונזערן פֿארעלטערן צום ערבטהייל איינצוגעבען. אונד זיא געגעססען פֿאן דיינען פריכטען,
אונד געזעטטיגט זיך פֿאן דיינעם גוטע. א ערבארמע דיך, עוויגער! אונזער גאטט! איבער ישראל דיין פֿאלק.
איבער ירושלים דיינע ערוואהלטע שטאדט. איבער ציון דיינע הערליכקייט. איבער דיינען אלטאר. אונד ערבויא
באלד אונד אין אונזערן טאגען נאך, דיינע הייליגע שטאדט ירושלים. דוא ברינגעסט אונס אלסדאן נו איהר היין, דאס
וויר אונס אין איהר אום יע מעהר פֿרייען, איבער איינען זאלכען (שבת אונד) פעסטטאג דעס אונגעזייערטען קוכענס.
יא דוא ביסט, עוויגער! איין גיטיגער גאטט! דער אללען וואהל טהוט. דארום דאנקען וויר דיר, פיר דאס לאנד, וויא

OSTROG · RUSSIA · 1819

The Illustrated Haggadah in Eastern Europe

Title page of the first Haggadah published in Eastern Europe with illustrations. It was printed in Ostrog in the government of Volhynia "under the rule of our lord . . . Emperor Alexander Pavlovitch [Tsar Alexander I] . . . with the permission of the royal censor of Vilna," and included several commentaries. In the original, the large words *Haggadah* and *Ostroha* (Ostrog) are printed in red.

The illustrations are all copied from the Amsterdam Haggadah, now redrawn as woodcuts.

YAARI NO. 419 JTSA 24:19

סדר

הגדה

של פסח

עם פירושים גדולים מפלגים עטרת עולם: ה"ה מהר"ם אלשיך: גבורות ה' עוללות אפרים:

ופי'

אברבנאל: על הברוז א רוב נסים: ואומץ גבורתך: ופי' על חד גדיא: ודיני בדיקת חמץ ודיני תענית בכורות: ודיני לישת מצות: ודיני הגעלה: ודיני סדר של פסח:

והכל באותיות גדולות ויפות בפנים ובר"ש"י: ובציורים נאים והדורים:

תחת ממשלת אדונינו הקיסר אוסע
פרסוויטליווסי דערזאווניסי
האסידאר אימפיראטר
אלכסנדר פאוולאוויטש
סאמאדערזיטס אוס' ראסיסקי האסידאר
ואוסע מילעסטיוויש יזוס הודו:

גדרוקט אין אוסטרוג אין וואליניען
גיבערמנט מיט באוויליגונג
איינר הערכבט פעררענטן קייזערליכן
צענז' אין ווילנא:
ע"פ רשיון הצענזור מן יום ז' סעפטעמבער
למספרם אלף תת"ו

באוסטרהא

בשנת לשנה הבאה בירושלים לפ"ק

OSTROG · 1819
[CONTINUED]
Departure from Egypt

The woodcut bears the biblical verse: "And the children of Israel journeyed from Rameses to Succoth, about six hundred thousand men on foot, beside children" (Exodus 12:37). To the right of the Hebrew text above is the commentary of the MaHaRaL of Prague; to the right, the commentary attributed to Moses Alshekh.

In another issue of the Ostrog Haggadah printed in the same year, the commentary of the Gaon Elijah of Vilna is included.

למדרש ועברתי ולא מלאך והכיתי ולא שרף ובכל אלקי מצרים אעשה שפטים אני ולא השליח :

והנה אומר באותות זה המטה ובמופתים זה הדם וביאר הדבר הזה בענין אות ומופ׳ דכתיב בקרא ונתן לך אות או מופת ובספרי בפרש׳ ראה ונתן לך אות בשמי׳ וכן הוא אומ׳ והיו לאותות ולמועדי׳ או מופת בארץ וכן הוא אומה אם יהי׳ טל על הגיזה לבדה ועל הארץ חורב : ויעש ה׳ כן בליל׳ ההוא וגומר ולפי זה קשיא מה שאמר כאן באותו׳ זה המט׳ אע״ג דאין זה אות בשמי׳ אבל יש לך לדעת כי כל שנוי אשר נראה בפועל נקרא אות כגון שיאמ׳ הנה הפועל הזה יפעול כך וכך וזה נקרא אות והשנוי אשר הוא במתפעל שיאמ׳ כי דבר זה מתפעל כך וכך וזה נקרא מופת ומפני זה אמרו חכמים ז״ל כי אות בשמים ומופתים בארץ ופירוש כי השמים הם פועלים ואינם מתפעלי׳ והארץ מתפעלת ואינה פועלת וכאשר יתן אות בשמים שהיו

אֶלָּא הַקָּדוֹשׁ בָּרוּךְ הוּא בִּכְבוֹדוֹ וּבְעַצְמוֹ שֶׁנֶּאֱמַר וְעָבַרְתִּי בְאֶרֶץ מִצְרַיִם בַּלַּיְלָה הַזֶּה וְהִכֵּיתִי כָל בְּכוֹר בְּאֶרֶץ מִצְרַיִם מֵאָדָם וְעַד בְּהֵמָה וּבְכָל אֱלֹהֵי מִצְרַיִם אֶעֱשֶׂה שְׁפָטִים אֲנִי יְיָ :

ועברתי

השמותם מהעבודה זרה שעבדו וזהו אשר יפלה ה׳ וכו׳ והוראה לזה היה מה שלא הרץ לאיש כלב את לשונו כמדובר ונבוא אל הענין והוא כי הנה הוקש׳ להם דכתוב שהיה ראוי יאמר ועברתי בארץ מצרי׳ והכתי כל בכור בלילה הזה מאד׳ וכו׳ ולמה הפסיק באומר בלילה הזה בין העבר׳ וההכא׳ ואמר בכל אחד בארץ מצרים : לך הוא שכל אחד ענין בפני עצמו וגם למה סמך לזה ענין שפטים שעש׳ באלהי מצרי׳ ועוד למה חזר ואמר אני ה׳ : על כן אמרו כי ג׳ עניינים הם א׳ מה שהפל׳ ה׳ בין מצרים וכו׳ שמתחבר ומתלו׳ שוא יתברך אל בנין לבל יאחזום כחות חיצונים בעידן ריתחא וילקו גם הם וזהו ועברתי בארץ מצרים בלילה הזה עוד חלוק׳ ב׳ היא הכא׳ האנשי׳ ג׳ הכאת אלהי מצרי׳ והנה ידו׳ כי כל מלאך שהם האמור בתורה הוא שר הפני׳ מט״ט ששמו כשם רבו כמז״ל על פסוק הנה אנכי שולח מלאך לפניך וכו׳ וכאומר הנה מלאכי ילך וכו׳ והנה היה הדעת

ויסעו בני ישראל מרעמסס סכתה כשש מאות אלף רגלי הגברים לבד מטף

BERLIN · PRUSSIA · 1830

A Missionary "Haggadah"

The work entitled *Gufo shel Pesaḥ, o Haggadat Pesaḥ le-tinokot Yisrael* ("The Essence of Passover; or, A Passover Haggadah for Jewish Children") is actually a Yiddish tract that aims at the conversion of Jewish youth to Christianity. Though anonymous, there is ample evidence that it was written by a Jewish apostate. It is probably the only piece of Christian missionary literature to utilize the theme of the Passover Haggadah as a springboard for its message.

On three nights of the Passover holiday a pious Jew and his son discuss the meaning of the paschal sacrifice. Though elaborated in a convoluted fashion, the core of the argument is fairly simple. It is stated in the Bible that the sacrifice of the paschal lamb is a statute to be observed for all generations. Why, then, do the Jews no longer fulfill it? Indeed, why has it ceased since ancient times? By implication and innuendo (though never explicitly) one is led toward the possibility that the biblical sacrifice has been superseded by that of Jesus.

The hallmark of the tract is its relatively muted approach. Christianity is rarely mentioned, and Judaism is presented, not as ignorant or vicious, but as radically problematic. The Christian conclusion is hinted at obliquely, but not stated. In effect, the "Haggadah" poses as a Jewish work.

The title page, reproduced here, is in Hebrew and Yiddish. This is, we are told, the Haggadah "which the preacher Reb Shelomo bar Menahem recited and explained to his children on three nights of Passover . . . in order to teach them the correct meaning of the Passover sacrifice . . . and he published this work in order to arouse the hearts of Jewish children to seek the paths of salvation, and to walk in the path of life."

The date is recorded in Jewish fashion by a biblical verse: "In the year *That gathereth the lambs in his arms, and carrieth them in his bosom*" (Isaiah 40:11).

HARVARD 21:12.5

גופו של פסח

או

הגדת - פסח
לתינוקות ישראל

שהיה מגיד אותה ומפרש ר״ שלמה ב״ר מנחם הדרשן לילדיו בשלשה לילות של פסח, דהיינו בליל השמורים אחרי סדרי ההסיבה ללמד אותם את תוכן כונת מלות קרבן-הפסח כראוי, והוסיף לפרש ולברר את הענין הזה בליל שביעי של פסח מכל צד וצד: והוציא לאור את החובר הזה, לעורר את לב ילדי ישראל לדרוש דרכי ישועה, ולהלך בנתיבות החיים:

בשלשה אופנים: או חלקים:

וויא ר״ שלמה ב״ר מנחם הדרשן האט ערציילט אונד מפרש גיוועזין זיינע קינדער נאך דיא סדרים פון ביידע נעכט פון פסח דיא כונות פון מלות קרבן-פסח, וויא עס גיהערט צו זיין: אונד אין שביעי של פסח, האט ער זיא נאך ווייטער גילערינט אונד מבאר גיוועזין, דיא גאנצע הנהגה פון דעם, וויא איר האלטין הייסט דען יו״ט פסח: אונד האט דיזען פרט מחבר גיוועזין, בכדי אויך צו וועקין דיא הערצען פון דיא קינדער ישראל, זייא זאלין זוכין דען וועג פון דער תשועה אונד זאלין גיין אויף דעם דרך החיים ·

אויף דרייא אפנים:

והיה כי יאמרו אליכם בניכם מה העבודה הזאת לכם: ואמרתם זבח-פסח ליי, אשר פסח על בתי בני ישראל במצרים בנגפו את מצרים ואת בתינו הציל:

סדרה בא: פרשה: ה״: פ׳: כו, כז:

נדפס

בשנת: בזרעו יקבץ טלאים ובחיקו ישא עלות ינהל:

LEGHORN · ITALY · 1837

The Posthumous Influence of Venice

At the end of the eighteenth century the Hebrew presses of Venice ceased to exist. Venice was now entirely replaced as a center of printing by Leghorn (Livorno), which had already been competing with it for more than a hundred years. In the nineteenth and twentieth centuries Leghorn was the chief supplier of Hebrew books to other Italian communities, and especially to those of the Near East.

The Livornese Hebrew printers created their own styles, and their title pages and typography are often readily distinguishable from others. In their Haggadahs, however, they created no new iconography of their own. They were content to copy the woodcuts of the Venetian editions of 1609 and 1629, and their subsequent reprints. Thus through Leghorn the Venetian illustrations achieved an unexpected immortality.

In the page reproduced here from the Leghorn Haggadah of 1837, both woodcuts are Venetian (as, indeed, are all the rest), but the format and layout are completely different.

Above: "And the children of Israel were fruitful, and increased abundantly, and multiplied" (Exodus 1:7).

Below: A continuation of the same theme, with reference to the verse: "I cause thee to increase, even as the growth of the field" (Ezekiel 16:7).

The text of the Haggadah is in Hebrew, with Ladino translation.

YAARI NO. 560 HARVARD 21:15

לְגוֹי גָּדוֹל וְעָצוּם כְּמוֹ שֶׁנֶּאֱמַר וּבְנֵי יִשְׂרָאֵל פָּרוּ וַיִּשְׁרְצוּ וַיִּרְבּוּ וַיַּעַצְמוּ בִּמְאֹד מְאֹד וַתִּמָּלֵא הָאָרֶץ אֹתָם׃

וָרָב כְּמָה שֶׁנֶּאֱמַר רְבָבָה כְּצֶמַח הַשָּׂדֶה נְתַתִּיךְ ותרבי

אליי פור גינטי גראנדי אי פואידטי · קומו דיזי איל פסוק אי איגוש די ישראל פרוגיגוארון אי מונייגוארונסי אי אינפורטיסייארונסי אין לו מוגו מוגו אי אינגוסי לה טיירה די אילייוש ׃ ורב אי מגו קומו דיזי איל פסוק מילאריא קומו אירמוליוו דיל קאמפו טי די

דינוטה קי מוגיגואבאן אין קאנטיראד ׃ אי קומו אירמוליוו די איל קאמפו פלוריסיאן ׃

אי

LEGHORN · 1837
[CONTINUED]
Pharaoh Bathing in the Blood of Infants

Reproduced here is an illustration that originally appeared in the Venetian Haggadahs, based on rabbinic legend. The Midrash relates that Pharaoh was afflicted with leprosy. Upon the advice of his counselors, he decided that the only remedy was to bathe in the blood of Israelite infants. The scene is graphically depicted in the large woodcut at the bottom of the page.

A woodcut of Pharaoh washing himself in blood while sitting in a tub already appeared in the Prague Haggadah of 1526 (see below).

The figure in the large initial letter printed in the upper right corner of the page is that of Moses, raising his wonder-working rod (Exodus 4:17). It was taken over from the Venetian Haggadahs.

Prague, 1526

באותות זה המטה כמה שנאמר ואת המטה הזה תקח בידך אשר תעשה בו את האתות: ובמופתים זה הדם כמה שנאמר ונתתי מופתים בשמים ובארץ דם ואש ותמרות עשן: דבר אחר ביד חזקה שתים ובזרוע נטויה שתים ובמורא גדול שתים ובאותות שתים ובמופתים שתים: אלו עשר מכות שהביא הקדוש ברוך הוא על המצריים במצרים ואלו הן:

דם

באותות אי קון שינייאליש אישטה לה וארה קומו דיזי איל פסוק אי ארה לה וארה לה אישטה טומאראש אין טו מאנו קי פאראש קון אילייה אה לאס סינייאליס:

אי קון מארא בילייאש אישטה לה סאנגרי קומו דיזי איל פסוק אי דארי מאראבילייאש אין לוש סיילוס אי אין לה טיירה סאנגרי אי פואיגו אי אטאמאראליש די אומו: דיקלארו אוטרו קון פודיר פואירטי דוש אי קון בראסו טינדידו דוש אי קון טימורידאר גראנדי דוש אי קון סינייאליס דוש אי קון מאראבילייאש דוש:

אלו אישטאש דיי׳ז פירידאש קי טרושו איל שאנטו בינדיגו איל שוברי לוש איג׳יפסייאנוס אין איג׳פטו אי אישטאש אילייאש:

פרעה קי שי לאבאבה אין לה סאנגרי די לוש ג׳יג׳ייוש פור סאנאר די לה סארנה:

NEW YORK · U.S.A. · 1837

The First American Haggadah

The Hebrew and English title pages of a bilingual Haggadah published in New York City in 1837, the first Haggadah ever to appear in the United States. Intended for the use of both Sephardic and Ashkenazic Jews, it was a reprint of an English translation by David Levi first published in London in 1794, and again in 1808 and 1831.

On the Hebrew title page the date is given as "in the year *Next year in Jerusalem*!"

YAARI NO. 562 HARVARD 16:10

Lavinia Phillips

סדר הגדה של פסח ׃

מתורגם מלשון הקודש ללשון ענגלאטירא

אשר כבר הובאה לדפוס

על ידי

המדקדק התורני כהרר דוד ב״ר מרדכי הלוי ז״ל ׃

בלונדן

ועתה הובאה לדפוס

על ידי

הצעיר שלמה בן צבי הירש ׃

נוא-יארק ׃

שנת

לשנה הבא בירושלים לפק ׃

SERVICE

FOR

THE TWO FIRST NIGHTS

OF THE

PASSOVER,

IN HEBREW AND ENGLISH:

ACCORDING TO THE

CUSTOM OF THE GERMAN & SPANISH JEWS.

TRANSLATED INTO ENGLISH BY THE LATE DAVID LEVI,

OF LONDON.

FIRST AMERICAN EDITION.

NEW-YORK.

PRINTED AND PUBLISHED BY S. H. JACKSON,

5597.

HARVARD UNIVERSITY LIBRARY

PLATE 94

COLOGNE · GERMANY · 1838

With Music by Offenbach, Père

A lithographed frontispiece for the Hebrew-German Haggadah published in Cologne in 1838. The special interest of this edition lies in its musical appendix, giving the score for some of the songs and hymns. These are described as "the old music which has come down to us through tradition, and some newly composed melodies."

The composer-arranger was Isaac Offenbach (1779–1850), born Isaac ben Judah in the town whose name he later adopted officially as his own. (During his youth he had been an itinerant musician and cantor, and on his travels people tended to call him "der Offenbacher.") Settling finally in Cologne in 1816, he became cantor of the community a decade later.

In his German preface, Offenbach makes some significant remarks concerning the translation:

> That, above all, a translation of Hebrew prayers and rituals into the German language and script has become a necessity for Jews, has already been learned from experience. . . . The so-called Judeo-German script is now understood by few, and the Hebrew only by a relatively meager number of our brothers, in a manner sufficient to enable the splendid prayers to fulfill their purpose—the lifting of the spirit to God. Unfortunately, worship, along with all other religious practices, has thereby become a formality. . . . We must vigorously strive to reform, not our religion, but its outer garb.

Isaac Offenbach and his wife had nine children, the seventh of whom was called Jacob. This son of the cantor of Cologne was to achieve, on the stages of Paris, a fame that the synagogue could not vouchsafe. He was Jacques Offenbach, the composer of such works as *Orpheus in the Underworld*, *La Vie Parisienne*, and *Tales of Hoffmann*.

YAARI NO. 578 HARVARD 20:13

הגדה
oder
ERZÄHLUNG
von
Israels Auszug
aus
AEGYPTEN
zum Gebrauche bei der im
Familienkreise stattfindenden
FEIERLICHKEIT
an den beiden ersten Abenden des
MATZOTH-FESTES
NEU BEARBEITET
Nebst einem Anhange zur Erklärung
fremder Ausdrücke und mit Musik-
-beilagen der alten durch Tradition
auf uns gekommenen und einigen
neu componirten Melodien
Moses.
Aaron
Salomon
David
von
J. OFFENBACH
Cantor der israelitischen Gemeinde
in CÖLN a. R.
1838
in Comiſsion bei Renard & Dubyen
Entw. u. lith.
von D. Levy Elkan
Gedr. bei
D. Levy Elkan

LONDON · ENGLAND · 1840

The Haggadah of the London Times

One of the most notorious outbreaks of the blood libel in modern times erupted in Damascus, Syria, in February 1840. With the connivance of the pasha and the French consul, a group of Jews were thrown into prison and accused of having murdered a Franciscan friar for ritual purposes. The news spread rapidly throughout the world, and while diplomatic and rescue efforts were being launched the "Damascus Affair" was everywhere discussed and argued. As might be expected, the *Times* of London gave the developing story extensive coverage, printed letters upholding or condemning the charge, and devoted several editorials of its own to the topic.

On August 17, 1840, the *Times* went further. On page 3 of the issue of that day it printed an English translation of the Passover Haggadah, complete except for some of the songs and hymns at the end. It was an obvious attempt to submit further evidence of the absurdity of the charge that Jews require Christian blood for the Passover ritual. Coincidentally, the *Times* also editorialized favorably on prospects for the restoration of the Jews to Palestine (for quotations and details, see the Introduction to this volume).

Of the Jews who had been imprisoned and tortured, one died and another accepted conversion to Islam in order to avoid further suffering. The rest were freed at the end of August, largely as a result of Sir Moses Montefiore's journey to the Near East in order to intercede personally in their behalf.

BOSTON ATHENÆUM

THE TIMES, MONDAY, AUGUST 17, 1840.

CELEBRATION OF THE PASSOVER BY THE JEWS.

A correspondent has furnished the annexed very minute account of this ceremony, which will be exceedingly curious in itself to most of our readers, and has at the same time an evident bearing on the Damascus case. It repels strongly the barbarous notion that human blood, or blood of any kind, is essential to its celebration:—

On the evening preceding the 14th day of the month of Nissan, immediately after the evening service, prior to entering on any occupation whatsoever, it is requisite for the master of every family to search after leavened bread in every place and apartment where leaven is usually kept, gathering all the leaven lying in his way. Before he begins the search he says the following:—

"Blessed art thou, O Lord our God, King of the universe, who hast sanctified us with thy commandments, and commanded us to remove the leaven."

He is not allowed to speak between the blessing and making the search, nor yet during the search; after he has done he secures the pieces of leaven which he has gathered and says—

"All manner of leaven that is in my possession which I have not seen nor removed shall be null, and accounted as the dust of the earth."

On the 14th day, after the 4th hour, about 10 o'clock in the morning, all manner of leaven must be removed, and that which was gathered the previous evening must be burnt.

On the first two nights the table of every family is decorated thus: the table-cloth being laid as usual, three plates are placed thereon; in one is put three passover cakes; in another the shank-bone of the shoulder of lamb (which is in commemoration of the Paschal lamb) and an egg, both roasted on the coals, the egg to commemorate the offering of the festival; in the third plate is put some lettuce and celery, or chervil and parsley, and a cup of vinegar or salt and water; some take the top of horseradish, which is in commemoration of the Egyptians making the lives of our ancestors bitter, likewise a compound formed of almonds and apples worked up to the consistency of lime, in memory of the bricks and water on which they laboured in Egypt. The table being thus formed, every one at table has a glass, or cup of wine placed before them, and during the night has the glass or cup filled four times. On these nights it is customary to allow even the meanest Hebrew servant to sit at the table during the ceremony; considering, as they were all equally alike in bondage, it is proper that they all return thanks to their God for their redemption.

On their return from synagogue the master of the house says the sanctification of the passover; they then drink the wine of the sanctification, leaning on the left side, after which they wash their hands; the master of the house then takes some parsley or chervil, and dips it into the vinegar or salt water, and distributing some to every one at table, and before they eat it, says the following grace:—

"Blessed art thou, O Lord, our God, King of the universe, Creator of the fruit of the earth." The master then breaks the middle cake in the dish, and, leaving one half of it there, he lays the other half by for the *aphicomin*, which is nothing more nor less than a piece of the Passover cake, and it is that which it is said human blood forms a portion of. He then takes the bone of the lamb and egg off the dish, and all at table lay hold of the dish and say,

"Lo, this is as the bread of affliction, which our ancestors ate in the land of Egypt, let all who are hungry, enter and eat thereof, and all who are necessitous come and celebrate the Passover. At present we celebrate it here, but the next year we hope to celebrate it in the land of Israel. This year we are servants here, but next year we hope to be freemen in the land of Israel."

They then fill the cup with wine a second time, when the youngest in company asks—

"Wherefore is this night distinguished from all other nights? On all other nights we may eat eat either leavened or unleavened bread, but on this night only unleavened bread; on all other nights we may eat any species of herbs, but on this night only bitter herbs; on all other nights we do not dip* even once, but on this night twice; on all other nights

"Rabbi Jose, the Galilean, saith, from whence art thou authorized to assert that the Egyptians were afflicted with 10 plagues in Egypt, and upon the sea they were smitten with 50 plagues? To which he answers, in Egypt it says, and the magician said unto Pharoah this is the finger of God; but at the sea it says, and Israel saw the mighty hand wherewith the Lord smote the Egyptians, and the people feared the Lord, and believed in the Lord and His servant Moses.

"Now, Rabbi Jose argues thus:—If by the finger only smitten with 10 plagues, hence it is deducible that in Egypt they were smitten with 10 plagues, and at sea they were smitten with 50 plagues. (This is founded on this argument:—In Egypt, they said this is the finger of God, but at sea it is said, "And they saw the mighty hand." If by the finger only they received 10 plagues, they must, of course have received 50 by the hand, as it contains five fingers.)

"Rabbi Eliezer saith from whence can it be proved that every plague which the Most Holy (blessed be He) brought upon the Egyptians in Egypt consisted of four different plagues? From what is said he sent forth against them, the fierceness of his anger, wrath, indignation, and trouble; also by sending evil angels amongst them. Now wrath is one, indignation two, trouble three, sending evil angels four. Hence it is deducible that in Egypt they were afflicted with 40 plagues, and at the sea they were smitten with 200 plagues. . . . .

"What abundant favours hath the Omnipresent conferred on us, for if He had but brought us forth from Egypt, and had not inflicted justice on the Egyptians, it would have been sufficient. If he had inflicted justice upon them, and had not executed judgment on their gods, it would have been sufficient. If He had executed judgment on their gods, and had not slain the first-born, it would have been sufficient. If he had slain their first-born, and had not bestowed their wealth on us, it would have been sufficient. If he had given us their wealth, and had not divided the sea for us, it would have been sufficient. If he had divided the sea for us, and had not caused us to pass through on dry land, it would have been sufficient. If he had caused us to pass through on dry land, and had not plagued our oppressors in the midst thereof, it would have been sufficient. If he had plunged our oppressors in the midst thereof, and had not supplied us with necessaries in the wilderness (40 years), it would have been sufficient. If he had supplied us with necessaries in the wilderness (40 years), and had not fed us on manna, it would have been sufficient. If he had fed us with manna, and had not given us the Sabbath, it would have been sufficient. If he had given us the Sabbath, and had not brought us near to Mount Sinai, it would have been sufficient. If he had brought us near to Mount Sinai, and had not given us his law, it would have been sufficient. If he had given us this law, and had not brought us to the land of Israel, it would have been sufficient. If he had brought us to the land of Israel, and had not built the temple, it would have been sufficient.

"How much, then, are we indebted for the manifold favours of the Omnipresent conferred on us. He brought us forth from Egypt, executed judgment on the Egyptians and on their gods, slew their first-born, gave us their wealth, divided the sea for us, caused us to pass through on dry land, plunged our oppressors in the midst thereof, supplied us with necessaries in the wilderness 40 years, gave us manna to eat, gave us the Sabbath, brought us near to Mount Sinai, gave us the law, brought us into the land of Israel, and built the chosen holy temple for us, to make atonement for all our sins.

"Rabbi Gamlieh saith, that whosoever doth not make mention of three things used in the passover hath not done his duty (Christian's blood is not mentioned): the paschal lamb, the unleavened cake, and bitter herb.

"The paschal lamb, which our ancestors ate during the existence of the holy temple, what did it denote? It denoted that the most Holy (blessed be He) passed over our fathers' houses in Egypt, as is said, (Exod. xii. 27,) and ye shall say it is the Lord's passover, because he passed over the houses of the children of Israel in Egypt, when he smote the Egyptians and delivered our houses. And the people bowed their heads and worshipped."

The master of the house then takes hold of the cake in the dish, and shows it to the company as a memorial of their freedom, and then says, "These unleavened cakes, wherefore do we eat them? Because there was not sufficient time for

PLATE 96

LONDON · ENGLAND · 1842

The First Reform Haggadah

Reform Judaism began in Germany in the early nineteenth century, and the first Reform prayer book appeared in Hamburg in 1818. However, the first separate edition of a Reform Haggadah did not appear until 1842 and was published, not in Germany, but in England. In the late 1830s some members of the Ancient Synagogue of Spanish and Portuguese Jews in London came into conflict with the communal leaders over the issue of reforms in the service. After several unsuccessful attempts at compromise, in 1840 the group formed an independent Reform congregation, known as the West London Synagogue of British Jews. Their first prayer book was published in 1841; the Haggadah, shown here, was published in the following year.

YAARI NO. 619 HARVARD 21.5:13

הגדה לפסח:

DOMESTIC SERVICE

FOR THE

FIRST NIGHT OF PASSOVER,

USED BY THE MEMBERS OF

THE WEST LONDON SYNAGOGUE

OF

BRITISH JEWS.

EDITED BY THE REV. D. W. MARKS,

MINISTER OF THE CONGREGATION.

LONDON:

PRINTED AND SOLD BY J. WERTHEIMER AND CO.,

CIRCUS PLACE, FINSBURY CIRCUS.

TO BE HAD ALSO OF THE EDITOR.

A.M. 5602.

BOMBAY · INDIA · 1846

For the Bene Israel of India

The origins of the indigenous Jews of India known as the Bene Israel ("Children of Israel") are veiled. For many centuries they were isolated from the rest of Jewry, yet they managed to maintain their identity amid the host of Indian religions that surrounded them. Living at first in villages, they began to settle in Bombay toward the end of the eighteenth century, partly as a result of their penchant for service in the British Army. Their first encounter with normative Judaism occurred in the same period through contact with the Cochin Jews of the Malabar coast. Eager now to assimilate the many elements of postbiblical rabbinic Judaism that had been lost to them, they built their first synagogue in Bombay in 1796. The subsequent arrival in the city of Jews from Cochin and from the oriental countries enriched their opportunities for Jewish learning and stimulated a religious revival of which the Haggadah of 1846 is but one example.

Like some of the other early Hebrew publications in Bombay, the Haggadah was lithographed. The title page, with the figures of Moses and Aaron at its sides, and the scene at the Burning Bush above, is an imitation of the frontispiece of the Amsterdam Haggadah of 1712 (Plate 66). The text of the Haggadah appears in Hebrew with a translation into Marathi, the Indian language of the Bene Israel.

YAARI NO. 656 JTSA 24:15

סדר הגדה

בלשון הקדש ועם פירוש של מרג״טי
ראה זה חדש הוא אשר לא היה לעולמים
אשר איזן ותיקר והוציא לאור כל ר׳ תער״ ומה
לזכות בו את הרבים וזכות הרבים תלוי בהם
ה״ה הרב המובהק כה״ר חיים
יוסף חליגואה יצ״ו מעיר
קוג״ין יע״א
ומשנהו לו מחבר
ביאורי של מר״אטי
שחיבר כה״ר חיים
יצחק ג״ל צורכר יצ״ו
ועם יד מתבר של לה״ק ושמו
למעלה אכ״יר
וגם הוא הוציא הכלי למעשה״ו
ה״ה כה״ר מחבר המר״אטי חיים
הי״ו ״׳ ושותפו היה למשען
לדפוס שהזיל זהב מכיסם
ה״ה כה״ר יחזקאל יוסף
טלכר הי״ו נרם יאיר אכ״יר
ועתה נדפס בפעם ראשון
על ידי הכותב כה״ר
אברהם בן יהודה גמ״ל
הי״ו ס״ט
בשנת ברוך אתה בבואיך וברוך
אתה בצאתיך לפ״ק
פה עיר בנדר בומ״באי
יע״א

PLATE 98

BOMBAY · 1846
[CONTINUED]

Venice—to Amsterdam—to Bombay

Six cuts, out of a series of thirteen in the Bombay Haggadah, show the order of the Seder. Under each Hebrew title is an explanation in Marathi characters.

The sequence is derived from the Amsterdam Haggadahs of 1695 and 1712, which, in turn, borrowed it from the Venetian Haggadahs of 1609 and 1629 (see Plate 54).

קַדֵּשׁ

स्नान करून जे मेज तयार करून ठेविले आहे तेथे बसोन किदुशाचे ग्लास भरून मग उभे राहून बराखा करावी मग खाली बसून किदुश प्यावे.

וּרְחַץ

किदोश पीवून हात धुवावे परंतु नेतीलाची बराखा करु नये

כַּרְפַּס

हात धुवुन करपासची भाजी घेउन अंबट रसांत बुडवोन आदामाची बराखा बोलोन खावी.

יַחַץ

करपास खाल्यावर ३ धरिलेल्या भाकरी तेथे मधील भाकर दुभागून एक भाग तेथे ठेवून दुसरा भाग कापडांत गुंडाळून कोणाजवळही ठेवावा.

מַגִּיד

दुसरे किदुशाचे ग्लास भरून ठेवावे आणि तदनंतर उच्च स्वराने हालाहम्यान या तीन वेळा बने होरीम पर्यंत पढावे.

רָחְצָה

किदुश पीवुन हात धुवावे आणि नेतीलाची बराखा करावी

136474

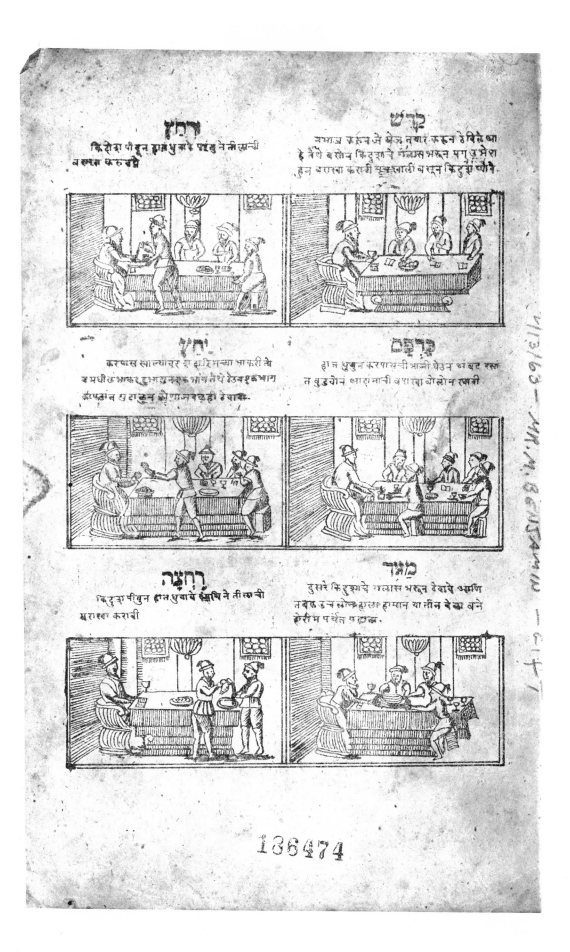

PLATE 99

NEW YORK · U.S.A. · 1851

Father and Son—à la Mode

Above: On the title page of this New York Haggadah a father and his son appear dressed in the height of mid-nineteenth-century elegance. Directly below them is the opening line of the Four Questions: "*Mah nishtanah ha-laylah ha-zeh mi-kol ha-leylot*?—How is this night different from all other nights?"

Below: A primitive woodcut, consisting of three panels, that appears on the verso of the title page; its significance is not entirely clear. From right to left are shown Moses and the Israelites at the Red Sea, the binding of sheaves (to be used for matzah?), and a most curious scene in which several men appear to be trimming their beards (in preparation for the holiday?!).

T. WIENER[1] NO. 20 HARVARD 18:10.5

סדר
הגדה של פסח

מה נשתנה הלילה הזה מכל הלילות ?

New York,
Druck u. Verlag der H. Frank's Buchdruckerei, 205 Houston St.
1851.

PLATE 100

FÜRTH · BAVARIA · 1857

English—in Germany

A Haggadah with English translation, published in Germany but obviously intended for export to England or America. Fürth was a center of Haggadah production, and issued more than seventy editions in the eighteenth and nineteenth centuries.

VARIANT OF YAARI NO. 777 HARVARD 19.5:14

Mrs Nathan Hart

סדר
ההגדה לליל שמורים׃

נמדויק היטב ומסודר יפה

ומתורגם ענגליש׃

SERVICE

FOR

THE FIRST TWO NIGHTS

OF

PASSOVER.

5617

Published by S. B. Gusdorfer in Fürth.
Printed by I. Sommer in Fürth.

NEW YORK · U.S.A. · 1860

German—in America

Unlike the English Haggadah published in Germany for export (Plate 100), this Hebrew-German edition was printed in New York for the domestic market. The second wave of Jewish immigration to the United States consisted of the German and Austrian Jews, beginning especially in the 1830s and 1840s. They retained the German language for several generations.

T. WIENER[1] NO. 29 HARVARD 18.5:11

סדר

הגדה של פסח.

Erzählung

von dem

Auszuge Israels

aus

Egypten,

an den

beiden ersten Pessach-Abenden.

NEW-YORK,

Druck und Verlag von L. H. Frank,

No. 3 Cedar & 185 Division Str.

5621—1860.

PLATE 102

TRIESTE · ITALY · 1864

A New Artistic Departure

The Trieste Haggadah is undoubtedly the most distinguished illustrated edition produced in Europe during the nineteenth century.

As the engraved Gothic title page already indicates, the Haggadah is different in format and design from any that preceded it, no mean achievement in an age when the Venetian and Amsterdam Haggadah illustrations were being copied and recopied in seemingly endless succession. Almost every page contains a large engraving above the text, drawn by C. Kirchmayr. Though inspired by the iconographic themes of the past, the Trieste engravings are not a mere aping of the stereotypes then current, but display a welcome freshness of design.

The Haggadah was edited by the journalist and publicist Abraham Ḥai (Vita) Morpurgo and was printed by Jonah Cohen. It was published simultaneously in two issues. One, reproduced here, is entirely in Hebrew; the other is accompanied by an Italian translation.

YAARI NO. 898 HARVARD 31:22

סדר
הגדה של פסח
עם ציורים
הוגה בעיון נמרץ
מאת
אברהם חי מורפורגו
ונדפס מחדש
בבית דפוס יונה כהן
פה טריאסטי
שנת ה'ת'ר'כ'ד'
MOSÈ
ARONNE
DAVIDE
SALOMONE
C. Kirchmayr inc.

PLATE 103

TRIESTE · 1864
[CONTINUED]
Ancient Afflictions

The illustration shows the distress of the Hebrew slaves, with the caption: "The children of Israel serve the Egyptians with hard labor."

בני ישראל עובדים את המצרים בפרך.

ומגביה את הכוס בידו ואומר:

לְפִיכָךְ אֲנַחְנוּ חַיָּבִים· לְהוֹדוֹת· לְהַלֵּל· לְשַׁבֵּחַ·
לְפָאֵר· לְרוֹמֵם· לְהַדֵּר· לְבָרֵךְ· לְעַלֵּה·
וּלְקַלֵּס· לְמִי שֶׁעָשָׂה לַאֲבוֹתֵינוּ וְלָנוּ אֶת כָּל
הַנִּסִּים הָאֵלּוּ· הוֹצִיאָנוּ מֵעַבְדוּת לְחֵרוּת·
מִיָּגוֹן לְשִׂמְחָה· מֵאֵבֶל לְיוֹם טוֹב· וּמֵאֲפֵלָה
לְאוֹר גָּדוֹל· וּמִשִּׁעְבּוּד לִגְאֻלָּה· וְנֹאמַר לְפָנָיו
(שִׁירָה חֲדָשָׁה) הַלְלוּיָהּ:

הַלְלוּיָהּ הַלְלוּ עַבְדֵי יְיָ הַלְלוּ אֶת־שֵׁם יְיָ: יְהִי
שֵׁם יְיָ מְבֹרָךְ מֵעַתָּה וְעַד־עוֹלָם: מִמִּזְרַח־
שֶׁמֶשׁ עַד־מְבוֹאוֹ מְהֻלָּל שֵׁם יְיָ: רָם עַל־
כָּל־גּוֹיִם יְיָ עַל־הַשָּׁמַיִם כְּבוֹדוֹ: מִי כַּייָ אֱלֹהֵינוּ
הַמַּגְבִּיהִי לָשָׁבֶת: הַמַּשְׁפִּילִי לִרְאוֹת בַּשָּׁמַיִם
וּבָאָרֶץ: מְקִימִי מֵעָפָר דָּל מֵאַשְׁפֹּת יָרִים
אֶבְיוֹן: לְהוֹשִׁיבִי עִם־נְדִיבִים עִם נְדִיבֵי
עַמּוֹ: מוֹשִׁיבִי עֲקֶרֶת הַבַּיִת אֵם־הַבָּנִים שְׂמֵחָה
הַלְלוּיָהּ:

בְּצֵאת יִשְׂרָאֵל מִמִּצְרָיִם בֵּית יַעֲקֹב מֵעַם
לֹעֵז: הָיְתָה יְהוּדָה לְקָדְשׁוֹ יִשְׂרָאֵל
מַמְשְׁלוֹתָיו: הַיָּם רָאָה וַיָּנֹס הַיַּרְדֵּן יִסֹּב
לְאָחוֹר: הֶהָרִים רָקְדוּ כְאֵילִים גְּבָעוֹת כִּבְנֵי־
צֹאן: מַה־לְּךָ הַיָּם כִּי תָנוּס הַיַּרְדֵּן תִּסֹּב
לְאָחוֹר: הֶהָרִים תִּרְקְדוּ כְאֵילִים גְּבָעוֹת
כִּבְנֵי־צֹאן: מִלִּפְנֵי אָדוֹן חוּלִי אָרֶץ מִלִּפְנֵי
אֱלוֹהַּ יַעֲקֹב: הַהֹפְכִי הַצּוּר אֲגַם־מָיִם חַלָּמִישׁ
לְמַעְיְנוֹ־מָיִם:

מכסין המצות ונוטלין הכוס בידם:

בָּרוּךְ אַתָּה יְיָ אֱלֹהֵינוּ מֶלֶךְ הָעוֹלָם אֲשֶׁר
גְּאָלָנוּ וְגָאַל אֶת אֲבוֹתֵינוּ מִמִּצְרַיִם· וְהִגִּיעָנוּ
לַלַּיְלָה הַזֶּה לֶאֱכָל בּוֹ מַצָּה וּמָרוֹר: כֵּן יְיָ
אֱלֹהֵינוּ וֵאלֹהֵי אֲבוֹתֵינוּ יַגִּיעֵנוּ לְמוֹעֲדִים
וְלִרְגָלִים אֲחֵרִים הַבָּאִים לִקְרָאתֵנוּ לְשָׁלוֹם
שְׂמֵחִים בְּבִנְיַן עִירֶךָ וְשָׂשִׂים בַּעֲבוֹדָתֶךָ
וְנֹאכַל־שָׁם מִן־הַזְּבָחִים וּמִן־הַפְּסָחִים אֲשֶׁר
יַגִּיעַ דָּמָם עַל קִיר מִזְבַּחֲךָ לְרָצוֹן· וְנוֹדֶה לְךָ
שִׁיר חָדָשׁ עַל גְּאֻלָּתֵנוּ וְעַל פְּדוּת נַפְשֵׁנוּ:
בָּרוּךְ אַתָּה יְיָ גָּאַל יִשְׂרָאֵל:

PLATE 104

TRIESTE · 1864
[CONTINUED]

"Jerusalem, the Holy City"

This illustration is closest to the visual conventions of the past, particularly in the rendering of the Temple in the form of the Dome of the Rock. (Compare Plates 18 and 55.)

ירושלם עיר הקדש.

הָרַחֲמָן הוּא יִשְׁתַּבַּח לְדוֹר דּוֹרִים וְיִתְפָּאַר בָּנוּ לָנֶצַח נְצָחִים וְיִתְהַדַּר בָּנוּ לָעַד וּלְעוֹלְמֵי עוֹלָמִים: הָרַחֲמָן הוּא יְפַרְנְסֵנוּ בְּכָבוֹד: הָרַחֲמָן הוּא יוֹלִיכֵנוּ קוֹמְמִיּוּת לְאַרְצֵנוּ: הָרַחֲמָן הוּא יִשְׁלַח בְּרָכָה מְרֻבָּה בַּבַּיִת הַזֶּה וְעַל שֻׁלְחָן זֶה שֶׁאָכַלְנוּ עָלָיו: הָרַחֲמָן הוּא יִשְׁלַח־לָנוּ אֶת־אֵלִיָּהוּ הַנָּבִיא זָכוּר לַטּוֹב וִיבַשֶּׂר־לָנוּ בְּשׂוֹרוֹת טוֹבוֹת יְשׁוּעוֹת וְנֶחָמוֹת: הָרַחֲמָן הוּא יְבָרֵךְ אֶת (אָבִי מוֹרִי) בַּעַל הַבַּיִת הַזֶּה וְאֶת (אִמִּי מוֹרָתִי) בַּעֲלַת הַבַּיִת הַזֶּה אוֹתָם וְאֶת־בֵּיתָם וְאֶת־זַרְעָם וְאֶת־כָּל־אֲשֶׁר לָהֶם אוֹתָנוּ וְאֶת־כָּל־אֲשֶׁר לָנוּ וּכְמוֹ שֶׁבֵּרַךְ אֲבוֹתֵינוּ אַבְרָהָם יִצְחָק וְיַעֲקֹב בַּכֹּל מִכֹּל כֹּל כֵּן יְבָרֵךְ אוֹתָנוּ כֻּלָּנוּ יַחַד בִּבְרָכָה שְׁלֵמָה וְנֹאמַר אָמֵן:

בַּמָּרוֹם יְלַמְּדוּ עֲלֵיהֶם וְעָלֵינוּ זְכוּת שֶׁתְּהֵא לְמִשְׁמֶרֶת שָׁלוֹם וְנִשָּׂא בְרָכָה מֵאֵת יְיָ וּצְדָקָה מֵאֱלֹהֵי יִשְׁעֵנוּ וְנִמְצָא־חֵן וְשֵׂכֶל־טוֹב בְּעֵינֵי אֱלֹהִים וְאָדָם:

בשבת אומרים.

הָרַחֲמָן הוּא יַנְחִילֵנוּ יוֹם שֶׁכֻּלּוֹ שַׁבָּת וּמְנוּחָה לְחַיֵּי הָעוֹלָמִים:

הָרַחֲמָן הוּא יַנְחִילֵנוּ יוֹם שֶׁכֻּלּוֹ טוֹב:

הָרַחֲמָן הוּא יְזַכֵּנוּ לִימוֹת הַמָּשִׁיחַ וּלְחַיֵּי הָעוֹלָם הַבָּא: מִגְדּוֹל יְשׁוּעוֹת מַלְכּוֹ וְעֹשֶׂה חֶסֶד לִמְשִׁיחוֹ לְדָוִד וּלְזַרְעוֹ עַד עוֹלָם: עֹשֶׂה שָׁלוֹם בִּמְרוֹמָיו הוּא יַעֲשֶׂה שָׁלוֹם עָלֵינוּ וְעַל כָּל־יִשְׂרָאֵל וְאִמְרוּ אָמֵן:

יְראוּ אֶת־יְיָ קְדשָׁיו כִּי־אֵין מַחְסוֹר לִירֵאָיו: כְּפִירִים רָשׁוּ וְרָעֵבוּ וְדֹרְשֵׁי יְיָ לֹא־יַחְסְרוּ כָל־־טוֹב: הוֹדוּ לַייָ כִּי־טוֹב כִּי לְעוֹלָם חַסְדּוֹ:

TRIESTE · 1864
[CONTINUED]

The Seder Scene—Updated

A scene showing the family around the Seder table had been a standard feature of almost all illustrated Haggadahs. In early printed editions the participants had been shown in contemporary dress (Plates 1, 6, 14, 35, 54). However, as certain influential Haggadahs began to be copied later, the representation of the Seder became increasingly anachronistic. For example, the late eighteenth-century Venetian reprints of the Haggadah of 1609 still show the family in the garb of that earlier age, as do many of the Livornese Haggadahs printed in the nineteenth and even the twentieth centuries. Indeed, with very few exceptions (Plate 84) this was the rule.

In the Trieste Haggadah the artist has clearly set out to present a middle-class Italian Jewish family of his own time. Not only are the men and women dressed in the current style, but each of them exhibits an individuality rarely encountered before.

ברכת המזון.

רְצֵה וְהַחֲלִיצֵנוּ יְיָ אֱלֹהֵינוּ בְּכָל מִצְוֹתֶיךָ וּבְמִצְוַת יוֹם הַשְּׁבִיעִי הַשַּׁבָּת הַגָּדוֹל וְהַקָּדוֹשׁ הַזֶּה כִּי יוֹם זֶה גָּדוֹל וְקָדוֹשׁ הוּא לְפָנֶיךָ לִשְׁבּוֹת בּוֹ וְלָנוּחַ בּוֹ בְּאַהֲבָה כְּמִצְוַת רְצוֹנֶךָ: בִּרְצוֹנְךָ הָנִיחַ לָנוּ יְיָ אֱלֹהֵינוּ וְאַל תְּהִי עָלֵינוּ צָרָה וְרָעָב וְיָגוֹן וַאֲנָחָה בְּיוֹם מְנוּחָתֵנוּ כִּי אָמַר דָּוִד הֵנִיחַ יְיָ אֱלֹהֵי־יִשְׂרָאֵל לְעַמּוֹ וַיִּשְׁכֹּן בִּירוּשָׁלַיִם עַד לְעוֹלָם: וְנֶאֱמַר שָׁם אַצְמִיחַ קֶרֶן לְדָוִד עָרַכְתִּי נֵר לִמְשִׁיחִי: וְתִמְלוֹךְ עָלֵינוּ אַתָּה לְבַדְּךָ וְהוֹשִׁיעֵנוּ לְמַעַן שְׁמֶךָ כִּי אַתָּה הוּא בַּעַל הַיְשׁוּעוֹת וּבַעַל הַנֶּחָמוֹת. וְשַׂמְּחֵנוּ בְּתוֹכָהּ וְנִרְאֶה בְּנֶחָמָתָהּ וּבְבִנְיָנָהּ:

אֱלֹהֵינוּ וֵאלֹהֵי אֲבוֹתֵינוּ יַעֲלֶה וְיָבֹא יַגִּיעַ וְיֵרָאֶה וְיֵרָצֶה וְיִשָּׁמַע וְיִפָּקֵד וְיִזָּכֵר זִכְרוֹנֵנוּ וְזִכְרוֹן אֲבוֹתֵינוּ וְזִכְרוֹן יְרוּשָׁלַיִם עִירֶךָ וְזִכְרוֹן מָשִׁיחַ בֶּן דָּוִד עַבְדֶּךָ וְזִכְרוֹן כָּל־עַמְּךָ בֵּית יִשְׂרָאֵל לְפָנֶיךָ לְטוֹבָה לְחֵן וּלְחֶסֶד וּלְרַחֲמִים וּלְרָצוֹן בְּיוֹם חַג הַמַּצּוֹת הַזֶּה. לְרַחֵם בּוֹ עָלֵינוּ וּלְהוֹשִׁיעֵנוּ. זָכְרֵנוּ יְיָ אֱלֹהֵינוּ בּוֹ לְטוֹבָה. וּפָקְדֵנוּ בוֹ לִבְרָכָה. וְהוֹשִׁיעֵנוּ בוֹ לְחַיִּים טוֹבִים. בִּדְבַר יְשׁוּעָה וְרַחֲמִים. חוּס וְחָנֵּנוּ. וְרַחֵם עָלֵינוּ וְהוֹשִׁיעֵנוּ. כִּי אֵלֶיךָ עֵינֵינוּ כִּי אֵל מֶלֶךְ חַנּוּן וְרַחוּם אָתָּה:

וּבְנֵה אֶת יְרוּשָׁלַיִם עִיר הַקֹּדֶשׁ בִּמְהֵרָה בְיָמֵינוּ. בָּרוּךְ אַתָּה יְיָ בּוֹנֶה בְּרַחֲמָיו בִּנְיַן יְרוּשָׁלָיִם אָמֵן: בְּחַיֵּינוּ בִּמְהֵרָה בְיָמֵינוּ יָבֹא גוֹאֵל וְיִגְאָלֵנוּ תִּבָּנֶה עִיר צִיּוֹן וְתִכּוֹן הָעֲבוֹדָה בִּירוּשָׁלָיִם. בָּרוּךְ אַתָּה יְיָ אֱלֹהֵינוּ מֶלֶךְ הָעוֹלָם יִתְבָּרַךְ לָעַד הָאֵל אָבִינוּ מַלְכֵּנוּ מַחְסֵנוּ אַדִּירֵנוּ בּוֹרְאֵנוּ גֹּאֲלֵנוּ יוֹצְרֵנוּ קְדוֹשֵׁנוּ קְדוֹשׁ יַעֲקֹב רוֹעֵנוּ רוֹעֵה יִשְׂרָאֵל רוֹעֶה נֶאֱמָן הַמֶּלֶךְ הַטּוֹב וְהַמֵּטִיב לַכֹּל אֵל שֶׁבְּכָל־יוֹם וָיוֹם עִמָּנוּ הוּא הֵטִיב לָנוּ הוּא מֵטִיב לָנוּ הוּא יֵיטִיב עִמָּנוּ: הוּא גְמָלָנוּ הוּא גוֹמְלֵנוּ הוּא יִגְמְלֵנוּ בְּרַחֲמָיו לָעַד חֵן וָחֶסֶד וְרַחֲמִים בְּרָכָה רְוָחָה וְהַצְלָחָה וְחַיִּים וְשָׁלוֹם וְכָל־טוֹב. וּמִכָּל־טוּב אַל־יְחַסְּרֵנוּ.

הָרַחֲמָן הוּא יִמְלוֹךְ עָלֵינוּ לְעוֹלָם וָעֶד:

LEGHORN · ITALY · 1867

Demons in Egypt

Another example of the remarkable persistence of Venetian illustrations in Livornese Haggadahs. The woodcut on this page first appeared in Venice in 1609, and thereafter in all later Venetian editions.

The Haggadah text, which is printed with a Ladino translation, cites a midrashic interpretation by Rabbi Akiba of Psalms 78:49. The verse, relating to the plagues of Egypt, states: "He sent forth upon them the fierceness of His anger, wrath, and indignation, and trouble, a sending of messengers of evil." These "messengers" are represented in the woodcut by demons, with the following rhymed caption in Ladino:

> Demonios deputados sobre los elementos,
> Por dar a *Mitzrayim* penas y tormentos.
>
> [Demons delegated over the elements,
> To give Egypt afflictions and torments.]

The folk element in both illustration and caption is readily apparent. See also Plate 47.

YAARI NO. 958 HARVARD 21:15

רַבִּי אֱלִיעֶזֶר אוֹמֵר מִנַּיִן שֶׁכָּל מַכָּה וּמַכָּה שֶׁהֵבִיא הַקָּדוֹשׁ
בָּרוּךְ הוּא עַל הַמִּצְרִיִּים בְּמִצְרַיִם הָיְתָה שֶׁל אַרְבַּע
מַכּוֹת שֶׁנֶּאֱמַר יְשַׁלַּח בָּם חֲרוֹן אַפּוֹ עֶבְרָה וָזַעַם וְצָרָה
מִשְׁלַחַת מַלְאֲכֵי רָעִים ׳ עֶבְרָה אַחַת ׳ וָזַעַם שְׁתַּיִם ׳ וְצָרָה
שָׁלֹשׁ ׳ מִשְׁלַחַת מַלְאֲכֵי רָעִים אַרְבַּע ׳ אֱמוֹר מֵעַתָּה בְּמִצְרַיִם
לָקוּ אַרְבָּעִים מַכּוֹת ׳ וְעַל הַיָּם לָקוּ מָאתַיִם מַכּוֹת :
רַבִּי עֲקִיבָא אוֹמֵר מִנַּיִן שֶׁכָּל מַכָּה וּמַכָּה שֶׁהֵבִיא הַקָּדוֹשׁ
בָּרוּךְ הוּא עַל הַמִּצְרִיִּים בְּמִצְרַיִם ׳ הָיְתָה שֶׁל חָמֵשׁ
מכות

רבי רִבִּי אֱלִיעֶזֶר דִיזְיין דֵי אַדוֹנְדֵי סֵי פְּרוּאֵיבָה קֵי טוֹדָה פֵּירִידָה אִי פֵּירִידָה קֵי טְרוּשוֹ
אֵיל סַאנְטוֹ בֵּינְדִיגוֹ אֵיל סִיבְּרֵי לוֹס אֵגִפְּסְיַאנוֹס אֵין אֵגִיפְּטוֹ ׳ אֵירָה דֵי קוּאַטְרוֹ
פֵּירִידַאס קוֹמוֹ דִיזֵי אֵיל פָּסוּק אֵינְבִּיאַרָה אֵין אֵילְיוֹס אֵירֵיסִימְיֵינְטוֹ דֵי סוּ פוּרוֹר סַאנְיָה
אִי אִירָה אִי אַנְגוּסְטְיָה אֵינְבִּיאַמְיֵינְטוֹ דֵי מֵינְסַאגֵירוֹש מַאלוֹס ׳ סַאנְיָה אוּנָה ׳ אִירָה
דוֹש ׳ אַנְגוּסְטְיָה טְרֵיש ׳ אֵינְבִּיאַמְיֵינְטוֹ דֵי מֵינְסַאגֵירוֹס מַאלוֹס קוּאַטְרוֹ ׳ דִי דֵי אַגוֹרָה
אֵין אֵגִיפְּטוֹ פוּאֵירוֹן פֵּירִידוֹס קוּאַרֵינְטָה פֵּירִידַאש ׳ אִי סוֹבְּרֵי לָה מַאר פוּאֵירוֹן פֵּירִידוֹש
דוּוֵיינְטַאש פֵּירִידַאשׁ :
רבי רִבִּי עֲקִיבָא דִיזְיין דֵי אַדוֹנְדֵי סֵי פְּרוּאֵיבָה קֵי טוֹדָה פֵּירִידָה אִי פֵּירִידָה קֵי טְרוּשוֹ
אֵיל סַאנְטוֹ בֵּינְדִיגוֹ אֵיל סִיבְּרֵי לוֹס אֵגִפְּסְיַאנוֹס אֵין אֵגִיפְּטוֹ ׳ אֵירָה דֵי סִינְקוֹ

רימוניוס ריפיטאדוס סיברי לוס אילימינטוס ׳ פור ראר אה מצרים פינאס אי טורמיינטוס

פירידאס

PLATE 107

POONA · INDIA · 1874

An Indian Passover

After Bombay, the second largest urban community of the Bene Israel of India was in the city of Poona, and a new edition of the Haggadah with Marathi translation appeared there in 1874. (For the Bombay edition of 1846, see Plates 97–98.)

The Poona Haggadah was "prepared and published by Moses Jacob Talkar and Aaron David Talkar according to the *Shulḥan Arukh* and the Haggadah published with Marathi by Rabbi Hayyeem Joseph Haleguva and Hayeem Isaac Galsulker. At Vital Sakharam Agnihorty's Press."

Besides some additions to the text, the major changes occurred in the illustrations. In the Bombay Haggadah the entire sequence of the Seder had been shown in two sets of six small illustrations, with a final scene on a third page. Now these illustrations were redrawn and considerably enlarged, with only two to a page. A completely new full-page illustration was also placed at the very outset, showing the preparation and baking of matzah.

While the Bombay illustrations were still closely linked to their Amsterdam prototypes, those in the Poona Haggadah have managed to drift into a sphere of their own. Even as they retain the basic pattern, they are now palpably Indian in tone and detail.

Above: The preparation and baking of the matzah. The women, their hair adorned with flowers, are dressed in saris. Note also the typical squatting positions of both men and women. The woman at the right, in particular, sits in a classic Indian position familiar from Hindu painting and sculpture.

Below: The Seder dish; and the actual beginning of the Seder sequence, each part of which bears the traditional Hebrew catchword with a Marathi explanation. Shown here is the first stage: KADESH (the sanctification over the wine).

YAARI NO. 1077 JTSA 20.5:14

כדיני החטים וטחינתם למצות וכדיני אפיית המצה וכו׳
आकृति
मस्सा करण्याचा प्रकार.

קדש

निमाज करूनजें मेज तयार करून ठेविलें आहे त्येवर बसून किदुशाचें गलास भरून मग उभे राहून बरासा करावी. मग खालीं बसून किदुश प्यावें.

PLATE 108

POONA · 1874
[CONTINUED]

Seder Sequence (Parts II–V)

RIGHT PAGE

Above: U-REḤATZ (the washing of hands).

Below: KARPAS (the eating of the vegetable).

LEFT PAGE

Above: YAḤATZ (the breaking of the middle of the three matzot placed before the celebrant).

Below: MAGGID (the recital of the Haggadah text).

וּרְחַץ

किदुशा पिऊन हात धवावे. परंतु नेतिलाची बराखा करूं नये.

כַּרְפַּס

हात धवून करपासाची भाजी घेऊन अंबट रसांत बुडवून आदामाची बराखा बोलून खावी.

יַחַץ

करपास खाल्यावर सेदारीमच्या भाकऱ्यांपैकीं व मधील भाकर दुभागून एक भाग तेथें ठेवून एक भाग कापडांत गुंडाळून कोणाजवळही ठेवावा.

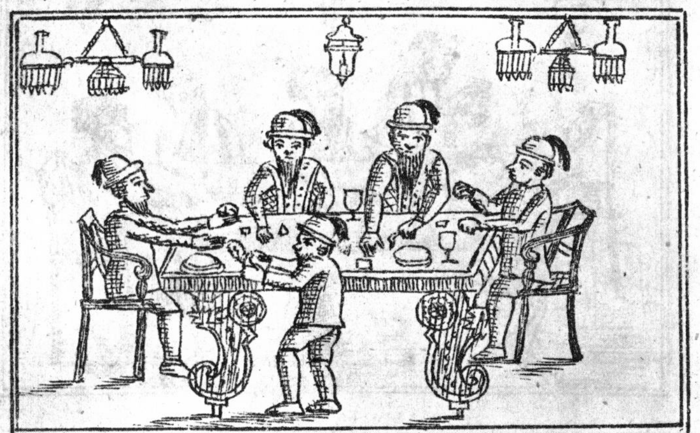

מַגִּיד

दुसरें किदुशाचें गलास भरून ठेवावें. आणि तबक उचलून हालाहामा या तीन वेळा बेने होरीम पर्यंत पढावा.

PLATE 109

POONA · 1874
[CONTINUED]

Seder Sequence (Parts VI–IX)

RIGHT PAGE

Above: RAḤATZAH (the washing of the hands prior to the meal).
Below: MOTZI; MATZAH (the blessings over the matzah).

LEFT PAGE

Above: MAROR (the tasting of the bitter herbs).
Below: KOREKH (the combining of matzah and bitter herbs).

רָחְצָה

किदुश पिऊन हात धवावें आणि नेतिलाची बराखा करावी.

מוֹצִיא מַצָּה

मेजावर जो मुख्य असेल त्यानें सेदारीमच्या आडीच भाकरी उचलून हामोसीची बराखा करावी. आणि वरचे दीड भाकरीतून तुकडा तुकडा सर्वांस देऊन मस्साची बराखा बोलून मिठांत बुडवून खावी.

מָרוֹר

कडवट भाजीचें पान सर्वत्रांही घेऊन खजूराचे शिऱ्यांत बुडवून मारोरची बराखा बोलून खावी.

כּוֹרֵךְ

खालची सर्व भाकर राहिली आहे तींतून तुकडा तुकडा सर्वांस देऊन सर्वांही तो तुकडा कडवट भाजीचे पानांत गुंडाळून खजूराचे शिऱ्यांत बुडवून जेखेर लेमिकदाश बोलून खावा.

PLATE 110

POONA · 1874
[CONTINUED]

Seder Sequence (Parts X–XIII)

RIGHT PAGE

Above: SHULḤAN OREKH (the partaking of the meal).

Below: TZAFUN (the half of the matzah secreted earlier and called the *afikoman* is now distributed, each participant eating a fragment to end the meal).

LEFT PAGE

Above: BAREKH (Grace after the meal).

Below: HALLEL; NIRTZAH (psalms of praise; and conclusion).

שלחן עורך

खावें प्यावें ईश्वराचे नामानें कीर्तन करावें. आनंद करावा. कारण त्याच रात्रीं आपण कष्टांतून सुटलों.

צפון

सर्व जेवण झाल्यावर अर्धी ठेवलेल्या भाकरींतून तुकडा तुकडा घेऊन खावा.

ברך

हात धुवून तिसरें किदूशाचें गलास भरून ठेवावें आणि नेबारेखची बराखा वेट्सरू आमेन पर्यंत झाली म्हणजे हगेफेनची बराखा बोलून किदूशा प्यावें.

הלל נרצה

चवथें किदूशाचें गलास भरून ठेवावें आणि शेफोक वाचावयास प्रारंभ करावा लो सेलेनू पासून हालेल बत्तीस पाहोत पर्यंत वाचावा आणि किदूशाचे गलास उचलून डावे बाजूस टेकून प्यावें. नंतर अल्हागेफेन ची बराखा वे आल पेरी हागेफेन पर्यंत बोलावी.

LEGHORN · ITALY · 1878

A Livornese Edition for the Jews of Tunis

This Haggadah, one of many brought in manuscript from North Africa to be printed in Leghorn, is according to the rite of Tunis. It is accompanied by a Judeo-Arabic translation in Hebrew characters.

The title page is in Judeo-Arabic and Hebrew. It records that the translation into the Arabic dialect of the Jews of Tunis was the work of Rabbi Elijah ben Joseph Gig. Moreover, this edition also includes

> much additional material, such as the evening prayer in large letters so that young and old will read it fluently; and we have also added the Song of Songs, and a poem on the miracle of the Exodus from Egypt and the Ten Plagues by Rabbi Joseph Gig, as well as a poem on the Exodus by the sage Solomon Zarka, and the Song of the Red Sea in Aramaic and Arabic, none of which was present in Haggadahs until now.

Printed in the year *Blessed be the name of the Lord.*

YAARI NO. 1133 HARVARD 26:18.5

סדר

הגדה של פסח

מעא תפסיר בלגווא מתע אלערבי
מתע **תונס** יע"א

חתא פייא תצוואר על גמיע אלאמאייר ואלעגאייב אלי נצארו לאבאתנא פי מאצר ועלא אלבאחר · וחתא סדר קדש ורחץ ועשר מכות ובאותיות מלאח יאסר · וחתא אתאצוואר אלי תמא מפסרין בלגווא מתע אלערבי מאכוד מן לגוואת אספניול :

מועתק ללשון ערבי של עו"בי **תונס** יע"א הכל כאשר לכל וגם ההגהה על ידי
אני הצעיר **אליהו** בכמהר"ר **יוסף גיג** זיע"א

ונזסף הוד תוספת מרובה תפלת ערבית כאותיות גרולות למען ירוץ קורא בו הקטנים עם הגדולים · וגם הוספנו **שיר השירים** ופיוט על נס יציאת מצרים ועשר מכות להח"ש רבי **יוסף גיג** וגם פיוט יציאת מצרים של החכם **שלמה זרקא** ושירת הים בתרגום וערבי מה שלא היה בהגדות עד עתה :

פה ליוורנו יע"א

שנת **יהי שם ה' מבורך** לפ"ק

ע"י **שלמה בילפורטי וחברו** הי"ו

סרפיסים ומוכרי ספרים

PLATE 112

LEGHORN · 1878
[CONTINUED]

The Woman Prepares the House

All the woodcuts in the Leghorn Haggadah of 1878 are copied from the old Venetian editions. They are, however, rearranged and accompanied by captions in Judeo-Arabic. (See Plate 113.)

HARVARD COLLEGE LIBRARY
TRANSFERRED FROM
SEMITIC LIBRARY
1937

האד אלמרא קעדא תכ̇סל פ̇ל
פ̇וכ̇אר ומאעון נחש

האד אלמרא קעדא תפ̇תש
פ̇ל חמץ מן אסנאדק
וקבלתא אסנדוק

האד אלמרא קעדא תכ̇סל פ̇ל
כ̇ודרא מתע פסח כאב תכול

האד אלמרא קעדא תג̇רבל-
פ̇טעאם כאס תעמ̇ל אלפ̇טאייר

LEGHORN · 1878
[CONTINUED]

Baking Matzah

These, as well as the illustrations reproduced in Plate 112, originally appeared together in the Venetian Haggadahs on one page. In the edition of 1609 they framed the title page, while in that of 1629 (Plate 49) they surrounded the introduction to Leone Modena's commentary.

סדר ביעור חמץ

אור לְאַרְבָּעָה עָשָׂר בְּנִיסָן בּוֹדְקִין אֶת הֶחָמֵץ בְּכָל הַמְּקוֹמוֹת שֶׁרְגִילִין לְהִשְׁתַּמֵּשׁ בָּהֶם אֲפִילוּ בַּחוֹרִין וּבַסְּדָקִין בְּנֵר שֶׁל שַׁעֲוָה וְלֹא לְאוֹר הָאֲבוּקָה · וְלֹא לְאוֹר הַלְּבָנָה · וְלֹא לְאוֹר הַחַמָּה · וְאֵין עוֹשִׂין מְלָאכָה עַד שֶׁיִּבְדּוֹק וַאֲפִילוּ בְּתַלְמוּד תּוֹרָה · וְקוֹדֶם שֶׁיַּתְחִיל לִבְדּוֹק מְבָרֵךְ :

פֿי לילת ארבעתש פֿי ניסן יפֿתשו פֿי כול מוואצֿע אלי מתלופֿין יתכֿדמו פֿיהום חתא פֿל גִיראן ופֿסקאת בצֿאו מתע אסמע ולייס לצֿאו אלאלייבא ולא לצֿאו לקמר ולא לצֿאו אשמש ומא יעמלו חתא כֿדמא חתא יפֿתש ולייס יקרא פֿי תורה וקבל מא יפֿתש יברך האד אלברכה ברוך אתה וכו׳ :

ברוך

PLATE 114

ODESSA · RUSSIA · 1883

The Karaite Haggadah—in Russian

The most enduring and creative of all Jewish sectarian movements, Karaism rejected the authority of the Talmud in favor of its own interpretations of biblical law. Arising first in Babylonia in the eighth century of the Common Era, in later ages Karaite centers emerged in Palestine, in Byzantium, and finally in Europe. Though always in a polemical relationship to rabbinic Judaism, Karaites often interacted, and at times even intermarried, with the majority. Indeed, despite occasional acrimony, the relationship between Rabbanites and Karaites stimulated renewed creativity on both sides in such fields as biblical exegesis, the study of the Hebrew language, and religious philosophy.

Like the rest of the Karaite liturgy, the Haggadah of the Karaites is composed entirely of biblical selections. The well-known talmudic and midrashic passages found in the normative Haggadah have no place in it.

In modern times the major concentrations of Karaites in Eastern Europe were in Lithuania and the Crimea. Shown here is the title page of a Karaite Haggadah in Hebrew and Russian published in Odessa in 1883. It was reprinted in St. Petersburg in 1889.

YAARI NO. 1210 HARVARD 25:15.5

הגדה של פסח

ע ם

תרגום בלשון רוסייא

כמנהג הקראים

מ א ת י

יהודה בלאו״ר דוד נ״ע כוכיזוב.

אודססא

שנת תרמ״ג לפ״ק.

ГАГАДА ШЕЛЬ ПЕСАХЪ,

то есть:

ПОСВЯЩЕНІЕ НА ПАСХУ

съ точнымъ русскимъ переводомъ

перевелъ

Ю. Д. Кокизовъ.

ОДЕССА.

Въ Тип. А. Шульце, Ланжероновская д. Карузо № 36.

1883.

CHICAGO · U.S.A. · 1883

The American Scene

One of the few nineteenth-century editions of the Haggadah to be printed in Chicago. The illustration shown here is curious and (perhaps unintentionally) even amusing.

Among the family seated around the table, the bearded father looks suitably patriarchal. The four young men would seem to represent the Four Sons (perhaps the only illustration in which they are together at the Seder meal). Seated beside the mother we obviously have the Wise Son, who is engrossed in following the Haggadah, the only son to be wearing a skullcap. The Wicked Son is the mature man at the extreme right, puffing away at a cigarette and raising his hand in a gesture of challenge. Between the remaining two sons it is hard to say which is Simple and which "he who knows not what to ask." Most striking is the contrast between the father and the Wicked Son. Did the illustrator intend to hint at the generation gap in an immigrant family?

This Haggadah was edited by the Reverend H. Lieberman and is printed in Hebrew and English. It was first published in 1879.

YAARI NO. 1228 HARVARD 17.5:14

יְמֵי חַיֶּיךָ, הָעוֹלָם הַזֶּה. כֹּל יְמֵי חַיֶּיךָ, לְהָבִיא לִימוֹת הַמָּשִׁיחַ:

בָּרוּךְ הַמָּקוֹם בָּרוּךְ הוּא. בָּרוּךְ שֶׁנָּתַן תּוֹרָה

denotes this time only; but ALL the days of thy life, denotes even at the time of the Messiah.

Blessed be the Omnipresent; blessed is he, blessed is he who hath given the law to his people Israel, blessed be he: the

ODESSA · RUSSIA · 1885

The Slavery of Jewish Teachers

A Hebrew parody, based on the text of the Haggadah, in which the penury and generally miserable conditions of Hebrew teachers in East European Jewish elementary schools are compared to the lot of the slaves in Egypt. The title page reads: "The Order of the Haggadah for teachers, according to the custom of Lithuania, Poland, Ruthenia, Galicia, and Romania. And so that the Haggadah should not remain a riddle with no solution, there has been added to it the commentary entitled *Bread of Affliction*."

The parody of the Four Questions will suffice to indicate the tenor of the whole:

> How does teaching differ from all other professions in the world?
>
> All the other professions enrich, and their practitioners eat and drink and are happy all the days of the year. But teachers groan and sorrow even on this night.
>
> In all other professions the workers do not dare to be brazen before their employers. But in teaching, the boys and girls constantly disrupt, and yet all find the teacher to be guilty.
>
> In all other professions there is peace. . . . But among teachers the opposite is true.
>
> All professions earn their livelihood with honor and receive their salary in full. But teachers acquire only a crust of bread and water, along with insults and abuses, and instead of a salary they receive hunger and famine.

The author of the parody was Levi Reuben Zimlin. It was published at the expense of Ephraim Deinard, bibliophile, Zionist, and publicist, who later emigrated to the United States and enjoyed a colorful career. His magnificent personal library of Hebraica was acquired by Harvard University. Some of the collections he helped form for others, notably that of Judge Mayer Sulzberger of Philadelphia, are now at the Jewish Theological Seminary of America.

HARVARD 20:15

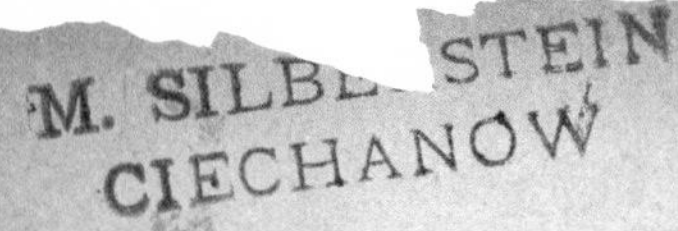
M. SILBERSTEIN
CIECHANOW

סדר

הגדה למלמדים

כמנהג

ליטא. פולין, רייסען, גאליציען ורומיניה.

ולמען לא תהיה ההגדה כחידה בלא פתרון נוסף עליה פירוש

לחם עוני

מאת לוי ראובן זימלין.

הוצאה שלישית

יצאה לאור בתקונים רבים בהוצאות אפרים דיינארד באדעססא
והזכות מכורה לו לצמיתות מאת המחבר.

אדעססא
בדפוס פ' א' זעליעני, ברחוב קראסנאיא נומ' 3

ГАГАДА ЛИМЛАМДИМЪ,
т. е. Сказаніе для учителей, соч. Л. Р. Зимлина.

ОДЕССА.
ТИПОГРАФІЯ П. А. ЗЕЛЕНАГО, КРАСНЫЙ ПЕРЕУЛОКЪ, ДОМЪ № 3.
1885.

VIENNA · AUSTRIA · 1889

For Algeria and Morocco

Though Leghorn, Italy, was the greatest source of Hebrew books printed for the Jews of North Africa in modern times, the Hebrew presses of Vienna occasionally issued books for the same market.

Shown here is the title page of a Haggadah published in the Austrian capital "with an Arabic [i.e., Judeo-Arabic] translation, as it is spoken in the cities of Algiers, Oran, and Constantine, and all the cities of the West, and with lovely illustrations, pleasing to the eye of the beholders." (The "West" [Hebrew, *Ma'arab*; Arabic, *Maghreb*] is generally a designation for Morocco, though it can include other parts of North Africa.)

In the page reproduced on the right, the Judeo-Arabic translation in Hebrew characters is printed in small type. The illustration of the departure of the Israelites from Egypt is derived from the Amsterdam Haggadahs of 1695 and 1712, and their later imitations. (See also Plate 89.)

YAARI NO. 1326 HARVARD 19:12

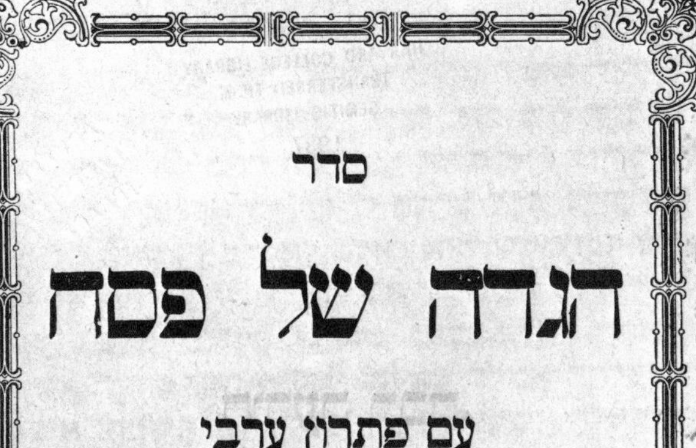

סדר

הגדה של פסח

עם פתרון ערבי

המדוברת בערי אלג׳יר ווהראן וקוסמטינא
וכל ערי המערב.

ועם ציורים נאים ויפים הנחמדים למראה
עין צופים.

בשנת **התרמ״ט** לפ״ג היא שנת 1889 לחשבונם.

מַצָּה זוֹ שֶׁאָנוּ אוֹכְלִים עַל שׁוּם מָה. עַל שׁוּם שֶׁלֹּא הִסְפִּיק בְּצֵקָם שֶׁל אֲבוֹתֵינוּ לְהַחְמִיץ. עַד שֶׁנִּגְלָה עֲלֵיהֶם מֶלֶךְ מַלְכֵי הַמְּלָכִים הַקָּדוֹשׁ בָּרוּךְ הוּא וּגְאָלָם מִיָּד. שֶׁנֶּאֱמַר. וַיֹּאפוּ אֶת הַבָּצֵק אֲשֶׁר הוֹצִיאוּ מִמִּצְרַיִם עֻגֹת מַצּוֹת כִּי לֹא חָמֵץ כִּי גֹרְשׁוּ מִמִּצְרַיִם וְלֹא יָכְלוּ לְהִתְמַהְמֵהַּ וְגַם צֵדָה לֹא עָשׂוּ לָהֶם:

לפטיר האדא די אחנא נאכלו עלא סבת האש. עלא סבת אדי לאם תעטל עג׳ינהום די ג׳דודנא לייכ׳מר חתא די אתג׳לא עליהום צולטאן מצלטן אצלאטין למוקדם מבארך הווא ופכ׳הום פיסאע. כיף אדי קאל לפסוק ועג׳נו לעג׳ין די כ׳ררג׳ו מן מאצר ג׳ראדק פטאייר אין לאם כ׳מיר אין אתטרדו מן מאצר ולאם קדרו לייתעטל וחתא לעווין לאם עמלו אילהום:

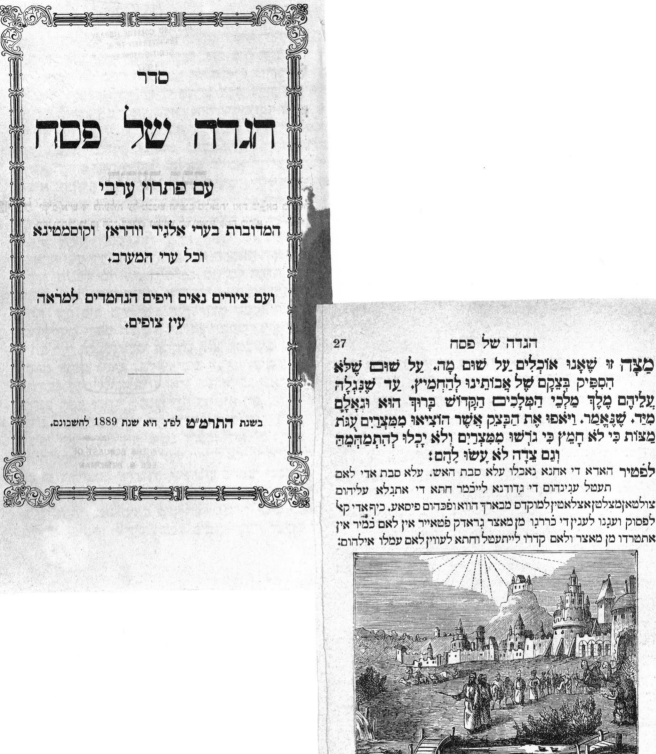

מָרוֹר זֶה שֶׁאָנוּ אוֹכְלִים עַל שׁוּם מָה. עַל שׁוּם שֶׁמֵּרְרוּ הַמִּצְרִיִּים אֶת חַיֵּי אֲבוֹתֵינוּ בְּמִצְרַיִם שֶׁנֶּאֱמַר וַיְמָרְרוּ אֶת חַיֵּיהֶם בַּעֲבוֹדָה קָשָׁה בְּחֹמֶר וּבִלְבֵנִים וּבְכָל עֲבֹדָה בַּשָּׂדֶה אֵת כָּל עֲבוֹדָתָם אֲשֶׁר עָבְדוּ בָהֶם בְּפָרֶךְ:

למראר האדא די אחנא נאכלו עלא סבת האש. עלא סבת די מררו למצריים חייאת גדודנא פי מאצר כיף די קאל לפסוק

PRAGUE · BOHEMIA · 1889

A Christian Illustrator of the Haggadah

The Prague Haggadah of 1889 was one of the very few editions in the nineteenth century in which an attempt was made to create new illustrations that departed from the Venetian and Amsterdam archetypes. The artist, Cyril Kutlik, was a Slovak Christian, son of a Protestant minister, and only nineteen years old at the time.

Twelve pictures were commissioned and executed. Done in the romantic style of the time, except for the Seder scene on the title page they manage to break with the conventional treatment of their themes. Unfortunately they were poorly reproduced in the printing, and thus must have lost much of their original quality. Kutlik, whose name is not even mentioned on the title page, died prematurely at the age of thirty-one.

Shown here, along with the title page, is Kutlik's illustration of the finding of the infant Moses.

The Haggadah was published with a new German translation by Alexander Kisch, rabbi of the Meisel Synagogue in Prague from 1885 to 1917.

YAARI NO. 1338 HARVARD 17:11

סדר

הַגָּדָה שֶׁל פֶּסַח

Die Peßach-Hagada,

Gebete und Gebräuche am Familientische für die beiden ersten Peßach-Abende. Mit 12 künstlerisch ausgeführten Illustrationen. Der althergebrachte hebräische Text mit

neuer deutscher Uebersetzung

und Erläuternng versehen

von

Phil.-Dr. **Alexander Kisch,**

Rabbiner und Prediger in Prag.

Der Sederabend.

Eigenthum und Verlag von Samuel W. Pascheles.

Buch-, Kunst- und Musikalienhandlung und hebr. Verlag.

Prag

PLATE 119

VILNA · RUSSIA · 1889–90

A Miniature from the Lithuanian Jerusalem

Vilna, called by the Jews *Yerushalayim de-Lita* ("The Jerusalem of Lithuania") was not only one of the greatest seats of Jewish learning and culture in modern times, it was also a major center of Hebrew printing. Among its presses none enjoyed more prestige than that of "The Widow and the Brothers Romm," whose editions of the Talmud and other major classics were regarded as authoritative throughout the world. In 1889–90 the firm published this miniature Haggadah, in format perhaps the smallest ever to appear. It is reproduced here in its actual size.

Above: The title page.

Below: The verso, in Russian, giving the permit of the tsarist censor of Kiev for the printing of the work and the first page of Hebrew text, with instructions and blessings for the burning of leaven.

YAARI NO. 1349 JTSA 7:5

סדר
הגדה
של פסח
עם
עירובי תבשילין

ווילנא
בדפוס והוצאות
האלמנה והאחים ראם
שנת תר״נ לפ״ק

סדר בדיקת חמץ   א

אור לי״ד (וכשחל בשבת אור לי״ג) מיד אחר ת״ע בודקין החמץ לאור הנר בכל המקומות שרגילים להשתמש שם אפי׳ בחורין ובסדקין. ובודקין בנר של שעוה. ואסור לאכול סעודת קבע באותה שעה אפי׳ התענה קודם שיבדוק. מיהו טעימה מותר. וקודם הבדיקה יאמר:

בָּרוּךְ אַתָּה יְיָ אֱלֹהֵינוּ מֶלֶךְ הָעוֹלָם אֲשֶׁר קִדְּשָׁנוּ בְּמִצְוֹתָיו וְצִוָּנוּ עַל בִּעוּר חָמֵץ:

ואחר הבדיקה מיד בלילה יבטלנו ויאמר זה:

כָּל חֲמִירָא וַחֲמִיעָא דְּאִכָּא בִרְשׁוּתִי דְּלָא חֲמִתֵּיהּ וּדְלָא בִעַרְתֵּיהּ וּדְלָא יְדַעְנָא לֵיהּ לִבָּטֵל וְלֶהֱוֵי הֶפְקֵר כְּעַפְרָא דְאַרְעָא:

ביום י״ד בניסן בשעה ה׳ יעשה מדורה בפני עצמו וישרפנו ואחר השריפה יבטלנו ויאמר:

כָּל חֲמִירָא וַחֲמִיעָא דְּאִכָּא בִרְשׁוּתִי דַּחֲזִתֵּיהּ וּדְלָא חֲזִתֵּיהּ דַּחֲמִתֵּיהּ וּדְלָא
חמתיה

Дозволено цензурою,
17 Іюля 1889 г. Кіевъ.

ГАГАДА ШЕЛЪ
ПЕСАХЪ.
Молитвенное чтеніе на первые два вечера Пасхи.
Второе извлеченіе изъ молитвенника Шалме-Тода съ Вилен. изданія
1888 г.

ВИЛЬНА.
Тип. Вдовы и бр. Роммъ.
Жмуд. пер. домъ № 328.
1889.

PLATE 120

BOMBAY · INDIA · 1890

A Marathi Seder Dish

The third edition of the Haggadah in the Marathi language of the Bene Israel of India was a revised translation by Elyoh Shalome Walwatkar. (For the earlier editions see Plates 97–98, 107–110.) It was published by Aaron Jacob Diweykar at the Anglo-Jewish and Vernacular Press in Bombay. Reproduced here are the title page (left) and the diagram and explanation of the Seder dish (right), all in Marathi. The Haggadah text is printed in Hebrew and Marathi, the translation following directly after each passage.

YAARI NO. 1341 HARVARD 18:13

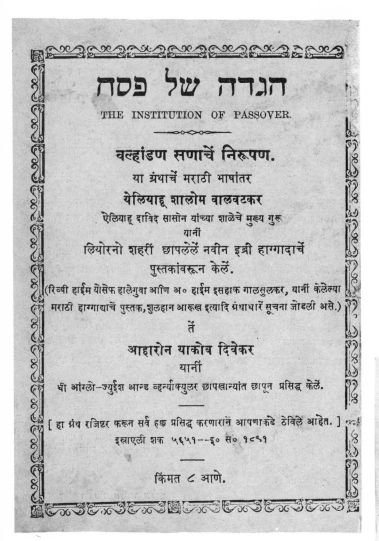

הגדה של פסח

THE INSTITUTION OF PASSOVER.

वल्हांडण सणाचें निरूपण.

या ग्रंथाचें मराठी भाषांतर

येलियाहू शालोम वालवटकर

ऐलियाहू दाविद सासोन यांच्या शाळेचे मुख्य गुरू

यानीं

लियोरनो शहरीं छापलेलें नवीन इब्री हाग्गादाचें

पुस्तकांवरून केलें.

(रिब्बी हाईम योसेफ हालेगुवा आणि अ० हाईम इसहाक गालसुलकर, यानीं केलेल्या मराठी हाग्गाद्याचें पुस्तक, शुलहान आरूख इत्यादि ग्रंथाधारें सूचना जोडली असे.)

तें

आहारोन याकोब दिवेकर

यानीं

धी आंग्लो–ज्युईश आन्ड व्हर्न्याक्युलर छापखान्यांत छापून प्रसिद्ध केलें.

[हा ग्रंथ रजिष्टर करून सर्व हक्क प्रसिद्ध करणारानें आपणाकडे ठेविले आहेत.]

इस्राएली शक ५६५१--इ० स० १८९१

किंमत ८ आणे.

१४ वे तारखेस आपल्या शक्तिप्रमाणें मेज तयारकरून मध्यें १ मोठें तबक ठेवून त्यांत एका जवळ एक असे ३ प्याले ठेवावे; एकांत मीठ, २ऱ्यांत खजुराचा शिरा, ३ऱ्यांत (लिंबाचा) अंबट रस ठेवून त्यावर सेदारिमच्या भाकरी ठेवाव्या. त्या अशा कीं, वर कोहेन, मध्यें लेवी आणि खालीं इस्राएल आणि समोरच्या दोन बाजूस एकिकडे जेरोवा, दुसरी कडेस ह्मणजे त्याच्या समोरच उकडलेलें अंडे ठेवावें. सर्व मनुष्यांस पुरेल इतका द्राक्षरस भांड्यांत भरून ठेवावा. गलास प्रत्येकास वेगवेगळेंच असावें व तबक वस्त्रानें झांकून ठेवावें.

शिरा करायाचा तो चांगला खजूर आणून त्यांतील बिया काढून टाकून एका भांड्यांत थंड पाणी घेऊन त्यांत तो टाकावा व चांगला फुगला म्हणजे त्याचा रस काढून चोथा टाकून द्यावा; मग तो एका भांड्यांत आटेपर्यंत शिजवावा. कित्येक लोक बदाम, अक्रोड इत्यादिकाच्या चार किंवा पांच बिया घेऊन त्या कुटून शिऱ्यांत मिळवून शिजवितात.

अंबट रस फक्त लिंबे कापून काढतात. जेरोवा म्हणजे बकऱ्याचे पुढचे पायाचा वरचा भाग घेऊन रीतिप्रमाणें शीरा काढून स्वच्छ करून मीठ लावून भाजावा.

तबक मांडण्याची रीत.

आंबट रस व मीठ

प्रार्थना करून येण्यापूर्वी मेज तयार ठेवावें परंतु रात्रीचें नक्षत्र निघाल्याशिवाय किदुश करूं नये. या रात्रीस ४दां किदुश प्यावा व बेखमीर भाकरी याच रात्रीं खाव्या; आधीं खाऊं नयेत.

ALEPPO · SYRIA · 1897

The Only Syrian Haggadah

One of the most venerable Jewish communities in the Near East was that of the city of Aleppo in Syria, called by the Jews *Aram Tzoba* (and abbreviated as AReTZ). Hebrew printing began in Aleppo in 1865 and continued until the persecution of Syrian Jewry in recent years. The Haggadah published in 1897 together with a Judeo-Arabic translation is the only one ever issued by the Aleppo press.

Left: The title page, announcing the book as a "Haggadah in the Arabic tongue." Around the flower is a Hebrew inscription: "Remember the Lord from afar, and let Jerusalem come into your mind" (Jeremiah 51:50).

Right: Instructions and blessings for the burning of leaven, and a diagram showing "the arrangement of the Seder dish according to the custom of the 'Ari' [Isaac Luria] of blessed memory."

YAARI NO. 1519 HARVARD 18:13

הגדה בלשון ערבי

זכרו את יי מרחוק וירושלים

תעלה על לבבכם

נדפסה בארץ יע"א

תרנ"ז

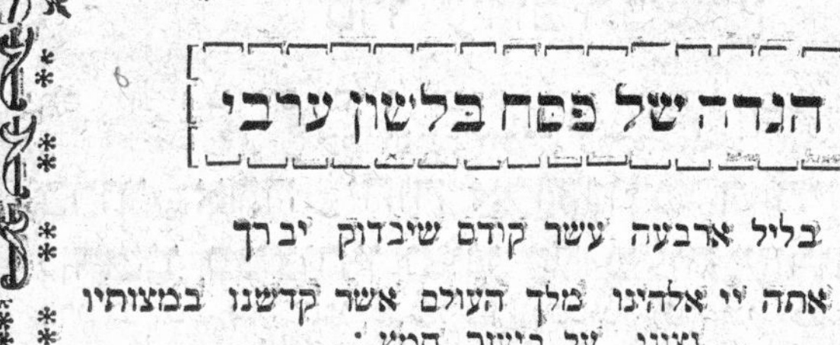

הגדה של פסח בלשון ערבי

בליל ארבעה עשר קודם שיבדוק יברך

ברוך אתה יי אלהינו מלך העולם אשר קדשנו במצותיו
וצונו על ביעור חמץ :

ואחר שיבדוק יאמר :

כל חמירא דאיכא ברשותי דלא חזיתיה ודלא ביערתיה ליבטיל
וליהוי כעפרא דארעא :

ביום ארבעה עשר אחר שליש היום ישרוף חמצו ויבטלנו בזה
הנוסח ויאמר :

כל חמירא דאיכא ברשותי דחזיתיה ודלא חזיתיה דביערתיה
ודלא ביערתיה ליבטיל וליהוי כעפרא דארעא :

סדר הקערה לפי מנהג האר"י ז"ל :

כי נר מצוה ותורה אור

נדפסה פי מטבעת אל דאהודייה פה ארצ"י

בשנת והגדת לבנך ביום ההוא לאמר לפ"ג

JERUSALEM · PALESTINE · 1904

For the Jews of Bukhara

A Haggadah commissioned by the Jews of the city of Bukhara in Central Asia and produced for their use by the Jerusalem printer Samuel Halevi Zuckerman. The edition is in Hebrew with a translation into Judeo-Persian (i.e., Persian in Hebrew characters), the vernacular of the Bukharan Jews. On the title page (left) it is described as

a version of the Haggadah in the Persian language, by the renowned translator Shimon Ḥakham, may the Lord guard and redeem him. Accompanied also by tales and songs relevant to the Passover holiday. All in an elegant and pure Persian rendition the like of which has never existed, in order to benefit the congregation of the Jewish community residing in the territory of Bukhara and its environs. At the order and expense of the faithful partners Azariah ben Yosef ha-Kohen and Yedidiah ben Yosef Harathi, booksellers in Bukhara.

Right: A page with an illustration of the Four Sons, taken from the Amsterdam Haggadah (Plate 60). The Judeo-Persian translation is printed in the smaller types.

YAARI NO. 1663 HARVARD 23:15

ספר

חקת הפסח

כולל

לימוד כל חדש ניסן שהם קרבנות הנשיאים והתפלות הראויות להם דבר יום ביומו. וברכת האילנות והגדה של פסח.

ונוסף בו מחדש

סדר קרבן פסח עם העתקה מהר"ש אסטרופלי זלה"ה ומ"ב מסעות המסוגלים לאומרם ביום י"ד. ודיני ביעור חמץ וסדר הקערה בציור יפה, ותפסיר ההגדה בשפת פרסי המתורגם מאת המתרגם המפורסם מוהר"ר מו' **שמעון חכם** הי"ו. גם אשו' נלוה עמם כמה ספורי מעשיות ופזמונים השייכים לחג הפסח. הכל בתפסיר פרסי צח ונקי אשר לא היה כמוהו לעולמים. כדי לזכות קהל עדת היהודים יושבי ארץ **בוכארא** ואגפיה :

במצות ובהוצאות השותפים הנאמנים

מו' **עזריה** יצ"ו בן מו' **יוסף הכהן** נ"ע ∴ ומו' **ידידיה** יצ"ו בן מו' **יוסף הראתי** נ"ע

מוכר ספרים בבוכארא

נדפס

פעה"ק **ירושלם** תובב"א

שנת **זאת חקת הפסח** לפ"ג

בדפוס ה"ר שמואל הלוי צוקערמאן הי"ו

תּוֹרָה. אֶחָד חָכָם. וְאֶחָד רָשָׁע. וְאֶחָד תָּם. וְאֶחָד שֶׁאֵינוֹ יוֹדֵעַ לִשְׁאֹל :

בְּאַפְּרִין הַקָּדוֹשׁ בָּרוּךְ הוּא בְּאַפְּרִין אוֹ. בְּאַפְּרִין אַנְגִ'י בִידָאד תוֹרָה בְקַוְמִי אוֹ יִשְׂרָאֵל בְאַפְּרִין אוֹ. גוּנ מוּקָאבִילִי גַהָאר פִּיסָרָאן. סוּכַן גוּפְתַה תוֹרָה, יַכִּי עָאקִיל, וְיַכִּי זָאלִים, וְיַכִּי סָאדַה, וְיַכִּי אַנְגִ'י גֵיסְתֵי אוֹ דָאנָא בְסַוָואל כַּרְדַן :

אין צורת הא שכלי אזאני ג'האר פיסראן מיבאשד :

חָכָם מַה הוּא אוֹמֵר. מָה הָעֵדֹת וְהַחֻקִּים וְהַמִּשְׁפָּטִים אֲשֶׁר צִוָּה יְהוָֹה אֱלֹהֵינוּ אֶתְכֶם. אַף אַתָּה אֱמוֹר לוֹ כְּהִלְכוֹת הַפֶּסַח. אֵין מַפְטִירִין אַחַר הַפֶּסַח אֲפִיקוֹמָן :

עָאקִיל גַי או גוֹיְיא. גִיסְת אָן שַהָאדַת הָא. וְאָן רַסְם הָא. וְאָן טַרִיקַת הָא. אַנְגִ'י בִיפַרְמוּד יְיָ כוּדָאיי אֵימָא שוּמָא רָא. גִיז תוּ בִיגוּי בְאוֹ גוּן רַוִישִי (טריקתי) אָן קָרְבַן פֶּסַח. גֵיסְתֵי דַהָאן כּוּשָׁאיְיָאן בַעְדִי אָן קָרְבַן פֶּסַח כּוּשׁ מֵיוַה הָא :

רָשָׁע מַה הוּא אוֹמֵר. מָה הָעֲבוֹדָה הַזֹּאת לָכֶם. לָכֶם וְלֹא לוֹ. וּלְפִי שֶׁהוֹצִיא אֶת עַצְמוֹ מִן הַכְּלָל כָּפַר בָּעִקָּר. אַף אַתָּה הַקְהֵה אֶת שִׁנָּיו. וֶאֱמוֹר לוֹ בַּעֲבוּר זֶה עָשָׂה יְהוָֹה לִי

בצאתי

PLATE 123

LEGHORN · ITALY · 1904

For the Jews of Bou Saada and Ghardaia

Most Livornese Haggadahs destined specifically for the North African market were published with texts according to the rites of major Jewish communities. This Haggadah, entitled *Ahabat ha-kadmonim* ("The Love of the Ancients"), is unusual in presenting the ritual of two of the smaller, lesser-known Algerian communities.

The title page is printed originally in red and black, with the description of the virtues of the edition in rhymed Hebrew prose. Within, a Judeo-Arabic translation appears together with the Hebrew text.

YAARI NO. 1665 HARVARD 19:13

לישועתך קויתי יי : ואעבור עליך

ספר

אהבת הקדמונים

הנותן אמרי שפר · אמרות טהורות · מפנינים
יקרות · הנהגות ישרות בעדי **בוסעאדא**
וגרדאייא יע״א ויחנו במוסרות · לדעת
טוב ורק בטובו חיינו קול קורא במדבר מדבר
קדמות · אסף אסיפים מספרי כ״י איש איש
ממקומו עירות המוקפות · למען ירוץ קול קורא
זקנים עם נערים · באותיות גדולות עם נקודות ·
ואתייא תוך תוך פיוטים למולות · שירו לאלהים
זמרו שמו בשיר המעלות :

פה **ליוורנו** יע״א

שנת **בשמחה ובששו״ן** לפ״ק

בדפוס חדש של הקכס רט״ל

אליהו בן אמוזג ובניו הי״ו

מדפיסים ומוכרי ספרים

ואראך מתבוססת בדמייך ואומר לך בדמייך חיי ואומר לך

בדמייך חיי : קול רנה וישועה

באהלי צדיקים : הנה אל ישועתי אבטח ולא אפחד : כי עזי וזמ׳

JERUSALEM · PALESTINE · 1905

Commissioned from Calcutta

A trilingual Jerusalem Haggadah, in Hebrew, Arabic, and English, was published in 1905. At this time, when Jerusalem was still under Ottoman rule, there was not a single Jewish community in the city that required a Haggadah with this particular combination of languages. The explanation is simply that it was intended, not for Jerusalem, but for someplace else.

The Haggadah was commissioned by a Jew of Calcutta, David Ḥai Eini, and reflects the needs of Jews in India. Beside the native Bene Israel, there were communities of Arabic-speaking Jews in India who had come there from the Muslim Orient. Living under British rule, they had acquired the English language as well.

There was no practical necessity for such an edition to be printed in Jerusalem. Calcutta had had a Hebrew press since 1841, and English types were, of course, also readily available. It was undoubtedly the symbolic value of a book printed in the Holy City that was uppermost in the mind of the sponsor. Perhaps the added attraction for potential customers also did not elude him.

Reproduced here are the title page and (right) a Hebrew advertisement that follows:

ANNOUNCEMENT

I am honored to inform our brothers and fellows in redemption in each and every city, that we have for sale all manner of lovely and important books, of the Leghorn press and the Vilna press, of many kinds, as well as from the presses of Vienna and Babylon [i.e., Baghdad]. There are also prayer shawls of lambs' wool, cotton and silk, all kinds of thread for fringes, phylacteries, the Jerusalem and Babylonian [Talmud], *mezuzot*, and other holy articles. . . . Those who buy from us or trade with us may be confident that they shall obtain satisfaction. Let them write according to this address.

The firm of David Sassoon, Ltd., mentioned in the address that follows, was that of the great Baghdadi family who made a fortune in India and came to be known as the "Rothschilds of the East."

Beneath are vignettes of two Palestinian holy places: Safed, and the synagogue at the tomb of Rabbi Meir Ba'al ha-Nes. A full-page photograph of David Ḥai Eini precedes the Haggadah text.

YAARI NO. 1688 HARVARD 18:13

הגדה של פסח

בעברי וערבי

עם העתקה אנגלית

כולה כסדר בשלימות

בהוצאות המלבה"ד

שאול דוד חי עיני ואחיו הי"ו

HAGADAH for PASSOVER

with English Translation

פעה"ק ירושלם תובב"א

תרס"ה–1905

JERUSALEM

כדפוס הרי"ד פרומקין הי"ו

Printed by J. B. Frumkin

מודעה!

אתכבד להודיע לאחינו אנשי גאולתינו דבכל עיר ועיר הי"ו יש אתנו כל מיני ספרים למכור, יפים וחשובים, מדפוס ליוורנו, ומדפוס ווילנא הרבה מינים, וגם מדפוס ווינא ובבל. כן נמצא טליתות צמר רחלים, וצמר גפן, ומשי, חוטים לציציות מכל המינים, תפילין ירושלמי ובבלי, ומזוזות, ושאר צרכי הק׳. גם יכולים בהזדמן אדם לקנות ספר תורה או ספר הפטרה יכולים להביא לו כתב נאה וחשוב ובערך השוה לכל נפש יכולים למכור. גם עדיין נמצא אתנו לוח העיבור לסוף ש׳ תרס"ז, ומחדש יצא לאור אצלנו הגדה של פסח השובה בתכלית היופי בשלשה לשונות וכולה בשלימות בעברי וערבי ואנגלית ביחד והקונה מאתנו לאחדים ... לעשרות ... למאות ... לאלפים ... כל אופן בערכו ימצא הנחה וראבאט הגון, ובטוחים יהיו הקונים מאתנו או המסתחרים אתנו במסחר הס׳ וכיוצא ישיגו נחת וישבעו רצון מאתנו ויכתבו על פי האדריסא זאת.

דוד חי עיני כלכתה הי"ו. ואזי כל א׳ ישיג שאלתו.

David Hai Einy 3/5 Bow Street Calcutta.
or through this address: c/o mesers. David Sassoon & Co. Ld. 37 Airly Placc Calcutta.

PODGÓRZE · GALICIA · 1905

"With 238 Commentaries"

Commentaries on the Haggadah, as on other classic Jewish texts, have been written throughout the centuries. Generally, the first edition of a commentary would appear by itself or with the Haggadah. In the eighteenth century it became the occasional practice to publish several important commentaries together, surrounding the text on the page. Later, some publishers began to vie with one another in the number they could crowd into a single edition.

Something of a record must have been set in 1905 by the Galician publisher Saul Hananiah Deutscher, who announces his Haggadah as printed "with 238 commentaries and additions." Naturally, each of these is represented by a mere fragment.

The title page, shown here, is printed in the original in green and red.

YAARI NO. 1696 HARVARD 21:15

בעה"י

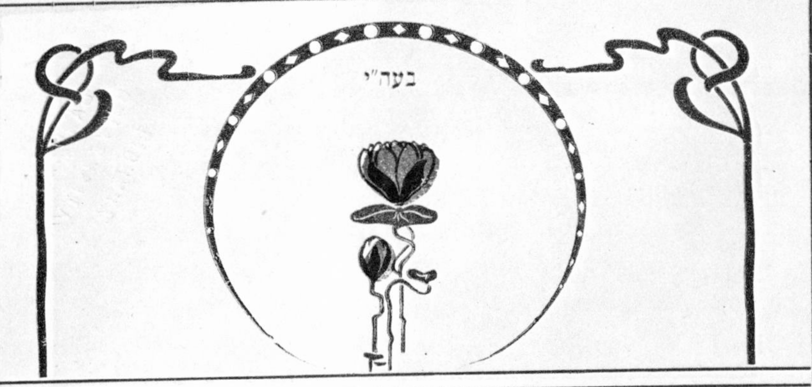

הגדה של פסח

עם

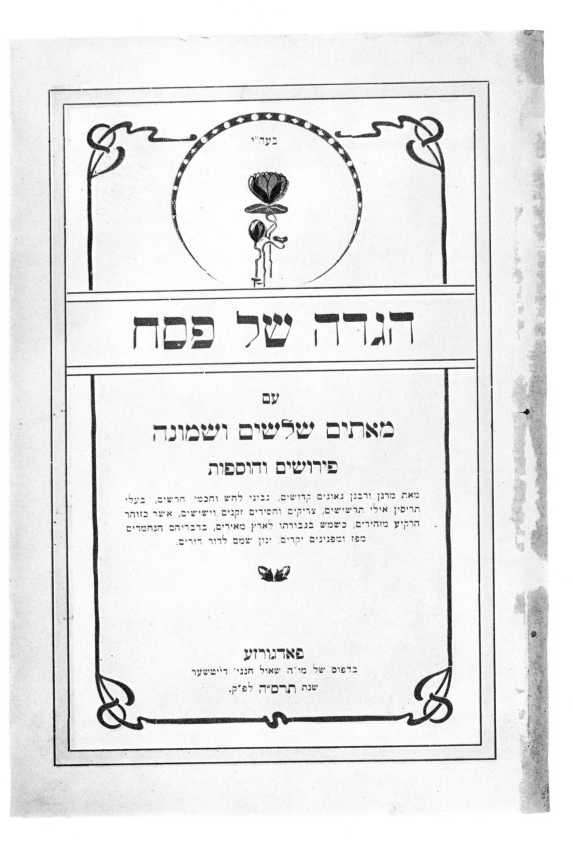

מאתים שלשים ושמונה

פירושים והוספות

מאת מרנן ורבנן גאונים קדושים, נבוני לחש וחכמי הרשים, בעלי תריסין אילי תרשישים, צדיקים וחסידים זקנים וישישים, אשר כזוהר הרקיע מזהירים, כשמש בגבורתו לארץ מאירים, בדבריהם הנחמדים מפז ומפנינים יקרים, ינון שמם לדור דורים.

פאדגורזע

בדפוס של מו"ה שאול חנני' דייטשער

שנת תרס"ה לפ"ק.

CINCINNATI · U.S.A. · 1907

The Reform Haggadah in America

The standardized American version of the Reform Haggadah was issued in 1907. Called the *Union Haggadah* (for the Union of American Hebrew Congregations), it was published by the Central Conference of American Rabbis in Cincinnati, Ohio, and printed at the press of L. H. Cahan and Co. in Philadelphia.

Most of the text is in English, with a minimal amount of Hebrew. In addition to a number of illustrations and musical selections, there are sections devoted to "Passover in History and Tradition" and "Passover in Literature." The frontispiece is reproduced here.

YAARI NO. 1735 HARVARD 20:13

The
Union
Haggadah
Max Rosenthal
1906.

BAGHDAD · IRAQ · 1908

Dated: "One Kid for Two Zuzim"

A Baghdad Haggadah in Hebrew and Judeo-Arabic, "printed in large letters . . . with vowels, and several additions: the laws for the burning of leaven, and the order of the night in the Arabic tongue, so that it may be understood by everyone, and so that Israel shall know what to do."

The traditional practice of dating a book by the numerical value of a biblical verse or a Hebrew phrase is here given an unusual twist. Recorded at the bottom of the title page are the opening words of the popular Haggadah song *Ḥad gadya*: "One kid . . . for two zuzim," which yields the year [5]668 on the Jewish calendar.

VARIANT OF YAARI NO. 1740 HARVARD 17.5:12

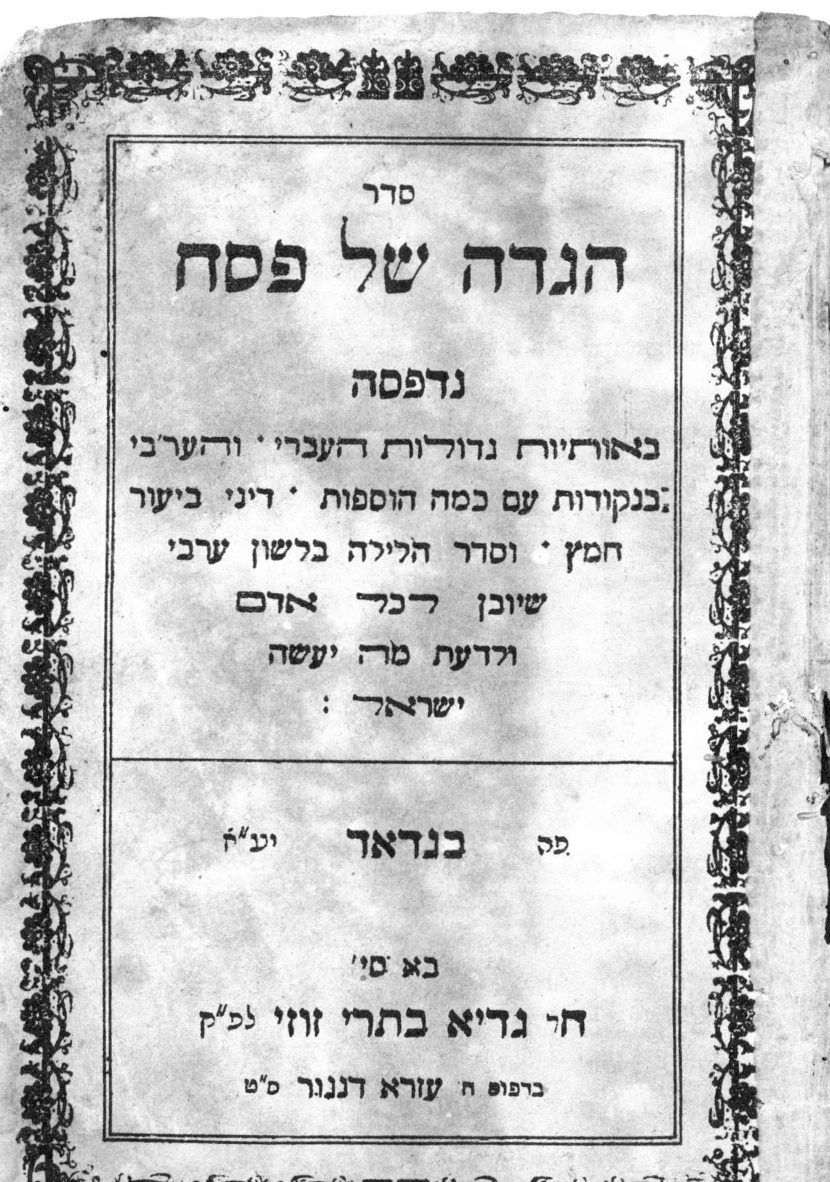

סדר

הגדה של פסח

נדפסה

באותיות גדולות העברי׳ והערבי
בנקודות עם כמה הוספות ׳ דיני ביעור
חמץ ׳ וסדר הלילה בלשון ערבי
שיובן לכל אדם
ולדעת מה יעשה
ישראל :

פה בגדאד יע״א

בא סי׳

חד גדיא בתרי זוזי לפ״ק

בדפוס ה׳ עזרא דנגור ס״ט

CAIRO · EGYPT · 1908

Passover in Form—Purim in Content

One of the most baffling genres of parody to the uninitiated employs the structure of the Passover Haggadah as a pretext for the irreverent mirth that is a byplay of the Purim festival. Shown here is the title page of such a "Purim Haggadah" composed and printed in Judeo-Arabic by Lazare M. Hami. There is nothing in it of Passover. It is all a kind of carnival humor which, even though using a hallowed text for purposes of mundane burlesque, is too obviously innocent to be considered sacrilege. The recurring motif is one of eating and drinking to extravagant excess. Toward the end, instead of the usual *Le-shanah ha-ba'ah bi-Yerushalayim* ("Next year in Jerusalem"), we read: *Le-shanah ha-ba'ah nishteh be-kiflayim* ("Next year we shall drink a double measure!").

HARVARD 25.5:17.5

הגדת פורים

בלשון ערבי

נוסכת פורים

בכ' ערבי

הזליה פכאהייה נוכאתייה ארבייה

תאליף

עזאר מורדוך חאמי

لا يجوز لاي احد خلافنا طبع هذه النسخه سوا بحروف عربي او
بحروف عبري ومن يخالف ذلك يتحاكم قانوناً ـ وكل نسخه لم تكن
مختومة بختمنا هذا تعتبر لاغيه

LAZARE M. HAMI

Lazare M. Hami

(טבע פי מטבעת אהרן אשר - בחארת א' יהוד במצר)

DJERBA · TUNISIA · 1917

An Island Community

According to the traditions of the Jews who live on the island of Djerba, near the Tunisian coast, their community was founded in the time of King Solomon, when Djerba was an important Phoenician trading post. Whatever its actual origins, the community is certainly very old.

As in most places outside of Europe, however, the Djerba press is of relatively recent origin, having begun in 1904. This is one of the earliest Haggadahs printed in Djerba (the first edition appeared in 1916). Entitled *'Arbey Pesaḥim* ("The Passover Evenings"), it is accompanied by a Judeo-Arabic translation and two commentaries: *Korban Pesaḥ* ("The Passover Sacrifice") and *Korban Ḥagigah* ("The Festival Sacrifice"), as well as other liturgical materials. (The Song of Songs with commentary, announced on the title page, does not actually appear within.)

YAARI NO. 1878 HARVARD 19:13

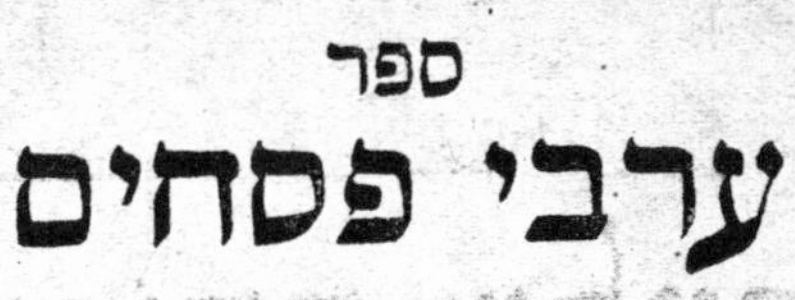

ספר

ערבי פסחים

והוא כ׳ פירושים על ההגדה קריאה נאמנה, שתקן המגיד לעדת
מי מנה, כליל התקדש חג מדי שנה בשנה, דישרן
המיכין עלוהי על לבו ועל שפתו, מזה ומזה לכסותו, שם האחד
קרבן פסח ושם השני קרבן חגיגה שניהם מגידי מישרים,
ביאורים פשוטים וברורים, כזוהר הרקיע
מזהירים, וכברקים מאירים, כדברים נוחים, כולם למבין נכוחים,
ובשמן הקדש משוחים, ונוסף גם אות פרטי דינים וענינים כל הדבר
השייך מר״ח ניסן עד ערב פסח ופרטי דיני הסדר מבוררים.

[ואזהרות לשבת הגדול מרבי יהודה הלוי זצ״ל
ראש המשוררים], כדברים יקרים, וסדר קרבן פסח וסדר אכילתו
ככל חקיו ומשפטיו סדורים, ונשלמה פרים שפתינו
ליוצר הרים, וביאור על דברי רבינו האר״י זצ״ל המאיר לארץ
ולדרים, ממהר״ש מאוסטרופולי זצ״ל
מבוארים, ורמזי סדר קדש ורחץ
חידושים ומוסרים, ופרטי ארבעים וחמשים מכות לר״א ולר״ע מבוררים,
וחמשים מכות על הים לר״א הגלילי על סדר המקרא מסודרים, הכל
נעשה יפה בעתו דבר דבור על אופניו כאשר עיני הקורא תחזינה
מישרים, כדברים נחים וברים, וענינים ישרים, מאירים כספירים
[ונוסף גם אות שיר השירים ופירושו לפי הנמשל מהדברים
ממפרשי הפשט מקובלים, להבין זקנים עם נערים], מידי יד כהם
היתה זאת לנו, בעזר מעוז לדלים ואביונים, ועלמה מרנה לאין
אונים, אנכי דל ורזה: כואב ונכוה, לא מזה ולא כן מזה, כי אם
בעזרת ה׳ באתי אות עוזי ומעוזי, אנכי איש צעיר שאול הכהן ס״ט

אי גרבה יע״א

שנת הבה לנו עזר״ת מלך לפ״ק

בדפוס החדש של רבי דוד עידאן הי״ו

מדפיס ומוכר ספרים

Rebbi DAVID AYDAN - Djerba

PLATE 130

VIENNA · AUSTRIA and BERLIN · GERMANY · 1921

Budko Haggadah: The Frontispiece

The first notable illustrated Haggadah of the twentieth century was created by the Jewish artist Joseph Budko and was published in 1921.

Budko was born in Poland in 1888 and, after a traditional education, went on to study art in Vilna and Berlin. A graphic artist in several media, he was also drawn to book illustration. In addition to the Haggadah he illustrated the collected works of the great modern Hebrew poet Chaim Nachman Bialik (Berlin, 1923). In 1933 he settled in Palestine, where he was associated with the Bezalel School of Arts and Crafts. He died in 1940.

Reproduced here is the frontispiece of the Haggadah. Placed against a background of almost oriental intricacy is what seems at first glance to be a Seder dish. However, it is merely a series of concentric circles. In the very middle is a fairly conventional portrayal of the Israelites at the Red Sea. Surrounding it are the Hebrew catchwords for the sequence of the Seder. In the rim is inscribed the opening reply to the Four Questions: "We were slaves unto Pharaoh in Egypt, and the Lord our God brought us forth from there with a mighty hand and an outstretched arm." This is complemented by the inscription in the outer square frame of the whole: "And even were we all wise, all understanding, all of us advanced in years, all endowed with knowledge of the Torah, it would still be our duty to tell the story of the Exodus from Egypt." In this highly compressed manner, both the structure and the basic themes of the Haggadah are announced.

YAARI NO. 1913 HARVARD 21:17

PLATE 131

VIENNA and BERLIN · 1921
[CONTINUED]

Budko Haggadah: Wandering

The Haggadah states: "And it is this [God's promise to Abraham] which has stood by our fathers and us. For not one man only has risen against us to destroy us, but in every generation they rise to destroy us, and the Holy One, blessed be He, saves us from their hand."

In the history of Haggadah illustration this theme is entirely new, and Budko treats it with great restraint. The persecuted Jewish people is embodied in the figure of a solitary Jew on a wintry road that stretches, as it were, from nowhere, and leads—one knows not where.

מכסה המצות ונוטל הכוס בידו ואומר:

וְהִיא שֶׁעָמְדָה

לַאֲבוֹתֵינוּ וְלָנוּ. שֶׁלֹּא אֶחָד בִּלְבָד עָמַד

עָלֵינוּ לְכַלּוֹתֵנוּ. אֶלָּא שֶׁבְּכָל־דּוֹר וָדוֹר

עוֹמְדִים עָלֵינוּ לְכַלּוֹתֵנוּ

וְהַקָּדוֹשׁ בָּרוּךְ הוּא

מַצִּילֵנוּ מִיָּדָם:

BERLIN · GERMANY · 1922

The First Danish Haggadah

The first edition of the Haggadah with a Danish translation was published, not in Denmark, but in Germany.

The translator, who also added some notes, was the Danish rabbi Marcus Melchior (1897–1969), who had just completed his rabbinic studies in Berlin the year before. In later decades he was to enjoy a distinguished career as rabbi of the Danish refugees in Sweden during World War II and, after 1947, as chief rabbi of Denmark.

In this Haggadah the Hebrew and Danish texts appear on facing pages.

YAARI NO. 1930 HARVARD 22:15

Lea Bjalle

סדר
הגדה של פסח
Hagadah schel Pesach

Dansk Oversættelse og forklarende Anmærkninger

af

Marcus Melchior

Lea Bjalle.
Chanuka 1934/5695

BERLIN 1922

M. Poppelauers Verlag

Eneforhandling for Skandinavien: „Israelitens" Ekspedition
Ny Kongensgade 6, Kjøbenhavn B.

CAIRO · EGYPT · 1922

Dayyenu—*in Arabic*

Agudat peraḥim ("A Bouquet of Flowers") is the title given this volume. It includes the Passover Haggadah, the Chapters of the Fathers (*Pirke Abot*), liturgical poems, and proverbs, all in Hebrew, with an Arabic translation by Dr. Hillel Jacob Farḥi.

Unlike the traditional Judeo-Arabic, which is always written in Hebrew characters, the translation in this edition appears in Arabic script.

Left: The title page.
Right: The hymn *Dayyenu* ("It would have sufficed us").

YAARI NO. 1947 HARVARD 21:14

אגודת פרחים
כוללת
הגדה של פסח . פרקי אבות
אזהרות . פתגמים
בעברית וערבית
מאת דר׳ הלל יעקב פרחי

שנת בעבור זה עשה יהוה לי בצאתי ממצרים לפ״ס

مجموعة فارحى
تحتوي على
رواية الفصح . حكم الاقدمين . الوصايا
وحكم بالعبري والعربي
جمع وتعريب
الدكتور فارحى
سنة ١٩٢٢

طبع بمطبعة الخواجه روبرتو موسكوفيتش ـ بمصر

bi Misr
(Cairo)

لو عمل فيهم احكاماً
.
ولم يعمل احكاماً بآلهتهم لكفانا :
لو عمل احكاماً بآلهتهم
.
ولم يقتل ابكارهم لكفانا :
لو قتل ابكارهم
.
ولم يعطنا مالهم لكفانا :
لو اعطانا مالهم
.
ولم يشق لنا البحر لكفانا :
لو شق لنا البحر
.
ولم يدخلنا في وسطه على اليابسة لكفانا :
لو ادخلنا في وسطه على اليابسة
.
ولم يغرق اعداءنا في وسطه لكفانا :
لو اغرق اعداءنا في وسطه
.
ولم يكف عوزنا في البر اربعين سنة لكفانا :
لو كفى عوزنا في البر اربعين سنة
.
ولم يطعمنا المن لكفانا :
لو اطعمنا المن
.
ولم يعطنا السبت لكفانا :
لو اعطانا السبت
.
ولم يقربنا امام جبل سينا لكفانا :
لو قربنا امام جبل سينا
.
ولم يعطنا التوراة لكفانا :

PLATE 134

BERLIN · GERMANY · 1923

Steinhardt Haggadah: The Four Sons

This is one of the most truly distinguished Haggadahs published in modern times, a milestone in Hebrew book production.

The artist responsible for the illustrations was Jacob Steinhardt (1887–1968). Born in Poland, he studied art in Berlin and Paris. In 1912 he returned to Berlin, where he began to exhibit. His career was interrupted by World War I, during which he served in the German Army. Returning to Germany, he remained there until the advent of Hitler in 1933, and then left to settle in Jerusalem. In 1949 he became head of the graphics department at the Bezalel School of Arts and Crafts and, from 1953 to 1957, he was its director. Most of Steinhardt's work was done in engraving and lithography, and, above all, in woodcut.

Shown here is Steinhardt's woodcut of the Four Sons, betraying the strong impact of German Expressionism at that phase in his work. The most striking single element in the composition is the figure of the Wicked Son. Reflecting a long tradition that began with the Prague Haggadah of 1526 (Plate 11), he appears here once again as a soldier, but dressed in a Prussian uniform with a spiked helmet on his head.

The beautiful Hebrew characters in the text of the Haggadah were drawn by the noted type designer Franziska Baruch and executed by Steinhardt in wood.

YAARI NO. 1952 HARVARD 26.5:19.5

לְסַפֵּר בִּיצִיאַת מִצְרַיִם · וְכָל־הַמַּרְבֶּה לְסַפֵּר בִּיצִיאַת מִצְרַיִם
הֲרֵי זֶה מְשֻׁבָּח:

מַעֲשֶׂה בְּרַבִּי אֱלִיעֶזֶר וְרַבִּי יְהוֹשֻׁעַ וְרַבִּי אֶלְעָזָר בֶּן־עֲזַרְיָה וְרַבִּי
עֲקִיבָא וְרַבִּי טַרְפוֹן שֶׁהָיוּ מְסֻבִּין בִּבְנֵי בְרַק · וְהָיוּ מְסַפְּרִים בִּיצִיאַת

מִצְרַיִם
כָּל אוֹתוֹ
הַלַּיְלָה ·
עַד שֶׁבָּאוּ
תַלְמִידֵיהֶם
וְאָמְרוּ לָהֶם
רַבּוֹתֵינוּ
הִגִּיעַ זְמַן
קְרִיאַת
שְׁמַע שֶׁל
שַׁחֲרִית:

אָמַר רַבִּי אֶלְעָזָר בֶּן עֲזַרְיָה · הֲרֵי אֲנִי כְּבֶן שִׁבְעִים שָׁנָה · וְלֹא זָכִיתִי
שֶׁתֵּאָמֵר יְצִיאַת מִצְרַיִם בַּלֵּילוֹת · עַד שֶׁדְּרָשָׁהּ בֶּן זוֹמָא · שֶׁנֶּאֱמַר
לְמַעַן תִּזְכֹּר אֶת יוֹם צֵאתְךָ מֵאֶרֶץ מִצְרַיִם כֹּל יְמֵי חַיֶּיךָ ·
יְמֵי חַיֶּיךָ הַיָּמִים · כֹּל יְמֵי חַיֶּיךָ הַלֵּילוֹת · וַחֲכָמִים אוֹמְרִים
יְמֵי חַיֶּיךָ הָעוֹלָם הַזֶּה · כֹּל יְמֵי חַיֶּיךָ לְהָבִיא לִימוֹת הַמָּשִׁיחַ:

בָּרוּךְ הַמָּקוֹם · בָּרוּךְ הוּא · בָּרוּךְ שֶׁנָּתַן תּוֹרָה לְעַמּוֹ יִשְׂרָאֵל.
בָּרוּךְ הוּא: כְּנֶגֶד אַרְבָּעָה בָנִים דִּבְּרָה תוֹרָה · אֶחָד חָכָם ·
וְאֶחָד רָשָׁע · וְאֶחָד תָּם · וְאֶחָד שֶׁאֵינוֹ יוֹדֵעַ לִשְׁאוֹל:

BERLIN · 1923
[CONTINUED]

Steinhardt Haggadah: Terror and Flight

Like Joseph Budko (Plate 131), Steinhardt also chose to illustrate the Haggadah passage concerning the perennial attempt to annihilate the Jews. Essentially, both artists have depicted the insecurity of Jewish life through the ages in terms of wandering. But where Budko was content to epitomize this in the figure of a single Jew whose face is not even revealed, Steinhardt has focused upon a group of Jews, their faces showing that they are overcome with fear, in flight from some horror they have witnessed. Both approaches—Budko's quiet pathos and Steinhardt's agitation and torment—are equally effective.

מכסין את המצות ומגביהין את הכוס.

וְהִיא שֶׁעָמְדָה לַאֲבוֹתֵינוּ וְלָנוּ. שֶׁלֹּא אֶחָד בִּלְבַד עָמַד עָלֵינוּ
לְכַלּוֹתֵינוּ. אֶלָּא שֶׁבְּכָל־דּוֹר וָדוֹר עוֹמְדִים עָלֵינוּ לְכַלּוֹתֵנוּ.
וְהַקָּדוֹשׁ בָּרוּךְ הוּא מַצִּילֵנוּ מִיָּדָם:

יניח הכוס מידו ויחזור ויגלה המצות

צֵא וּלְמַד. מַה בִּקֵּשׁ לָבָן הָאֲרַמִּי לַעֲשׂוֹת לְיַעֲקֹב אָבִינוּ. שֶׁפַּרְעֹה
לֹא גָזַר אֶלָּא עַל־הַזְּכָרִים וְלָבָן בִּקֵּשׁ לַעֲקוֹר אֶת־הַכֹּל. שֶׁנֶּאֱמַר
אֲרַמִּי אֹבֵד אָבִי וַיֵּרֶד מִצְרַיְמָה וַיָּגָר שָׁם בִּמְתֵי מְעָט וַיְהִי־שָׁם לְגוֹי
גָּדוֹל עָצוּם וָרָב: וַיֵּרֶד מִצְרַיְמָה. אָנוּס עַל פִּי הַדִּבּוּר. וַיָּגָר שָׁם.

BERLIN · 1923
[CONTINUED]

Steinhardt Haggadah: The Slaying of the Angel of Death

Then came the Holy One, blessed be He,
And smote the angel of death
That slew the slaughterer
That slaughtered the ox
That drank the water
That quenched the fire
That burned the stick
That beat the dog
That bit the cat
That ate the kid
That father bought for two zuzim.

This half-playful half-grim summary of a chain of absolute retribution ends the most popular Passover song, *Ḥad gadya*, and with it the Haggadah itself closes.

Though much ink has been spilled in an effort to fathom the profound "mystery" of *Ḥad gadya* (there are entire books devoted to the subject), it is basically a folk song, almost a nursery rhyme of the type represented in English by "This Is the House That Jack Built." Therein, perhaps, lies the clue to its inclusion in the Seder; like so much else, it would appeal to children. As for its interpretation, any number of possibilities exist, all plausible, none completely satisfactory. But no literal correspondence need be sought. At its core, at least, the song suggests that all must render an eventual account, and that God is the judge of all, even of the angel of death.

Shown here is the last of Steinhardt's series of illustrations to the song. At the end of the text, in large letters, is the Hebrew abbreviation that traditionally appears at the end of a book: *T*am *V*e-nishlam, *SH*ebaḥ *L*a-El *B*orey Olam—"It is ended and completed; praise unto the Lord, Creator of the world."

וְאָתָא הַקָּדוֹשׁ בָּרוּךְ הוּא · וְשָׁחַט לְמַלְאַךְ הַמָּוֶת · דְּשָׁחַט לְשׁוֹחֵט · דְּשָׁחַט לְתוֹרָא · דְּשָׁתָא לְמַיָּא · דְּכָבָה לְנוּרָא · דְּשָׂרַף לְחוּטְרָא · דְּהִכָּה לְכַלְבָּא · דְּנָשַׁךְ לְשׁוּנְרָא · דְּאָכְלָה לְגַדְיָא · דְּזַבִּין אַבָּא בִּתְרֵי זוּזֵי · חַד גַּדְיָא חַד גַּדְיָא:

תושלבע:

BUDAPEST · HUNGARY · 1924

A Hungarian Haggadah

A title page of an illustrated Haggadah sponsored in 1924 by the Society for Jewish Culture in Hungary. The text is in Hebrew and Hungarian, translated by Dr. Ferenc Hevesi, rabbi of the town of Szekes Fejérvár. This Haggadah was profusely illustrated by István Zádor with a series of highly original woodcuts. Each page is surrounded by a mauve border with stylized floral or Egyptian motifs.

YAARI NO. 1977 HARVARD 24:17

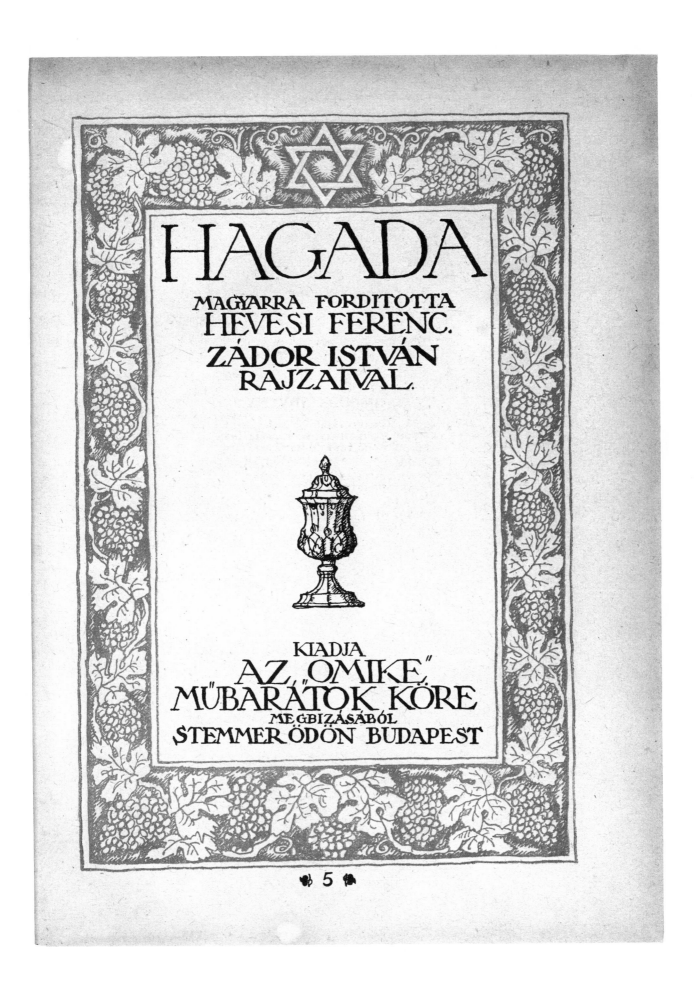

MAGYARRA FORDITOTTA
HEVESI FERENC.
ZÁDOR ISTVÁN
RAJZAIVAL.

KIADJA
AZ „OMIKE"
MŰBARÁTOK KÖRE
MEGBIZÁSÁBÓL
STEMMER ÖDÖN BUDAPEST

PLATE 138

BUDAPEST · 1924
[CONTINUED]

The Four Sons

One of the novelties in the Zádor illustrations is the manner in which the Four Sons are depicted. In the Haggadahs of prior centuries the Sons had been differentiated by their dress or by their gestures. Zádor, however, draws only their faces and relies upon the facial expression to identify each of them.

In the Haggadah itself, each face appears on a different page. All four are reproduced here on one plate in order to facilitate comparison.

ABOVE

Left: The Wise Son (p. 19).

Right: The Wicked Son (p. 20).

BELOW

Left: The Simple Son (p. 21).

Right: The son "who knows not what to ask" (p. 22).

PLATE 139

BUDAPEST · 1924
[CONTINUED]

"Pour Out Thy Wrath . . ."

Traditionally, illustrations of *Shefokh ḥamatkha* either centered around the figure of the Messiah or else they portrayed a restored Jerusalem in the Messianic era. Here the emphasis shifts back into history, in a somber and powerful allegory. Jews, surrounded by the grotesque and bestial forms of their persecutors, raise their arms to invoke God's retribution against the nations that have sought to destroy them.

AZ Ő BÁLVÁNYAIK EZÜST ÉS ARANY,
EMBERI KÉZNEK MÜVE. DE TE IZRAEL!
BIZZ AZ ÖRÖKKÉVALÓBAN
SEGITSÉGED Ő ÉS PAJZSOD!

BUDAPEST · 1924
[CONTINUED]

Ḥad Gadya

Reproduced here are the first three stanzas of the song *Ḥad gadya*, showing the kid, the cat, and the dog. The text is in Hungarian.

VOLT EGYSZER
EGY BÁRÁNY
חַד גַּדְיָא
VOLT EGYSZER EGY
BÁRÁNYKA,
UGY VETTE MEG APÁCSKA
KÉT EZÜST TALLÉRON,
EGY PICZI KIS
BÁRÁNY,
EGY PICZI KIS
BÁRÁNY.
JÖTT EGY GONOSZ
VADMACSKA,
NAGY DÜHÖSEN FÖLFALTA
DARABOKRA TÉPTE,
SZEGÉNY SZÉP
BÁRÁNYKA.
SZEGÉNY SZÉP
BÁRÁNYKA.
MACSKA IS MEG
BÜNHÖDÖTT,
EGY NAGY KUTYA ARRA JÖTT,
SZÉTTÉPTE A MACSKÁT—
Ó SZEGÉNY
BÁRÁNYKA,
Ó SZEGÉNY
BÁRÁNYKA.

SOUSSE · TUNISIA · 1924

A Typographical Flourish

A Tunisian Haggadah, in Hebrew and Judeo-Arabic, published in the town of Sousse. Following the title page there is an unusual feature: an announcement by the publisher (in Judeo-Arabic) of other liturgical works he has issued, with the types set in the shape of a tree.

VARIANT OF YAARI NO. 1995 HARVARD 19:13

בס"ד

הגדה גדולה

והייא

הגדה של פסח

מע שרח ערבי

כאמלה בגמיע דינים אלאזמין בחרוף כשאן ובלא נקודות · והתא קדוש וברכת המזון תרגמנאהם כדאלך בערבי · וחכינא פיהא בקאפיה מוהממה אכבאר עשרה צרבאת ופי אכרהא פיוט כי לו נאה ומפי אל ופזמון חד גדיא בתפסיר ואיצן שיר השירים וכתמנאהא במלזומה גדידה באסם כליני נסכר ונזיד אין וצפנא פיהא מדח מוהם ללגאיה:

פה סוסה יע"א

בדפוס מכלוף נגאר הי"ו

מדפ"ס ומוכר ספרים

MAKLOUF NADJAR - SOUSSE

אעלאן מן מטבעת מכלוף נגאר אלכאינה בסוסה

אן
אלדי
יכון פי עלם
גמלת מעאריף
נא אלדי אסדאדר
אדי כרגו מן מטבעת
נא מרתאע סוסה כללהם
אנטבעו בתרתיב מופיד גדן
עלא קד מנהג צלאואתנא ואן כל
סדור אנטבע כאמל פי סירתהו בגיר
מא ינקץ חתא שאי ולא ילזם פיה חתא
פתיח. ראש השנה. כפור. מועדים. האדו
אנטבעו בתרתיב וכמא לם סבקו אבדן. סדור
שומע תפלה. אדי פיה תסעה עמידות חול ושבת
ומועד. ואדי כל צלאה כאמלה בגיר פתיח. צאר הווא
אסדור אאכתר מכתאר בין גמלת יהוד בר תונס. בר אל
גזאיר. בר תראבלס ואגרב. סדור מנחה וערבית אצגייר אדי
יוזן אתנאש גראם. וסדור מנחה וערבית בכמסה עמידות. וכל
מן אנטלע עלא סדאדרנא אסתחסן תרתיבהם אדי ליסהם מכצוצין
פי שאי. ולהאדא
תמא פאידה כביר
רה ללשאריין אדי
ילקאו אסואמנא
רכיצה באלנסבה
לאסואם גיתארת
אוכרין וירבחו אדי
יכון אסדור פי איד
כאמל פי כל שאי
ומטבוע פי אחסן
אנצאפה ואתספיר אצחיח. ואן מטבעתנא
תבעת אכאתאלוג בגיר פלוס לכל מן יטלבהו

Maklouf Nadjar, 26, Rue de France - Sousse

PLATE 142

BERLIN · GERMANY · 1925

The Liebermann Haggadah

Except for a German title page, this Haggadah is entirely in Hebrew. The illustrations, as well as the lettering on most of the pages, were created by Julian Liebermann.

In general, the designs attempt to evoke a Near Eastern atmosphere. Stones and monuments predominate as borders and backgrounds. Text and illustrations are intermingled, and flow into one another.

On this page is shown *Ha laḥma anya* ("This is the bread of affliction"), preceded by instructions for washing the hands, eating the vegetable, and the division of the middle matzah, each ritual illustrated by an appropriate symbol. In the lower left is a banner inscribed *Degel maḥaneh Yehudah* ("the standard of the camp of Judah"), referring to the encampment of the Israelite tribes in the desert (Numbers 2:3).

YAARI NO. 1999 | HARVARD | 34:25

נוטל ידיו בלי ברכה נטילת ידים:
ורחץ
כרפס
לוקח כרפס פחות מכזית
ויטבול במי מלח או בחומץ ויברך:
בָּרוּךְ אַתָּה יְיָ
אֱלֹהֵינוּ מֶלֶךְ הָעוֹלָם בּוֹרֵא פְּרִי
הָאֲדָמָה:
יחץ
ויבצע מצה שניה
ויניח חציה הקטנה
במקומה
והגדולה
יצפין
לאפיקומן:
דגל
מחנה
יהודה
מגיד
מגלין המצה ונוטלין
הביצה והזרוע
מעל הקערה ומגביהין
אותה ואומרין הא לחמא
בקול רם:
הָא לַחְמָא
עַנְיָא דִי אֲכָלוּ
אַבְהָתָנָא בְּאַרְעָא דְמִצְרָיִם. כָּל
דִכְפִין יֵיתֵי וְיֵיכוּל. כָּל דִצְרִיךְ
יֵיתֵי וְיִפְסַח. הַשַּׁתָּא הָכָא. לְשָׁנָה
הַבָּאָה בְּאַרְעָא דְיִשְׂרָאֵל. הַשַּׁתָּא
עַבְדֵי. לְשָׁנָה הַבָּאָה בְּנֵי חוֹרִין:

PLATE 143

PARIS · FRANCE · 1925

Finding the Infant Moses

The Paris Haggadah of 1925 is memorable for its lovely illustrations, as well as the French translation that faces the Hebrew text. Janine Aghion was the artist. The translator was Edmond Fleg (1874–1963), the famous French poet, playwright, and essayist, whose dramatic return from assimilation to Jewish commitment was a result of the Dreyfus Affair and the rise of Zionism. Fleg's subsequent Jewish writings influenced several generations of French Jews.

Shown here is the finding of the infant Moses. The original is in color, with a predominant use of black backgrounds.

Five issues of this Haggadah were published, each on different papers, with one issue on vellum.

YAARI NO. 2013 HARVARD 29:19

MOSCOW · U.S.S.R. · 1927

A Communist "Haggadah" in the Soviet Union

In the decade following the Bolshevik Revolution a zealous campaign to eradicate Zionism, Hebrew culture, and the Jewish religion was conducted by the members of the Yevsektsiia, (the Jewish section in the Commissariat of Nationalities of the Council of Commissars), with local branches throughout the Soviet Union. Although relatively few in number, these were delegated to guide the cultural destinies of the mass of Soviet Jews, whose aspirations they did not represent. Jewish nationalism and religion were anathematized under the slogan of proletarian universalism. Yiddish alone was now tolerated as a Jewish language, but even then largely as a vehicle through which to inculcate Communist ideology.

Regarding Judaism as an archaic obstacle to proletarian progress, the Yevsektsiia heartily joined in the general antireligious campaign then under way. The Communist parody of the Haggadah shown here is a striking example of the mentality and techniques involved.

The "Haggadah," published in Moscow in 1927, is entitled *Hagodeh far Gloiber un Apikorsim*—"Haggadah for Believers and Atheists." Its text, written by M. Altshuler, is entirely in Yiddish, with illustrations by A. Tishler. The order of the traditional Haggadah is adhered to, from the preliminary preparations through the Four Questions, and is then followed by a long section called "Our Haggadah."

A few characteristic selections will indicate the thrust of the rest.

The traditional declaration over the burning of leaven is rendered:

> May all the aristocrats, bourgeois, and their helpers—Mensheviks, . . . Cadets, Bundists, Zionists, . . . Poale Zion, . . . and other counterrevolutionaries—be consumed in the fire of the revolution. May those who have been burned never rise again. The rest, which have remained, we abandon and hand over to the jurisdiction of the GPU [the Soviet secret police].

Directions for the Seder sequence are paraphrased:

> U-REḤATZ [the washing of hands]:
>
> Wash away, workers and peasants, the entire bourgeois filth, wash off the mildew of the ages and say—not a blessing—but a curse: May annihilation overcome all the outdated rabbinic laws and customs, yeshivas and ḥeders [the traditional Jewish elementary schools], which blacken and enslave the people.
>
> MAGGID [the recital]:
>
> *Ha laḥma anya*—for the bread of affliction did every capitalist buy our blood and sweat. Driven by hunger, we became voluntary slaves to capital. Our Jewish caretakers, lovely pillars of the community and rabbis, taught us to be patient. They wanted to persuade us that we are hungry and lonely only because we are in exile. They transformed their festivals into a means for the benighting and enslavement of the people.

The new "Haggadah," which comes later, consists largely of a pseudohistorical account of the origin and evolution of Passover. It is designed to demonstrate that, far from being a festival of freedom, Passover was used by Jewish leaders throughout the ages as a means to chain the masses, and even to indoctrinate them with hatred of gentiles. Passover must therefore be abolished.

At the very end, the traditional elements are parodied again:

> KOREKH [in a real Seder, the combining of matzah and bitter herbs]:
>
> Put together the Second International and the League of Nations. Between them place Zionism, and say—"Let them be eaten." May they be eaten up by the world revolutionary uprising of the proletariat.
>
> HALLEL [psalms of praise]:
>
> Sing the "International" and say—
> Down with the mildew of the ages!
> Down with clerical nationalistic festivals!
> Long live the revolutionary workers' holidays.

The illustrations reproduced on this plate are:

Left: The frontispiece. Jews are seated at a Seder table, surrounded by the spectral shapes of demons and devils.

Right: *Biur ḥametz*, the burning of "leaven," that is, all the counterrevolutionary elements castigated in the passages quoted above. The Hebrew words here, as throughout the work, are spelled according to Yiddish orthography.

HARVARD 19.5:13.5

בּיער כאָמעץ

PLATE 145

WARSAW · POLAND · 1928

The Haggadah in Polish

An illustrated edition of the Haggadah in Hebrew and Polish, translated by Chanan Neszer, and edited with a Polish introduction and commentary by Chaim A. Kaplan. Portrayed on the title page is the kid of the song *Ḥad gadya.*

T. WIENER[1] NO. 172 HARVARD 21:15

ILUSTROWANA

HAGADA

NA

PESACH

Opracował naukowo
we wstęp i objaśnienia
zaopatrzył Ch. A. Kapłan

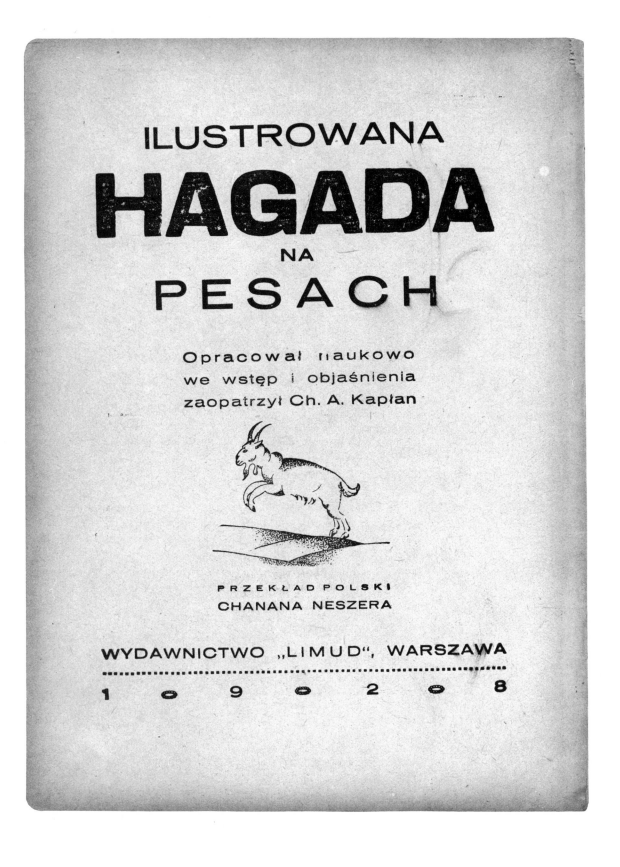

PRZEKŁAD POLSKI
CHANANA NESZERA

WYDAWNICTWO „LIMUD“, WARSZAWA

1 9 2 8

WARSAW · 1928
[CONTINUED]

"We Cried unto the Lord"

The woodcut illustrates the text "And we cried unto the Lord, the God of our fathers, and the Lord heard our voice, and saw our affliction, and our toil, and our oppression" (Deuteronomy 26:7). The Hebrew is followed below by the Polish translation.

וַנִּצְעַק

אֶל יְיָ אֱלֹהֵי אֲבוֹתֵינוּ. וַיִּשְׁמַע יְיָ אֶת קֹלֵנוּ. וַיַּרְא אֶת עָנְיֵנוּ וְאֶת עֲמָלֵנוּ וְאֶת לַחֲצֵנוּ.

„וַנִּצְעַק אֶל יְיָ אֱלֹהֵי אֲבוֹתֵינוּ״—כְּמָה שֶׁנֶּאֱמַר: וַיְהִי בַיָּמִים הָרַבִּים הָהֵם. וַיָּמָת מֶלֶךְ מִצְרַיִם. וַיֵּאָנְחוּ בְנֵי יִשְׂרָאֵל מִן

I zawodziliśmy do Wiekuistego, Boga praojców naszych. Wysłuchał też Adonaj głosu naszego i przyjrzał się naszej niedoli, cierpieniom naszym i naszej udręce.

„I zawodziliśmy do Wiekuistego, Boga praojców naszych" — jako powiedziane:

Zdarzyło się, że wśród długiego okresu niewoli zmarł jeden z królów egipskich.

(Zaś pod panowaniem jego następcy) uginali się

PLATE 147

BERLIN · GERMANY · 1928

Geismar Haggadah: Searching for Leaven, and Havdalah

In 1927 a Haggadah was published in Berlin (and printed in Leipzig) with illustrations by Otto Geismar. The following year it appeared again in an expanded edition published simultaneously in Berlin in two issues. One, reproduced here, included a Dutch translation. The other was translated into German.

The Geismar illustrations are among the most unusual ever to adorn a Haggadah text. They are essentially black-and-white line drawings that depict their themes in deceptively simple strokes, and therein lies their unique impact. Everything is reduced to bare essentials, as it were, and yet all is present, in a virtuoso display of sheer inventiveness and wit.

ABOVE: A panel that appears on one of the preliminary unnumbered pages of the Haggadah. It shows the search for leaven in the house by the light of a candle.

BELOW: *Havdalah,* the ceremony for concluding the Sabbath at a Seder that occurs on a Saturday night. The head of the house raises the cup of wine. The child holds the *Havdalah* candle. A spice box stands on the table. The Dutch translation appears underneath.

YAARI NO. 2078 HARVARD 22:17

Indien de eerste avond van het Pesachfeest op een Zaterdagavond valt, zegt men:

Geloofd zijt Gij, Eeuwige, onze God, Koning der wereld, die de lichtgevende stralen van het vuur geschapen heeft.

Geloofd zijt Gij, Eeuwige, onze God, Koning der wereld, die een onderscheid maakt tusschen heilig en ongewijd, tusschen licht en duisternis, tusschen Israël en de volkeren, tusschen den zevenden dag en de zes werkdagen, tusschen de heiligheid van den Sjabbos en de heiligheid van den feestdag hebt Gij een onderscheid gemaakt en den zevenden dag hebt Gij na afloop der zes werkdagen geheiligd. Zoo hebt Gij Uw volk Israël onderscheiden en met Uw heiligheid geheiligd. Geloofd zijt Gij, Eeuwige, die onderscheid maakt tusschen heilig en heilig.

PLATE 148

BERLIN · 1928
[CONTINUED]

Geismar Haggadah: Scenes from the Seder and the Passover Story

The panels reproduced on this plate appear on separate facing pages in the Haggadah. (Out of considerations of space they have been slightly reduced.)

ABOVE

Right: The family around the Seder table.
Left: The son asks the Four Questions.

CENTER

Right: The slaves build an Egyptian city.
Left: Pharaoh on his throne.

BELOW

Right and left : The hard labor and affliction of the slaves.

PLATE 149

BERLIN · 1928
[CONTINUED]

Geismar Haggadah: The Four Sons

Geismar's line drawings showing the Four Sons in the corners of the page illustrate the Hebrew text.

Upper right: The Wise Son, with his books.
Upper left: The Wicked Son, thumbing his nose.
Lower right: The Simple Son sits and bounces a ball in his hand.
Lower left: He "who knows not what to ask" merely stands and does nothing.

אֶחָד חָכָם. וְאֶחָד רָשָׁע. וְאֶחָד תָּם. וְאֶחָד שֶׁאֵינוֹ יוֹדֵעַ לִשְׁאוֹל:

חָכָם

חָכָם מַה הוּא אוֹמֵר (דברים ו׳ כ׳) מָה הָעֵדֹת וְהַחֻקִּים וְהַמִּשְׁפָּטִים אֲשֶׁר צִוָּה יְיָ אֱלֹהֵינוּ אֶתְכֶם: וְאַף אַתָּה אֱמָר־לוֹ כְּהִלְכוֹת הַפֶּסַח אֵין מַפְטִירִין אַחַר הַפֶּסַח אֲפִיקוֹמָן:

רָשָׁע

רָשָׁע מַה הוּא אוֹמֵר (שמות י״ב כ״ו) מָה הָעֲבֹדָה הַזֹּאת לָכֶם: לָכֶם וְלֹא לוֹ. וּלְפִי שֶׁהוֹצִיא אֶת עַצְמוֹ מִן הַכְּלָל כָּפַר בָּעִקָּר. וְאַף אַתָּה הַקְהֵה אֶת שִׁנָּיו וֶאֱמָר־לוֹ (שם י״ג ח׳) בַּעֲבוּר זֶה עָשָׂה יְיָ לִי בְּצֵאתִי מִמִּצְרָיִם. לִי וְלֹא לוֹ. אִלּוּ הָיָה שָׁם לֹא הָיָה נִגְאָל:

תָּם

תָּם מַה הוּא אוֹמֵר (שם י״ג י״ד) מַה־זֹּאת, וְאָמַרְתָּ אֵלָיו (שם) בְּחֹזֶק יָד הוֹצִיאָנוּ יְיָ מִמִּצְרַיִם מִבֵּית עֲבָדִים:

וְשֶׁאֵינוֹ יוֹדֵעַ לִשְׁאוֹל

אַתְּ פְּתַח לוֹ. שֶׁנֶּאֱמַר וְהִגַּדְתָּ לְבִנְךָ בַּיּוֹם הַהוּא לֵאמֹר: בַּעֲבוּר זֶה עָשָׂה יְיָ לִי בְּצֵאתִי מִמִּצְרָיִם:

BERLIN · 1928
[CONTINUED]

Geismar Haggadah: The Ten Plagues

Like his drawings of the Four Sons, Geismar's version of the Ten Plagues is full of ingenuity. The plague of blood is portrayed in the central oval above, with the other plagues occupying the next three rows, each progressing from right to left.

First row: frogs, lice, beasts.
Second row: blight, boils, hail.
Third row: locusts, darkness, and the slaying of the firstborn.

ככל אחת מעשר המכות מטיף באצבעו טפה מן היין

וכן בסימנים רַבִּי יְהוּדָה הָיָה נוֹתֵן בָּהֶם סִמָּנִים. דצ״ך עד״ש באח״ב.

דצך עדש באחב

PLATE 151

PÔRTO · PORTUGAL · 1928

The Haggadah of the Portuguese Marranos

In 1497 the Jews of Portugal were dragged to the baptismal fonts by royal decree and forcibly converted. Christians against their will, they now began to live the agonized dual life of secret Jews, or "Marranos." Remarkably, not only they but many of their descendants over the next four centuries managed to maintain some form of subterranean Judaism.

The Inquisition was finally abolished in Portugal around 1778. Paradoxically, by the end of the eighteenth century it appeared that the Portuguese Marranos had been fully and voluntarily assimilated to Catholic orthodoxy. Little or nothing was now heard of crypto-Judaism, and it was taken for granted in the nineteenth century that the phenomenon no longer existed.

However, Portuguese Marranism had not disappeared; with the extinction of the Inquisition, the Marranos were simply no longer objects of special attention. Through the nineteenth century and into our own, Marrano communities still secretly maintained their traditions in the northeastern provinces of Portugal. To be sure, time, persecution, and isolation had eroded much of the content of the Judaism they had inherited. But these remote scions of a once-proud Jewry were still conscious of themselves as Jews and clung tenaciously to the "Law of Moses" as they interpreted it.

They were rediscovered after the First World War by Samuel Schwarz, a Jewish engineer who had come to Portugal from Poland, and he now brought them to the attention of the outside world. From abroad came offers to help bring these twentieth-century Marranos back within the fold of the Jewish people. A charismatic leader arose, a Marrano officer in the Portuguese Army named Arthur Carlos de Barros-Basto.

With the cooperation of the Lisbon Jewish community and Sephardic Jews in other lands, a center for the return of Marranos to Judaism was established in the city of Pôrto; it eventually included a school and a synagogue. Barros-Basto, who adopted the Hebrew name Ben-Rosh, threw himself enthusiastically into the task of reclaiming and reeducating his brethren. He traveled to their remote villages, urging them to proclaim themselves openly as Jews. He edited a periodical advocating the Marrano cause. And he translated Jewish texts into Portuguese in order to bring the Marranos into direct contact with the basic sources of Judaism. Among his translations of the liturgy was a Portuguese version of the Haggadah published in Pôrto in 1928. Its title page is displayed here.

For a while the Portuguese Marrano revival had considerable success. Later, because of changes in the general religious and political climate in the country, the innate timorousness of the Marranos themselves, and perhaps also because of certain problematic aspects of Barros-Basto's own personality, the movement waned and dissipated. Barros-Basto himself died in 1961.

YAARI NO. 2106 | HARVARD | 19:12.5

HAGADAH

SHEL PESSAH'

(RITUAL DA CEIA PASCAL)

TRADUÇÃO E ARRANJO
DE A. C. DE BARROS
BASTO (BEN-ROSH)

5688 (1928 E. V.) EDIÇÃO DA
COMUNIDADE ISRAELITA
PORTO

COMPOSTO E IMPRESSO NA TIPOGRAFIA DO DIARIO DO PORTO

CAIRO · EGYPT · 1931

The Plagues—in Arabic

A Cairo Haggadah according to the Sephardic rite, with an Arabic translation in Arabic characters. The illustrations are derived from the Venetian Haggadahs. On the facing pages reproduced here are the first five plagues.

BEN MENAHEM[1] NO. 162 HARVARD 18.5:12

אֵלּוּ עֶשֶׂר מַכּוֹת שֶׁהֵבִיא הַקָּדוֹשׁ בָּרוּךְ הוּא . עַל הַמִּצְרִיִּים בְּמִצְרַיִם . וְאֵלּוּ הֵן :

דָּם צְפַרְדֵּעַ . כִּנִּים . עָרוֹב . דֶּבֶר . שְׁחִין . בָּרָד . אַרְבֶּה . חשֶׁךְ . מַכַּת-בְּכוֹרוֹת :

هذه العشرة ضربات الذي انزلها المقدّس تبارك هو على المصريين في مصر . وهذه هما :

دم . ضفادع . قمل . خلط . فناء . حكه . برد . جراد . ظلام . ضربة الابكار

דם دم

ماء المصريين رجع دم ونشف ريقهم من عدم الماء حيث انقلب كله دم .

צפרדע ضفادع

الضفادع الذى جاؤا في مصر كان في كل موضع من محلات المصريين حتى في طعامهم وشرابهم وملبوساتهم

כנים قمل

القمل كثر حتى ملا ملابسهم ورؤوسهم وجميع حوايجهم حتى أقروا وقالوا هذه الاية من الله

ערוב خلط

وحوش كانوا يجروا وراء المصريين يعضوهم ويعذبوهم وهكذا في كل برية للمصريين حتى ضجوا من شدة العذاب

דבר فناء

البهايم تعلق المصريين كانوا يموتوا من الفناء واما تعلق بني اسرائيل لم يحصل لهم اذى

PLATE 153

ISTANBUL · TURKEY · 1932

Linguistic Mutations

The Haggadah text in this Istanbul edition appears in two languages: Hebrew and Ladino (Judeo-Spanish). Except for occasional catchwords, however, both are printed in the Latin alphabet and spelled according to the rules of modern Turkish. In the case of the Ladino, which was originally Spanish written in Hebrew characters, the result is in effect a double transliteration.

Shown here is the beginning of the Seder sequence. The illustrations are copied from the Venetian Haggadahs.

YAARI NO. 2164 HARVARD 22:15

ברוך Baruh ata Adonay Eloenu Meleh aolam aşer kideşanu bemisvotav vesivanu al ahilat maror.

i se la komen.

כורך Koreh, tomaran la una masa ke resto en la meza i daran a kada uno serka de nueve dramas, i serka de nueve dramas de leçuga, i encuntos lo untan en el haroset; i antes de komerselos, diran:

זכר Zeher lamikdaş keillel azaken şeaya korhan ve ohlan bevad ahat lekayem ma şeneemar al masot umrorim yohelu u.

שלחן עורך Şulhan oreh, aprontan la meza i komen kon buena gana.

צפון Safun, tomaran la medya masa ke guadraron en una tovaja, i daran a kada uno serka nueve dramas i diran.

זכר Zeher lekorban pesah afikomin aneehal al asova.

i se lo komeran arimados.

ברך Bareh, inçiran los vazos de vino i diran Birkat-amazon.

BUENOS AIRES · ARGENTINA · 1934

The Haggadah in South America

The title page of a Hebrew Haggadah printed in Buenos Aires with a commentary by Yekutiel Weiss, published by his son Ḥayyim Jacob Villa. Weiss's preface ends with a personal hope "to come to Zion and Jerusalem, speedily and in our own days."

Regarded until recently as the first Haggadah issued in the Argentine capital, an earlier one has now been discovered. It was published in 1919, and a copy of it is in the possession of the YIVO Institute for Jewish Research in New York. The Haggadah of 1934 may now be regarded as the second edition, not only in Argentina, but in the whole of South America.

YAARI NO. 2181 HARVARD 23:15

ב"ה

הגדת פסח

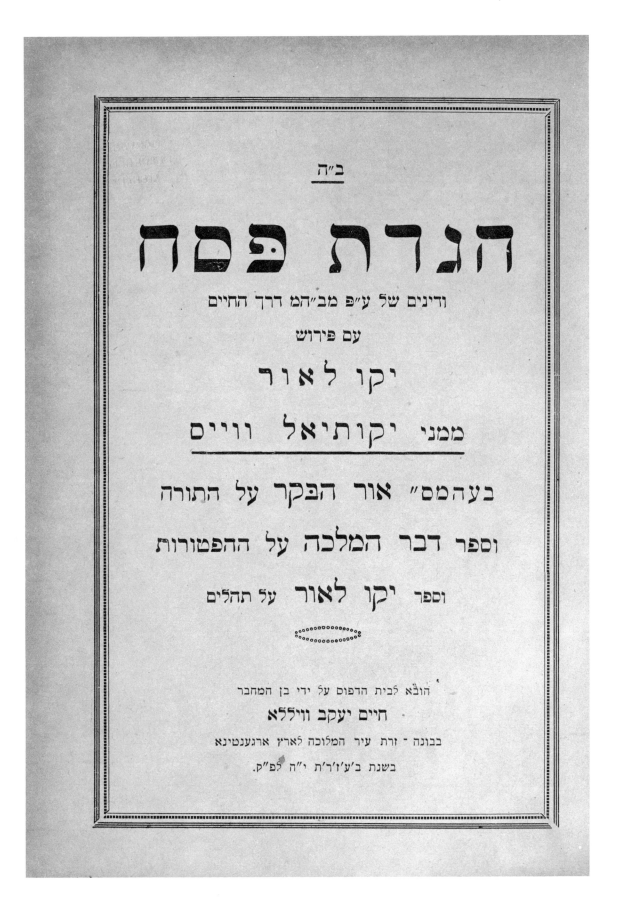

ודינים של ע"פ מב"המ דרך החיים

עם פירוש

יקו לאור

ממני יקותיאל ווייס

בעהמס" אור הבקר על התורה

וספר דבר המלכה על ההפטורות

וספר יקו לאור על תהלים

הובא לבית הדפוס על ידי בן המחבר

חיים יעקב ווילא

בבונה - זרת עיר המלוכה לארץ ארגענטינא

בשנת ב'ע'ז'ר'ת י"ה לפ"ק.

WARSAW · POLAND · 1934

Let My People In!

A Zionist Haggadah parody appeared in a Warsaw satirical journal issued for the Passover holiday in 1934. Entitled *Kulo maror* ("Only bitter herbs"—a quotation from the Four Questions), it was written in Yiddish under the pseudonym "Bontche" and illustrated by S. Feigenboim. The dish of "bitter herbs" shown under the title is concocted of "Hitlerism," "racial theory," and the discriminatory economic measures then being promulgated against Polish Jewry.

The lower half is devoted to a caricature called *Der moderner Moishe* ("The Modern Moses"). Its background lies in the events of the time. Jews were already fleeing from Nazi Germany. Despite the earlier assurances of the Balfour Declaration, British commissions on Palestine were recommending restrictions on Jewish immigration. Pharaoh is shown here as "the English king" (George V) seated upon his throne. The "modern Moses" is the great Zionist Revisionist leader Vladimir (Ze'eb) Jabotinsky, holding a petition in his hand. The caption underneath reads: "Instead of demanding that the Jews be allowed to leave, he demands that they be permitted to enter . . . into the Land of Israel."

HARVARD 36:24

„KULO MAROR" Dodatek do „Momentu" № 77 פּרייז 20 גראָשען · וואַרשאַ, פּסח תרצ"ד.

הומאָריסטיש־סאַטיריש פּסח־בלאַט

פון באַנטשע.

אילוסטרירט: ש. פיינענבוים

דער מאַרערבער משה...

אַנשטאָט צו פאָדערן מ׳זאָל אַרויסלאָזן די יודען, פאָדערט ער מ׳זאָל אַריינלאָזן די יודען... קיין ארץ־ישראל.

NITRE · CZECHOSLOVAKIA · 1934

The Haggadah in Slovak

This edition of the Haggadah was translated into the Slovak language by Vladimir Wetzler, with commentary by Dr. Lazar Schweiger, rabbi of Nitre in Czechoslovakia.

HARVARD 19:13

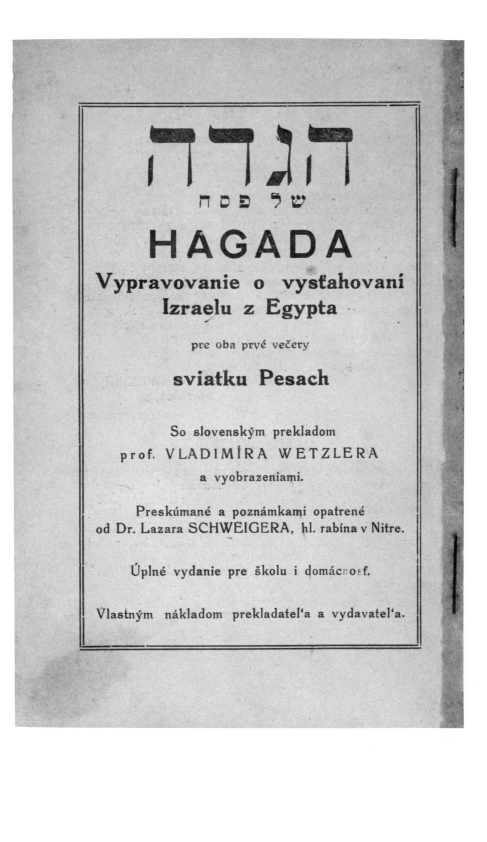

של פסח

HAGADA

Vypravovanie o vysťahovaní Izraelu z Egypta

pre oba prvé večery

sviatku Pesach

So slovenským prekladom
prof. VLADIMÍRA WETZLERA
a vyobrazeniami.

Preskúmané a poznámkami opatrené
od Dr. Lazara SCHWEIGERA, hl. rabína v Nitre.

Úplné vydanie pre školu i domácnosť.

Vlastným nákladom prekladateľa a vydavateľa.

TUNIS · TUNISIA · ca. 1941

The First Seder

A trilingual Haggadah (Hebrew, Judeo-Arabic, and French), published in Tunis.

The illustration, copied from the Venetian Haggadahs, depicts the eating of the Passover sacrifice in haste on the eve of the departure from Egypt, with all the participants standing. It represents the biblical verse "And thus shall ye eat it: with your loins girded, your shoes on your feet, and your staff in your hand" (Exodus 12:11).

YAARI NO. 2653 HARVARD 24.5:16

הגדה של פסח

בתלת לוגאת

פ׳שט ، ערבי ופראנצ׳יץ

דאכלהא תרתיב אסיסתו ואקדוש ותרתיב אסדר באפשט ובאערבי
ואחגדה מתרגמה ומפהומה מליח יאסר באלוגה אערבייה
ואלוגה אלפראנצאוייה וברכת המזון
וכדאך פזמון חד גדיא וכלל׳ני
נסכר יא יהודי

AGADA POUR PAQUE

avec Traductions Judeo-Arabe et Français

מטבעת כאסתרו נהג באב קרטאגנה עדד 4 בתונס

TUNIS - Imprimerie Castro, 4, Rue Bab-Carthagène

GURS · FRANCE · 1941

In a Vichy Concentration Camp

The first page of a Haggadah handwritten and mimeographed by Rabbi Leo Ansbacher for the inmates of the Vichy internment camp at Gurs, near the Pyrenees. Like the Haggadahs produced in the same year in Nice and Toulouse (Plates 160–162), it is a witness to the beginning of the dark night of European Jewry during World War II.

The camp at Gurs was one of several established by the Vichy government into which were huddled German Jews expelled by the Nazis from Baden, foreign Jews residing in France, the stateless, the homeless, and all manner of "undesirables." No printing press, of course, was available. With the approach of Passover, this Haggadah was produced under the makeshift conditions that obtained.

YAARI NO. 2290 JTSA 27:20

ב"ה

הַגָּדָה שֶׁל פֶּסַח

Jewish Theological Seminary LIBRARY

	קַדֵּשׁ
מַגִּיד	וּרְחַץ
רָחְצָה	כַּרְפַּס
מוֹצִיא	יַחַץ
מַצָּה	

מָרוֹר כּוֹרֵךְ שֻׁלְחָן עוֹרֵךְ צָפוּן בָּרֵךְ הַלֵּל נִרְצָה

(יוֹם הַשִּׁשִּׁי) וַיְכֻלּוּ הַשָּׁמַיִם וְהָאָרֶץ וְכָל צְבָאָם: וַיְכַל אֱלֹהִים בַּיּוֹם הַשְּׁבִיעִי מְלַאכְתּוֹ אֲשֶׁר עָשָׂה. וַיִּשְׁבֹּת בַּיּוֹם הַשְּׁבִיעִי מִכָּל מְלַאכְתּוֹ אֲשֶׁר עָשָׂה: וַיְבָרֶךְ אֱלֹהִים אֶת יוֹם הַשְּׁבִיעִי וַיְקַדֵּשׁ אֹתוֹ כִּי בוֹ שָׁבַת מִכָּל מְלַאכְתּוֹ אֲשֶׁר בָּרָא אֱלֹהִים לַעֲשׂוֹת:) בָּ"א יְיָ אֱ"מ"ה" בּוֹרֵא פְּרִי הַגָּפֶן:

בָּ"א יְיָ אֱ"מ"ה" אֲשֶׁר בָּחַר בָּנוּ מִכָּל עָם וְרוֹמְמָנוּ מִכָּל לָשׁוֹן וְקִדְּשָׁנוּ בְּמִצְוֹתָיו. וַתִּתֶּן לָנוּ יְיָ אֱלֹהֵינוּ בְּאַהֲבָה (שַׁבָּתוֹת לִמְנוּחָה וּ) מוֹעֲדִים לְשִׂמְחָה חַגִּים וּזְמַנִּים לְשָׂשׂוֹן אֶת יוֹם (הַשַּׁבָּת הַזֶּה וְאֶת יוֹם) חַג הַמַּצּוֹת הַזֶּה. זְמַן חֵרוּתֵינוּ (בְּאַהֲבָה) מִקְרָא קֹדֶשׁ זֵכֶר לִיצִיאַת מִצְרָיִם: כִּי בָנוּ בָחַרְתָּ וְאוֹתָנוּ קִדַּשְׁתָּ מִכָּל הָעַמִּים (וְשַׁבָּת) וּמוֹעֲדֵי קָדְשְׁךָ (בְּאַהֲבָה וּבְרָצוֹן) בְּשִׂמְחָה וּבְשָׂשׂוֹן הִנְחַלְתָּנוּ. בָּרוּךְ אַתָּה יְיָ מְקַדֵּשׁ (הַשַּׁבָּת וְ) יִשְׂרָאֵל וְהַזְּמַנִּים: (בָּ"א יְיָ אֱ"מ"ה" בּוֹרֵא מְאוֹרֵי הָאֵשׁ

בָּ"א יְיָ אֱ"מ"ה" הַמַּבְדִּיל בֵּין קֹדֶשׁ לְחוֹל בֵּין אוֹר לְחֹשֶׁךְ בֵּין יִשְׂרָאֵל לָעַמִּים בֵּין יוֹם הַשְּׁבִיעִי לְשֵׁשֶׁת יְמֵי הַמַּעֲשֶׂה. בֵּין קְדֻשַּׁת שַׁבָּת לִקְדֻשַּׁת יוֹם טוֹב הִבְדַּלְתָּ וְאֶת יוֹם הַשְּׁבִיעִי מִשֵּׁשֶׁת יְמֵי הַמַּעֲשֶׂה קִדַּשְׁתָּ. הִבְדַּלְתָּ וְקִדַּשְׁתָּ אֶת עַמְּךָ יִשְׂרָאֵל בִּקְדֻשָּׁתֶךָ. בָּ"א יְיָ מַּבְדִּיל בֵּין קֹדֶשׁ לְקֹדֶשׁ:

בָּ"א יְיָ אֱ"מ"ה" שֶׁהֶחֱיָנוּ וְקִיְּמָנוּ וְהִגִּיעָנוּ לַזְּמַן הַזֶּה:

בָּ"א יְיָ אֱ"מ"ה" בּוֹרֵא פְּרִי הָאֲדָמָה:

הָא לַחְמָא עַנְיָא דִּי אֲכָלוּ אַבְהָתָנָא בְּאַרְעָא דְמִצְרָיִם. כָּל דִּכְפִין יֵיתֵי וְיֵיכוֹל. כָּל דִּצְרִיךְ יֵיתֵי וְיִפְסַח. הָשַׁתָּא הָכָא לְשָׁנָה הַבָּאָה בְּאַרְעָא דְיִשְׂרָאֵל. הָשַׁתָּא עַבְדֵי לְשָׁנָה הַבָּאָה בְּנֵי חוֹרִין:

PLATE 159

GURS · 1941
[CONTINUED]

So That All May Sing

While the main text of the Gurs Haggadah was written in Hebrew, the songs at the end were transliterated and produced on a typewriter so that everyone could join in the singing. On this last page are seen the end of the song *Eḥad mi yodea*, as well as *Ḥad gadya*. At the very bottom is a one-line colophon, giving the barest details of where and by whom the Haggadah was produced. No mention is made of the tragic circumstances that surrounded it.

Rabbi Leo Ansbacher, himself an inmate of the camp, managed to survive the war and eventually went to Israel. A copy of this Haggadah was presented to the Jewish National and University Library in Jerusalem, along with the Nice Haggadah (Plates 160–161). Both were thought by the bibliographer Abraham Yaari to be the only ones extant. However, second copies (from which the present facsimiles have been made) are in the possession of the Jewish Theological Seminary of America.

Arba mi jaudeia,arba ani jaudea,arba imohaus,schlauscho ::::
Chamischo mi jaudea,chamischo ani jaudea,chamischo chumsche tauro,arba :::::
tauroSchischo mi jaudea,schischo ani jaudea,schischo sidre mischno,cham.::::
Schiwo mi jaudea,schiwoani jaudea,schiwo jme schabato,schischo::::
Schmauno mi jaudea,schmauno ani jaudea,schmauno jme milo,schiwo::::
Tischo mi jaudea,tischo ani jaudea,tischo jarche ledo,schmauno::::
Asoro mi jaudea,asoro ani jaudea,asoro dibrajo,tischo::::
Achod osor,mi jaudea,achad osor ani jaudea,achad osor kauchwajo,asoro:::
Schnem osor mi jaudea,schnem osor ani jaudea,schnem osor schiwtajo,achad oso
Schlauscho osor mi jaudea,schlauscho osor ani jaudea,schlauscho osor midajo,
scnem osor etc.

Chad gadjo, chad gadjo desabin abo bitre susei, chad gadjo, chad gadjo
weosso schunro weochlo le gadjo desabinabo::::::::::::::
weosso chalbo wenoschach leschunro deochlo gadjo::::::::::::
weosso chutro wehiko lechalbo denoschach leschunro::::::::::::
weosso nuro wessoraf lechutro dehiko lechalbo denohchach leschunroh::::
weosso majo wechowo lenuro dessoraf lechutro dehiko lechalbo denoschach
leschunro
weosso ssauro weschosso lemajo dechowo lenuro dessoraf lechutro dehiko
lechalbo denoschach leschunro::::::::::::
weosso haschauched weschochad lessauro deschosso lemajo dechowo lenuro
dessoraf lechutro dehiko lechalbode denoschach leschunro:
weosso malach hamowes weschochad leschauched deschochad lessauro
deschosso lemajo dechowo lenuro dessoraf lechutro dehiko lechalbo::::
Weosso Hakodausch boruch hu weschochat lemalach hamowes deschochad leschauched deschochad lessauro deschosso lemajo dechowo lenuro dessoraf
lechutro dehiko lechalbo denoschach leschunro deochlo legadjo desabin
abo bitre susei chad gadjo chad gadjo.

Edité du Rabbinat du Rabbin LEO ANSBACHER, GURS (France) NISSAN 5701.

....

03420

PLATE 160

NICE · FRANCE · 1941

The Parisian Rabbinate at the Hotel Roosevelt in Nice

Another handwritten and mimeographed Haggadah from Vichy France.

The south of France in 1941 was still part of a "free" zone, not under direct German administration. Among thousands of other Jewish refugees who had fled there from Paris and other northern cities were members of the Parisian rabbinate, who were installed in Nice with headquarters at the Hotel Roosevelt. With Passover approaching, they decided to issue a Haggadah. Not only were there no Hebrew printing facilities at their disposal, but apparently no copies of the Haggadah were available from which to reproduce the text. Accordingly, they mimeographed the text of the Haggadah that is included as part of the *Mishneh Torah*, the code of Jewish law by Moses Maimonides. The actual handwriting is that of the cantor of the synagogue at Nice, whose name was Cohen.

Shown here is the first page. The heading reads: "The Passover Haggadah, according to the version of Maimonides, published by the Rabbinic Association of Paris, which is currently in Nice."

YAARI NO. 2289 | JTSA | 30:20

הגדה של פסח

על פי נוסח הרמב״ם :

יצא לאור ע״י אגודת הרבנים דפאריז בעת בניצא

קדש. ורחץ. כרפס. יחץ. מגיד. רחצה. מוציא. מצה. מרור. כורך. שלחן עורך.

צפון. ברך. הלל. נרצה :

(כשבת מתחילין יום הששי)

סברי מרנן ורבנן ורבותי :

ברוך אתה יי אלהינו מלך העולם, בורא פרי הגפן :

ברוך אתה יי, אלהינו מלך העולם, אשר בחר בנו מכל עם, ורוממנו מכל לשון, וקדשנו במצותיו ותתן לנו יי אלהינו באהבה (שבתות למנוחה ו)מועדים לשמחה, חגים וזמנים לששון, את יום (השבת הזה ואת יום) חג המצות הזה. זמן חרותנו (באהבה) מקרא קודש זכר ליציאת מצרים : כי בנו בחרת ואותנו קדשת מכל העמים (ושבת ו)מועדי קדשך (באהבה וברצון) בשמחה ובששון הנחלתנו : ברוך אתה יי, מקדש (השבת ו)ישראל והזמנים :

ברוך אתה יי, אלהינו מלך העולם, שהחיינו וקימנו והגיענו לזמן הזה :

ורחץ. — כרפס. — (בורא פרי האדמה) יחץ. - מגיד.

הא לחמא עניא די אכלו אבהתנא בארעא דמצרים כל דכפין ייתי ויכול כל דצריך ייתי ויפסח. השתא הכא לשנה הבאה בארעא דישראל. השתא עבדי לשנה הבאה בני חורין :

מה נשתנה הלילה הזה מכל הלילות : שבכל הלילות אנו אוכלין חמץ ומצה. הלילה הזה כלו מצה : שבכל הלילות אנו אוכלין שאר ירקות. הלילה הזה מרור : שבכל הלילות אין אנו מטבילין אפילו פעם אחת. הלילה הזה שתי פעמים : שבכל הלילות אנו אוכלין בין יושבין ובין מסבין. הלילה הזה כלנו מסבין :

עבדים היינו לפרעה במצרים ויוציאנו יי אלהינו משם ביד חזקה ובזרוע נטויה. ואלו לא הוציא הקדוש ברוך הוא את אבותינו ממצרים הרי אנו ובנינו ובני בנינו משועבדים היינו לפרעה במצרים. ואפילו כלנו חכמים כלנו נבונים כלנו זקנים כלנו יודעים את התורה מצוה עלינו לספר ביציאת מצרים. וכל המרבה לספר ביציאת מצרים הרי זה משובח :

מעשה ברבי אליעזר ורבי יהושע ורבי אלעזר בן עזריה ורבי עקיבא ורבי טרפון שהיו מסובין בבני ברק והיו מספרים ביציאת מצרים כל אותו הלילה. עד שבאו תלמידיהם ואמרו להם רבותינו הגיע זמן קריאת שמע של שחרית :

אמר רבי אלעזר בן עזריה הרי אני כבן שבעים שנה ולא זכיתי שתאמר יציאת מצרים בלילות עד שדרשה בן זומא שנאמר למען תזכור את יום צאתך מארץ מצרים כל ימי חייך. ימי חייך הימים כל ימי חייך הלילות והחכמים אומרים ימי חייך העולם הזה כל ימי חייך להביא לימות המשיח :

ברוך המקום ברוך הוא ברוך שנתן תורה לעמו ישראל ברוך הוא. כנגד ארבעה בנים דברה תורה. אחד חכם. ואחד רשע. ואחד תם. ואחד שאינו יודע לשאול :

חכם מה הוא אומר. מה העדות והחוקים והמשפטים אשר צוה יי אלהינו אתכם. ואף אתה אמור לו כהלכות הפסח אין מפטירין אחר הפסח אפיקומן :

רשע מה הוא אומר. מה העבודה הזאת לכם. לכם ולא לו ולפי שהוציא את עצמו מן הכלל כפר בעיקר ואף אתה הקהה את שיניו ואמור לו בעבור זה עשה יי לי בצאתי ממצרים. לי ולא לו אלו היה שם לא היה נגאל :

תם מה הוא אומר מה זאת. ואמרת אליו בחוזק יד הוציאנו יי ממצרים מבית עבדים :

PLATE 161

NICE · 1941
[CONTINUED]
Passover Regulations in a Time of Travail

Appended to the Nice Haggadah is a sheet with emergency instructions for the coming Passover. It offers a vivid glimpse into the conditions in which French Jewry then found itself. It begins:

With the help of God

THE DECISION OF THE COMMITTEE OF THE RABBINIC ASSOCIATION OF PARIS CURRENTLY IN NICE, CONCERNING PASSOVER OF THIS YEAR, THE YEAR [5]701 IN FRANCE:

At a meeting of the committee of the Rabbinic Association of Paris on the first day of [the weekly Torah portion] *tetzaveh*, the third of Adar II, with the participation of other scholars expert in Jewish law, we have pondered the state of our brothers, the children of Israel, who find themselves in the cities, towns, villages and hamlets, taking note of the drought which (God save us) grows worse daily, and there has been no famine greater than this. Therefore we have decided after long debate, reaching a conclusion according to the Law, to alleviate what can be alleviated regarding the approaching Passover in accordance with the *Shulḥan Arukh* [the authoritative code of Jewish law] and the early and later authorities in the great hour of need which has occurred this year. But we hereby proclaim that this applies only: TO HIM WHO CANNOT GET ALONG WITHOUT IT, AND ONLY IN THIS YEAR, A YEAR OF WAR.

The regulations that follow relax some of the stringencies which ordinarily obtain in foods and utensils to be used on Passover. Various kinds of beans and grains are now permitted, though not their flour, as well as some dried fruits, milk (for children and the sick), and oils (if bought before Passover and strained in a Passover vessel). Since most Jews now have no other fuel for cooking, spirits and alcohol may be used, but care must be taken that none of this spills on food or utensils. Metal cooking and frying pans used during the year may be rendered fit for Passover by scalding, but this must be done carefully and properly, and if there is any doubt a rabbi should be consulted. Glass vessels, if they have not been used for spirits or alcohol, are permitted if new ones cannot be bought, but only after having been rinsed three times. Anyone who has no wine or other beverage fit for Passover may fulfill the requirement of the Four Cups with sweet tea, substituting for the *Kiddush* the blessing "That all came into being by His word."

Finally, all leaven that cannot be disposed of must be sold, with the traditional document of sale. Otherwise this can be effected through a general sale document (which had apparently been distributed), even if no actual transaction takes place and it is merely sent by mail to the rabbis M. Shochtman, A. Hofstein, and S. Rubinstein at the Hotel Roosevelt in Nice.

ב"ה

החלטות ועד אגודת הרבנים דפאריז, בנוגע לפסח שנה זו שנת תש"א בצרפת.

בישיבת ועד אגודת הרבנים דפאריז, כעת בניצא, א' תצוה ג' אדר ש"ז בצירוף עוד תלמידי חכמים יודעי דת ודין, דנו על מצבם של אחינו בני ישראל הנתונים בערים, עירות, כפרים ומושבות, בתשומת לב על הבצורות ההולך ומתחזק בכל יום ויום ר"ל ואין לך שנת רעבון גדול מזה, לכן החלטנו אחרי ויכוחים ארוכים לאסיקי שמעתתא אליבא דהלכתא להקל מה שיש להקל על פסח הבע"ל, ע"פ השלחן ערוך והפוסקים ראשונים ואחרונים בשעת הדחק הגדול אשר בשנה זו, אבל הנני מודיעים שזה, רק :

" למי שאי אפשר לו מבלעדי זה ורק בשנה זו שנת מלחמה "

ההחלטות

א) קטניות: התרנו לפסח זו כל מיני קטניות (לבד אורז ודוחן) כמו ארבים, באבים, פאסאליס, קאקאראזע (מאיס), גריקע (רעצקי, מאטריקי) וגרויפין מהקטניות הללו אבל לא הקמח שלהם, וצריכים לברר היטב את הקטניות או הגרויפין שלהם קודם הפסח שלא יהיה מין אחר מעורב בהם וגם צריך להחליט אותם ברותחין קודם הבישול.

ב) אנחנו מזהירים שיש הרבה מיני גרויפין וגרייפליך כמו פעריל-גרויפין קוסקעס סמאל, אבערפלאקען וכדומה, אינם ממיני גרויפין שהתרנו כי הם מחמשת מיני דגן, והם חמץ גמור מדאוריתא.

ג) פירות יבשים התרנו בשנה זו והם תאנים (פייגין) תמרים (טייטלין) שזופים, תפוחים, ואגסים (פלאמין, עפיל, בארניס) יבשים, כמהין ופטריות. (שוועמליך) אך צריכים להדיח אותם היטב קודם הפסח.

ד) דגים מלוחים והערינג גדולים וקטנים התרנו לאוכלם בפסח זה רק בתנאי שידיחם היטב שלשה פעמים במים קרים לפני הפסח ובכלי פסח.

ה) חלב התרנו בשנה זו לקטנים ולחולים אף שאין בהם סכנה, וחמאה, אם יקנו אותה קודם הפסח וידיחנה היטב קודם הפסח ג' פעמים.

ו) בסאחארין אפשר להשתמש בשנה זו ורק בקריסטאל מפני שאין בו שום תערובת.

ז) שמן, כל מיני שמנים הנמצאים במדינותנו התרנו אבל צריכים לקנותם קודם הפסח ולסננם קודם הפסח בכלי פסח.

ח) דענאטוראט, (ברען ספירט, אלקאהל) היות שרוב היהודים במדינתנו אין להם חמרי הסקה מבלעדי זה, ולכן סמכנו בזה על שני גדולי דורנו הרב הגאון צירלסון, רב הכולל דמדינת בסרביה והרב הגאון ה' רובינשטיין אבד"ק ווילנא שהתירו בספריהם את האלקאהל הזה להשתמש בו בפסח לבשל על ידו, ועל סמך זה התרנו גם אנו לפסח הבע"ל למי שאין לו שום אמצעי אחר לבשל, אך שיהיו זהירים מאוד שלא ישפך ח"ו על הכלים ובפרט על המאכלים.

ט) התרנו בשנה זו להגעיל כל כלי מתכות וגם אלאמיניום, ועמאייל וגם כלי בישול אם הם ממתכות. גם כלים שמטגנים בו מותרים להגעיל אבל צריך להזהר מאד שההגעלה תהיה כדת, בכל אופן אם יש למי שהיא איזה ספק טוב לעשות שאלת חכם.

י) סכינים אם הלהב והקתא מגוש אחד אפשר להגעילם בענין אחר עשה ש"ח.

יא) כלי זכוכית, אם לא נשתמש בהם בדבר חריף כמו ספירטוס שכר וכדומה אם אין לו אפשרות לקנות חדשים יש להתירם אבל במלוי ועירוי שלשה פעמים במים.

יב) למי שאין לו יין ולא שום משקה אחרת הכשרים לשם פסח, התרנו בהסכמת „גדולי פולין לצאת ידי ארבע כוסות בטיי מחוק ויברך שהכל.

יג) הננו מזהירים לכל מי שנמצא אצלו מיני חמוצים, לעשות עליהם שטר מכירה או להצטרף עם ההרשאה הכללית של מכירת חמץ אפילו ע"י הפאסט ובלא תשלום גמול, ויוכל לשלוח ישר על האדריסה שלנו

הרבנים :

מ. שוחטמן

א. הופשטיין

ש. רובינשטיין

Hotel Rosevelt
Nice
Marechal Joffre 16.
Rabbinat.

TOULOUSE · FRANCE · 1941

"The Last Haggadah in Exile"

The Haggadah shown here has hitherto remained unknown to bibliographers. Like those of Gurs and Nice (Plates 158–161), this one was also mimeographed. It was produced in the southern French city of Toulouse, apparently in the same year, by Rabbi S. R. Kapel. Formerly rabbi of Mülhausen in Alsace, he now describes himself as "chaplain to the camps" (*Aumonier des Camps*). At the bottom, in large letters is the traditional exclamation *Le-shanah ha-ba'ah bi-Yerushalayim* ("Next year in Jerusalem"), followed by the colophon. In the very last line the name Bindiger appears (probably the person who actually wrote the text). Finally, there is yet another cry, this time in Yiddish:

Die Hagodeh zol zayn die letzte in Goles!
[This Haggadah should be the last one in Exile!]

JTSA 29:21.5

שפוך

שפוך חמתך אל הגוים אשר לא ידעוך ועל ממלכות אשר בשמך לא קראו: כי אכל את יעקב ואת נוהו השמו: שפך עליהם זעמך וחרון אפך ישיגם: תרדוף באף ותשמידם מתחת שמי יי:

(הלל) לא לנו עד סוף

הודו ליי כי טוב כי לעולם חסדו:

הודו לאלקי האלקים כל״ח. הודו לאדוני האדונים כל״ח: לעושה נפלאות גדולות לבדו כל״ח: לעושה השמים בתבונה כל״ח: לרוקע הארץ על המים כל״ח: לעושה אורים גדולים כל״ח: את השמש לממשלת ביום כל״ח: את הירח וכוכבים לממשלות בלילה כל״ח: למכה מצרים בבכוריהם כל״ח: ויוצא ישראל מתוכם כל״ח: ביד חזקה ובזרוע נטויה כל״ח: לגוזר ים סוף לגזרים כל״ח: והעביר ישראל בתוכו כל״ח: ונער פרעה וחילו בים סוף כל״ח: למוליך עמו במדבר כל״ח: למכה מלכים גדולים כל״ח: ויהרוג מלכים אדירים כל״ח: לסיחון מלך האמורי כל״ח: ולעוג מלך הבשן כל״ח: ונתן ארצם לנחלה כל״ח: נחלה לישראל עבדו כל״ח: שבשפלנו זכר לנו כי ל״ח: ויפרקנו מצרינו כל״ח: נותן לחם לכל בשר כל״ח

הודו לאל השמים כי לעולם חסדו:

(נשמת כל חי... עד חי העולמים.)

כי לו נאה כי לו יאה

אדיר במלוכה בחור כהלכה גדודיו יאמרו לו, לך ולך, לך כי לך, לך אף לך, לך יי הממלכה כי לו נאה כי לו יאה: דגול, הדור, ותיקיו: זכאי, חסין, טפסריו: יחיד, כביר, למודיו: מלך, נורא, סביביו: עניו פודה, צדיקיו: קדוש, רחום, שנאניו: תקיף, תומך, תמימיו:

(כוס רביעי) ברוך אתה יי אמ״ה. בורא פרי הגפן. (על הגפן)

חסל

חסל סדור פסח כהלכתו, ככל משפטו וחקתו, כאשר זכינו לסדר אותו כן נזכה לעשותו: זך שוכן מעונה, קומם קהל עדת מי מנה, בקרוב נהל נטעי כנה. פדוים לציון ברנה:

לשנה הבאה בירושלים!

S.R.KAPEL - RABBIN DE MULHOUSE - AUMONIER DES CAMPS - TOULOUSE.

די הגדה זאל זיין די לעצטע אין גלות! קינדער.

178335

PLATE 163

BUDAPEST · HUNGARY · 1942
[EDITION A]
In the Shadow of the Holocaust

In 1942 the bulk of European Jewry were already marked for extermination. Hundreds of thousands had been systematically slaughtered in the *Einsatzgruppen* massacres that accompanied the Nazi drive into the Baltic countries and Russia. The death camps were already established, and deportations from the Polish ghettos had begun. In southeastern Europe, Jews were being killed in Serbia, Croatia, and other areas. Hungary, until 1944, could still offer temporary safety.

The Haggadah whose pages are reproduced here was published in Budapest in 1942 in two editions. Except for the additional materials found in one of them (Plate 164) they are identical. Both are of folio size. The text is printed in Hebrew and Hungarian on facing pages, translated and annotated by Dr. Zoltán Kahn. Most of the illustrations are reproductions, in red and black, of ancient Egyptian art. The page borders and other ornaments continue the Egyptian motif and were designed by B. Gandor.

Shown here is the Hungarian translation of *Ha laḥma anya* ("This is the bread of affliction"), ending: "Now we are here; next year may we be in the Land of Israel. Now we are slaves; next year may we be free men."

VARIANT OF YAARI NO. 2293 HARVARD 34:24

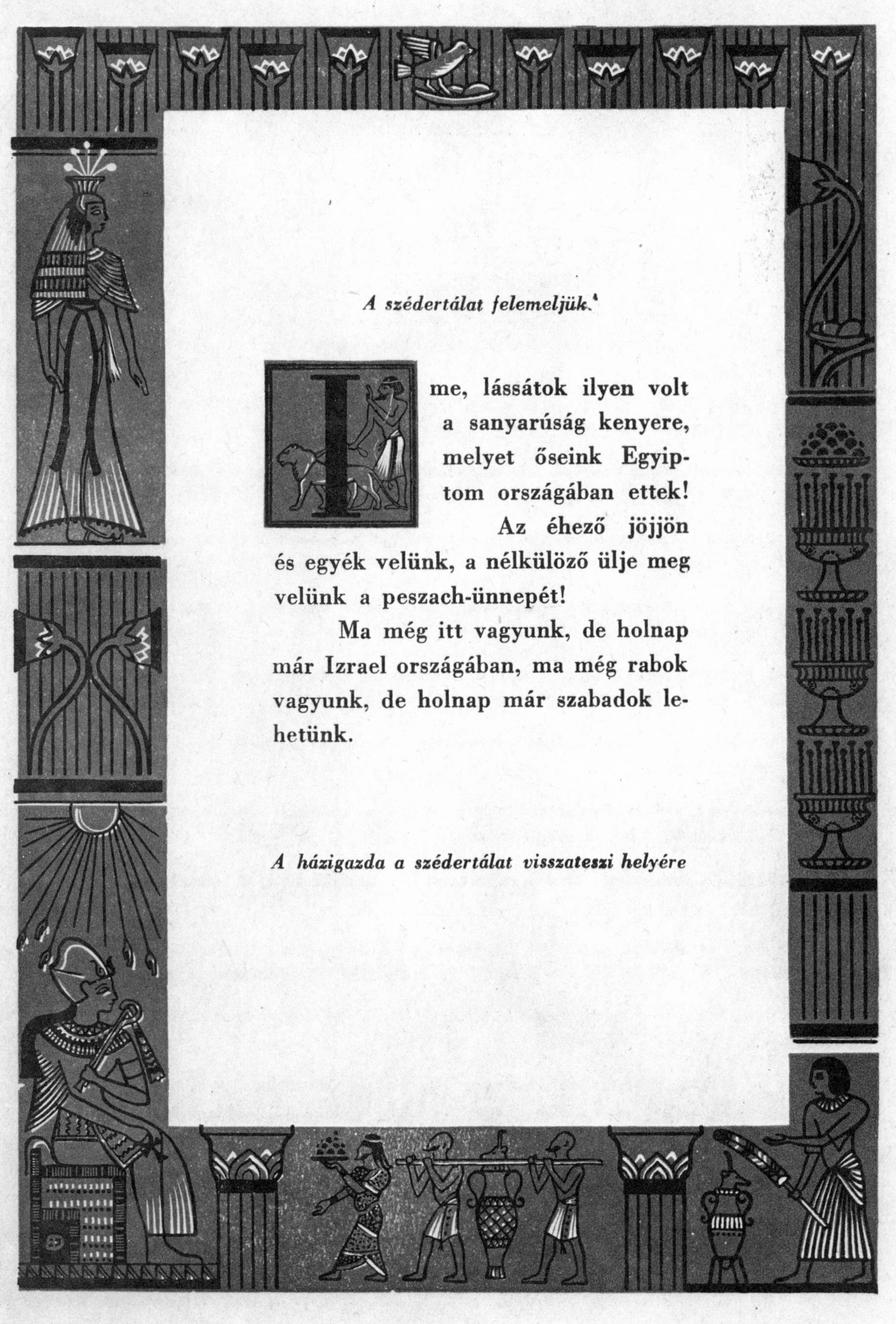

A szédertálat felemeljük.

Íme, lássátok ilyen volt a sanyarúság kenyere, melyet őseink Egyiptom országában ettek!

Az éhező jöjjön és egyék velünk, a nélkülöző ülje meg velünk a peszach-ünnepét!

Ma még itt vagyunk, de holnap már Izrael országában, ma még rabok vagyunk, de holnap már szabadok lehetünk.

A házigazda a szédertálat visszateszi helyére

BUDAPEST · HUNGARY · 1942
[EDITION B]
As Though He Had Emerged from Egypt

The other edition of the Budapest Haggadah of 1942 contains additional sections which precede and follow the text itself. These include an introduction by Dr. Géza (Moshe) Ribady; two historical essays (one of them on Haggadah illustrations) by Dr. Ernö Munkácsi; music for some of the hymns and songs; and even reproductions of some pages from old Haggadahs, both printed and manuscript. A thousand numbered and signed copies were printed, one hundred on paper of extra fine quality.

Both editions are examples of sumptuous bookcraft, executed with loving attention to quality and detail. Considering the time in which they were produced, they are also affecting reminders of the resilience of the Jewish spirit in the midst of historical adversity, and of the power of the Haggadah itself to sustain the hopes of Jews for a brighter future.

Shown here is a Hebrew page of the Haggadah ending with the passage: "In each and every generation one should regard oneself as though he had emerged from Egypt."

YAARI NO. 2293 HARVARD 34:24

זֶה שֶׁאָנוּ אוֹכְלִים, עַל שׁוּם מָה. עַל שׁוּם שֶׁלֹּא הִסְפִּיק בְּצֵקָם
שֶׁל אֲבוֹתֵינוּ לְהַחֲמִיץ עַד שֶׁנִּגְלָה עֲלֵיהֶם מֶלֶךְ מַלְכֵי
הַמְּלָכִים הַקָּדוֹשׁ בָּרוּךְ הוּא וּגְאָלָם. שֶׁנֶּאֱמַר וַיֹּאפוּ אֶת
הַבָּצֵק אֲשֶׁר הוֹצִיאוּ מִמִּצְרַיִם עֻגֹת מַצּוֹת כִּי לֹא חָמֵץ כִּי
גֹרְשׁוּ מִמִּצְרַיִם וְלֹא יָכְלוּ לְהִתְמַהְמֵהַּ וְגַם צֵדָה לֹא עָשׂוּ לָהֶם:
מָרוֹר זֶה שֶׁאָנוּ אוֹכְלִים. עַל שׁוּם מָה. עַל שׁוּם שֶׁמֵּרְרוּ
הַמִּצְרִיִּים אֶת חַיֵּי אֲבוֹתֵינוּ בְּמִצְרָיִם. שֶׁנֶּאֱמַר וַיְמָרְרוּ אֶת
חַיֵּיהֶם בַּעֲבֹדָה קָשָׁה בְּחֹמֶר וּבִלְבֵנִים וּבְכָל עֲבֹדָה בַּשָּׂדֶה
אֵת כָּל עֲבֹדָתָם אֲשֶׁר עָבְדוּ בָהֶם בְּפָרֶךְ:

בְּכָל דּוֹר וָדוֹר חַיָּב אָדָם לִרְאוֹת אֶת עַצְמוֹ כְּאִלּוּ הוּא
יָצָא מִמִּצְרָיִם. שֶׁנֶּאֱמַר וְהִגַּדְתָּ לְבִנְךָ בַּיּוֹם הַהוּא לֵאמֹר.
בַּעֲבוּר זֶה עָשָׂה יְיָ לִי בְּצֵאתִי מִמִּצְרָיִם. לֹא אֶת אֲבוֹתֵינוּ
בִּלְבַד גָּאַל הַקָּדוֹשׁ בָּרוּךְ הוּא. אֶלָּא אַף אוֹתָנוּ גָּאַל עִמָּהֶם.
שֶׁנֶּאֱמַר וְאוֹתָנוּ הוֹצִיא מִשָּׁם לְמַעַן הָבִיא אֹתָנוּ לָתֶת לָנוּ
אֶת הָאָרֶץ אֲשֶׁר נִשְׁבַּע לַאֲבוֹתֵינוּ:

NORTH AFRICA · 1942
The Palestine Jewish Brigade

The attitude of Palestinian Jewry toward Britain during World War II was necessarily ambivalent. The same nation that was a prime factor in the war against Nazi Germany was also, in Palestine itself, an occupying power whose policies were increasingly inimical to Jewish aspirations. Tens of thousands of young Palestinian Jews volunteered, nevertheless, for service in the British Army, and a campaign was begun for the creation of an all-Palestinian Jewish unit that would fight under its own flag.

The British were opposed to this. Jewish companies were formed in 1940, but they were assigned to auxiliary and transport duties, and were not identified as a national unit. Only after sustained pressure by the Palestinian volunteers were they allowed to participate in combat, and eventually to display the Jewish flag. The Haggadah reproduced here was mimeographed in North Africa in 1942, in the dark days of the Allied struggle against Rommel's forces. It is the earliest example of its genre.

ABOVE: The title page, inscribed "M. T. [Military Transport?] Hebrew Transport Unit, Middle East Forces. Passover Haggadah. In the Field. [5]702."

BELOW: Introduction to the Seder.

As the festival of freedom begins on this night, the night of the 14th of Nisan, 1942, we sit together, soldiers of Hebrew Drivers Unit no. 5, our hearts filled with emotion and celebration. The heart rages because "Egypt" has not ended for Israel. For us, the entire world has become "Egypt."

With burning grief and the wrath of vengeance let us recall, above our highest joy this evening, the Jewish houses throughout the Diaspora in which the holiday has turned to terror. Let us remember the storm-tossed ship of Jewry which no shores will accept, and the one toward which it yearns is locked with bars. So let the joy of the festival of freedom be muted and restrained, for the destroyer has risen against the House of Israel.

As we sit together, hundreds of Hebrew soldiers, in an alien place, far from our land, our heart is with that home in whose mission we have gone forth, and it celebrates and shines to us from afar. We remember our comrades who rallied to the banner and fell along the way, those who were the first to fall in battle, and those who fell prisoners to the enemy.

Let us recall our home this evening, the struggles to build it, and the exertions to develop it. Let us see it from afar, radiant and luminous, and let us believe that it will be felt ever more strongly as the last haven for a people wallowing in its own blood, so that there be an end to weakness and withdrawal from the demand to trust in it and to rebuild it.

As the night of the festival arrives, let us remember the Seder night a year ago, when we celebrated the holiday crouching on the rocks while Tobruk lay terrified in siege, and we felt that the siege had not broken but had enclosed us all around.

And let there stand fast in us the faith in "despite everything." The faith that we shall really prevail over the "Egyptian" siege which has closed about us. When the next Passover arrives may it find us standing over the ruins of those who enslave freedom, prepared for the future, and ready for the burden of building, in whatever way the destiny of Israel shall impose it upon us. Amen.

Next year in Jerusalem!

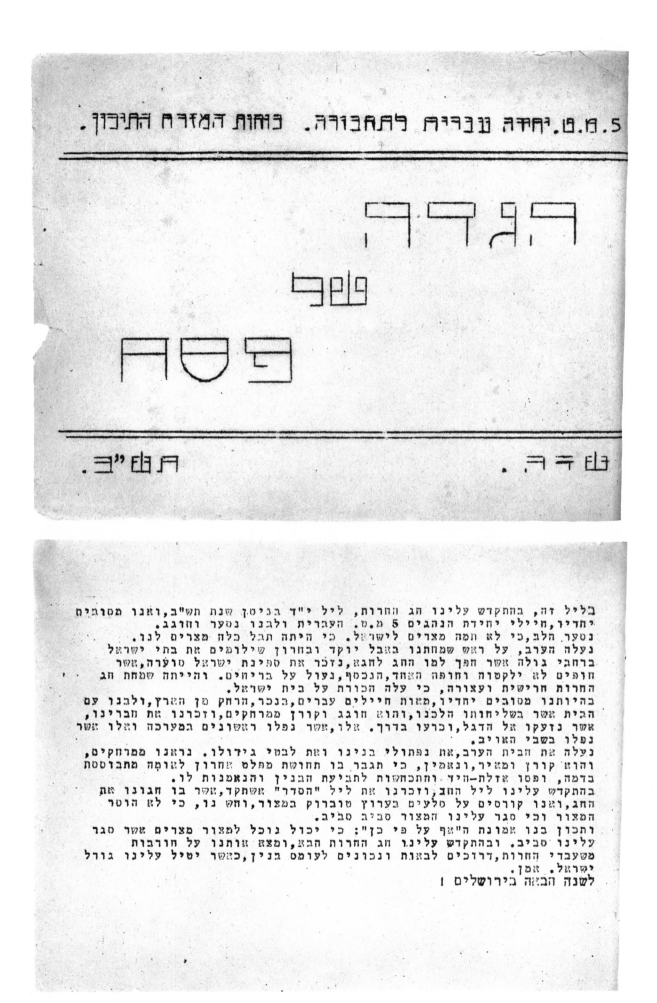

5.מ.ט. יחידה עברית לתחבורה. בחזית המזרח התיכון.

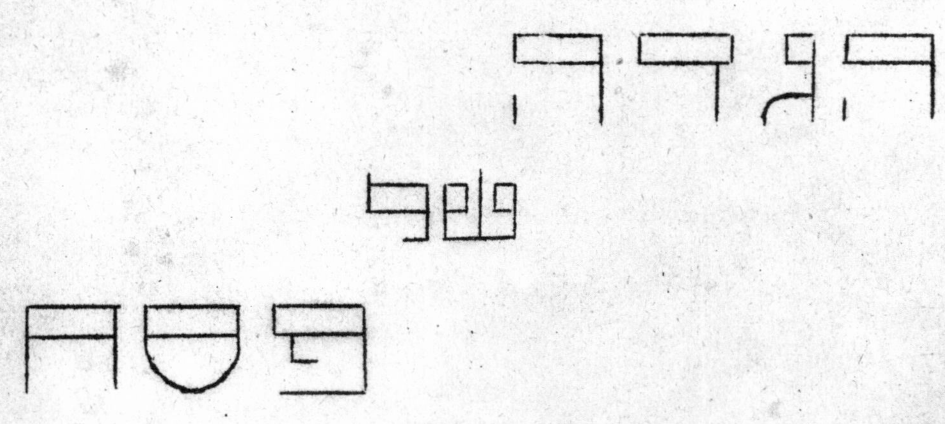

שדה. תש"ב.

בליל זה, בהתקדש עלינו חג החרות, ליל י"ד בניסן שנת תש"ב, ואנו מסובים יחדיו, חיילי יחידת הנהגים 5 מ.ט. העברית ולבנו נסער והוגג. נסער הלב, כי לא תמה מצרים לישראל. כי היתה תבל כלה מצרים לנו.

נעלה הערב, על ראש שמחתנו באבל יוקד ובחרון שילומים את בתי ישראל ברחבי גולה אשר הפך למו החג לחגא, נזכר את ספינת ישראל סוערה, אשר חופים לא ילקטוה וחופה האחד, הנכסף, נעול על בריחים. והייתה שמחת חג החרות חרישית ועצורה, כי עלה הכורת על בית ישראל.

בהיותנו מסובים יחדיו, מאות חיילים עברים, בנכר, הרחק מן הארץ, ולבנו עם הבית אשר בשליחותו הלכנו, והוא חוגג וקורן ממרחקים, וזכרנו את חברינו, אשר נזעקו אל הדגל, וכרעו בדרך. אלו, אשר נפלו ראשונים במערכה ואלו אשר נפלו בשבי האויב.

נעלה את הבית הערב, את נפתולי בנינו ואת לבטי גידולו. נראנו ממרחקים, והוא קורן ומאיר, ונאמין, כי תגבר בו תחושת מפלט אחרון לאומה מתבוססת בדמה, ופסו אזלת-היד והתכחשות לתביעת הבנין והנאמנות לו.

בהתקדש עלינו ליל החג, וזכרנו את ליל "הסדר" אשתקד, אשר בו חגונו את החג, ואנו קורסים על סלעים בערוץ טוברוק במצור, וחש נו, כי לא הוסר המצור וכי סגר עלינו המצור סביב סביב.

ותכון בנו אמונת ה"אף על פי כן": כי יכול נוכל למצור מצרים אשר סגר עלינו סביב. ובהתקדש עלינו חג החרות הבא, ומצא אותנו על חורבות משעבדי החרות, דרוכים לבאות ונכונים לעומס בנין, כאשר יטיל עלינו גורל ישראל. אמן.

לשנה הבאה בירושלים!

NAAN · PALESTINE · 1942

Four New Questions

The modern Jewish renaissance in the Land of Israel was intimately bound up with the creation of a new form of community: the kibbutz. Fully aware of their pioneering role, not only in reclaiming the land, but in the creation of a mode of life without precedent in almost two millennia, the members of the kibbutzim have also sought a new relation to Jewish tradition. The classic festivals, for example, have been reinterpreted, and Passover is celebrated in varying patterns which combine both old and new features.

These changes are epitomized in the kibbutz Haggadahs, of which more than a thousand different editions have appeared. They reflect, not only the many new approaches to the holiday, but the very spirit of the kibbutz itself.

Shown here is a mimeographed Haggadah from Naan, a kibbutz founded in 1930 and situated not far from Rehovoth. It was produced in the midst of World War II. On this page we find a new version of the Four Questions:

Why does this night differ from all other nights? For on all other nights the children eat in their own dining hall; but on this night we are all seated together, parents, children, and comrades.

Why is the position of the Jews different from that of all the nations? For every nation dwells in its house and homeland, but the Jews are scattered throughout the world, hated, persecuted, and even to the Land of Israel, their homeland, they are not permitted to come without hindrance.

Why are there in the world poor and rich, well-fed and hungry, workers and idlers? And why do men fight instead of giving a helping hand to one another so as to be happy and joyful together?

When shall the day come in which Naan will be large, beautiful, expanded with much land about, and many brothers from exile will come to build it together with all its comrades?

HARVARD 21.5:16

מה נשתנה
הלילה הזה מכל הלילות, שבכל הלילות
הילדים סועדים בחדר האכל שלהם והלילה
הזה אנו מסבין כאן כולנו יחדיו, הורים, ילדים
וחברים?
מדוע שונה מצבם של היהודים ממצב
כל העמים, שכל עם יושב בביתו
ובמולדתו, והיהודים מפוזרים בכל העולם,
שנואים ונרדפים ואפילו לארץ-ישראל
מולדתם לא יתנו להם לבוא באין מפריע?
מדוע יש בעולם עניים ועשירים, שבעים
ורעבים, עובדים והולכי בטל, ומדוע
נלחמים האנשים זה בזה במקום לתת יד ולעזור
זה לזה ויחדיו להיות מאושרים ושמחים?
מתי יבוא היום ונען תהיה גדולה, יפה
ורחבת ידים ואדמה רבה לה מסביב
ואחים רבים מן הגולה באים אליה
לבנותה יחד עם כל חבריה?

RABAT · MOROCCO · ca. 1943

"Hitler's Haggadah"

The title page of one of the most exotic of Haggadah parodies. Written in Judeo-Arabic, it is entitled *Haggadah de Hitler* (literally, "Hitler's Haggadah") and was published in Rabat, Morocco, sometime after June of 1943. By then Morocco had passed from Vichy rule to that of General de Gaulle, and the Vichy anti-Jewish laws were no longer in effect.

Reflecting the joy of Moroccan Jewry at their liberation from an oppressive regime, the parody is exuberant to the point of allowing itself every possible license with the traditional text. The cast of characters runs riot. Of the Four Sons, the Wise Son is—"the English." The Wicked Son is, of course, Hitler. The Simple Son (with no pejorative implications intended) is interpreted as "the Americans." And he "who knows not what to ask" is Mussolini. Rabbi Eleazar is Roosevelt, Rabbi Yosi the Galilean is Stalin, and Rabbi Akiba is General Montgomery. The verse "And the Lord brought us forth out of Egypt" is reserved for General de Gaulle himself!

HARVARD 15.5:10.5

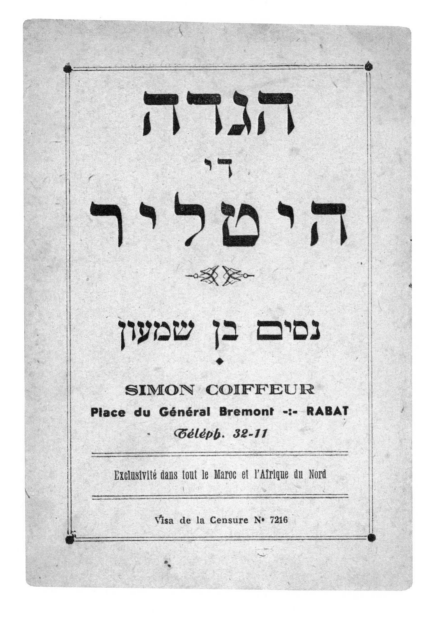

הגדה
די
היטליר

נסים בן שמעון

SIMON COIFFEUR
Place du Général Bremont -:- RABAT
Téléph. 32-11

Exclusivité dans tout le Maroc et l'Afrique du Nord

Visa de la Censure N° 7216

MELBOURNE · AUSTRALIA · 1945

For the Australian Armed Forces

A Haggadah published for use by Australian Jewish servicemen. The title page (left) bears the date 1943. However, both the preface and the Hebrew cover (right) are dated 1945. This is the only Haggadah published in Australia.

YAARI NO. 2316 JTSA 15.5:11

HAGGADAH

HOME SERVICE
FOR
THE FIRST TWO NIGHTS OF PASSOVER

AUSTRALIAN SAILORS', SOLDIERS' & AIRMEN'S EDITION

Published by the
AUSTRALIAN ARMY CHAPLAINS' DEPARTMENT
under the supervision of the
AUSTRALIAN HEBREW CHAPLAINS' CONFERENCE,
JANUARY, 1943

Text selected and reprinted from the Fourth Edition of the Haggadah in Hebrew and English by the late Rev. A. P. Mendes, as published by P. Vallentine, London, 1878, with additional notes from the Haggadah published by the American Jewish Welfare Board, 1919.

McLARENS Melbourne
1943

Jewish Theological Seminary of America
LIBRARY

PLATE 169

GERMANY · 1945
The Rainbow Haggadah

A Haggadah was printed in Germany by Jewish soldiers in the famed Rainbow Division of the United States Infantry. Inserted in the copy now at the Jewish Theological Seminary library is a letter addressed to Professor Alexander Marx, the Seminary librarian, explaining the circumstances under which the Haggadah appeared:

Chaplain Eli A. Bohnen
Hq 42nd (Rainbow) Infantry Division
APO 411, c/o PM, New York, N.Y.

April, 1945

Professor Alexander Marx
3080 Broadway
New York, N.Y.

Dear Dr. Marx,

I thought that perhaps you might be interested in the enclosed Haggadah. It was printed by the press which prints our division newspaper. The press uses the photo-offset method. The Hebrew text was taken from the prayer book for soldiers issued by the Jewish Welfare Board. It was prepared to be used at our division Seder which was held in Dahn, Germany.

The Haggadah has significance for this reason, I believe. I am confident that it is the first Hebrew religious work printed in Germany since the beginning of the war. You may also be interested to learn that the soldiers who did the actual printing told us that when they had to clean the press before printing the Haggadah, the only rags available were some Nazi flags, which for once served a useful purpose.

With kindest regards I remain

Sincerely yours,
Eli A. Bohnen

The Haggadah was prepared by Rabbi Bohnen and his assistant, Corporal Eli Heimberg. On the verso of the cover there is a letter from the division commander, dated March 28, 1945:

To my Jewish soldiers:

The celebration of Passover should have unusual significance for you at this time, for like your ancestors of old, you too are now engaged in a battle for freedom against a modern Pharaoh. This Pharaoh has sought, not only to enslave your people, but to make slaves of the whole world.

God grant that victory for us will make it possible for you to celebrate the next Passover with your loved ones at home, in a world you helped make free.

(signed) Harry J. Collins
Major General, U. S. Army

The Hebrew text of the Haggadah is followed by an English "Prayer for Home" and the hymn "America."

T. WIENER[1] NO. 27 JTSA 13:10.5

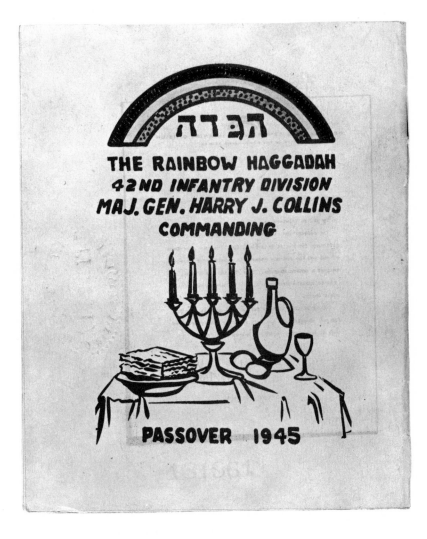

THE RAINBOW HAGGADAH
42ND INFANTRY DIVISION
MAJ. GEN. HARRY J. COLLINS
COMMANDING

PASSOVER 1945

ALEXANDRIA · EGYPT · 1945

For Egyptian Zionist Youth

This Haggadah was published in Alexandria by the Egyptian Zionist scout organization *He-ḥalutz ha-tzair* ("The Young Pioneer"). The text is in Hebrew and in French.

Left: The title page.
Right: The French preface (which also appears in Hebrew):

"NEXT YEAR IN JERUSALEM"

For the fifth time in this Second World War, in these days of destruction and distress for our people, we celebrate *Pesaḥ* [Passover]. Thousands of years have passed since our liberation from the yoke of slavery, but the recollection of it remains no less profoundly anchored in our hearts.

On this day in which we relate the *Yetziat Mitzrayim* [the Exodus from Egypt] and eat the bread which was eaten by our pursued ancestors, each of us considers himself as one of the Jews who departed from Egypt.

Pesaḥ has become the most cherished of Jewish holidays, the most beautiful and important, because in it the Jewish people sees its perennial aspirations.

From generation to generation they rise against us to exterminate us, and always we are saved because we love liberty and know how to die for it. The memory of *Yetziat Mitzrayim* is for us at this tragic moment a consolation for our bitter fate in exile.

Each year, while celebrating *Pesaḥ* far from our much-beloved Zion, our yearning increases. We promise ourselves always to be "next year in Jerusalem." Remembering the Passovers we celebrated in Eretz-Yisrael, our joy cannot be complete since its destruction and the beginning of our exile, for we have not recovered our well-being.

As we celebrate the festival of freedom this year, let us remember those who can no longer join us because a brutal hand has torn life from them. May they not have fallen in vain.

While relating the story of *Yetziat Mitzrayim*, let us understand its true sense in reminding ourselves that we are not yet all free.

LET US LEARN TO LOVE FREEDOM AT THE FESTIVAL OF FREEDOM,
FOR ONLY IT CAN SAVE US!

BEN MENAHEM[2] NO. 82 HARVARD 21:13.5

5705

HAGGADAH
DE
PESSAH

בהוצאת הסתדרות הצופים "החלוץ הצעיר" אלכסנדריה

Edité par le groupement des Éclaireurs Israélites

« Hehaloutz Hatzaïr »

ALEXANDRIE

"Lashanah Habaà Biyeruchalaïm"

Pour la cinquième fois en cette seconde guerre mondiale, dans ces jours de destruction et de détresse pour notre peuple, nous célébrons Pessah. Des milliers d'années ont passé depuis notre libération du joug de l'esclavage mais le souvenir n'en reste pas moins profondément ancré dans nos cœurs.

En ce jour où nous racontons la «yetsiat Mitsraïm» et où nous mangeons le pain qu'ont mangé nos ancêtres pourchassés, chacun de nous se considère comme l'un de ces juifs qui ont quitté l'Egypte.

Pessah est devenue la plus chère des fêtes d'Israél, la plus belle et la plus importante, parce que c'est en elle que le peuple juif voit l'essence de ses aspirations de tous temps.

De génération en génération on s'élève contre nous pour nous exterminer et toujours nous sommes sauvés parce que nous aimons la liberté et savons mourir pour elle. Le souvenir de «yetsiat Mitsraim» est pour nous en ce moment tragique une consolation pour notre sort amer dans la Gola (Exil).

Chaque année, en célébrant Pessah loin de Sion bien-aimé, notre nostalgie augmente ; nous nous promettons toujours d'être «l'an prochain à Jérusalem". Au souvenir des Pâques que nous avons fêtées en Eretz-Israél depuis sa destruction et le début de notre exil, notre joie ne peut être complète, tant que nous n'avons pas retrouvé notre salut.

Cette année, en célébrant la fête de la liberté, souvenons-nous de ceux qui ne peuvent plus le faire avec nous parce qu'une main brutale les a arrachés à la vie. Qu'ils ne soient pas tombés en vain.

En racontant l'histoire de la «yetsiat Mitsraim», comprenons son vrai sens et rappelons-nous que nous ne sommes pas encore tous libres.

Apprenons à aimer la Liberté à la Fête de la Liberté, elle seule nous sauvera !

MEXICO CITY · MEXICO · 1946

The First Mexican Haggadah

An illustrated Haggadah published in Mexico in Hebrew and Spanish, with notes in Yiddish. The translator was Professor Zelik Shifmanovich, director of the local Yavneh school. The name of the artist is not recorded.

Opposite: "We were slaves unto Pharaoh in Egypt."

YAARI NO. 2329 HARVARD 24:17

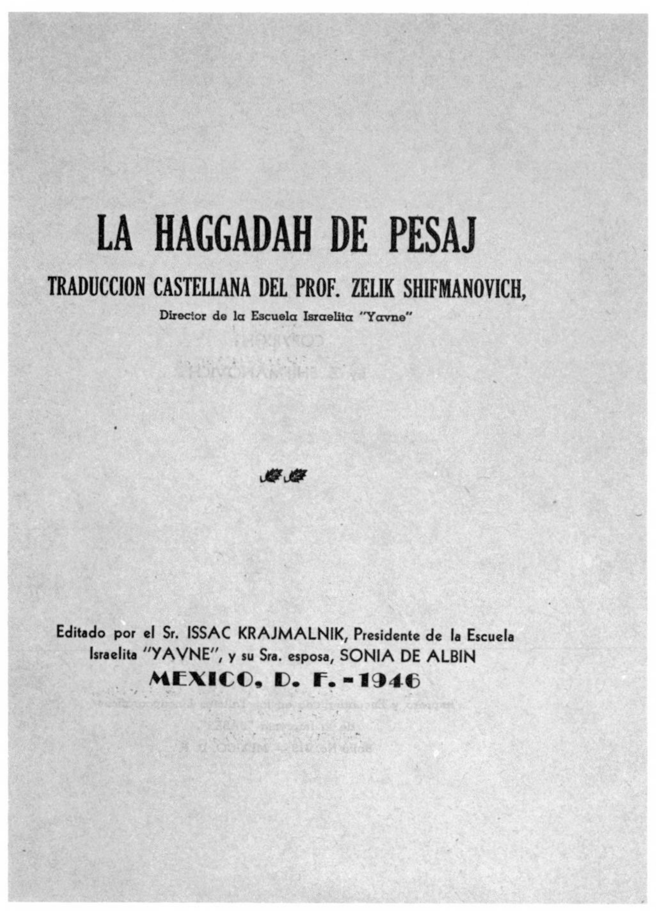

LA HAGGADAH DE PESAJ

TRADUCCION CASTELLANA DEL PROF. ZELIK SHIFMANOVICH,

Director de la Escuela Israelita "Yavne"

Editado por el Sr. ISSAC KRAJMALNIK, Presidente de la Escuela Israelita "YAVNE", y su Sra. esposa, SONIA DE ALBIN

MEXICO, D. F. - 1946

Title Page (Reduced)

עבדים היינו
לפרעה
במצרים

LANDSBERG · GERMANY · 1947

Between Slavery and Freedom

The Allied victory over Nazi Germany in 1945 brought an end to the war in Europe and ushered in a new period of trial for those Jews who had survived. The Holocaust was followed by the desperate search to find a home for the homeless. In the eyes of world Jewry the survivors were the *She'erit ha-pleitah*—literally, the "saved remnant." To the governments of the world they were "DP's": "displaced persons."

Only one country was eager to have them: Jewish Palestine. The British Mandatory power, however, was almost equally determined to keep them out. Thus began the macabre spectacle of leaky ships loaded with Jewish refugees running the British blockade. Some succeeded. Others were caught and forced to turn back to Europe. Meanwhile, the bulk of the survivors awaited their salvation in camps and refugee centers established on the now accursed soil of Germany and Austria.

In those very places Passover was celebrated again, an ancient festival of freedom suddenly infused with an urgently contemporary relevance. Haggadahs were published there, some by Jewish relief organizations from abroad, others by the refugees themselves.

Reproduced on this plate is the title page of a Haggadah issued in the camp at Landsberg, Germany. Across the top are the words: "The Saved Remnant in Landsberg." In the upper left the pyramids indicate the ancient Egyptian bondage, while in the upper right a concentration camp is sketched. The chains are broken, however, and below there is a vision of the Land of Israel.

HARVARD 28:20

שארית הפליטה בלנדסברג
הגדה
של
פסח

TEL AVIV · PALESTINE · 1947

For Those Who Wait in Cyprus

On the island of Cyprus the British established detention camps for Jewish refugees caught in the attempt to reach Palestine. This is the title page of a Haggadah published in Tel Aviv for their use. The seal displaying a ship is that of the Committee for the Cyprus Exiles, established by the Jewish Agency and the National Council in Palestine, in cooperation with the Joint Distribution Committee.

VARIANT OF BEN MENAHEM[1] NO. 50 HARVARD 21:13

הגדה
של
פסח

ביסודם של הסוכנות היהודית
הועד הלאומי לכנסת ישראל בא״י
בשיתוף פעולה עם הג׳וינט

הוצאת „יבנה", תל־אביב

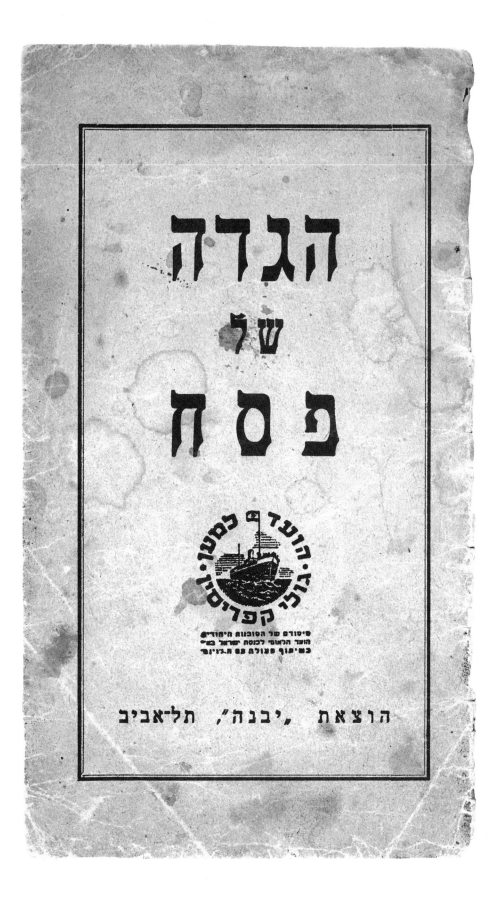

BET HA-SHITAH · PALESTINE · 1947

To All Who Are Hungry

A kibbutz Haggadah from Bet Ha-Shitah in the Valley of Jezreel, founded in 1935.

On this page the traditional Haggadah text begins: "Let all who are hungry enter and eat; let all who are needy come to the Passover feast."

The illustration depicts the communal Seder in the Kibbutz dining hall.

HARVARD 24:15.5

כָּל דִּכְפִין יֵיתֵי וְיֵיכוֹל:
כָּל דִּצְרִיךְ יֵיתֵי וְיִפְסַח:
הַשַּׁתָּא עַבְדֵי:
לַשָּׁנָה הַבָּאָה בְּנֵי חוֹרִין:

אוֹכְלִים מַצָּה וּמָרוֹר:
שׁוֹתִים כּוֹס רִאשׁוֹנָה:

PLATE 175

BET HA-SHITAH · 1947
[CONTINUED]

Mourning the Holocaust

Some of the most poignant expressions of grief over the Holocaust are to be found in kibbutz Haggadahs. In the Bet Ha-Shitah edition of 1947, as in those of some other kibbutzim, the following poem appears:

I dreamed a most terrible dream—
My people no longer exists, it is no more.
I rose with a cry—Woe, woe!
That which I dreamed has come to pass.
O God above! I called with a shudder,
For what and why has my people died?
For what and why has it died in vain,
Not even in war nor in battle?
Young and old, women and children,
They are no more—strike hands in grief!
I weep in my anguish by day and by night,
Why, my Lord, wherefore, O God?

The author was Yitzhak Katzenelson (1886–1944), the Hebrew and Yiddish poet and dramatist. Early in World War II he was in the Warsaw Ghetto, where his wife and two sons died. Later he was transferred to the Vittel concentration camp in France, where, in 1943, he wrote this poem. He was finally deported to Auschwitz, and was killed there together with his only surviving son.

חֲלוֹם חָלַמְתִּי נוֹרָא מְאֹד —
אֵין עַמִּי, עַמִּי אֵינֶנּוּ עוֹד;
בִּצְעָקָה קַמְתִּי — אֲהָהּ! אֲהָהּ!
אֲשֶׁר חָלַמְתִּי, בָּא לִי, בָּא!
„הָהּ, אֵל בָּרָמָה!” אֶקְרָא רֶתֶת:
„עַל מָה וְלָמָּה עַמִּי מֵת?!
עַל מָה וְלָמָּה מֵת לַשָּׁוְא?
לֹא בַּמִּלְחָמָה, לֹא בַּקְּרָב...
נְעָרִים, זְקֵנִים, גַּם נָשִׁים וָטַף
כְּבָר אֵינָם, אֵינָם — סִפְקוּ כַּף!”
כֹּה אֵבְךְּ בִּיגוֹנִי, גַּם יוֹם, גַּם לֵיל —
עַל מָה רִבּוֹנִי? וְלָמָּה, אֵל?

PLATE 176

MUNICH · GERMANY · 1948
[VAAD HA-HATZALAH EDITION]
A Gift to the "Saved Remnant"

A Haggadah was issued in Munich by the *Vaad Ha-Hatzalah* ("Rescue Committee") and distributed as "a gift . . . to the saved remnant." The text of the Haggadah, with a commentary by Rabbi Jacob of Lissa, was photographed from a prayer book that was printed in Stettin in 1864.

YAARI NO. 2361 HARVARD 20.5:14

הגדה לפסח

עם פירוש דרך חיים ונ"ש
מאת הגאון ר' יעקב מליסא זצ"ל

מתנה מאת ועד ההצלה
להשארית הפליטה

נדפס ע"י הועד להוצאות ספרים אצל
ועד ההצלה

הרב נפתלי בארוך, הרב אביעזר בורשטין

מינכן, תש"ח

PRINTED BY VAAD HATZALA,
GERMANY 1948.

MUNICH · GERMANY · 1948

[JOINT DISTRIBUTION COMMITTEE EDITION]

To the Promised Land

Another Munich Haggadah for the "saved remnant" was published by the American Joint Distribution Committee. By the time Passover was celebrated in 1948, the United Nations had already partitioned Palestine, the State of Israel was shortly to proclaim its independence, and among the refugees there was widespread anticipation of momentous events.

Left: Moses showing the way into the Promised Land. (The map, which includes Tel Aviv, is of course pointedly contemporary.)

Right: The preface:

> This year the festival of freedom acquires an exalted form and lofty content for world Jewry in general, and for the Saved Remnant in particular.
>
> Again we stand upon the threshold of the fulfillment of the prophetic promise concerning eternal peace and absolute freedom. . . .
>
> Today we see the fulfillment of the prayers and hopes of Jewry in bitter exile: "Now we are here; next year in the Land of Israel. Now we are slaves; next year we shall be free men."

BEN-MENAHEM[1] NO. 51 HARVARD 14.5:9.5

ב"ה מינכן בחודש האיתנים

חג החרות בשנה זו מקבלת צורה רוממה ותוכן נשגב בעד היהדות העולמית בכלל ובעד "שארית הפלימה" בפרט.

עוד הפעם אנו עומדים על טף הגשמת היעוד הנבואי ע"ד השלום הנצחי והחרות המוחלטת.

עוד הפעם אנו רואים בעליל את אצבע אלוקים המראה לנו את ארץ־ישראל בתור בית לעם שבע־רוגז ומלא־נדודים.

היום אנו רואים את המלוי של תפילת ותקות ישראל בגלות המרה: השתא הכא, לשנה הבאה בארעא דישראל, השתא עבדי, לשנה הבאה בני חורין".

היהדות האמריקאית ו"הועד האמריקאי לעזרה"־„דזוינט" מתאחד עמכם בתקוה הנאמנה שחג הפסח הזה יהיה חג גאולת עמנו וארצנו וגאולת הצדק והחרות.

הרב שלמה שפירא	מר. שמואל הבר
מנהל „משרד דתי"	מנהל ה„דזוינט"
בגרמניה	בגרמניה

RVARD
VERSITY
BRARY
Y 1968

PLATE 178

MUNICH · GERMANY · 1948
[NOAR ḤALUTZI EDITION]

Zionist Youth on German Soil

Unlike the two previous Munich Haggadahs (Plates 176–177), the edition whose title page is reproduced here contains a nontraditional text. It was produced by the Noar Ḥalutzi Meuḥad ("United Pioneer Youth") in Germany, and reflects the particular passion of the young to free themselves from the shackles of exile and make their way to the Jewish state, which was about to be born. For other pages from this Haggadah, see Plates 179–181.

HARVARD 21:14

הוצאת נוער חלוצי
מאוחד (נוחם) בגרמניה

MUNICH · 1948

[NOAR ḤALUTZI EDITION · CONTINUED]

"And They Afflicted Us"

The Egyptian enslavement as a concentration camp. From the Haggadah text comes the caption: "And they afflicted us, and laid upon us hard bondage."

בן - בנימין

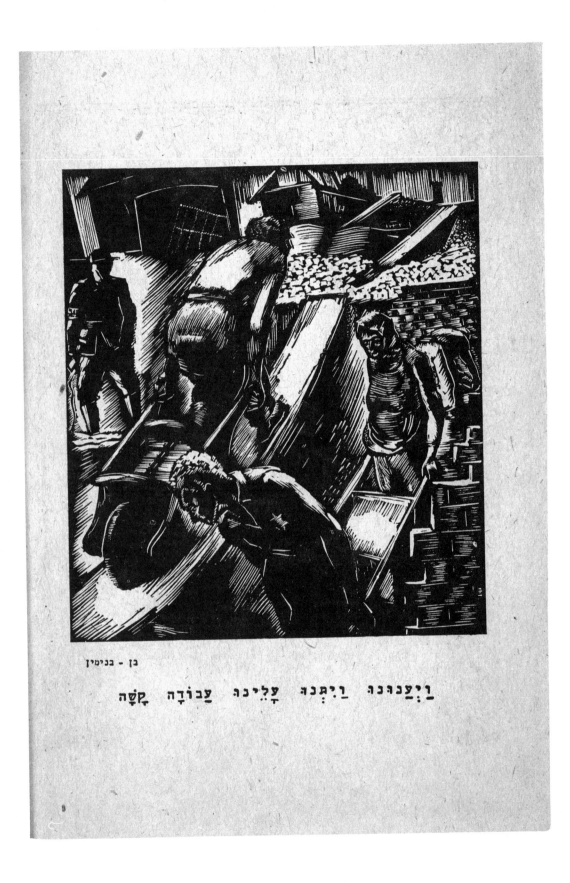

וַיְעַנּוּנוּ וַיִּתְּנוּ עָלֵינוּ עֲבֹודָה קָשָׁה

MUNICH · 1948
[NOAR ḤALUTZI EDITION · CONTINUED]
Egypt—Ancient and Modern

"In each and every generation one should regard himself as though he had emerged from Egypt."

Within the top of the huge Hebrew letter *bet* which encloses this text are the pyramids of Egypt; within the bottom panel—a concentration camp.

ב
כָל דוֹר וָדוֹר
חַיָּב אָדָם
לִרְאוֹת אֶת
עַצְמוֹ כְּאִלּוּ
הוּא יָצָא מִמִּצְרַיִם.
BAD

MUNICH · 1948

[NOAR ḤALUTZI EDITION · CONTINUED]

Exile and Redemption

The last page of the Haggadah published by the union of Zionist youth in Germany is occupied by the following Yiddish text:

> There is no such thing as a "bad" or a "good" exile. Every exile leads to annihilation.
>
> With blood of our heart, by the light of our faith, and with a final hope, we will break through every wall. We will break through and go up [to the Land of Israel].

ניטא קיין
שלעכטער און גוטער
גלות. יעדער
גלות פירט צום
אונטערגאנג.
מיט בלוט
פון אונדזער הארץ,
ביים ליכט פון
אונדזער גלויבן
און מיט דער
לעצטער האפנונג
וועלן מיר דורכ-
ברעכן יעדע
וואנט, דורכברעכן
און עולה זיין.

NAAN · ISRAEL · 1949

After Independence

Passover of 1949 was the first to be celebrated after the State of Israel had achieved its full independence. In kibbutz Naan the change was reflected in a further revision of the Four Questions:

Why does this night differ from all other nights? For on this, the night of Passover, we are all seated together at the meal, parents and children . . . and like us, so also all the Jews in the Land and in all parts of the Diaspora, wherever they are, since ancient times and to this day.

Why does this night differ from all other nights? For in all previous years we performed the Seder of our freedom festival while we were in the hands of an alien and oppressive rule, struggling for development and immigration. Now—we are as free men in the State of Israel, the gates are open to those who return from exile, and the expanses of our land are ours to settle.

Why does this night differ from all other nights? For we are rejoicing in our freedom, and sitting securely in our home, but most of our people are still scattered and separated among the nations, prey to the destiny of exile, and all our dispersed have not yet been gathered into the Land.

Why does this night differ from all other nights? For we here rejoice in the spring, in the freedom of work, of human society, of the Hebrew kibbutz, while the end has not yet come to the enslavement of the laborer, the oppression of man, and the exploitation of the child; while nation still lifts the sword over nation; and the redemption of man in the kingdom of labor and equality in our land and in the entire world has not yet arisen, nor has it been completed.

HARVARD 24:16

מה נשתנה הלילה הזה

מכל הלילות, שבלילה זה, ליל הפסח, אנו מסובין
כאן בסעודה כלנו יחדיו, אבות ובנים, שבת אחים,
וכמונו כן עושים כל בני־ישראל אשר בארץ ואשר
בכל תפוצות הגולה באשר הם שם, מאז הימים ועד
היום הזה?

מה נשתנה הלילה הזה מכל הלילות, שבכל השנים היינו
עורכים את סדר חג־חירותנו כשאנו בידי שלטון זר וצורר
נאבקים על הבנין והעליה, והשתא - אנו כבני־חורין במדינת
ישראל, השערים פתוחים לשבי־גולה ומרחבי ארצנו בידנו
להתישב בהם?

מה נשתנה הלילה הזה מכל הלילות, שבו אנו שמחים ב-
חירותנו ומסובין לבטח בביתנו, - ומרבית עמנו עודו מפוזר
ומפורד בין הגוים נתון לגורל גלותו ועוד טרם נתקבצו ובאו
כל גלויותיו לארצנו?

מה נשתנה הלילה הזה מכל הלילות, שבו אנו שמ-
חים באביב, בחירות־העמל וחברת־האדם
בקבוץ העברי, - ועוד טרם הקיץ
הקץ על שעבוד העמל ודכוי
האדם ונצול הילד, וגוי אל
גוי עוד ישא חרב, וגאו-
לת האדם במולדת
העבודה והשויון בארצנו
ובמלוא התבל, טרם
קמה וטרם
נשלמה?

מה נשתנה הלילה הזה?

NAAN · 1949
[CONTINUED]
The Price of Sovereignty

The ancient rabbis had stated: "In blood and fire Judea fell; in blood and fire shall it rise again." The events of 1948 were almost a literal fulfillment of these words, as Israel fought its War of Independence and achieved its existence as a state. Victory was won, however, at a heavy cost. In every kibbutz fathers, sons, brothers, and comrades were absent at the Seder of 1949. In the Naan Haggadah the last stanzas of a poem by Saul Tchernichovsky expressed the sorrow that was felt in the midst of rejoicing:

BEHOLD, O EARTH
Here you have the best of our sons,
Youth of pure dreams,
Clean of heart and hands,
Untouched by mundane filth,
The cloth of their years still weaving
The hopes of a day yet to come.
We have none better than these.
Earth, have you? Then where?

And you shall cover them all.
Then may the plant spring forth in its time!
A hundred gates of strength and glory
Sacred to the homeland's people!

Blessed be the sacrifice of their unseen death,
Price of our lives in splendor.

האי אדמה
הא לך הטובים בבנינו,
נוער טהר חלומות,
ברי לב, נקיי כפים,
טרם חלאת אדמות,
וארג יומם עודו שתי,
ארג תקוות יום יבוא,
אין לנו טובים מכל אלה.
את הראית? ואיפה?
ואת תכסי על כל אלה.
יעל הצמח בעתו!
מאה שערים הוד וכח,
קדש לעם מכורתו!
ברוך קרבם בסוד מות,
כפר חיים בהוד...
<ש. טשרניחובסקי>
כו

NE'OT MORDECAI · ISRAEL · 1949

A New Calendar

The cover of a mimeographed Haggadah produced in kibbutz Ne'ot Mordecai in northern Israel "for the year [5]709—which is the first year of the State of Israel."

HARVARD 23:17

#6

נאות מרדכי

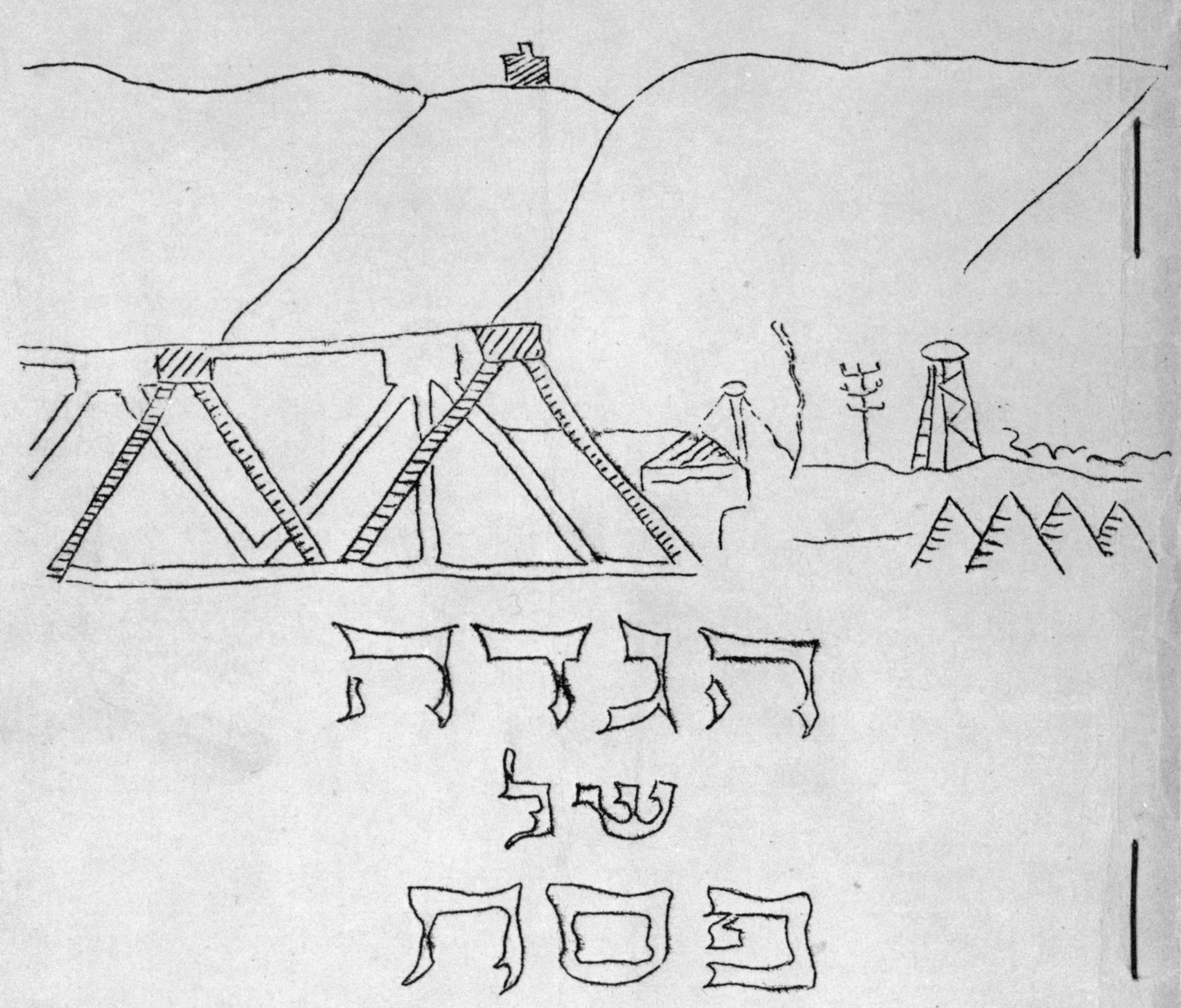

הגדה של פסח

לשנת תש"ט

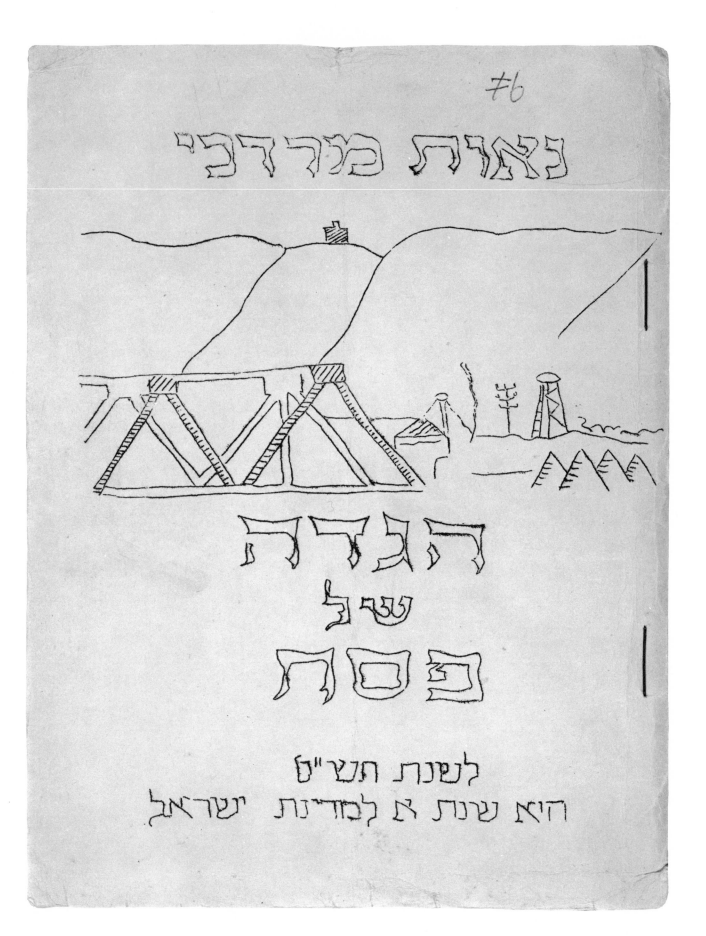

היא שנת א למדינת ישראל

PLATE 185

NE'OT MORDECAI · 1949
[CONTINUED]

For Fallen Warriors

Another elegiac evocation of those who fell in the War of Independence appears in this Haggadah:

Let us raise above our highest joy
The memory of all those
Whose blood was spilled
Over the foundation stones
Of our political liberation,
For with their death
They bequeathed life to us.

"And when I . . . saw thee wallowing in thy blood,
I said unto thee: In thy blood, live."
—Ezekiel 16:6

"Oh that my head were waters,
And mine eyes a fountain of tears,
That I might weep day and night
For the slain of the daughter of my people!"
—Jeremiah 8:23

נעלה על ראש שמחתו
את זכר כל אלה
אשר דמם נשפך
על אבני היסוד
של חרותנו המדינית
אשר במותם
צוו לנו את החיים.

ואראך מתבוססת בדמיך, ואמר לך
בדמיך חיי.

י יתן ראשי מים
ועיני מקור דמעה
ואבכה יומם ולילה
את חללי בת עמי.

TEL AVIV · ISRAEL · 1952

Zim Haggadah: The Four Sons

A distinctive modern Israeli Haggadah in large folio, illustrated by Jacob Zimberknopf (Zim). Most striking are the beautifully designed letters of various sizes, which were created by the artist for this edition. In their variety and startling alternations they call to mind the Prague Haggadah of 1526.

The Four Sons, shown here, are fairly conventional in inspiration, except for the Wicked Son, who has become a purse-snatcher.

YAARI NO. 2422 HARVARD 36:24

כְּנֶגֶד אַרְבָּעָה בָנִים דִּבְּרָה תוֹרָה, אֶחָד
חָכָם, וְאֶחָד רָשָׁע, וְאֶחָד תָּם, וְאֶחָד
שֶׁאֵינוֹ יוֹדֵעַ לִשְׁאוֹל:

חָכָם מַה הוּא אוֹמֵר;

מָה הָעֵדֹת וְהַחֻקִּים וְהַמִּשְׁפָּטִים אֲשֶׁר
צִוָּה יְיָ אֱלֹהֵינוּ אֶתְכֶם, וְאַף אַתָּה אֱמָר־
לוֹ כְּהִלְכוֹת הַפֶּסַח, אֵין מַפְטִירִין אַחַר
הַפֶּסַח אֲפִיקוֹמָן:

רָשָׁע מַה הוּא אוֹמֵר;

מָה הָעֲבוֹדָה הַזֹּאת לָכֶם, לָכֶם וְלֹא לֹה
וּלְפִי שֶׁהוֹצִיא אֶת עַצְמוֹ מִן הַכְּלָל כָּפַר
בְּעִקָּר, וְאַף אַתָּה הַקְהֵה אֶת שִׁנָּיו וֶאֱמָר־

PLATE 187

TEL AVIV · 1952
[CONTINUED]

Zim Haggadah: "In a Rebuilt *Jerusalem"*

For Israelis, the exclamation "Next year in Jerusalem" is somewhat incongruous. The version in Israel is therefore *Le-shanah ha-ba'ah bi-Yerushalayim ha-benuyah*—"Next year in a *rebuilt* Jerusalem."

נרצה

חסל

סדור פסח כהלכתו, ככל
משפטו וחקתו, כאשר זכינו
לסדר אותו, כן נזכה לעשותו.
זך שוכן מעונה, קומם קהל
עדת מי מנה, בקרוב נהל
נטעי כנה, פדוים לציון
ברנה:

לשנה
הבאה
בירושלים
הבנויה

PLATE 188

ISRAEL · 1956

A Seder of the Israeli Army

A page with the Four Questions from a Haggadah issued in a unified version for use by the Israel Defense Forces. In the illustration soldiers are seated around the Seder table, with their chaplain at the right. The artist was Jacob Zimberknopf.

YAARI NO. 2462 HARVARD 23:16

מחזיר הקערה, מוזג כוס שניה והצעיר שבין המסובים שואל

צעיר המסובים

מה
נשתנה הלילה הזה
מכל הלילות

א. שֶׁבְּכָל הַלֵּילוֹת אָנוּ אוֹכְלִין חָמֵץ וּמַצָּה, הַלַּיְלָה הַזֶּה כֻּלוֹ מַצָּה.

ב. שֶׁבְּכָל הַלֵּילוֹת אָנוּ אוֹכְלִין שְׁאָר יְרָקוֹת, הַלַּיְלָה הַזֶּה מָרוֹר?

ג. שֶׁבְּכָל הַלֵּילוֹת אֵין אָנוּ מַטְבִּילִין אֲפִילוּ פַּעַם אֶחָת, הַלַּיְלָה הַזֶּה שְׁתֵּי פְעָמִים?

ד. שֶׁבְּכָל הַלֵּילוֹת אָנוּ אוֹכְלִין בֵּין יוֹשְׁבִין וּבֵין מְסֻבִּין, הַלַּיְלָה הַזֶּה כֻּלָּנוּ מְסֻבִּין?

TEL AVIV · ISRAEL · 1957

Wechsler Haggadah: The Egyptian Bondage

A Haggadah edited by Dr. Hayyim Gamzu and illustrated by Jacob Wechsler. The lettering of the text was created by a Torah scribe, Samuel ben Barukh.

YAARI NO. 2449 HARVARD 24:23

עֲבָדִים הָיִינוּ לְפַרְעֹה בְּמִצְרָיִם וַיּוֹצִיאֵנוּ
יְיָ אֱלֹהֵינוּ מִשָּׁם בְּיָד חֲזָקָה וּבִזְרוֹעַ נְטוּיָה.
וְאִלּוּ לֹא הוֹצִיא הַקָּדוֹשׁ בָּרוּךְ הוּא אֶת
אֲבוֹתֵינוּ מִמִּצְרַיִם הֲרֵי אָנוּ וּבָנֵינוּ וּבְנֵי בָנֵינוּ —
מְשֻׁעְבָּדִים הָיִינוּ לְפַרְעֹה בְּמִצְרָיִם. וַאֲפִילוּ כֻּלָּנוּ
חֲכָמִים כֻּלָּנוּ נְבוֹנִים כֻּלָּנוּ זְקֵנִים כֻּלָּנוּ יוֹדְעִים אֶת
הַתּוֹרָה. מִצְוָה עָלֵינוּ לְסַפֵּר בִּיצִיאַת מִצְרָיִם. וְכָל
הַמַּרְבֶּה לְסַפֵּר בִּיצִיאַת מִצְרַיִם הֲרֵי זֶה מְשֻׁבָּח:

ISRAEL · 1958

In Memoriam

This Haggadah was published as a standardized edition for use in the kibbutzim affiliated with the left-wing *Ha-Shomer Ha-Tzair* movement, and was illustrated by Moshe Proops. The two pages reproduced here face one another in the original. The text reads:

Let us remember the myriad souls of our brothers and sisters who were cut down before their time, who fell in the lines of battle and perished under ruins and heaps of debris, who raised the banner of revolt and sanctified the name of Israel while fighting and dying amid the walls of the burning ghetto, their hearts filled with the vision of coming to the homeland, and with faith in man and in the redemption of Israel. Let the Jewish people remember the best of its sons, clean of heart and pure of vision, the first fruits of our strength in the Land, and the last of our portion in the Diaspora, who grasped weapons in order to defend Israel's honor and independence, those who fell guarding its borders, who were killed from ambush, or perished in enemy prisons and in captivity. May the people of Israel remember all those who fell in the battles for its redemption and who, by their death, bequeathed life to us.

HARVARD 16:23

נזכר

את רבבות הנשמות של אחינו ואחיותינו
שנכרתו בלי עתם, אשר נפלו במערכות הקרב
ואשר אבדו תחת החרבות ועיי המפלת. אשר
הרימו את נס המרד ויקדשו את שם ישראל בלחמם
ובנפלם בין חומות הגיטו הבוער ובלבם החזון
העליה למולדת, אמונה באדם ובגאולת
ישראל. יזכר עם-ישראל את הטובים בבניו, ברי-לב
וטהורי-חזון, ראשית אוננו בארץ ושארית גחלתנו
מן הגולה שאחזו בנשק להגן על כבודו ועל
עצמאותו; אשר נפלו על משמר גבורותיו
ואשר נרצחו מן המארב ואשר נספו בכלא
אויב ובשבי-צר. יזכר עם ישראל את כל שנפלו
במערכות גאלתו ובמותם צוו לנו את החיים!

JERUSALEM · ISRAEL · 1959

For the Kurdish Jews in Israel

The "ingathering of exiles" into Israel following the establishment of the state included the most varied and exotic Jewish groups. Among those who arrived from the far-flung oriental diasporas were the Jews of Kurdistan in Iraq. In addition to Arabic, these Jews employed a dialect of ancient Aramaic.

Reproduced here is the title page of a Haggadah in Hebrew and Kurdish-Aramaic published by Ash'ab Abidani in 1959, "which is the tenth year of the State of Israel, may the Lord establish it well."

YAARI NO. 2697 HARVARD 16.5:12

ב"ה

סדר

הגדה של פסח

עברי - כורדי

מהדורה ראשונה

פעה"ק ירושלים תובב"א

שנת ה'תשי"ט לפ"ג

היא שנת העשור למדינת ישראל יע"א

הוציא לאור

עש"ב אבידני

כל הזכויות שמורות למוציא לאור

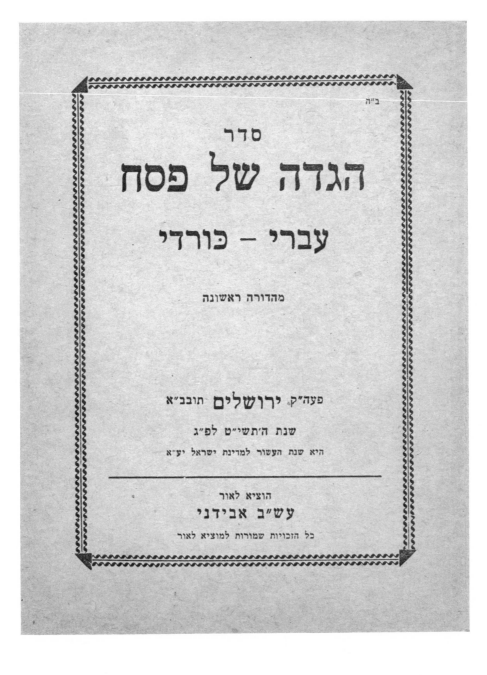

PLATE 192

FEZ · MOROCCO · 1960

The Temple—by Way of Amsterdam

This Moroccan Haggadah was published and sold in Fez, though possibly printed in Casablanca. On the title page the restored Temple in the end of days appears, yet another copy of the illustration in the Amsterdam Haggadah of 1695 (Plate 62).

HARVARD 21.5:13.5

הַגָּדָה שֶׁל פֶּסַח

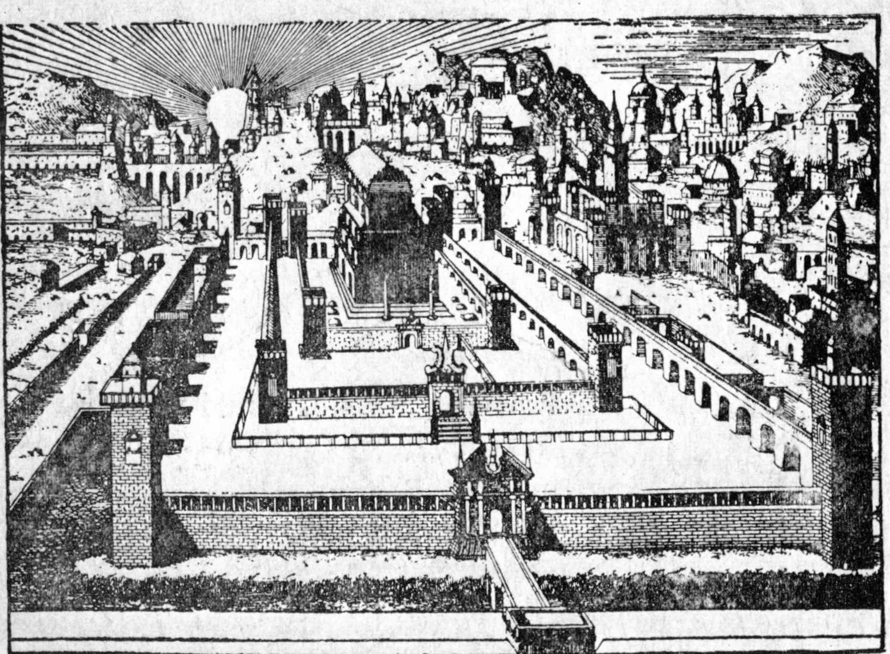

צורת בה״מ ועיר ירושלים תובב״א אכי״ר

בית מסחר ספרים וואחנון

LIBRAIRIE WAHNOUN

FEZ (Mellah) פאס

SANTIAGO · CHILE · 1961

A Bessarabian "Third Seder" in Chile

In many parts of the Jewish world, but especially in the Western Hemisphere, it has become a practice of communities and organizations to celebrate a "Third Seder." On such occasions funds are raised for Israel, and sometimes a special "Haggadah" is prepared.

Shown here are the Hebrew-Yiddish and Spanish covers of such a Haggadah, issued for a Third Seder of the Association of Bessarabian Jews in the capital of Chile. (Bessarabia was a province in southwest Russia, bordering on Romania.) The text within is in Yiddish.

HARVARD 16:21

פאראיין פון בעסאראבער יידן
הגדה של פסח
טשילע
דריטער סדר

שלש עשרה שנה לתקומת ישראל

ה. ת. ש. כ״א

SOCIEDAD ISRAELITA BESARABIA

Hagada Schel Pesaj

Tercer Seder

SANTIAGO DE CHILE

1961

TEL AVIV · ISRAEL · 1962

The Most Ancient Sect

The Samaritans are a Jewish sect that originated after the fall of the Northern Kingdom of ancient Israel and later broke off from the rest of Jewry. They have preserved their own form of Judaism down to the present, including the actual sacrifice of paschal lambs on Mount Gerizim, south of the city of Shechem. Between 1948 and 1967 they were divided between two centers, one in Jordan, the other in Israel. Since the Six-Day War, however, all the Samaritans live within Israeli territory, where they have been relocated and united in permanent living quarters in Holon. Israel's Law of Return recognizes them as citizens of the state. In 1970 they numbered 430 in all. This figure marked, nevertheless, a decided increase since the previous decade.

Both the Pentateuch and the liturgy of the Samaritans are in Hebrew, though the latter has an admixture of Aramaic and is influenced by the Samaritan Arabic vernacular. Of particular interest is the fact that the Samaritans alone have retained the forms of the ancient Hebrew alphabet.

The Samaritan Passover festival has been described, and the hymns printed in Samaritan and in Hebrew, in a book by Abraham Tzedakah.

ABOVE: The title page, with a photograph of Samaritans celebrating Passover on Mount Gerizim.

BELOW: A page of hymns in the Samaritan script.

HARVARD 20:15.5

אברהם צדקה

קרבן־הפסח
אצל השומרונים

•••

THE CELEBRATION OF PASSOVER BY THE SAMARITANS

TEL-AVIV, 1962 • תל־אביב, תשכ״ב

SOUTH AFRICA · 1968

The Haggadah in Afrikaans

A Haggadah published in Hebrew, English, and Afrikaans, the South African language derived from the Dutch of the Boer settlers. This is a second edition of a Haggadah that first appeared in Paarl, near Capetown, in 1943.

HARVARD 22.5:15

Die Paasfeesverhaal

Eerste Afrikaanse Vertaling

deur

Roman B. Egert

Met die Hebreeuse teks en 'n moderne
Engelse Vertaling

VOORWOORD

deur

Hoofrabbyn Professor Israel Abrahams

en

INLEIDING

deur

Dr. H. Abt

Tekeninge deur

Henry Meyer

TWEEDE UITGAWE

1968 5728

VariTyping deur Artset (Edms.) Bpk.
Gedruk deur B & B Drukkers (Edms.) Bpk.
en Copystat Services (Edms.) Bpk.

ISRAEL · 1968
After the Six-Day War

ABOVE: The title page of an Israeli Army Haggadah published for the first Passover celebrated since the Six-Day War of June 1967. It is entitled "Haggadah for a Time of Emergency, for the Soldier on Active Military Duty."

BELOW: The preface of the then chief chaplain, Rabbi Shlomoh Goren:

Dear soldiers:

We have been found worthy this year by the grace of God to celebrate Passover, the nation's festival of freedom throughout the ages, in a liberated Land of Israel and in a united Jerusalem, the site of the Temple, the Temple Mount, and the city of the Lord being in the hands of Israel. The soldiers of the Israel Defense Forces stand prepared in guarding the nation, and observe the Seder night from the river of Egypt to Mount Hermon.

Nevertheless, we have not yet attained the hoped-for peace. The enemies of Israel still stand at the gate to destroy us as a nation. We must continue with might and heroism, and out of trust in the God of Israel, to stand ready and prepared to guard and defend our lives.

Regrettably, in view of the state of security in guarding the borders we cannot promise all of you full participation in the Passover Seder. To you, dear soldiers, who find yourselves on the "Night of Watching" [Exodus 12:42] in emergency tasks on the borders of Israel, lying in wait, on patrols, and in positions facing the enemy, we present this abridged Haggadah issued by the chief chaplaincy. We have also prepared for you individual Seder portions, including the main Seder accessories. We have edited this abridged Haggadah version which will enable you to fulfill the requirements from the point of view of Jewish law, by observing a Passover Seder similar to the first Passover in Egypt, as the verse states: "And thus shall ye eat it: with your loins girded, your shoes on your feet, and your staff in your hand; and ye shall eat it in haste—it is the Lord's passover" [Exodus 12:11].

The year [5]728
The year 20 of the State of Israel
The year 1 of united Jerusalem

With the blessing of peace, salvation, and redemption
General Shlomoh Goren
Chief Rabbi of the Israel Defense Forces

HARVARD 21.5:16.5

הגדה לשעת חרום

לחייל בתעסוקה מבצעית

ערוכה ע"י הרבנות הצבאית הראשית

ערב פסח תשכ״ח
כ׳ למדינת ישראל
שנה א׳ לירושלים השלמה

ב״ה

ברכת הרב הראשי לצה"ל

חיילים יקרים

זוכים אנו השנה בחסדי ה׳ לחוג את חג הפסח חג החרות של העם מדור דור בארץ ישראל המשוחררת ובירושלים השלימה כאשר מקום המקדש, הר הבית ועיר האלהים נתונים בידי ישראל. וחיילי צה״ל עומדים הכן על משמרת העם ועורכים את ליל הסדר מנחל מצרים ועד הר חרמון.

לעומת זאת טרם זכינו לשלום המקווה, אויבי ישראל עדיין עומדים בשער להכחידנו מגוי. עלינו להמשיך בעוז ובגבורה מתוך בטחון באלהי ישראל, לעמוד דרוכים וערוכים לשמור ולהגן על חיינו.

לאור המצב הבטחוני בשמירת הגבולות לא נוכל לצערינו להבטיח לכלכם את ההשתתפות המלאה בסדר ליל פסח. לכם חיילים יקרים הנמצאים בליל השמורים בתפקידי חרום על גבולות ישראל במארבים. בפטרולים ובעמדות מול האויב. אנו מגישים את ההגדה המקוצרת המוצאת בזה לאור על ידי הרבנות הצבאית הראשית, עבורכם הכינונו מנות סדר אישיות, הכוללות את אביזרי הסדר העקריים, וערכנו את נוסח ההגדה המקוצרת אשר תאפשר לכם לצאת ידי חובה מבחינת ההלכה, ע״י עריכת סדר פסח מעין פסח מצרים ככתוב ״וככה תאכלו אותו מתניכם חגורים נעליכם ברגליכם ומקלכם בידכם ואכלתם אותו בחפזון פסח הוא לה׳״.

ער״פ תשכ״ח
כ׳ למדינת ישראל
שנה א׳ לירושלים השלימה

בברכת השלום הגאולה והפדות
שלמה גורן — אלוף
הרב הראשי לצה״ל

HAIFA · ISRAEL · 1968
Jerusalem Reunited

Of all the results of the 1967 war, none had a greater emotional impact than the reconquest of the Old City of Jerusalem, and the unification of the entire city for the first time since 1948. Reproduced here is a panel that forms part of a folding triptych in a "Jerusalem Haggadah," illustrated by Shmuel Boneh and published in Haifa. An Israeli paratrooper stands near the Tower of David. Inscribed above are the words *Le-ḥerut Yisrael u-ge'ulat Yerushalayim*—"In the year of Israel's freedom and the redemption of Jerusalem." The motto derives from inscriptions found on the coins struck by Bar Kokhba, leader of the great revolt against Rome in the second century.

HARVARD 30:20

לחדות ישראל וגאולת ירושלים

PLATE 198

SALONIKA · GREECE · 1970

The Languages of Jewish Salonika

In the century following the Spanish Expulsion, Salonika became one of the greatest Jewish centers ever to arise in the Diaspora (see Plate 32). Although by the twentieth century its cultural primacy was a thing of the past, Salonika itself was still almost a "Jewish city." Its more than 55,000 Jews made up the bulk of the population.

Tragically, Salonikan Jewry was all but destroyed in the Holocaust. Between March 15 and May 9, 1943, the Germans deported some 45,000 Jews from Salonika to Auschwitz in consecutive convoys. The trip lasted ten days. Considered "poor human material" by Rudolph Hoess, the commandant of the death camp, they were often exterminated en masse immediately upon arrival, with no selection whatever.

Though decimated by the slaughter, an organized and active Jewish community still exists in Salonika today. Remarkably, in 1970 the community published one of the most luxurious editions of the Haggadah to appear within recent memory.

It contains no new illustrations. However, it is adorned throughout with a profusion of reproductions, in monochrome and color, of old manuscript and printed Haggadahs, as well as ancient Jewish mosaics and Egyptian art. There are also contemporary photographs showing views of the synagogue of Salonika, the monument to its Jewish martyrs, and a group of Jews praying at the Western Wall in Jerusalem following its recovery in 1967. Several pages of music are provided for the songs and hymns. Toward the end there is a map of the city of Salonika in 1943, showing the points of Jewish interest that existed before the Nazi occupation.

Of singular interest are the languages in which the Haggadah is printed: Hebrew, Ladino in Hebrew characters, modern Greek, and Ladino transcribed into Latin characters. The latter two, of course, are reflections of modern developments within Salonikan Jewry. The Greek appears for those Jews who no longer know Hebrew or Ladino; the transliterated Ladino, for those who know the language but cannot read it in the Hebrew alphabet.

Reproduced on the plate opposite is a typical page of text. The passage is that which explains the *maror*, the bitter herbs. The first paragraph is in Hebrew, the second is Ladino in its traditional Hebrew characters. These are followed by the Greek translation, and the Ladino rendered in the Latin alphabet. At the bottom of the page are small facsimiles of the title pages of two Salonikan Haggadahs printed in 1927 and 1929.

HARVARD 28:20

אי טומארה לה ליג׳וגה אין לה מאנו אי דירה.

מרור זה שאנו אוכלין. על שום מה. על שום שמררו המצרים את חיי אבתינו במצרים שנאמר. וימררו את חייהם בעבדה קשה. בחמר ובלבנים ובכל עבדה בשדה את כל עבדתם אשר עבדו בהם בפרך:

ליג׳וגה איסטה קי נוס קומיינטים. פור קאב׳זה די קי. פור קאב׳זה קי אמארגארון לוס איסייאנוס אה ב׳ידה די מואיסטרוס פאדריס אין איפ׳טו. קי אנסי דיזי איל פסוק. אי אמארגארון אה סוס ב׳ידאס קון סירב׳יסייו דורו. קון בארו אי קון לאדריאוס. אי קון טודו סירב׳יסייו קי אין איל קאמפו. אה טודוס סוס סירב׳יסייוס קי סירב׳יירון אין אילייוס קון דוריזה:

Παίρνομε τὸ μαροῦλι στὸ χέρι καὶ λέμε:

Τοῦτο τὸ μαροῦλι ποὺ τρῶμε, γιὰ ποιὸ λόγο; Γιατὶ οἱ Αἰγύπτιοι κάναν πικρὴ τὴ ζωὴ τῶν πατέρων μας στὴν Αἴγυπτο. Καθὼς λένε οἱ Γραφές: (1) «Καὶ πίκραναν τὴ ζωή τους μὲ σκληρὴ δουλειά, μὲ τὸν ἄργιλο καὶ τὸ τοῦβλο, μὲ ἀγροτικὲς ἀγγαρεῖες καὶ ἄλλες δουλειὲς ποὺ τοὺς ἐπέβαλαν μὲ σκληρότητα».

Y TOMARA LA LITCHOUGA EN LA MANO Y DIRAN:

Litchouga esta que nos coumientes, por cavsa deque? Por cavsa que amargàron los Ayissianos a vidas de nuestros Padres en Ayifto. Que ansi dize el passouk: Y amargàron sus vidas con servicio duro, con barro y con adôves, y con todo servicio que en el campo, a todos sus servisios que servieron a eyos con dureza.

---

(1) Ἔξοδος 1, 14.

Ἐξώφυλλο τῆς Ἀγκαδᾶ ποὺ τυπώθηκε στὴ Θεσσαλονίκη τὸ 1927 (5687) Τυπογραφεῖο Μπεζές).

Ἐξώφυλλο τῆς Ἀγκαδᾶ ποὺ τυπώθηκε στὴ Θεσσαλονίκη τὸ 1929 (5689) Τυπογραφεῖο Μπεζές).

PLATE 199

SALONIKA · 1970
[CONTINUED]

The Route of the Exodus—in Greek

The first Hebrew map of the Exodus from Egypt appeared in the Amsterdam Haggadahs of 1695 and 1712 (Plate 69). In the Salonika edition of 1970 the route from Egypt to Canaan is presented, for the first time on a map printed by Jews, in Greek. The colors of the original are green and orange.

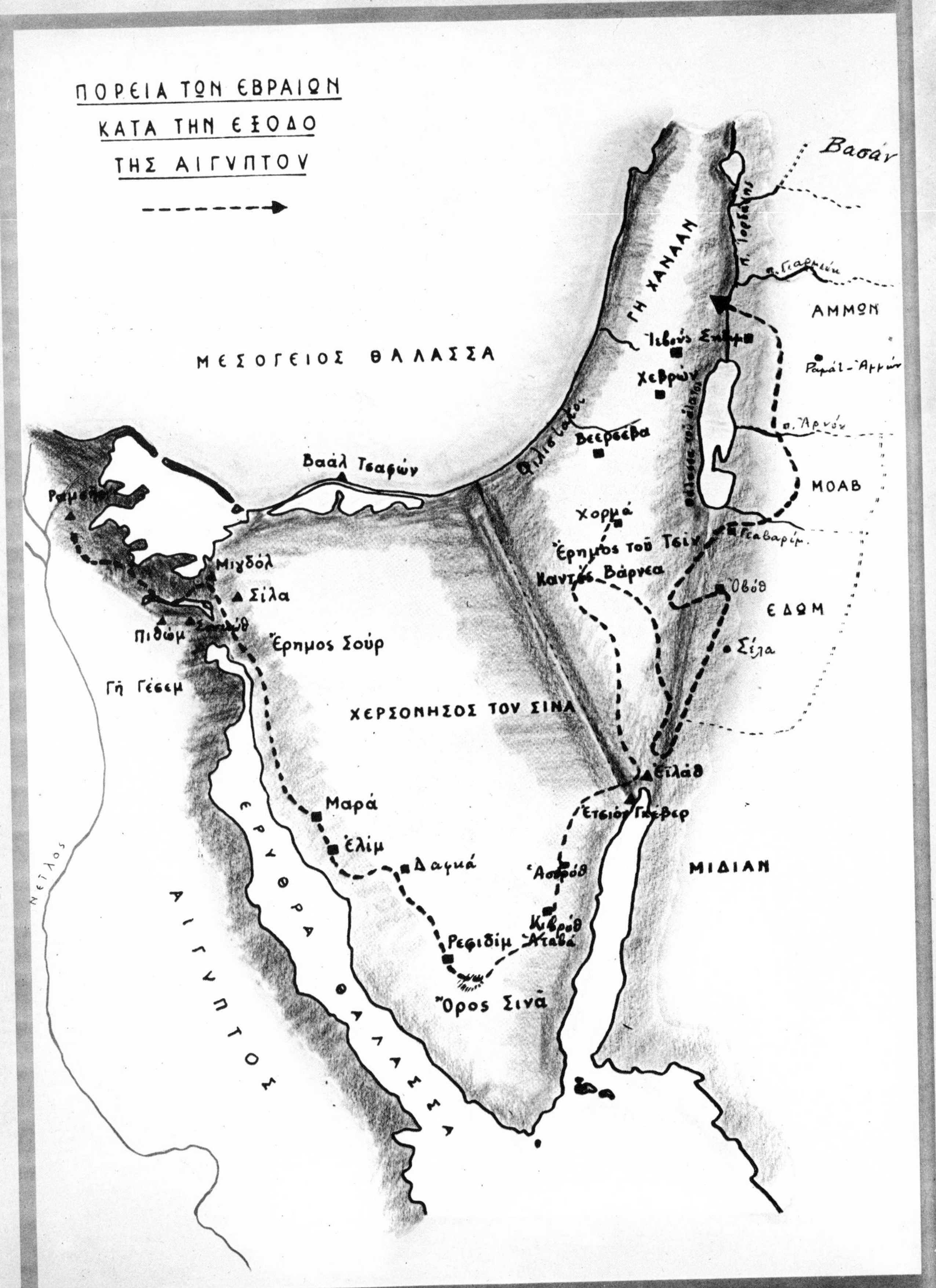

ΠΟΡΕΙΑ ΤΩΝ ΕΒΡΑΙΩΝ
ΚΑΤΑ ΤΗΝ ΕΞΟΔΟ
ΤΗΣ ΑΙΓΥΠΤΟΥ
ΜΕΣΟΓΕΙΟΣ ΘΑΛΑΣΣΑ
ΓΗ ΧΑΝΑΑΝ
Βασάν
ΑΜΜΩΝ
ΜΟΑΒ
ΕΔΩΜ
ΜΙΔΙΑΝ
Βαάλ Τσεφών
Χεβρών
Βεερσέβα
Χορμά
Έρημος τού Τσιν
Καντές Βάρνεα
Όβώθ
Σίλα
Έλάθ
Μιγδόλ
Σίλα
Πιθώμ
Έρημος Σούρ
Γή Γέσεμ
ΧΕΡΣΟΝΗΣΟΣ ΤΟΥ ΣΙΝΑ
Μαρά
Έλίμ
Δαφκά
Άσηρώθ
Ρεφιδίμ
Όρος Σινά
ΕΡΥΘΡΑ ΘΑΛΑΣΣΑ
ΑΙΓΥΠΤΟΣ
Νείλος

[TEL AVIV?] · ISRAEL · 1972

The Latest Exodus

The ongoing exodus of Jews from the Soviet Union, permitted by the Soviet authorities only within the last few years, has already taken thousands of Jews into Israel. At this moment it is still premature to speculate as to how long this migration will continue, whether it will be allowed to continue at all, or what dimensions it may ultimately attain.

For those Soviet Jews who have arrived in Israel, several Haggadahs have already appeared. One of them is reproduced here. The text is printed throughout in Hebrew and Russian. This is the final page, ending—"Next year in Jerusalem"—in both languages. At the bottom is a cut taken from an Israeli Army Haggadah, with the line repeated in Hebrew in its updated form: "Next year in a rebuilt Jerusalem!"

HARVARD 24:10.5

נִרְצָה

ЗАКЛЮЧЕНИЕ

חֲסַל סִדּוּר פֶּסַח כְּהִלְכָתוֹ,
כְּכָל מִשְׁפָּטוֹ וְחֻקָּתוֹ;
כַּאֲשֶׁר זָכִינוּ לְסַדֵּר אוֹתוֹ,
כֵּן נִזְכֶּה לַעֲשׂוֹתוֹ.

זָךְ שׁוֹכֵן מְעוֹנָה,
קוֹמֵם קְהַל עֲדַת מִי מָנָה;
בְּקָרוֹב נַהֵל נִטְעֵי כַנָּה,
פְּדוּיִם לְצִיּוֹן בְּרִנָּה.

На этом кончается Седер Песах согласно соблюдаемым традициям. И так же как мы заслужили того, чтобы праздновать его сегодня, так мы должны заслужить, чтобы отпраздновать его снова. Чистый, обитающий высоко, собери собрание народа бесчисленного — веди, не медля, отпрыск Твой, Израиль, с песнею возрождения — к Сиону!

לְשָׁנָה הַבָּאָה בִּירוּשָׁלַיִם

В БУДУЩЕМ ГОДУ — В ИЕРУСАЛИМЕ!

מתוך הגדת צה״ל לא. אלואיל

SELECTED BIBLIOGRAPHY

I. *Bibliographies of the Printed Haggadah*

Yaari, Abraham. *Bibliografiah shel Haggadot Pesaḥ mi-reshit ha-Defus ve-ad ha-Yom* [Bibliography of the Passover Haggadah from the Earliest Printed Edition to 1960]. Jerusalem: 1960. (The standard bibliography.)

SUPPLEMENTS TO YAARI

Ben-Menahem, Naphtali. "Abraham Yaari, Bibliografiah shel Haggadot Pesaḥ," *Areshet*, III (1961), 442–65.

———. "Be-shaarey ha-Haggadah shel Pesaḥ," *Sinai*, LVII (1965), 56–67.

———. "Bibliografiah shel Haggadot Pesaḥ," *Areshet*, IV (1966), 518–44.

Habermann, A. M. [Review of Yaari], *Kirjath Sepher*, XXXVI (1961), 419–22.

Wiener, Theodore. "Addenda to Yaari's *Bibliography of the Passover Haggadah*," *Studies in Bibliography and Booklore*, VII (1965), 90–129.

———. "Addenda to Yaari's *Bibliography of the Passover Haggadah* from the Library of Congress Hebraica Collection," *Studies in Jewish Bibliography, History and Literature, in Honor of I. Edward Kiev*, edited by Charles Berlin (New York, 1971), 511–16.

SPECIALIZED

Ben-Menahem, Naphtali. *Ha-Haggadah shel Pesaḥ bi-Ẓefon Afrika: Reshimah Bibliografit.* [French title: *La Haggada de Pessah en Afrique du Nord: Bibliographie.*] Jerusalem: 1969.

Steiner, Nathan. "Haggadot kibbuẓiyot" [Kibbutz Haggadahs], *Studies in Bibliography and Booklore*, VII (1965): Hebrew section, 10–31.

II. *Haggadah Exhibitions*

[Berlin, Charles.] *Haggadahs from Harvard.* Cambridge, Massachusetts: 1972. (An exhibition held at the B'nai B'rith Building, Washington, D.C., March 8 – April 28, 1972.)

Hirschhorn, Harry J. *Mah Nishtana.* Chicago: 1964. (Contains additions to Yaari's *Bibliography.*)

Schocken Library, Jerusalem. *Sifrey Haggadah: Ta'arukhat Ḥag ha-Pesaḥ, 5715* [Catalogue of an Exhibition of Haggadahs held at the Schocken Library in 1955]. Jerusalem: 1955.

Steiner, Nathan. *Ta'arukhat Haggadot Pesaḥ me-'osfo shel R. Nathan Steiner* [Exhibition of Passover Haggadahs from the Steiner Collection]. Tel Aviv: 1964.

Witting, Nancy. "Passover Haggadahs, and Other Gems from Harvard's Judaica Collection," *Harvard*, LXXIII, no. 9 (March 22, 1971), 41–44.

III. *Other Bibliographical Works*

Freimann, Aron. *A Gazetteer of Hebrew Printing*. New York: 1946.

Harvard University Library. *Catalogue of Hebrew Books*. 6 vols. Cambridge, Massachusetts: 1968. *Supplement*, 3 vols. Cambridge: 1972.

Kayserling, Meyer. *Biblioteca Española-Portugueza-Judaica and Other Studies in Ibero-Jewish Bibliography by the Author, and by J. S. da Silva Rosa* . . . Selected with a Prolegomenon by Yosef Hayim Yerushalmi. New York: 1971.

Mayer, L. A. *Bibliography of Jewish Art*, edited by Otto Kurz. Jerusalem: 1967.

Rivkind, Isaac. "Sifrut ha-Haggadah shel Pesaḥ" [Bibliography of Studies of the Haggadah], *Kirjath Sefer*, XII (1935–36), 230–37, 360–67.

———. "Sifrut ha-Haggadah shel Pesaḥ." [Bibliography of Studies of the Haggadah], *Studies in Bibliography and Booklore*, VII (1965); Hebrew section, 1–9.

Roth, Cecil. *Magna Bibliotheca Anglo-Judaica: A Bibliographical Guide to Anglo-Jewish History*. London: 1937.

Shmeruk, Kh., editor. *Pirsumim Yehudiim bi-Berit ha-Mo'aẓot* [Jewish Publications in the Soviet Union]. Jerusalem: 1961.

Yaari, Abraham. *Ha-defus ha-'ibri be-arẓot ha-mizraḥ* [Hebrew Printing in the East]. 2 vols. Jerusalem: 1936, 1940.

Zedner, J. *Catalogue of Hebrew Books in the Library of the British Museum*. London: 1867. Reprint, 1964.

IV. *Haggadah Illustration*

Habermann, A. M. "Ha-Haggadah ha-meẓuyeret ba-defus ha-'ibri" [The Illustrated Haggadah in Hebrew Printing], *Hed Ha-Defus*, XI (1957), 38–44.

Marx, Alexander. "Illustrated Haggadahs," *Jewish Quarterly Review*, n.s., XIII (1922–23), 513–19. Reprinted in his *Studies in Jewish History and Booklore* (New York: 1944), 271–76.

Müller, D. H., and J. v. Schlosser. *Die Haggadah von Sarajevo*. Vienna: 1898.

Narkiss, M. "Haggadat Pesaḥ ha-meẓuyeret" [The Illustrated Passover Haggadah], *Moznayim* IV (1933), no. 41–42 [191–92], 9–12.

Rivkind, Isaac. *Haggadat Pesaḥ ba-aspaklariah shel ha-dorot* [The Passover Haggadah in the Mirror of the Ages]. New York: 1961. (Originally appeared in *Hadoar*, Adar 1961, pp. 313–14, 331–33.)

Roth, Cecil. "Ha-Haggadah ha-meẓuyeret she-bi-defus" [The Illustrated Printed Haggadah], *Areshet*, III (1961), 7–30.

———. "The Illustrated Haggadah," *Studies in Bibliography and Booklore*, VII (1965), 37–56. (Abridged translation of his Hebrew study in *Areshet*, III.)

Wischnitzer-Bernstein Rachel. "Hagada: Illustration," *Encyclopaedia Judaica*, VII, 794–813.

———. "Haggadah, Passover: Illustration," *Universal Jewish Encyclopedia*, V, 157b–163a.

v. *Individual Haggadahs*

Abrahams, Israel. "Some Egyptian Fragments of the Passover Hagada," *Jewish Quarterly Review*, o.s., X (1898), 41–51.

Goldschmidt, Lazarus. *The Earliest Printed Haggadah*. London: 1940. (Goldschmidt had acquired some leaves of the Prague Haggadah which he judged to be an earlier issue than that commonly known. These are, however, probably proof pages. See Italiener, Bruno.)

Habermann, A. M. "Daf nosaf la-Haggadah ha-meẓuyeret, Kushta? 1515?" [An Additional Leaf to the Illustrated Haggadah Attributed to Constantinople 1515], *Kirjath Sefer*, XXXVIII (1963), 273. (The new leaf was discovered at Cambridge University. See also: Scheiber, Alexander.)

Italiener, Bruno. "Which is the Oldest Woodcut Haggadah?" *Journal of Jewish Studies*, VI (1955), 227–35.

Kisch, Guido. "An Innovator of Haggadah Illustration—Cyril Kutlik," *Studies in Jewish Bibliography, History and Literature, in Honor of I. Edward Kiev*, edited by Charles Berlin (New York: 1971), 211–15.

Loewe, Heinrich. *Die Pessach Haggadah des Gershom Kohen*. Berlin: 1925. (Booklet accompanying the facsimile of the Prague Haggadah issued by the Soncino-Gesellschaft.)

Marx, Alexander. "Die Soncino-Haggada und das Sidorello 1486," *Zeitschrift für Hebräische Bibliographie*, VIII (1905), 58.

Munk, L. "Die Pesach Hagada der Bene Israel," *Festschrift zum siebzigsten Geburstage David Hoffmann's* (Berlin: 1914), pp. 257–66.

Scheiber, Alexander. "New Pages from the First Printed Illustrated Haggadah," *Studies in Bibliography and Booklore*, VII (1965), 26–36.

Soncino-Gesellschaft. *Haggadah. Das fragment der ältesten mit Illustrationen gedruckten Haggadah wurde nach dem Original aus der Sammlung Elkan Nathan Adler, jetzt im Besitze der Bibliothek des Theological Seminary zu New York, reproduziert und als Publikation Sieben der Soncino-Gesellschaft der Freunde des Judischen Buches E. V. ihren Freunden und Mitgliedern zu Chanukkah 5687 überreicht*. Berlin: 1926.

Weil, E. "Venezianische Haggadah-Holzschnitte aus dem 15. Jahrhundert." *Soncino-Blätter*, I (1925), 45–46.

Wengrow, Charles. *Haggadah and Woodcut: An Introduction to the Passover Haggadah Completed by Gershom Cohen in Prague, Sunday, 26 Teveth, 5287 / December 30, 1526*. New York: 1967.

Wischnitzer-Bernstein, Rachel. "Autour du mystère de la Haggadah de Venise," *Revue des études juives*, XCIV (1933), 184–92.

———. "Von der Holbeinbibel zur Amsterdamer Haggadah," *Monatsschrift für Geschichte und Wissenschaft des Judentums*, LXXV (1931), 269–86.

———. "Zur Amsterdamer Haggadah," *Monatsschrift für Geschichte und Wissenschaft des Judentums*, LXXVI (1932), 239–41. (Addenda to the preceding article.)

Yaari, Abraham. "Tofes meyuḥad shel Haggadah shel Pesaḥ, Veneẓiah SHaSaT, 'al klaf" [A Special Copy of the Venice Haggadah of 1609 on Vellum], *Kirjath Sefer*, XXX (1954–55), 113–17.

Zlocisti, Theodor. "Die Haggadah von Mantua (1560)," *Ost und West*, IV (1904), cols. 265–82.

VI. *History of Hebrew Printing*

Benayahu, Meir. *Ha-defus ha-'ibri be-Cremona* [Hebrew Printing at Cremona]. Jerusalem: 1971.

Bloch, Joshua. *Hebrew Printing in Riva di Trento*. New York: 1933.

Friedberg, Ch. B. *Toledot ha-defus ha-'ibri be-Polaniah* [History of Hebrew Typography in Poland]. Tel Aviv: 1950.

Habermann, A. M. *Sha'arey sefarim 'ibrim* [Title Pages of Hebrew Books]. Safed: 1969.

Rivkind, Isaac. "Yidish in hebrayishe drukn bizn yor TaḤ" [Yiddish in Hebrew printed works up to 1648], *Pinkas*, I (1927–28), 34–38, 263–65.

Roth, Cecil. *Studies in Books and Booklore: Essays in Jewish Bibliography and Allied Subjects*. Westmead, Farnborough, England: 1972.

Yaari, Abraham. *Digley ha-madpisim ha- 'ibrim* [Hebrew Printers' Marks]. Jerusalem: 1943.

———. "Mappot Ereẓ Yisrael ba-Haggadah shel Pesaḥ" [Maps of the Land of Israel in the Passover Haggadah], *Maḥanayim*, LV (1961), 151–55.

———. *Meḥkerey sefer* [Studies in Hebrew Booklore]. Jerusalem: 1958.

INDEX

Figures refer to plate numbers

Places of Printing

Languages

HAGGADAH AND HISTORY was bound by Robert Burlen and Son. The book was composed, and the Introduction printed, in Monotype Bembo, by The Stinehour Press; the plate section by The Meriden Gravure Company. The paper, Mohawk Superfine, was supplied by The Pratt Paper Company. The cartouches and the title engraving were drawn by Stephen Harvard. The planning, production and design of the book were supervised by the Design Associates of David R. Godine.

Of the total edition, two hundred and fifty-two copies have been set aside for a special bibliophilic issue, boxed in half leather, of which two hundred are numbered, and fifty-two copies, *hors commerce*, are marked I–LII. In addition to *Haggadah and History*, this issue contains a portfolio of sixteen plates reproducing the eight extant leaves of the oldest illustrated printed Haggadah, with an introductory study by Yosef Hayim Yerushalmi.

תם ונשלם
שבח לאל בורא עולם

ENDLEAF ILLUSTRATIONS FROM: Bernard Picart, *Histoire générale des cérémonies, moeurs, et coûtumes religieuses de tous les peuples du monde*, Vol. I, Paris, 1741 (Houghton Library, Harvard University.)

FRONT: Searching for leaven

BACK: A Passover Seder among the Portuguese Jews of Amsterdam